THE CREATION OF HISTORY
IN ANCIENT ISRAEL

THE CREATION OF HISTORY IN ANCIENT ISRAEL

Marc Zvi Brettler

London and New York

First published 1995
by Routledge
11 New Fetter Lane, London EC4P 4EE

Simultaneously published in the USA and Canada
by Routledge
29 West 35th Street, New York, NY 10001

© 1995 Marc Zvi Brettler

Phototypeset in Garamond by Intype, London

Printed and bound in Great Britain by
T. J. Press (Padstow) Ltd, Padstow, Cornwall

British Library Cataloguing in Publication Data
Brettler, Marc Zvi
Creation of History in Ancient Israel
I. Title
221.95

Library of Congress Cataloguing in Publication Data
Brettler, Marc Zvi
The creation of history in Ancient Israel / Marc Zvi Brettler.
p.   cm.
Includes bibliographical references and index.
1. Bible. O.T. – Historiography.   2. Jews – History – To 70 A.D. –
Historiography.   3. Bible as literature.   I. Title.
BS1197.B756   1995
221.6′7 – dc20   94–39144

ISBN 0–415–11860–3

To my parents,
Miriam and Sidney Brettler,
my first teachers

CONTENTS

CONTENTS

PREFACE

This book has allowed me to realize how indebted an author can really be to other scholars, students, professional organizations and family.

I would like to thank the various institutions that offered me financial support at various stages: a Bernstein Fellowship from Brandeis University allowed me to take a leave for Spring 1991, a travel grant from the American Philosophical Society allowed me to travel to England in 1991, to use the libraries there and to discuss my work with various scholars from the United Kingdom, and a summer stipend from the National Endowment for the Arts allowed me to spend the summer of 1991 thinking, reading and writing.

Many librarians have helped me; I would like especially to acknowledge Dr Charles Cutter and Mr James Rosenbloom of the Brandeis University Judaica division, various Interlibrary Loan librarians at Brandeis University, and the librarians at the British Library and the School of Oriental and African Studies in London.

Many colleagues discussed certain problems with me and read parts of the manuscript; I would like to thank especially Professors John Barton, David Clines, Philip Davies, Keith Whitelam and Hugh Williamson from Great Britain. While in London, Esther and Willie Ungar offered me a home away from home with a wonderful atmosphere in which this book began to take shape. Professors Stephen Geller, Nahum Sarna, Alan Cooper, Gary Knoppers and Jack Sasson, and Mr Edward Tripp read and critiqued earlier versions of the manuscript. Scholars and students have heard sections of this book presented at the Annual Conferences of the Association for Jewish Studies, and at lectures at the University of Chicago, Hebrew Union College, Cornell University, Brown University and the Boston Theological Institute. The questions after these lectures have helped to sharpen my thinking on many issues.

Michael Carasik, Michael Rosenbaum and Susan Tanchel, graduate students at Brandeis University, read the manuscript with great care. They offered many insightful comments, and questioned my arguments where they were vague, helping to clarify my thoughts. William Schniedewind offered very helpful comments on Chronicles. Mr David Bernat assisted me in correcting the proofs and compiling the indices. Various undergraduate and graduate students have taken different versions of my course on biblical historiography, where many of the ideas expressed here began to develop; these students have always challenged me, and deserve recognition.

The editors of *Journal of Biblical Literature*, *Vetus Testamentum* and *Hebrew Union College Annual*, and of the volume *The Hebrew Bible as Sacred Text and Literature* have granted me permission to reuse in a revised form material published earlier.

My family has been greatly supportive as I struggled to complete this book. They have foregone family time, and have spent too much time with me while I was thinking about the past rather than the present and the future. I am greatly indebted to Talya, Ezra and especially to Monica for their understanding while living with someone who was, over a period of several years, trying to articulate on paper the ideas which existed somewhere in his head. Finally, I would like to dedicate this book to my parents, my first teachers in Judaica, Hebrew and almost everything else, for whom education was important and fun. For many reasons, without them this book would never have been written.

A short bibliographical note: the literature on the various topics probed in this book is immense. It was impossible to cover, let alone acknowledge, all of the literature written on history, ideology, literature, Genesis, Deuteronomy, Judges, Samuel, Kings and Chronicles. Bibliographical references to the individual topics covered may be found in the notes to the individual chapters. For comprehensive bibliographies of general works on biblical historiography, two recent *Journal for the Study of the Old Testament* Supplements are especially useful: K. Lawson Younger, Jr, *Ancient Conquest Accounts: A Study in Ancient Near Eastern and Biblical History Writing*, JSOTSup 98 (Sheffield: Sheffield Academic Press, 1990) and *The Fabric of History: Text, Artifact and Israel's Past*, ed. Diana Vikander Edelman, JSOTSup 127 (Sheffield: Sheffield Academic Press, 1991). Much recent work has been written on the early history of Israel, which has raised many fundamental questions concerning the historicity of the biblical account; see especially Thomas L. Thompson, *Early History of the Israelite People From the Written and Archaeological Sources*, Studies in the History of the Ancient Near East, 4 (Leiden: E. J. Brill, 1992).

ABBREVIATIONS

AB	Anchor Bible
ABD	*Anchor Bible Dictionary*
AnBib	Analecta Biblica
ANET	*Ancient Near Eastern Texts Relating to the Old Testament*, ed. J. B. Pritchard, Princeton: Princeton University Press, 1969
AnOr	Analecta Orientalia
AOAT	Alter Orient und Altes Testament
ASOR	American Schools of Oriental Research
ASTI	*Annual of the Swedish Theological Institute*
ATANT	Abhandlungen zur Theologie des Alten und Neuen Testament
ATD	Das Alte Testament Deutsch
BA	*Biblical Archaeologist*
BAReader	*Biblical Archaeologist Reader*
BARev	*Biblical Archaeology Review*
BBB	Bonner biblische Beiträge
BDB	F. Brown, S. R. Driver and S. A. Briggs, *A Hebrew and English Lexicon of the Old Testament*, Oxford: Oxford University Press, 1907
BHS	*Biblia hebraica stuttgartensia*
BI	*Biblical Interpretation*
Bib	*Biblica*
BJS	Brown Judaic Studies
BN	*Biblische Notizen*
BSAOS	*Bulletin of the School of Oriental and African Studies*
BWANT	Beiträge zur Wissenschaft vom Alten und Neuen Testament
BZAW	Beihefte zur *ZAW*
BzEATAJ	Beiträge zur Erforschung des Alten Testament und des antiken Judentums

CAD	*The Assyrian Dictionary of the Oriental Institute of the University of Chicago*
CBC	Cambridge Bible Commentary
CBOT	Coniectanea Biblica Old Testament Series
CBQ	*Catholic Biblical Quarterly*
CBQMS	*CBQ Monograph Series*
CJ	*Concordia Journal*
CTM	*Concordia Theological Monthly*
DJD	Discoveries in the Judaean Desert
EB	*Encyclopaedia Biblica* (= Hebrew אנציקלופדיה מקראית)
Ebib	Études bibliques
EI	*Eretz Israel*
EJ	*Encyclopedia Judaica*
ErFor	Erträge der Forschung
FOTL	Forms of Old Testament Literature
FRLANT	Forschungen zur Religion und Literatur des Alten und Neuen Testaments
H and T	*History and Theory*
HALAT	*Hebräisches und aramäisches Lexikon zum Alten Testament*, 4 vols., ed. W. Baumgartner *et al.*, Leiden: E. J. Brill, 1967–90
HAR	*Hebrew Annual Review*
HAT	Handbuch zum Alten Testament
HKAT	Handkommentar zum Alten Testament
HSM	Harvard Semitic Monographs
HSS	Harvard Semitic Studies
HTR	*Harvard Theological Review*
HUCA	*Hebrew Union College Annual*
ICC	International Critical Commentary
IEJ	*Israel Exploration Journal*
Int	*Interpretation*
JANESCU	*Journal of the Ancient Near Eastern Society of Columbia University*
JAOS	*Journal of the American Oriental Society*
JB	Jerusalem Bible
JBL	*Journal of Biblical Literature*
JCS	*Journal of Cuneiform Studies*
JHI	*Journal of the History of Ideas*
JJS	*Journal of Jewish Studies*
JNES	*Journal of Near Eastern Studies*
JPS	Jewish Publication Society
JQR	*Jewish Quarterly Review*
JR	*Journal of Religion*
JSJ	*Journal for the Study of Judaism in the Persian,*

	Hellenistic and Roman Period
JSNTSup	*Journal for the Study of the New Testament Supplement Series*
JSOT	*Journal for the Study of the Old Testament*
JSOTSup	*JSOT Supplement Series*
JSP	*Journal for the Study of Pseudepigrapha*
JSQ	*Jewish Studies Quarterly*
JSS	*Journal of Semitic Studies*
JTS	*Journal of Theological Studies*
KAI	*Kanaanäische und aramäische Inschriften*, 3 vols, ed. H. Donner and W. Röllig, Wiesbaden: Otto Harrasowitz, 1962
KHAT	Kurzer Hand commentar zum Alten Testament
KJV	King James Version
MT	Masoretic Text
NCBC	New Century Bible Commentary
NEB	New English Bible
NJPS	New JPS Bible translation (*Tanakh: A New Translation of the Holy Scriptures According to the Traditional Hebrew Text*)
NLH	*New Literary History*
NRSV	*New Revised Standard Version*
NS	*New Series*
OBO	*Orbis biblicus et orientalis*
OBT	*Overtures to Biblical Theology*
Or	*Orientalia*
OTL	Old Testament Library
OTP	*Old Testament Pseudepigrapha*, 2 vols, ed. J. Charlesworth, Garden City, NY: Doubleday, 1983–7
OTS	*Oudtestamentische Studiën*
PAAJR	*Proceedings of the American Academy for Jewish Research*
RB	*Revue biblique*
REB	Revised English Bible
RGG	*Religion in Geschichte und Gegenwart*
RSV	Revised Standard Version
SBL	Society of Biblical Literature
SBLDS	SBL Dissertation Series
SBLMS	SBL Monograph Series
SBLSCSS	SBL: Septuagint and Cognate Studies
SBT	Studies in Biblical Theology
ScrHier	*Scripta Hierosolymitana*
Sem	*Semeia*
SJOT	*Scandinavian Journal of the Old Testament*

SNTSMS	Society for New Testament Studies Monograph Series
SVT	Supplement to *VT*
SWBA	The Social World of Biblical Antiquity
TAPS	Transactions of the American Philosophical Society
TCS	Texts from Cuneiform Sources
TDNT	*Theological Dictionary of the New Testament*, ed. G. Kittel and G. Friedrich, trans. G. W. Bromiley, Grand Rapids: Eerdmans, 1964–76
TDOT	*Theological Dictionary of the Old Testament*, ed. G. J. Botterweck *et al.*, trans. J. T. Willis *et al.*, Grand Rapids: Eerdmans, 1974–
ThStud	Theologische Studien
TLZ	*Theologische Literaturzeitung*
TWAT	*Theologisches Wörterbuch zum Alten Testament*, ed. G. J. Botterweck *et al.*, Stuttgart: Kohlhammer, 1970–
VT	*Vetus Testamentum*
WMANT	Wissenschaftliche Monographien zum Alten und Neuen Testament
YNER	Yale Near Eastern Researches
ZA	*Zeitschrift für Assyriologie*
ZAW	*Zeitschrift für die alttestamentliche Wissenschaft*

The abbreviations of biblical books, pseudepigraphical and rabbinic literature follow the conventions of *JBL*, as found most recently in *American Academy of Religion – Society of Biblical Literature Membership Directory and Handbook* (Atlanta and Decatur, GA: Society of Biblical Literature, 1993), 386–90. For the sake of convenience, the abbreviations of the books of the Hebrew Bible are presented below:

Gen	Genesis
Exod	Exodus
Lev	Leviticus
Num	Numbers
Deut	Deuteronomy
Josh	Joshua
Judg	Judges
1–2 Sam	1–2 Samuel
1–2 Kgs	1–2 Kings
Isa	Isaiah
Jer	Jeremiah
Ezek	Ezekiel
Hos	Hosea
Joel	Joel
Amos	Amos

Obad	Obadiah
Jonah	Jonah
Mic	Micah
Nah	Nahum
Hab	Habakkuk
Zeph	Zephaniah
Hag	Haggai
Zech	Zechariah
Mal	Malachi
Ps	Psalms
Job	Job
Prov	Proverbs
Ruth	Ruth
Cant	Canticles (Song of Songs)
Qoh	Qohelet (Ecclesiastes)
Lam	Lamentations
Esth	Esther
Dan	Daniel
Ezra	Ezra
Neh	Nehemiah
1–2 Chr	1–2 Chronicles

INTRODUCTION
The new biblical historiography

First of all it should be understood that we are not
here interested in the "historical David," as though we could
isolate and identify the real thing. That is not available to
us.

Walter Brueggemann, *David's Truth in Israel's Imagination
and Memory* (Philadelphia: Fortress, 1985), 13

All history is created.[1] Events transpire, but people tell and record, select
and reshape them, creating historical texts. The nature of these texts varies
widely, reflecting the interests and skills of their authors. Some retellings
of the past attempt to depict the events as they transpired, others cloak a
particular ideology in historical garb, while still others aim primarily to
enlighten or to entertain. These functions are not necessarily mutually
exclusive; one person may compose an entertaining ideological text, or a
text which was originally interested in the actual past may be reshaped by
a later author with didactic aims.

In this book, I will explore a selection of biblical texts in an attempt to
discover how the texts might have functioned in antiquity. I will study the
texts themselves rather than the events which lie behind them.[2] The importance of this type of inquiry has been recognized in several recent studies.
K. Lawson Younger, Jr explores the historical, ideological and literary
aspects of ancient Near Eastern texts, noting:

> While it is perfectly valid (and important) to ask questions concerning
> which events were narrated, it is equally valid and important to ask
> questions concerning the way in which events were narrated. In fact
> it is the latter questions which reveal the texts' ultimate purpose.[3]

A similar idea has been expressed concerning Islamic historical texts:

> Instead of asking what a premodern Muslim author was trying to do
> as a historian and how he accomplished his goals, the scholar of

1

Islamicate history has usually been content to ask what information the source provides that can be useful in solving *his own* problems.[4]

Throughout this book I will show what various biblical authors were "trying to do" when they wrote works which we typically categorize as historical.

The approach I suggest questions the traditional assumption that ancient Israelite and early Jewish religions were fundamentally historical religions in the sense of being primarily concerned with, and based on, actual events in history.[5] A strong impetus for my dissenting perspective comes from a study by Moshe David Herr, "The Conception of History among the Sages."[6] He points to an idiom in rabbinic literature: "what was, was," which shows the rabbis" complete disregard for actual events of the past.[7] Based on the use of that idiom and other rabbinic evidence, he notes, "there was no question more meaningless or boring [to the rabbis] than the purpose and usefulness of an exact description of what actually transpired."[8]

Modern scholarship has begun to emphasize the significant continuities between biblical Israel and rabbinic Judaism.[9] This suggests that the attitude of the rabbis might well be true for the earlier biblical period as well;[10] this is supported by a close examination of biblical texts. Why, then, does so much much of the Bible look like historical literature? Why and how was this "history-like"[11] material composed?

THE NEW BIBLICAL HISTORIOGRAPHY

My analysis builds upon the newer views that have developed over the last two decades concerning the way in which texts which purport to narrate the Israelite past have been understood. Biblical books that were previously viewed as history in the sense of a generally accurate depiction of the Israelite past are now seen as historiography, literally "history writing," a term typically used to emphasize the creative nature of historical texts.[12] This change is not entirely new; in many ways, it is a return to the position espoused by Julius Wellhausen over a century ago. Wellhausen's position, however, was relatively short-lived due to the tremendous influence of scholars such as Albrecht Alt and William Foxwell Albright.[13]

The more recent return to the skepticism of Wellhausen can be traced by comparing the three Bible survey volumes published this century by the Society for Old Testament Study. The relevant section in *Record and Revelation*, published in 1938, is entitled "The History of Israel," and attempts a short reconstruction of the history of Israel.[14] The comparable chapter in *The Old Testament and Modern Study*, published in 1951, is entitled "The Historical Books" and is primarily concerned with the date and sources of these books.[15] The most recent chapter, in *Tradition and*

Interpretation, published in 1979, is entitled "Old Testament Historiography";[16] it probes the relation between biblical and ancient Near Eastern historiography and explores the theology of large blocks of biblical historiographic material. These changes reflect a movement from history in the sense of a reconstruction of the past to history as a narrative which is influenced by its authors' religious and political ideologies.

The change reflected in the titles and contents of these surveys may be seen in other ways. For example, in the last twenty years, scholars have begun to write articles on topics which are fundamentally different from those of their predecessors. Typical works from the middle portion of this century attempted to reconstruct the actual history of Israel, and sometimes used ancient Near Eastern texts toward this purpose. Classic articles such as Roland de Vaux's "The Prophets of Baal on Mount Carmel"[17] or Albrecht Alt's "The Monarchy in the Kingdoms of Israel and Judah"[18] typify this genre. While similar works continue to be written, especially in Europe, these have been supplemented by studies such as W. Lee Humphrey's "From Tragic Hero to Villain: A Study of the Figure of Saul and the Development of 1 Samuel"[19] and Lillian R. Klein's *The Triumph of Irony in the Book of Judges*.[20] Works of this sort, dealing with literary or rhetorical aspects of texts such as Judges, Samuel and Kings, are now regularly published in the mainstream scholarly journals; they were largely absent before the 1970s.

A further significant indication of the changes of the last decades may be seen in the reactions to *A History of Ancient Israel and Judah* by J. Maxwell Miller and John Hayes, published in 1986.[21] More than fifty pages of review articles on Miller and Hayes were published in a leading journal, most of which questioned the working assumptions of the authors in their attempt to recreate the ancient Israelite past.[22] Many reviewers wondered if a history of Israel could be written or is worth writing. The book's authors were especially criticized for paying too much attention to the biblical text and too little attention to sociological modeling. These criticisms were seen as so fundamental to the traditional venture of writing the history of Israel, that one of the book's authors entitled his response "In Defense of Writing a History of Israel."[23] This is the first time that the publication of such a volume evoked such questions. It is possible that this book's explicit treatment of methodological issues created a new awareness of the basic methodological problems involved in the writing of Israelite history, inviting scholars to criticize it. The criticism continues. Thompson's recent *Early History of the Israelite People From Written and Archaeological Sources* has "deconstruction" as its *Leitwort*, and another recent work has claimed that the genre History of Israel "is probably obsolete."[24]

The changes of the last several decades may be symbolized by the contrasting treatments in 1944 and 1985 of the biblical narrative about

King David. In Gerhard von Rad's classic 1944 essay, "The Beginning of History Writing in Ancient Israel,"[25] he calls the succession narrative, the biblical story in Samuel and Kings concerning the fight for the throne of David, "The oldest piece of ancient Israelite historical writing,"[26] by which he means that it contains "acute perception of the realities of a nation's situation" and use of "historical contingency [and] . . . cause and effect."[27] Much more recently, Walter Brueggemann introduces his book *David's Truth in Israel's Imagination and Memory* with the following: "First of all it should be understood that we are not here interested in the 'historical David,' as though we could isolate and identify the real thing. That is not available to us."[28] These two studies typify the changing attitudes over the last half-century.

The changes reflect a shift away from concern with texts as a source for the social, political or religious history of the Israelite past to an interest in the literary merits or ideological underpinnings of the texts.[29] Several factors working together are responsible for this shift.

Over the last few decades, scholars have paid more attention to questions concerning the Deuteronomist, the supposed author or editor of the books Deuteronomy through Kings. Until the nineteenth century, most Bible readers saw the first five books of the Bible, namely the Pentateuch or Torah, as a unit. As a result of the critical study of the Bible, which saw the Pentateuchal sources continuing into the book of Joshua, it became customary to speak of the Hexateuch, that is the six books from Genesis through Joshua.[30] This was changed with the publication in 1943 of Martin Noth's *Überlieferungsgeschichtliche Studien*,[31] which remains a classic of biblical scholarship, and suggests that the first four books of Genesis through Numbers are a unit, and must be distinguished from Deuteronomy through Kings, which are labeled the Deuteronomistic History. Noth's study is essential in that the attribution of such a large corpus, namely Deuteronomy though Kings, to a single hand must be defended by examining how the editor reworked earlier materials[32] using a consistent ideology. As a result, the ideology of a historical work became a more central focus of attention than the text's historicity or sources. This was a catalyst for a debate concerning the text's ideology and the extent of its pervasiveness.[33] As other scholars began to cast doubts on the unity of this corpus, they advanced their arguments by noting the multiplicity of ideologies within the Deuteronomistic History.[34] Thus, the isolation of the Deuteronomistic History as a separate corpus and the debate concerning the number and provenience of the Deuteronomistic Historians have helped to accentuate the role of ideology in the writing of biblical historical texts.[35]

A second factor responsible for the shift of focus from history to historiography is the introduction of social scientific models into biblical studies. While there were some early experiments in this direction at the turn of the century, George Mendenhall's 1962 article on "The Hebrew Conquest of Palestine"[36] has served as a catalyst for further studies which apply social scientific methods to biblical texts.[37] The authors of these studies vary widely in terms of their methodologies, but they frequently emphasize the lack of historicity of major blocks of the biblical text.

This negative assessment has been centered around the claims of archeologists that the predominant biblical account of Joshua conquering Canaan should be rejected in favor of the peaceful settlement of Canaan.[38] Some biblical scholars are now moving beyond the early history of Israel, and are questioning the historicity of an ever-increasing number of texts. For example, Thomas L. Thompson notes in reference to the reconstruction of Israelite history, including that of the monarchy, "One cannot but question any alleged 'reliable pool of information.' "[39] He follows a position advocated by Niels Peter Lemche, "I propose that we decline to be led by the biblical account and instead regard it, like other legendary materials, as formally ahistorical; that is, as a source which only exceptionally can be verified by other information."[40] While the positions of Lemche, Davies[41] and Thompson have not gained general assent, these three scholars have begun to make contemporary scholars who attempt to reconstruct ancient Israelite history much more aware of the fundamental problems involved in their task.

Two external developments have begun to change the direction of study of biblical historical texts. The "New History" or *"annales* school," which emphasizes social rather than political history,[42] has recently begun to influence the work of several biblical scholars.[43] This has happened especially in the United States, as biblicists have moved away from theological models and interests and have become a more integral part of the university, open to newer developments outside of the theological disciplines.[44] The second external development is the rise of the study of rhetoric within general historiography. This movement is especially associated with Hayden White in the States and Paul Veyne in France, and has produced works such as "The Fictions of Factual Representation"[45] and "Plots, Not Facts . . . ,"[46] which defend the literary and ideological nature of all history writing. To the extent that biblical scholars are becoming more attuned to the intellectual world of the university, they are increasingly influenced by these general developments.[47]

A final factor influencing the changing viewpoints of scholars concerning texts narrating Israel's past is the rise of the movement to study the Bible as literature.[48] This movement began to develop in the 1960s under the influence of such figures as Meir Weiss,[49] Luis Alonso Schökel[50] and James Muilenberg.[51] The movement gained momentum and extensively dealt with prose texts in the mid-1970s. The publication in 1975 of J. P. Fokkelman's *Narrative Art in Genesis: Specimens of Stylistic and Structural Analysis,*[52] the first book-length study in a European language to apply new-critical insights to biblical narrative texts, is an important landmark in this respect.

5

Two of the earliest applications of this method to longer historical episodes are by David Gunn, who wrote literary analyses of the stories of King David and Saul.[53] The literary treatment of biblical historical texts reached broader audiences with the publication in 1981 of Robert Alter's *The Art of Biblical Narrative*.[54] Thus, by the early 1980s, literary, largely new-critical methodologies were applied to narrative texts that were previously considered historical. This movement has gained many adherents, causing a massive shift in how texts narrating Israel's past are studied.[55]

The various changes suggested above have acted in concert to alter radically the way in which we study biblical texts concerned with Israel's past. Until the early 1970s, there was a general consensus that the best way to study texts such as Judges or Kings was to use the tools of the historian, for these texts are in some sense "historical." For many American scholars, especially those sympathetic to the work of William Foxwell Albright, the texts were "historical" in the sense of being reasonably accurate depictions of the history of ancient Israel.[56] American scholarship has now moved quite far from this position, but there is no single unifying figure or position which has replaced the Albright school. The old consensus is gone, and there is no indication that a new one is developing to replace it.

I do not presume to hope that the following study will offer the beginning of a new consensus concerning the nature of biblical historical texts. My goals are much more modest – I propose to illustrate what I believe to be the four central factors responsible for the production of ancient Israelite biblical texts: the use of typologies, the interpretation of earlier texts, what others have considered literary shaping, and ideological influence.[57] These factors will be illustrated through selected examples in Chapters Three through Six. These principles, however, do not work in isolation; this will be illustrated in Chapter Seven, which shows how the four factors may be seen working together in 2 Kings 17.

A different way of studying these four factors would have been to examine an entire corpus of biblical texts, such as the Deuteronomistic History, following the model of John van Seters' *In Search of History*[58] or, in a related field, Charles William Fornara's *The Nature of History in Ancient Greece and Rome*.[59] I do not feel that enough of the groundwork has been laid to allow such a survey of biblical history writing to be completed. Instead, I have used as a model T. P. Wiseman's *Clio's Cosmetics: Three Studies in Greco-Roman Literature*,[60] which analyzes key texts to illuminate the outstanding features of classical history writing. I have chosen texts that highlight particular issues in Israelite history writing, while 2 Kings 17 shows how various concerns are shared in a single complex unit.

These extended case studies, which are the core of this book, are framed by sections which consider methodological issues. I begin with an examination of the terms most closely associated with the type of study I am pursuing: "history," 'ideology" and "literature" (Chapter One). I follow this with a study of the Book of Chronicles (Chapter Two), which is the only biblical text whose methods of composition can be observed with relative certainty because its sources are still extant. These first two chapters thus offer the theoretical underpinnings of the book.

I conclude with an examination of the entailments of my analysis of texts for the modern biblical historian. Though my focus in this book is not on the writing of modern histories of Judah and Israel, my understanding of the nature of biblical texts has significant ramifications for how such histories should be written. Exploring these implications is worthwhile given the importance of biblical history within both ancient Near Eastern history and the study of Israelite theology.

1

DEFINING HISTORY, IDEOLOGY AND LITERATURE

The ability of the ancients to invent and their capacity to believe
are persistently underestimated.

M. I. Finley, *Ancient History: Evidence and Models* (New
York: Viking, 1986), 9

ON DEFINITIONS

The three terms "history," 'ideology" and "literature" have played a central
role in scholarly literature on biblical historical texts, yet there is no
uniform understanding of these terms. For example, different volumes in
the series The Forms of the Old Testament Literature[1] present different
definitions of the genre history. One volume defines it as "Designed to
record events of the past as they actually occurred. The structure is controlled by chronological stages or cause–effect sequences of events as the
author(s) understood them."[2] Another considers "history":

> An extensive, continuous, written composition made up of and based
> upon various materials, some originally traditional and oral, others
> written, and devoted to a particular subject or historical period.
> The author of history links together his materials and unifies the
> whole by imposing overarching structural and thematic connections.
> History is dominated by a concern with chronology and cause–effect
> relationships; it seeks to place events and how they occurred with-
> in a framework of interpretation and in relation to the author's
> own time. For purposes of literary definition, it is not important
> whether, from our modern point of view, the events actually occur-
> red as reported. . . . Writers of history intended to document, reflect
> on, and organize the past in order to understand, legitimate, or
> define in some way the institutional and social reality of their own
> time.[3]

The two different definitions would yield quite different lists of biblical

8

texts that should be considered "history"; examination of additional definitions by other biblical scholars would yield more diversity.

This lack of consensus might suggest that it is pointless to propose definitions of history or of other central terms. Indeed, some eminent historians have suggested that definitions of history are counterproductive, and only act as a "prison."[4] I disagree, since I feel that a "definition . . . [i]f properly formulated . . . can become an efficient tool for clear thinking."[5] Furthermore, I believe that the process of evaluating various proposed definitions helps to clarify for the reader my stance on several central issues.[6]

A definition should be concise, and just broad enough to include what is typically considered essential.[7] Thus, definitions of the type of Long's second, "longer" definition, cited above, should be avoided. Additionally, although it is interesting to see the etymological meaning of central terms such as "history," and the use of its cognate predecessors in Greek and Latin literature,[8] definitions must reflect usage and not etymology.

This notion of "definition" as a heuristic instrument useful within a particular discipline rather than as an objective description of an absolute reality underscores the subjectivity and partial circularity of biblical studies. A definition is chosen with a corpus of texts in mind and a (pre-) understanding of those texts; that definition is then used to understand those texts. This process, which is central to scholarship, is described clearly by John Barton, in his study of the methodologies of biblical scholarship:

> Biblical "methods" are *theories* rather than methods: theories which result from the formalizing of intelligent intuitions about the meaning of biblical texts. Texts are perceived as having certain sorts of meaning – or, just as interestingly, as failing to convey meaning – by reading them with certain vague expectations . . . which are either confirmed and clarified, or disappointed and frustrated. The reading begins again, this time with a sharper focus; and at the end of the process there emerges a distinct impression of what the text means, together with an explanatory theory as to how it comes to mean it. But the theory . . . is logically subsequent to the intuitions about meaning. It may lead to useful insights into other texts, when they are approached in a similar frame of mind, and so may greatly shorten the quest to understand them.[9]

My definitions, reached after many readings of the biblical historical corpus, attempt to reflect my crystallization of the "vague expectations" of how that corpus should be interpreted; their success will be judged by the extent to which they offer others a useful "frame of mind" for understanding biblical historical texts.

However, the subjectivity involved in biblical scholarship should not suggest a state of anarchy, where all definitions, theories and interpretations are equally valid.[10] Instead, I would side with Jon Levenson, who believes that though "we all have biases," theories may be evaluated by the extent to which they agree with the data, which we may evaluate because the idea that "all we have is biases" is false.[11] Ultimately, the definitions proposed here must be judged by their usefulness in understanding the biblical texts, the data that we possess.

HISTORY

A century ago, the great American historian Frederick Jackson Turner wrote, "The conceptions of history have been almost as numerous as the men who have written history."[12] Conceptions of history have multiplied even further since Turner wrote, especially with the growth of social history and cliometrics.[13] Rather than surveying all of the proposed conceptions of history that might be useful to biblical scholars,[14] I will examine Collingwood's influential understanding of history, as representative of the notion that biblical texts should not be considered history. I will then concentrate on two definitions of history used by biblical scholars. A discussion of the problems with these definitions offers the backdrop for my proposal concerning the definition of history within biblical studies.

In *The Idea of History*, R. G. Collingwood claims that "history is a kind of research or inquiry" whose object is "*res gestae*: actions of human beings that have been done in the past"; it "proceeds by the interpretation of evidence" and has as its object "human self-knowledge."[15] The scientific nature of history is crucial for Collingwood, who sees Herodotus as the first historian and entitles one of his chapters: "The Creation of Scientific History by Herodotus."[16] He explicitly rejects the possibility that Mesopotamian or biblical texts might be categorized as history.[17]

Collingwood's definition is unnecessarily restrictive. It reflects a modern bias toward scientific history, a bias which reflects the relatively recent growth of history as a university academic discipline.[18] Few, if any, premodern works would be characterized as history if we rigidly followed Collingwood; as M. I. Finley has noted, "The ability of the ancients to invent and their capacity to believe are persistently underestimated."[19] A recent article focussing on Herodotus notes that many ancient historians believed that truth is not essential for history.[20] Indeed, many classical scholars deny that Herodotus was a scientific historian in Collingwood's sense.[21] Even the reputation of Thucydides, who is often seen as the first objective historian by those skeptical of Herodotus, has begun to wane.[22] For example, Virginia J. Hunter has noted: "Factual accuracy and objectivity have long been considered the major qualities of Thucydides" *History*. This is a one-sided, if not totally distorted view of the historian and his method of composition."[23] At times, she notes, Thucydides fits events into patterns, "generat[ing] facts for which he had no evidence."[24] To the extent that Thucydides might have been interested in objectivity, he was very atypical of classical historians.[25] In sum, Collingwood misrepresents Herodotus and other pre-modern historians, and his understanding of history is not useful in examining the conception of history in antiquity.[26]

John van Seters' *In Search of History: Historiography in the Ancient World and the Origins of Biblical History*[27] is the most significant recent synthetic work on ancient Near Eastern history writing. It offers both a survey of Israelite history within its ancient Near Eastern background and an exploration of the historiographical nature of the books Joshua–Kings. He begins with a precise definition of history,[28] that of the Dutch historian, Johan Huizinga, "*History is the intellectual form in which a civilization renders account to itself of its past.*"[29] Rather than evaluating the secondary use of Huizinga's definition by van Seters, I will turn to Huizinga's original article, where the implications of the definition are adumbrated.[30] Huizinga sees a "sharp distinction between history and literature," and claims that history "is almost entirely lacking in that element of play which underlies literature from beginning to end."[31] As we shall see later in this chapter, this sharp dichotomy between literature and history is rightly rejected by most scholars of ancient texts, and by many who study modern historical writing as well. An additional problem of applying Huizinga's definition to the Hebrew Bible is that we often know so little of the event which stands behind the biblical historical narrative, that we cannot discern the extent of the "element of play." Any understanding of history which depends on historicity cannot be profitably applied to the biblical corpus.[32] In sum, to the extent that Huizinga's definition of history implicitly emphasizes a correct self-understanding by the civilization, it is unsuitable for the Bible, which typically cannot be evaluated in these terms.[33]

A more recent attempt at understanding biblical history, published in 1988, is Baruch Halpern's *The First Historians: The Hebrew Bible and History*.[34] Halpern sidesteps the issue of historicity, and defines history on the basis of the intention of the text's author: "Whether a text is history, then, depends on what its author meant to do."[35] More specifically, a text's classification as history depends on its "author's relationship to the evidence."[36] True history is typified by its "antiquarian interest,"[37] and should be contrasted with "romance," which contains elaborations "unnecessary to the presentation of a reconstruction from the evidence."[38] Phrased differently, the central issue for us to consider in determining whether to label a biblical text "history" is whether "the narrator ha[d] reason to believe what he or she wrote."[39]

This type of definition is highly problematic. How do we know if an elaboration goes beyond the evidence the author had, especially when that evidence is no longer available to us? Furthermore, if in "elaboration" he includes literary embellishment, it is noteworthy that relatively few biblical texts are lists; the biblical historians did embellish their works, fashioning facts and traditions into a narrative that people would listen to or read.

The "author's relationship to the evidence" is central to Halpern's understanding of history, but it is difficult, if not impossible, to judge whether a biblical author was working from sources. The Chronicler provides an instructive analogy: there are still many places where it is seriously debated whether he based his narrative on sources, or might have fabricated material for ideological reasons.[40] Even with our knowledge of the Chronicler, whose historical period is generally agreed upon, and many of whose sources are extant, we cannot always decide whether he was writing in Halpern's terms "history" or "romance"; the case of the Deuteronomistic History, whose dating is debated and whose sources are (generally) no longer extant, is certainly more difficult to determine. Phrased differently, Halpern's definition is useless because in much of the Deuteronomistic History, we have no ability to determine whether the author "ha[d] reason to believe what he or she wrote."

Finally, Halpern's definition relies upon our ability to reconstruct the intentions of the biblical authors. The criterion of "intentionality" has been found to be wanting in determining whether classical texts are history;[41] the case would be similar for biblical texts. In their revised statement concerning the intentional fallacy, W. K. Wimsatt and Monroe C. Beardsley claim, "The design or the intention of the author is neither available nor desirable as a standard for judging either the meaning or the value of a work of literary art."[42] Though it is true that we must try, through careful analysis of texts, to figure out the purposes that particular biblical historical texts had in antiquity, and it is thus difficult to sidestep totally the issue of intentionality, Halpern's model is especially problematic because it places intentionality in such a central role.

In sum, definitions that emphasize the scientific nature of history, its fundamental differences from literature, or the intentions of an author, are problematic. For these reasons, I propose defining a historical narrative within biblical studies as "a narrative that presents a past."[43] The group of "narratives that present a past" delimits a meaningful corpus of biblical texts which may be distinguished from other corpora, such as law, proverbs, psalms and (most of) prophecy. It does not, one may object, allow for the traditional distinction between myth or legend and history; however, as Matitiahu Tsevat notes, there is no internal biblical reason to distinguish between these genres; from the perspective of the Israelite, "the waters of Noah are no less real than the waters of Shiloah."[44]

IDEOLOGY

There is no accepted definition of "ideology"; indeed, "There are few words in our language as frequently used (at least in some contexts), and at the same time as ambiguous, as open to contrary interpretations, as the words 'ideology' and 'ideological.' "[45] The issue is further complicated by the fact that the understanding of ideology, as noted by Clifford Geertz, has become highly ideological.[46]

"Ideology" frequently is understood in a derogatory fashion,[47] often as "a system of illusory beliefs – false ideas or false consciousness – which can be contrasted with true or scientific knowledge."[48] This derogatory connotation is connected to the use of the term by Marx.[49] Originally, the word was positive rather than negative; it has its origins in the late nine-teenth-century *idéologie* in the sense of "science of ideas," though it soon gained a new sense.[50] In finding a definition of ideology for biblical studies, it is desirable to avoid both the original, overly general, and the more recent pejorative sense of the word.[51] Overly narrow definitions,[52] or long descriptions that present themselves as definitions, must also be avoided.[53]

Several scholars of antiquity have adopted definitions of ideology that are appropriate for ancient texts. For example, Eric Carlton, in his comparative study of the relationship between ideology and social order in Egypt and Athens,[54] uses Julius Gould's definition from *A Dictionary of the Social Sciences*, "*Ideology* is a pattern of beliefs and concepts (both factual and normative) which purport to explain complex social phenomena with a view to directing and simplifying socio-political choices facing individuals and groups."[55] This definition has been applied to biblical texts by Younger,[56] but is cumbersome. More suitable is a modification of Althusser's definition of ideology suggested by the French historian George Duby in a survey of "Ideologies in Social History": "a system (possessing its own logic and structure) of representations (images, myths, ideas or concepts) existing and playing a historical role within a given society."[57] This definition highlights the systemic nature of ideologies, the various forms in which they may manifest themselves and the importance of seeing them within their social and historical context. This definition of Duby would fit the uses of the term "ideology" in Assyriological studies[58] and the use by biblical scholars of terms such as "Davidic ideology."[59] Furthermore, it is general enough to incorporate both religious and political patterns of belief under a single rubric.[60] This definition of "ideology" offers a convenient umbrella for understanding how religious and political belief systems shaped the writing of history in Israel.

The term "propaganda" is often associated with "ideology." Although it might be prudent to avoid the word altogether because of its strongly negative contemporary connotation,[61] propaganda is a useful term when applied to the production of literature in antiquity.[62] Propaganda was originally a neutral term, used especially within the Church in relation to the propagation of ideas.[63] Although the definition of propaganda continues to be debated,[64] much scholarly literature continues to use it in a neutral sense, even recognizing that it is a fundamental part of human communication[65] and has certain positive features. For example, Jacques Ellul claims that people need propaganda,[66] as it reduces tension "by making man live in a familiar climate of opinion." It is used during times of peace as well as war, and has both defensive and offensive purposes.[67] The word, in the sense of an attempt to persuade a group to follow a particular ideology,[68] can be used profitably in relation to the Bible and other religious texts.

The connection between propaganda and ideology has been made in biblical studies by Keith Whitelam,[69] in rabbinics by Robert Goldenberg[70] and in the study of Assyrian palace reliefs by Irene Winter.[71] It also has been noted in general studies of propaganda by Jacques Ellul[72] and others.[73] Following the lead of these scholars, ideology will here refer to a specific type of sets of beliefs, while propaganda will refer to the methods used to disseminate and to foster those beliefs.

LITERATURE

It has become commonplace to treat sections of the Bible as literature. This is by no means a new development; a century ago, Richard Moulton published *The Literary Study of the Bible*,[74] which argued that the Bible shows the same literary forms as the great Western literary works. Among turn-of-the-century biblicists, Hermann Gunkel emphasized certain literary features of the biblical text.[75] Literary treatments of the Bible have proliferated since the 1970s. These have been written by biblical scholars as well as scholars of comparative literature such as Robert Alter,[76] Northrop Frye[77] and Meir Sternberg.[78] The influence of Alter on biblical scholars has been especially important; this may be seen, for example, by the space given to his works in academic journals.[79] The focus of biblical studies has changed through this method,[80] and many studies of Judges and Samuel as literature have appeared in the last decade,[81] especially in English-speaking countries.[82]

Most of these studies have applied to the Bible the word "literature" or terms derived from literary study. James L. Kugel incisively called attention to the problem of considering the Bible as literature,[83] though few have paid attention to his critique. With Kugel's critique in mind, I begin with a discussion of the term "literature" and will then examine the applicability of this term to the Bible.

The word "literature" originates from the Latin *litteratura*, "a knowledge of reading and writing," which reflects the Greek *grammatiké*.[84] It began to be used "as a designation for a body of literature" in the 1730s,[85] and by the eighteenth century, it frequently referred to a subcategory of everything written.[86] How, then, is this subcategory to be determined? Some have despaired and insisted that the word "literature" be used only in its broadest, etymological sense of "all written works"[87]; others, like Tzvetan Todorov have moved in the opposite direction and have wondered, "could it be that . . . literature does not exist?"[88]

Definitions of "literature" emphasize either: (1) the language of the text, (2) its literary organization, or (3) the social phenomena relating to its reception.[89] The first two types of definition may be considered structural, in that they find something intrinsic to the structure of the literary work itself that makes it literature,[90] while the last approach may be considered functional.[91]

The approach that concentrates on the language of the text is most closely associated with the movements of the Russian Formalists, especially the group called The Prague School.[92] However, that school typically uses poetic texts to illustrate the nature of literature, and does not offer a useful definition of what might make historical prose texts of the Bible literary.[93] Furthermore, any definition which concentrates solely on a text's language would probably not be able to differentiate between what is typically perceived as the successful, "literary" use of these devices in what is some-times called Literature, and their stock or hackneyed use in non-literary works.[94] For these reasons, a definition of literature which relies on the formal study of the use of language is not satisfactory for our purposes.

Definitions that emphasize a text's "literary organization," suggesting that literature is a particular type of artistic or aesthetic text, are highly subjective.[95] These definitions depend on the definitions of "artistic" or "aesthetic"; there is, however, no accepted definition of these terms among art historians and philosophers who study aesthetics, and many scholars have argued that aesthetics itself must be defined functionally rather than structurally.[96]

The objectionable nature of definitions of "literature'" which are based on aesthetic judgement may be seen by examining two such definitions by significant literary scholars. In their classic work *Theory of Literature*, René Wellek and Austin Warren contrast literary to scientific language.[97] The former is connotative, aesthetic and relatively unpragmatic, while the latter is denotative.[98] In sum, "a literary work of art is not a simple object but rather a highly complex organization of a stratified character with multiple meanings and relationships."[99] Although this type of definition satisfies some of the qualities that we typically see in literary texts, it contains too many vague terms to be useful – "simple object," 'highly complex" and "multiple meanings." Not only do these terms defy the type of clear delimitation that we expect of definitions, they are highly subjec-tive[100] – who determines whether a text has multiple meanings? What type of stratification makes a text literary?

Similar problems may be found in Robert Alter's conception of literature as developed in his recent *The Pleasures of Reading in an Ideological Age*.[101] Alter notes:

If any purposeful ordering of language implies some intention of communication, literature is remarkable for its densely layered communication, its capacity to open up multifarious connections and multiple interpretations to the recipient of the communication, and for the pleasure it produces in making the instrument of communication a satisfying aesthetic object – or more precisely, the pleasure it gives us as we experience the nice interplay between the verbal aesthetic form and the complex meanings involved.[102] ... But this general quality of *cohesion*, as some linguists call it, is heightened to such a degree in literary texts that it becomes a difference in kind.[103] ... But it is only the literary text that as a matter of intrinsic purpose marshals all these resources for the construction of a "world" – a reordering through language, and language made prominent, of the elements of experience in order to express a certain vision or understanding or visceral apprehension of them.[104]

Alter's definition is quite beautiful and initially compelling, but is ultimately problematic. For example, how "densely layered" must the work be to qualify, and who decides? After all, the extent of a text's layering is often open to dispute among critics. Who is the ultimate arbiter concerning the extent to which the text's language is "made prominent"? At what point does the use of literary devices become not merely a difference of extent, but a "difference in kind" that can make a work literary?

The questions provoked by Wellek and Warren and by Alter suggest that literature is best defined functionally rather than structurally. This position has been articulated most clearly by Marxist critics, such as Terry Eagleton[105] and Raymond Williams.[106] For example, the latter notes:

The shift from "learning" to "taste" or "sensibility" was in effect the final stage of a shift from a para-national scholarly profession, with its original base in the church and then in the universities, and with the classical languages as its shared material, to a profession increasingly defined by its class position, from which essentially general criteria, applicable in fields other than literature, were derived.[107]

Although the explicit connection of "literature" to "class position" may be particular to Marxists, the recognition of the social basis of literature, and the value of offering a functional definition of it, are frequently recognized by theorists and critics who are not typically considered Marxist.

A compelling analysis of literature as a social category is John Ellis, *The Theory of Literary Criticism: A Logical Analysis*. He writes: "literary texts are defined as those that are used by the society in such a way that *the text is not taken as specifically relevant to the immediate context of its origin.*"[108] Literary texts are determined by the community, not by their authors; this explains how historical works such as Gibbon's *Decline and*

Fall of the Roman Empire are later recognized as works of literature.[109] Ellis' definition, as he recognizes, has the distinct advantage of avoiding the issue of aesthetics.[110] Ellis offers a strong extended analogy between "literature" and "weed"[111]; both are defined differently by different communities according to specific concerns and needs.

Similar conceptions based on the audience of literature and the social setting in which literature has been produced have been offered by other scholars.[112] Some have used the term "honorific" to express the exalted social status presumed by the groups who see specific texts as literary.[113] Several scholars have observed that the concept of "literature" is connected to the death of the classical curriculum at the turn of the century.[114] In this view, the determination of what is "literature" is neither a personal decision[115] nor a popular decision,[116] but is institutionally determined. The process of change through which post-classical works became recognized as worthy of university study and became classified as "literature" has been illustrated in detail by Gerald Graf, *Professing Literature: An Institutional History.*[117]

Since the structural definitions of literature may not be applied to the Bible, we are left with functional definitions, which recognize that what is literature is socially determined, in contemporary times, often by the universities. We may therefore speak of the Bible as part of the contemporary literary canon,[118] but it would be anachronistic to consider it literature from a historical-critical perspective, since we have no reason to believe that some ancient Israelite texts were considered literary while others were not.[119] Various rhetorical or literary devices and genres which are known from modern literature may be isolated in the Bible,[120] but as we saw, such structural arguments are not decisive in determining whether a work is literature, since the term "literature" should be understood from a functional perspective. For these reasons, I will avoid the term "literature" in this study; this contrasts with the terms "history" and "ideology," which may be defined, and have here been defined, to bring out *fundamental* similarities between biblical and other ancient, medieval and modern texts.

This position does not deny that there are structures (such as chiasm) in biblical texts. Nor am I suggesting that the Bible lacks extensive figuration, such as metaphor. What I am suggesting is that the presence of these devices does not legitimize labeling the Bible as "literature," since this term must be defined functionally, and should not be applied to the Hebrew Bible. In addition, business letters are highly structured, and television commercials contain metaphors, but these are hardly considered "literature" by most people. Instead of focussing on the aesthetic accomplishments of biblical texts, we should explore the social dimensions of biblical rhetorical devices, as suggested by Keith Whitelam.[121] This will often force us to consider what others have considered literary under the rubric of ideology.[122]

HISTORY, IDEOLOGY AND RHETORIC IN THE BIBLE

This exploration of appropriate definitions for history, ideology and literature suggests that the authors of historical texts are typically influenced by ideologies. Additionally, though I have rejected the term "literature', narrative devices are used in texts depicting a past, often for ideological purposes. There is nothing new in these observations; outside of biblical studies, the ideological nature of much of history is recognized,[123] and the narrative dimension of almost all history writing is acknowledged.[124]

My position concerning the use of what others would call literary devices in historical texts is very close to Peter Gay, who has studied the styles of great historians in *Style in History*. He claims: "Style ... is the bridge to substance"[125] and observes that narrative devices in historical texts often "become signposts to larger, deeper matters."[126] Similar positions have been advocated in reference to the great classical historians.[127] For example, Thucydides structures his *History* using certain patterns to lead "his reader to make comparisons and contrasts that reveal the meaning of the events he describes"[128] or "to convey the truth about the war in a way which we cannot refute."[129] Others have emphasized that Thucydides" composed speeches are not "for the sake of mere ornament; their inclusion and placement form part of this same process of organization for the purpose of illuminating Thucydides" insights into the development of the war."[130]

The connection between history and ideology is emphasized by Robert Anchor:

> Narrative theory shows beyond a doubt that the world is never given to us in the form of well-made stories, that we make up such stories, that we give them referentiality by imagining that in them the world yields up its various meanings, and that historical narratives, no less than fictional narratives, always serve, in one way or another, to legitimize an actual or ideal social reality.[131]

This has been appreciated by scholars of classical antiquity, especially by M. I. Finley: "The study and writing of history, in short, is a form of ideology."[132] Even Charles Fornara, whose major (ideological) interest as a modern historian of classical history is in showing these works" historicity, is forced to concede:

> Fortunately or unfortunately, history was harnessed early on to "higher purpose," was made to subserve ethics and patriotism.... Although none of this is theoretically incompatible with a strictly veracious account, the reader will readily perceive that the potential for distortion, even unintentional distortion, was great.[133]

Several scholars have explored the ideological nature of rabbinic and medieval Jewish texts.[134] Ivan G. Marcus has depicted the communal and social dimension of history, and thus its openness to ideological influence.[135] In "History and Ideology in Talmudic Narrative," Robert Goldenberg examines the rabbinic stories concerning the Hillelite dynasty as "ideological propaganda."[136] Similar analyses have been written by A. I. Baumgarten in reference to the status of Akiba and Rabbi Judah.[137] William Scott Green, in the essay "History Fabricated: The Social Uses of Narrative in Early Rabbinic Judaism,"[138] has begun to put forward a more synthetic picture of the fundamentally ideological perspective of the rabbis as they wrote history.

These studies make it abundantly clear that I am not claiming originality in combining the realms of ideology, history and rhetoric or narrative.[139] Several biblical studies have examined the connections between history and rhetoric, and have commented on the etymological connections between "story" and "history."[140] The understanding of literature in these articles, however, differs significantly from the one I have presented here. The connection between literature and ideology is the focus of Harold Fisch, *Poetry With a Purpose: Biblical Poetics and Interpretation*.[141] This book is especially valuable because Fisch is very cognizant of the problems in calling the Bible literature, though his approach differs from mine in that his primary ideological focus is on religion rather than on politics. In terms of connecting all three realms, Meir Sternberg in *The Poetics of Biblical Narrative: Ideological Literature and the Drama of Reading* explicitly notes, "ideology, historiography, and aesthetics [are] a trio of functional principles,"[142] and he explores the relationship between them.[143] However, his understanding of ideology is different from mine, and he spends little space examining the role of political ideologies in ancient Israel. In addition, many of his critics have correctly perceived his literary readings as modern, and thus of limited use in studies that are historical-critical, such as this one.[144] An approach which is more kindred to my own is by Keith Whitelam, "Between History and Literature," which advocates: "the historian has to build up a whole network of interrelationships based upon reasoned arguments drawing upon historical, literary, anthropological and sociological evidence."[145]

My "reasoned arguments" begin from the Book of Chronicles. There is a strong consensus concerning the date of Chronicles, its sources are (largely) extant and its methods of composition are known: by examining it first, we are beginning with the (relatively) known and moving to the (relatively) unknown, using Chronicles as a model for what to search for in analyzing other texts. Rather than searching for exact parallels between Chronicles and earlier texts, I will use this work as a general model, concentrating on how the author of Chronicles wrote his history, and on some of the fundamental differences between ancient and modern history writing, especially in reference to chronology and to the use of sources.[146]

2

CHRONICLES AS A MODEL FOR BIBLICAL HISTORY

The Chronicler ... gives such information concerning the past as appears to him most probable, and corrects the sources in conformity with his own historical standards.

Elias Bickerman, *From Ezra to the Last of the Maccabees: Foundations of Postbiblical Judaism* (New York: Schocken, 1962), 22

CHRONICLES: THE BASICS

Most previous treatments of biblical historiography, such as John van Seters" *In Search of History* and Baruch Halpern's *The First Historians*, have ignored Chronicles in favor of the earlier Deuteronomistic History.[1] Their omission of Chronicles is to some extent justified, because their interest is in the beginning of historical writing in Israel. I would, however, advise returning to the position of Julius Wellhausen, who suggested: "We begin the inquiry where the matter is the clearest – namely with the Book of Chronicles,"[2] for it is the Book of Chronicles that provides clear examples of how at least one biblical historian worked, and may shed light on the work of the earlier historians.[3]

The use of post-exilic texts to elucidate earlier texts is especially relevant if there is continuity between pre-exilic and post-exilic Israel. Classical biblical scholarship often drew a clear line between pre-exilic and post-exilic texts, associating the former with ancient Israel, and the latter with Judaism. In some cases, this reflected a strong pro-Christian ideology, which allowed Christianity to be the true continuation of ancient Israelite religion, in contrast to Judaism, which was sometimes depicted as "twisted and perverted."[4] Now, however, many scholars admit the continuity between pre-exilic and post-exilic Judaism.[5] Certainly, the Babylonian deportation was a traumatic experience and Israelite religion changed in some fundamental ways as a result of Israel's deportation from the land of, and its direct contact with, Babylon and various peoples in the cosmopolitan neo-Babylonian world.[6] However, the exile did not cause a clean break with what preceded, nor is there any obvious reason why the exile would change the conceptions of Israelite history writing. These considerations suggest the appropriateness of using Chronicles as a model for other, earlier Israelite historiographical texts. It is especially useful because its date is roughly known,[7] we have contemporaneous texts which reflect the historical background of its author,[8] and many of its sources are extant. These three factors allow us clearly to see how the ideology of the author's time-period influenced his recasting of earlier traditions.

Howard Macy has discerned four general views concerning the Chronicler's[9] use of sources[10]: (1) he had only texts from the Hebrew Bible, and any deviation from this is tendentious; (2) he supplemented the biblical texts with some minimal external sources; (3) he supplemented the biblical texts with fairly extensive external sources; (4) Chronicles and Samuel–Kings both derive from a no longer extant source.[11] The first position is typically identified with Charles C. Torrey,[12] but has been largely abandoned by scholars. As scholars have isolated groups of texts in Chronicles that share similar characteristics, have no parallel in Samuel–Kings, but do not fully represent the Chronicler's ideology and language, a consensus has begun to emerge that the Chronicler did have sources which were not included in the biblical canon.[13] The contemporary debate concerns the relative merits of Macy's second and third positions, namely on the extent of the Chronicler's dependence on sources as opposed to his free creation of traditions. Whatever his dependence on sources, it is important to remember Williamson's observation: "But overall the Chronicler shows himself as the master, not the servant, of his sources. His is the last example of Israel's genius for retelling her sacred history in a way which applies its lessons creatively to the demands of a developing community."[14]

Given the problems of determining the exact form of the sources used by the Chronicler,[15] I will choose my examples from Chronicles with care, trying to use cases where we are relatively confident that the Chronicler has used earlier biblical texts in a form close to the extant Hebrew text (MT). These will provide a sketch of how the Chronicler wrote history, which may serve as a basis for understanding the methods used by other ancient Israelite historians.[16]

RESHAPING THE KNOWN

The Chronicler, writing in the post-exilic period, could not hope to write a new history that would replace the old. The books of Samuel and Kings were well known to his contemporaries, and were probably in some sense authoritative.[17] Some scholars suggest that these books were already canonical.[18] Thus, the Chronicler was most likely not writing a history to replace Samuel and Kings, but desired to reshape the way in which these books would be read and remembered. In other words, the Chronicler assumed that his readers knew these books, or at the very least, considered as authoritative the traditions now found in them, and he attempted to supplement them and to revise sections of them so that his readers would have a "better" idea of what actually happened.[19] In this sense Chronicles may be considered a *"corrective"* to the earlier history.[20]

Different types of evidence suggest that the Chronicler intended his work as a supplement to rather than as a replacement for Samuel–Kings.[21] Many passages in Chronicles make no sense unless the reader is familiar with Samuel–Kings. For example 1 Chronicles 10 narrates the death of Saul, and at the end of the chapter, notes that Saul died for consulting a medium. However, Saul is not properly introduced in Chronicles, and none of the long story of Saul and the necromancer, found in 1 Samuel 28, is told in Chronicles. It is sufficient for the Chronicler to allude to Saul and to that story without fully retelling it because he could assume that his audience was already familiar with it, probably from (some form of) the Book of Samuel.[22]

In addition, the extent of the material covered in Chronicles does not overlap exactly with Samuel–Kings, but begins with Genesis. Thus, if one were to argue that Chronicles was written to replace an earlier work, that work would have to be seen as Genesis–Kings. However, given the interest of Chronicles in the laws of the Torah, which are used and occasionally cited but not systematically repeated, Chronicles can certainly not be seen as a replacement of Genesis–Kings. Rather, it is an attempt to *reshape* the way these books are seen. The Chronicler hoped that his book would be read after Genesis–Kings, and to the extent that it was different, the Chronicler wanted his account to be the one remembered by the reader. It was written as an "authoritative commentary,"[23] to be read in conjunction with its sources.

Initially it seems remarkable that a historian would attempt this venture, and even more remarkable that he should succeed. However, though the Chronicler might look idiosyncratic to us, he was not idiosyncratic from the perspective of his contemporaries. He shares so many ideas with the author(s) of Ezra–Nehemiah, with whom he is probably more or less contemporaneous, that for generations scholars assumed that these books were the product of the same author.[24] Thus, he is re-presenting the history in a way that made his contemporaries likely to sympathize with him.[25] In addition, the book contains over twenty source citations, which serve to support its authority.[26] Although some modern scholars have doubted the existence of these sources, in antiquity these citations likely bolstered the readers" belief in the work's reliability.[27] Thus, to the extent that the Chronicler's contemporaries might have felt that his account differed from the traditions that they knew, predominantly Samuel–Kings, he was reassuring them that his history too was based on old, reliable, authoritative traditions, and thus was as genuine or reasonable as Samuel–Kings. The combination of authoritative "footnoting" and adherence to the values of his contemporaries allowed Chronicles to become accepted, and eventually canonical. It is only in more recent times, with the rise of historical-critical scholarship, the growing interest in early texts among biblical scholars, and our distance from the ideologies and theologies of the Persian period, that we have such difficulty understanding how the Chronicler could possibly have succeeded in "foisting" on his contemporaries this new version of history.

THE CHRONICLER AND "HISTORICAL PROBABILITY"

Lately there has been a great deal of emphasis on the Chronicler as a theologian rather than as a historian.[28] This position has been recently criticized by Mordechai Cogan: "Modern biblical historians would do well if they studied the ancient Chronicler's work not only as a theological statement based on history – the focus of most major investigations during the last two decades – but also as an example of historiographic writing which mirrors the canons of ancient Near Eastern literature."[29] Given the understanding of history developed in the previous chapters, the titles "historian" and "theologian" should not be understood as mutually exclusive, for historians are influenced by ideologies, including religious ideologies, that is, theology. The Chronicler's perception of the past was shaped by a combination of what his earlier sources claimed as seen within his (largely theological) framework. Viewed this way, the Chronicler was a typical, mainstream historian.[30]

When there was no conflict between tradition and his beliefs, the Chronicler let the old version stand. He did not omit the old version, for this might have implied that the earlier tradition was irrelevant or incorrect. Instead, he copied it, though not always slavishly. Sometimes the language was revised slightly or modernized.[31] This is not surprising; in antiquity the notion of textual authority did not automatically presume that the earlier text must be copied word for word.[32] When the Chronicler disagreed with the source or felt it was irrelevant, he omitted it, as may be seen, for example, in the cases of the history of much of the northern kingdom or of David's affair with Bathsheba (2 Sam 11:2ff.).

Fundamental to the world-view of the Chronicler is the authoritative nature of Torah legislation.[33] This may be seen, for example, from cases where he revised texts from Samuel and Kings, which were composed before the Torah as a whole was canonized, and are not consistent with Torah legislation. The clearest example of this, already pointed out by Wellhausen,[34] concerns the relationship between 1 Kgs 8:65 and 2 Chr

7:8–10. Both texts are describing the dedication of Solomon's Temple, which they agree transpired on *Sukkot*, the ingathering festival. According to Kings, this was a seven-day festival;[35] this agrees with the legislation found in Deut 16:15. However, Lev 23:36, 39 and Num 29:35–38 describe an eighth day of the festival. It is likely that Kings was written before the practice narrated in Leviticus and Numbers became common. This had changed, however, by the time of the Chronicler, and he "naturally" revises his source to incorporate this additional festival day. He thus adds (2 Chr 7:9–10), "On the eighth day they had a sacred convocation ... and on the twenty-third of the seventh month he sent the people home to their tents."[36]

The special status of the Torah in Chronicles is particularly clear from a comparison of 1 Kgs 8:25 with 2 Chr 6:16. These parallel texts both contain obedience formulae which Solomon is reciting to YHWH. Kings notes the obligation "to walk before me," while the Chronicler revises this to "to walk in the way of my Torah."[37] This small change is quite significant, and reflects the fact that by the time of the Chronicler, walking in YHWH's way was defined quite specifically as following the Torah. I. L. Seeligmann phrases the reason for the change aptly, "Almost against his will, the Chronicler reflects his worldview, and the very heart and center of this worldview is the idea of the Torah."[38] Thus, like the rabbis who followed him, the Chronicler believed in the absolute centrality of the Mosaic Torah. It was thus natural for the Chronicler to reshape the depiction of the past to conform to the legal norms of the Torah.

This was not always an easy task. Sometimes the Torah traditions conflicted with each other, and the Chronicler somehow had to decide how to reconcile them. When possible, he conflated them, adhering to a theme found later in rabbinic Judaism, that all Torah texts are equally authoritative.[39] The clearest example of this process is in 2 Chr 35:13, a description of Josiah's Passover offering.[40] Two equally authoritative Torah texts presented the Chronicler with a serious problem: Exod 12:9 prohibits the sacrifice from being eaten raw or boiled,[41] and insists that it must be roasted in fire. Deut 16:7, however, suggests that it must be boiled. From the critical perspective, we suspect that these differences reflect diverse customs; however, from the perspective of the Chronicler, who believed that they were both Torah, how should the Passover sacrifice be prepared? 2 Chr 35:13 reads, "They boiled the Passover sacrifice in the fire, just as they were supposed to."[42] This creates a wonderful image of a caldron consumed with flames, somehow fulfilling the laws of both Exodus and Deuteronomy.

Finally, there are many cases where the Chronicler changed texts because they differed from the political, theological or cultic norms of his period. For example, he believed that David and Solomon, who founded a long-lasting dynasty, were heroic figures.[43] Additionally, he did not understand religion in historical terms, as a developing system of beliefs. Religious practice was unchanging; thus, from his perspective, if an earlier text contained a norm which differed from his own, that source must be mistaken.[44] It was thus natural for him to retroject his contemporaneous religious practices and political beliefs. For example, he knew 1 Kings 1–2, which describes the battle for the throne between Solomon and his brothers. However, his political ideology precluded him from believing that account. He knew that Solomon could have no enemies and that there was a smooth transition between David and Solomon. Therefore, Kings was wrong; he advised his readers of that by writing polemically against Kings (1 Chr 29:24): "All of the officers, warriors and all of the sons of King David supported Solomon the king."

Two simple, unambiguous examples of how the Chronicler's religious beliefs caused him to rewrite earlier traditions are provided in 2 Chronicles 2. V. 11a reads, "Huram said, 'Blessed is YHWH, God of Israel, who made the heavens and the earth, who gave to David a wise son.' " This is based on 1 Kgs 5:21: "He said, 'Blessed is YHWH today, who gave David a wise son.' " The Chronicler has given YHWH a new title, "who made the heavens and the earth." This phrase is rare in pre-exilic prose texts,[45] but is found several times in the last two books of Psalms,[46] and in Neh 9:6. This phrase was well known to the Chronicler from its liturgical use in psalms, and its attestation in Nehemiah indicates that it was used in the Persian period. The Chronicler naturally assumed that the Israelite concept of God and his epithets had not changed over the centuries. This allowed, indeed encouraged him (either consciously or subconsciously), to insert this phrase, reflecting his own viewpoint and liturgical custom, into Huram's mouth.

A different way in which the Chronicler anachronistically imposed his ideology on the older text is shown in 2 Chr 2:3. The source for the text, 1 Kgs 5:19, merely describes the building of the Temple. The Chronicler has elaborated on that text, and offered a list of functions that the Temple served. This list, however, was not based on his source, Kings, but is a collection of various Tabernacle functions from P texts, especially from Numbers 28–9. Critical scholarship would suggest that these texts postdate Solomon by close to half a millennium, but the Chronicler connected the Tabernacle and Temple, and assumed that these Torah texts were followed by Solomon.[47] His error here was probably a naive one, based on his belief that the entire Torah functioned as *torah*, "teaching," already in the time of Solomon.

A useful phrase summarizing one way of understanding how the Chronicler wrote history is "historical probability." This was coined by Elias Bickerman, who says:

The Chronicler, like Hecataeus of Miletus or Herodotus, gives such information concerning the past as appears to him most probable, and corrects the sources in conformity with his own historical standards. . . . Following his rule of historical probability, he cannot believe that Solomon turned over cities to Hiram of Tyre (I Kings 9:12); so he changes the text: the cities were given by Hiram to Solomon (II Chron. 8:2).[48]

Bickerman emphasizes that the Chronicler, in reshaping the past, weighed his sources against his beliefs, and used his beliefs to help decide whether his sources were accurate. This is what all historians do when they speak of "evaluating evidence."[49] The Chronicler, as a pre-modern historian, used pre-modern criteria for that evaluation, which led him to conclude that the author of substantial sections of Samuel and Kings was wrong.

THE CHRONICLER AT WORK: A CASE STUDY

I have selected sections of 1 Chr 15:1–26 as my sample text, choosing to exclude the lists that comprise almost half of the text, as these would lead us too far afield. 1 Chr 15:1–26 is appropriate for analysis since it contains both synoptic and non-synoptic sections,[50] in other words sections that have (some form of) Samuel as their source, and others that do not reflect Samuel. Although the non-synoptic sections are not a direct reworking of a Samuel text, most are not totally free compositions, but are heavily influenced by several biblical texts.

The non-synoptic section is comprised of 15:1–24, and is primarily concerned with the role of the Levites in conveying the ark. The synoptic section, 15:25–6, is related to 2 Sam 6:12b–13; it begins a section which has as its focus David's actions during the conveyance of the ark.

Here is the relevant section of the text of Chronicles:

(1) He [David] built for himself houses in the City of David, and prepared a place for the ark of God, and pitched a tent for it. (2) Then David said that the ark should only be carried by the Levites, for YHWH had chosen them to carry the ark of God and to serve him in perpetuity. (3) David assembled all of Israel to Jerusalem, to bring the ark of YHWH to its place which he had prepared for it. [Verses 4–11 list the priests and Levites.] (12) He [David] said to them, "You are the heads of the clans of the Levites; sanctify yourselves along with your kinsmen, and bring up the ark of YHWH the God of Israel to [the place][51] which I have prepared for it." (13) Because, initially, you did not {bring it up}[52] YHWH our God broke out against us, because we did not serve him properly. (14) The priests and Levites sanctified themselves in order to bring up the ark of YHWH the God of Israel. (15) The Levites carried the ark of God just as Moses had commanded, according to the word of YHWH

– on their shoulders, with poles upon themselves. [Verses 16–24 discuss the establishment of the Levitical singers.] (25) David, and the elders of Israel, and the officers of one thousand went to bring the ark of the covenant of YHWH joyfully up from the house of Obed-Edom. (26) When God helped the Levites, who were carrying the ark of the covenant of YHWH, they sacrificed seven cows and seven rams.

The main theme of 2 Samuel 6, our author's source, is the conveyance of the ark from Gibeah to Jerusalem, which sets the stage for David's wish to build for the ark a permanent home, namely the Temple. The first verse of our section reads (1 Chr 15:1): "He [David] built for himself houses in the City of David, and prepared a place for the ark of God, and pitched a tent for it." The opening phrase, which notes that David built houses, is somewhat unexpected; the Bible elsewhere, both in Samuel and Chronicles, suggests that David had only one house or palace in the City of David (2 Sam 7:1//1 Chr 17:1). Various scholars have noted in a different context that the reigns of David and Solomon are viewed together by the Chronicler as the united monarchy[53]; this is made explicit by several texts such as 2 Chr 7:10, which speaks of "the goodness which YHWH has bestowed on David and Solomon" (cf. 2 Chr 35:4). Sara Japhet has noted several cases where the Chronicles "takes something which was clearly ascribed to Solomon in the Book of Kings and transfers it to David."[54] Sometimes the process is reversed; for example, the phrase "and YHWH his God was with him" is characteristic of David in Samuel (1 Sam 16:18; 18:12; 2 Sam 5:10), but the Chronicler applies it to Solomon in 2 Chr 1:1. It is thus quite possible that this notice concerning David's "palaces" or "houses" reflects Solomon's palace, which had a number of "buildings" or "houses."[55] This possibility will be bolstered later by showing several other, more obvious connections between 1 Chronicles 15, which is about David, and passages concerning Solomon.

V. 1b "he prepared a place for the ark of God" reflects the usage "to prepare," which is "a favourite word of the Chronicler,"[56] especially in contexts that develop the idea that David performed most of the preparatory work for the construction of the Temple. It reflects a notion – developed in great detail in Chronicles – that David was intimately involved in the planning and gathering of materials for the Temple and organized the functionaries who later served in the Temple under his son Solomon.[57]

This idea of the Chronicler is not found explicitly in Samuel or Kings. However, 1 Kgs 7:51 refers to some sanctified objects of David which Solomon transferred to the Temple. Furthermore, in 2 Samuel 7, when David wants to build the Temple, he is told that he may not, but there is no injunction against his involvement in the planning phase. It is likely that an overly close and expansionistic reading of these texts was a major factor influencing the Chronicler's belief that David prepared all of the groundwork for the Temple.

V. 1bβ "and pitched a tent for it" is based on 2 Sam 6:17, which is our text's main source. 2 Sam 6:17 notes that when the ark was brought to Jerusalem, it was placed in the tent which David *had* pitched for it. The text in 2 Samuel 6 describes the event of pitching the tent in the pluperfect[58]; the Chronicler relates this information in 16:1, following his *Vorlage*, but also presented it here (15:1bβ), where he felt it belonged chronologically, by incorporating it into the introduction to the chapter. The same event is told again, retrospectively, in 2 Chr 1:4. The Chronicler elsewhere repeats information in a second relevant context; for example, in 1 Chr 11:3, which describes the coronation of David, the Chronicler adds to his *Vorlage* the words "according to the word of YHWH through Samuel," a reference to 1 Sam 16:13, which is not reflected earlier in Chronicles, in a location parallel to where it appears in Samuel. Correct information has been copied into a relevant place.[59] This repetition and restructuring of material based on logic typifies historians working with sources.[60]

V. 2 can only be understood in relationship to an earlier chapter, 1 Chronicles 13//2 Samuel 6, which narrates a previous, failed attempt to bring the ark to Jerusalem. That chapter tells of the death of Uzza, who attempted to steady the ark when the cattle pulling it on a cart stopped. The exact reason for Uzza's death is unclear in Samuel;[61] however, for the Chronicler, living in a period after the Torah had become authoritative, an obvious reason supplied itself: the ark was not carried according to the laws specified in the Torah.[62] Although this is not spelled out by the Chronicler in ch. 13, which narrates the Uzza episode,[63] it is implied by 15:2: "Then David said that the ark should only be carried by the Levites, for YHWH had chosen them to carry the ark of YHWH and to serve him in perpetuity." The medieval Jewish commentator on Chronicles printed in the Rabbinic Bible under the name Rashi[64] recognized this issue.[65] In fact, the language of v. 2 directly reflects the legislation of Deut 10:8, "At that time Moses set apart the tribe of Levi to carry the ark of the covenant of YHWH, to stand before YHWH and to bless in his name to this very day."[66] The Chronicler has quoted selectively from the verse; he omits the sections concerning the Levitical roles of standing before YHWH and blessing in his name, which are irrelevant to this context. The change from Deuteronomy's "the ark of the covenant of YHWH" to "the ark of God" is not significant; the Chronicler uses many different terms for the ark, even within a single pericope.[67] The end of 1 Chr 15:2, "in perpetuity," replaces the end of Deut 10:8, "until this very day." The Chronicler felt that Deuteronomy was correct, but insufficient, so he extended it by using "in perpetuity."[68] This change reflects the theology of the Chronicler: for him the Torah is an eternal guide, and he uses this opportunity to revise the typical Deuteronomic phrase, "until this very day," to explicitly reinforce that point.

V. 3 reads: "David assembled all of Israel to Jerusalem, to bring the ark of YHWH to its place which he had prepared for it." The second part of the verse reflects the notion mentioned above, that David made preparations for the Temple, which was actually only completed by Solomon. The first part of the verse, which states that all Israel participated in this event, has no parallel in Samuel, but is reflected elsewhere in 1 Chr 13:5, "David assembled all of Israel from Shichor in Egypt to Lebo Hamath, to bring the ark of God from Kiryat Yearim." This verse too finds no parallel in Samuel. The closest parallel may be found in 1 Kgs 8:1–2 (//2 Chr 5:2–3): "Then Solomon gathered the elders of Israel, all the heads of the tribes, the chiefs of the Israelites to King Solomon in Jerusalem, to bring the ark of the covenant of YHWH from the City of David, that is, Zion. Every Israelite gathered to Solomon in the month of Ethanim, at the festival – that is, the seventh month." These verses describe the people assembling when the ark was being transported from the City of David to the newly constructed Temple. The similarities between this passage and 1 Chr 13:5 and 15:3 are substantial, and include the presence of "all Israel," the use of "to gather,"[69] and the phrase "to bring the ark up from." The similarities suggest that these verses in Chronicles are patterned after 1 Kgs 8:1–2, and were created on the basis of the notion that the details of Solomon's and David's reign are similar. Finally, it is noteworthy that the borders adduced here are unique within the Bible, and reflect the Chronicler's ideology that the territory of ideal Israel was in Israelite possession at the beginning of David's reign.[70]

Vv. 4–11 list the priests and the Levites who have a special role in carrying the ark. This material is not in Samuel, and seems to reflect a combination of Torah material and the realities of the Chronicler's period.[71]

After calling together a small group of priests and Levites (v. 11), the text continues (v. 12): "He [David] said to them, 'You are the heads of the clans of the Levites; sanctify yourselves along with your kinsmen, and bring up the ark of YHWH the God of Israel to [the place] which I have prepared for it.' " The verse seems to indicate that all of the Levites are to prepare themselves for the task of transporting the ark; why then is the command phrased giving such prominence to "the heads of the clans of the Levites"? This group appears elsewhere in Chronicles only once (in the genealogy of 1 Chr 9:33, 34).[72] It is thus likely that our verse has been influenced by 1 Kgs 8:1, the description of the conveyance of the ark by Solomon to the Temple. That verse reads: "Then Solomon gathered all of the elders of Israel, all the heads of the tribes, chiefs of the clans of Israel . . . to bring up the ark of the covenant of YHWH." We saw above how this verse from Kings influenced v. 3 of our chapter; it has shaped the language of this verse ("heads of the clans," "bring up") as well. Here again the

Chronicler has used the story concerning the conveyance of the ark by Solomon to fill in the details concerning its conveyance by David. One detail from Kings, however, is rewritten to reflect the theological notions of the Chronicler: the heads of the clans of Israel are replaced by the heads of the clans of the Levites.

David tells the Levites to sanctify themselves. Williamson suggests that this reflects Exod 19:22, which reads, "The priests who approach YHWH should also sanctify themselves, lest YHWH break out against them."[73] He properly notes that the relatively unusual root *prṣ* for "breaking out" is used in both texts, and was important in the two previous chapters of Chronicles. This, according to Williamson, encouraged the author to import the notion of Levites sanctifying themselves. There are, however, additional possible reasons for the Chronicler's deduction that the Levites needed to sanctify themselves. Josh 3:5–6 discusses the conveyance of the ark across the Jordan River; it reads, "Joshua said to the people, 'Sanctify yourselves' . . . Joshua said to the priests, 'Carry the ark of the covenant and pass in front of the people.' " This offers a close parallel to the situation of 1 Chronicles 15 – sanctification prior to the conveyance of the ark. The Chronicler may have transported this to his situation, though, following his theology, only the (priests and) Levites rather than the entire population had to sanctify themselves.

However, it is quite possible that the Chronicler is not exclusively basing himself on either the Exodus or the Joshua text, but on contemporaneous practice as well. Several times he notes that Levites or priests consecrate themselves before performing sacred tasks (e.g. 2 Chr 5:11; 29:34; 30:3, 24), and the language of our text may reflect this reality. This short exploration of the Chronicler's use of the term "consecrate oneself" illustrates in a nutshell the problems of determining whether the Chronicler, in revising earlier sources, is basing himself on a single biblical text, several texts, his contemporaneous practice, or some combination of these factors.

The rest of v. 12 has already been touched on. The reference to "bringing the ark up" is based on 1 Kings 8, and the mention of "the place which I have prepared for it" reflects the language and notion already seen in v. 1, that David was intimately involved in the preparations for building the Temple.

V. 13, emended slightly,[74] reads: "Because, initially, you did not {bring it up} YHWH our God broke out against us, because we did not serve him properly." The use of the verb "to break out" reflects the previous chapters, both based on Samuel, where YHWH "breaks out" against the people because of Uzza (1 Chr 13:11//2 Sam 6:8) and then "breaks out" against the Philistines (1 Chr 14:11//2 Sam 5:20). The final phrase, "because we did not serve him properly," reflects the language and the beliefs of the Chronicler. The term "to serve" [YHWH] was "a favourite of the Chronicler,"[75] which may be used by the Chronicler to indicate what makes an individual a "true" Israelite. "Properly" or "just as they were supposed to" is used predominantly in late texts,[76] and reflects a common ancient Near Eastern notion which is emphasized in post-exilic texts: that certain rituals must be performed properly, otherwise they will not be effective.[77] Proper cultic behavior is emphasized here because, as the text notes, improper behavior resulted in the death of Uzza.

Vv. 14–15 read: "The priests and Levites sanctified themselves in order to bring up the ark of YHWH the God of Israel. The Levites carried the ark of God just as Moses had commanded, according to the word of YHWH – on their shoulders, with poles upon themselves." V. 14 notes the fulfillment of v. 12. The author specifies that the priests as well as the Levites sanctified themselves, though v. 12 only mentioned Levites sanctifying themselves to carry the ark. The slight discrepancy between the verses is apparent only, since the Chronicler uses the term Levites in two ways; sometimes he means Levites plus priests, where elsewhere he means Levites to the exclusion of priests.[78] In composing v. 14, the Chronicler may have been influenced by Josh 3:6a, noted above, which reads "Joshua said to the priests, 'Carry the ark of the covenant and pass in front of the people.' " This may explain the explicit reference to priests in this verse, as well as the use of the verb "to carry" which is found in Joshua, rather than the verb "to bring up"[79] which is used elsewhere in the unit. Here as well as in other places, one gets the impression that the Chronicler knew by heart much of his Bible, which included at least the Torah, the Former Prophets, most of the Latter Prophets, and Psalms. He is not composing his text mechanistically, by looking up verses and applying this language to his context. He knows these works so well that they naturally and constantly influence his language and thought, creating a mosaic of sorts comprised of biblical citations.[80] This is quite similar to the modern historian who is totally at home with his or her sources. In including the priests, the Chronicler is also basing himself on Num 4:19–20, which suggests that the priests had some role in preparing the ark for travel.

V. 15 contains a two-part fulfillment formula: "just as Moses had commanded, according to the word of YHWH." Similar expressions such as "according to all that YHWH commanded Moses" and "as YHWH commanded Moses" are frequently found in the Torah. The Chronicler instead has used "according to the word" as part of his formula. This term fits in with the Chronicler's new understanding of "the *word* of YHWH," which is connected to the interpretation of Torah *texts* rather than to prophetic revelation.[81]

The end of the verse notes specifically that the Levites carried the ark on their shoulders, in contrast to the cart used in the Uzza episode. Conveyance on the shoulders is not commanded in the Torah,[82] but matches exactly the narrative of Num 7:9, "and to the descendents of

Kohath he did not give [any carts], for they were responsible for the holy place, and carried with their shoulders." This verse is also reflected in 2 Chr 35:3. Finally, the use of poles is mentioned in the directions for the construction of the ark in Exodus (25:13 and elsewhere) and in the description of Solomon's Temple in 1 Kgs 8:8. The word for poles used in both these places is *baddîm*; the Chronicler has substituted the word *mōṭôt* (15:15). This is of no theological or historical significance, but reflects a case where the Chronicler naturally slipped into his own dialect; *mōṭôt* in the sense of "pole" is a late usage.[83]

The replacement of *baddîm* with *mōṭôt* is characteristic of the way in which the Chronicler generally functioned. He had authoritative texts, but also lived in a real world which differed from those texts. Sometimes the difference between the authoritative texts and his own world was merely terminological. The Chronicler would sometimes be conservative and careful, and would retain the earlier terminology, although it was alien to him and to his community.[84] Frequently, however, he would replace old terms with those in contemporaneous use, as evidenced here. This process occurred not only on the lexical level. Sometimes the earlier history itself, as preserved in his sources, was at variance with his beliefs. When the conservatism of the Chronicler won out, the earlier picture would stand, creating a contradiction between the Chronicler's beliefs and what he wrote in the Book of Chronicles, leaving an internal contradiction in the Book of Chronicles itself. More often the Chronicler's idea would naturally replace what his *Vorlage* said, in just the same way that a contemporaneous word would replace one no longer in use.

In sum, although 1 Chr 15:1–15 are non-synoptic, that is, they are not directly based on an earlier version of the same story, they do reflect several biblical texts which are relevant to the historical events at hand according to the Chronicler's principles. The guiding principle behind this section is the notion that David and Solomon parallel each other, so David's conveyance of the ark should parallel what is depicted in 1 Kings 8, concerning Solomon's conveyance of the ark. Thus, according to the Chronicler, David, like Solomon, had a large, public ceremony for the occasion. Central to the ceremony is the idea that David, although he did not build the Temple, prepared for it in every way possible. This idea is absent in Samuel, but was probably developed by the Chronicler on the basis of a careful close reading of earlier texts. The details of the ark conveyance ceremony are adjusted according to the norms of the Torah, which from the Chronicler's perspective, was already given to Moses, and existed for the pious David to follow. Thus, the misfortune with Uzza was because the ark was carried in a cart, as opposed to being properly carried on the shoulders of Levites. This time, David did it correctly, with the Levites carrying the ark on their shoulders. Certain details have several possible origins. For example, the consecration of the priests may be based on Exodus, on Joshua, on contemporaneous practice, or on some combination of these factors. Finally, certain features of the narrative, such as the structure and roles of the Levitical and priestly families in vv. 4–11, reflect an anachronistic transposition of the norms of the Chronicler. Thus 1 Chr 15:1–15 reflect a combination of historical patterning (David after Solomon), various Torah and prophetic phrases and verses, and a projection of the Chronicler's norms back to the period of David.

The synoptic section begins with v. 25: "David, and the elders of Israel, and the officers of one thousand went to bring the ark of the covenant of YHWH joyfully up from the house of Obed-Edom." The parallel in 2 Sam 6:12b[85] reads: "David went and joyfully brought the ark of God from the house of Obed-Edom to the City of David." The Chronicler has omitted the reference to the City of David; there is no obvious or tendentious reason for this omission, since he elsewhere makes reference to it.[86] More significant is his change of 2 Sam 6:12, which made David alone responsible for the transfer of the ark, to a communal act, in which the elders of Israel and the officers of one thousand participated. The basis for this innovation is 1 Kgs 8:1, the story of Solomon bringing the ark into the Temple.[87] That text states explicitly that Solomon assembled "the elders of Israel, all the heads of the tribes of the clans of Israel." This is the origin of the "elders of Israel" in 1 Chr 15:25. Similarly, it is likely that the phrase "the officers of one thousand" reflects the group referred to in Kings" 'all the heads of the tribes of the clans of Israel." The term *maṭṭôt* for tribes is not favored by the Chronicler, who uses it only once;[88] here he uses a more contemporaneous phrase ("the officers of one thousand") to refer to the same group.[89] Thus, the Chronicler has rewritten his *Vorlage* in line with 1 Kings 8, updating some of the terminology found there.

V. 26 reads: "When God helped the Levites, who were carrying the ark of the covenant of YHWH, they sacrificed seven cows and seven rams." This varies in several details from 2 Sam 6:13: "When those who carried the ark of YHWH marched six steps, he sacrificed a ram and a fatling." The Chronicler omits the section that mentions marching six paces; this probably described an unfamiliar ritual that made little sense, so he left it out. There are several other cases where he omits sections of his *Vorlage* that were probably unclear to him.[90]

The Chronicler compensates for what he omits by noting that there was divine help in carrying the ark. The Chronicler here is concerned with practical issues that a logical reader might raise,[91] and realized that the ark as described in Exodus was quite heavy. For him, this is probably the reason that David had earlier arranged (1 Chronicles 13) to have it carried by cart. The Chronicler uses one of his favorite roots, "to help,"[92] to convey the notion that God helped the Levites – even if something is too heavy or difficult, with God's help, it can be done. This major theme of the Chronicler may be seen, for example, in 2 Chr 32:8 (a non-synoptic passage), when Hezekiah confronts the mighty Assyrians and tells his people, "With him [Sennacherib, King of Assyria] is a shoulder of flesh, but with us is YHWH, our God, to help us[93] and to fight our battle." The rabbis understood the purpose of the Chronicler's reference to divine help; a midrash cited by both pseudo-Rashi and Qimhi notes that "the ark carried itself."

The Chronicler also changes the number of animals used for the offering and the person responsible for sacrificing them. Sacrificial prerogatives typically belong in the post-exilic age to the priests and not to the kings, and there is a tendency for the Chronicler to alter his source to reflect this.[94] The change in the number and type of animals offered seems to reflect the post-exilic reality of the Chronicler. There is no mandated number according to the Torah for the type of offering described in 1 Chr 15:26, but Job 42:8, which on linguistic grounds should be dated to the post-exilic period,[95] also notes a general offering of seven cows and seven rams. A case of various offerings of seven animals each is also offered in 2 Chr 29:21. However, it has been suggested that the change reflected here in Chronicles was not made by the Chronicler himself, but reflects his *Vorlage*. According to Lemke, a Samuel Qumran fragment from cave 4 contains the reading "seven cows and seve[n rams]," which agrees with Chronicles.[96] In this case, the Chronicler might have inherited the text in its current form, and did not change his *Vorlage*.

This examination of a short synoptic passage shows that the Chronicler was not enslaved to his *Vorlage*. This case is typical in that the general outlines of the Chronicler's story and his *Vorlage* agree: an individual or group joyously brings the ark up to the accompaniment of a sacrifice. However, the active party is changed to the secular leaders of the people under the influence of 1 Kings 8, and the nature of the sacrifice is changed to conform to the practice performed in the Chronicler's own time. A difficult detail was left out, and a practical problem was addressed by claiming that it was only with God's help that the Levites carried the ark. The solution to the problem incorporated one of the Chronicler's favorite themes: with God as your helper, all will go well. All of these changes are fostered by the Chronicler's interpretation of his *Vorlage* as influenced by his ideological agenda.

TYPOLOGIES AND PATTERNS OF HISTORY

Events themselves do not typically occur in patterns. It is the historian who sees patterns in events or in traditions concerning events, and writes a historical account that reflects these perceived patterns. We have just seen how the Chronicler patterned the conveyance of the ark by David after a similar event performed by Solomon. In this particular case, the two events were made comparable to each other because the Chronicler believed that

David and Solomon, as the two kings of the united monarchy, led similar lives.

Other cases of patterning within the book of Chronicles have been observed by scholars. For example, it has been noted that Hezekiah is patterned after Solomon, and that the transition from David to Solomon is modeled after that from Moses to Joshua. I will briefly examine these two complex cases of patterning, which are important because they show that patterning is fundamental to Chronicles. I will first offer two short examples of literary patterning in Chronicles which will help to establish different uses for this device.

The verses 1 Chr 21:22–5 concern the purchase of the Temple site by David from Ornan the Jebusite. The Chronicler's source in 2 Samuel 24 notes that David insisted on paying for this site (v. 24). This idea is taken over by the Chronicler, but has been formulated differently; the Chronicler notes twice that David pays "the full price" for the threshing floor (vv. 22, 24). In v. 22, this appears as an addition of the Chronicler to Samuel, while in v. 24, it replaces its source's phrase "for a price." The phrase used by the Chronicler, "the full price," is found elsewhere only in Gen 23:9, in connection to the negotiations between Abraham and the Hittites for the Cave of Machpelah, where Abraham insists on paying them (v. 9) "at the full price." The Chronicler probably borrowed the phrase because Genesis 23 described a similar situation to that of David: being offered some land for free, but insisting that it nevertheless be paid for fully.[97] It is unlikely that the Chronicler is drawing a meaningful parallel between David and Abraham; there are insufficient additional parallels between the two contexts to suggest this, and in general, the Chronicler has downplayed the importance of Abraham.[98] Rather, this is likely a case where the Chronicler, due to his great familiarity with the Torah narrative, naturally (and probably subconsciously) used thematically appropriate details from the Torah to fill in his story.[99] Such use of earlier material is best considered an echo rather than a full-fledged allusion.[100]

A different type of literary patterning may be seen in 2 Chr 7:1–3, which describes the events after Solomon's dedication of the Temple and accompanying prayer. The text reads:

> When Solomon had finished praying, a fire descended from heaven and devoured the burnt offering and the sacrifices, and the glory of YHWH filled the house. The priests could not enter the house of YHWH because the glory of YHWH had filled the house of YHWH. All Israel saw as the fire descended and the glory of YHWH was upon the house; they prostrated themselves to the earth upon the floor and bowed, "thanking YHWH, for he is good, for his lovingkindness is forever."

The verses in Chronicles are based on 1 Kgs 8:54, 10–11 (in that order)[101] and, as noted by Williamson and others,[102] various events that according to the Torah are connected to the completion of the Tabernacle are moved by the Chronicler to the Temple. For example, 2 Chr 7:1b–2 have been influenced by 1 Kgs 8:10–11: "When the priests left the Holy Place, the cloud filled the House of YHWH. The priests could not stand and minister because of the cloud, because the glory of YHWH had filled the House of YHWH." These verses in Kings are in turn patterned after Exod 40:34–5: "The cloud covered the Tent of Meeting, and the glory of YHWH filled the Tabernacle. Moses could not come into the Tent of Meeting because the cloud dwelled on it, and the glory of YHWH filled the Tabernacle." In Chronicles, the cloud of Exodus and Kings has been expunged. This is probably because the "glory" continued to play a major role in post-exilic theology, while the cloud had no such role.[103]

However, 2 Chr 7:1a, which describes the fire consuming the offerings, does not reflect Kings and the last chapter of Exodus. It is influenced instead by Leviticus 9, which describes the consecration of the priests, the final ritual that prepared the Tabernacle for proper use. Vv. 23b–24 read: "The glory of YHWH appeared to the people. A fire went out from before YHWH and devoured what was on the altar – the burnt offering and the fat; the people saw, and cried out, and fell upon their faces." The similarity between the two situations is striking – in both cases a fire suddenly devours the inaugural offerings, as a sign of divine favor. There are slight differences between the accounts; according to Leviticus, the fire originated "from before YHWH," probably a technical term for before the ark. The Chronicler does not use "before YHWH," in this technical sense,[104] and he probably understood the term according to his norms, as referring to where YHWH resides, namely in heaven.[105] In addition, perhaps he shared the notion of divine fire descending from heaven with the post-exilic Job 1:16. The type of sacrifice is changed to fit what had been earlier narrated in 1 Kgs 8:62–4. Despite these minor differences, it is clear that 2 Chr 7:1a is based on Leviticus 9. A quick look at 2 Chr 7:3 shows the continuing influence of that context.

It reads: "All Israel saw as the fire descended and the glory of YHWH was upon the house; they prostrated themselves to the earth upon the floor and bowed, 'thanking YHWH for he is good, for his lovingkindness is forever.' " With the exception of its first three words, this verse is derived from Lev 9:24b: "the entire nation saw and cried out, and they fell upon their faces." All of the elements of this verse are preserved by the Chronicler, though somewhat differently. He too notes that the people saw, but uses the opportunity to restate what the people saw – the fire and the glory. For the bowing, he uses the phrase "they prostrated themselves fully to the earth upon the floor and bowed" instead of his source's "and they fell upon their faces." This probably reflects a change to an expression more favored by the Chronicler (2 Chr 29:29) and his period (cf. Esth 3:2,

5). The single word "they cried out" is replaced by a formula which states the content of that call: "thanking YHWH for he is good, for his lovingkindness is forever." The root "to cry out"[106] is predominantly used in poetic texts, and is only once found in Chronicles, when a psalm is quoted (1 Chr 16:33//Ps 96:12). The Chronicler has replaced it with what he assumed the cry of the people was: a call of praise or thanksgiving to YHWH. We know from several contexts that one of the Chronicler's favorite cultic expressions was "thank/praise YHWH for he is good, for his lovingkindness is forever."[107] He has interpreted the "crying out" of his *Vorlage* in line with that expression.

This case of literary patterning in 2 Chronicles 7 differs from the one discussed above. The borrowing from Abraham's purchase of the Cave of Machpelah represented the shift of thematically appropriate Torah material to a different context. There is no sense, however, that the context in Genesis is being recalled, nor is there an (obvious) theological or historical significance to that borrowing. Here, however, the author of 2 Chronicles 7 wanted to convey the point that the Temple was as important as the Tabernacle, and thus he claims that it received the same signs of divine blessing as the Tabernacle. The more similarities between Temple and Tabernacle the better – for this reason, sources referring to signs of divine approval at different stages of the Tabernacle's completion and dedication from both Exodus and Leviticus are used.[108] Solomon's Temple was not merely of antiquarian interest; rather, the Chronicler was very interested in the Second Temple, which was standing in his own period, its proper functioning and legitimacy.[109] He viewed the Second Temple as a direct continuation of the First.[110] He emphasized the legitimacy of the First Temple by rewriting his *Vorlage* in order to legitimate, by extension, his own Temple. This is all accomplished by making the Temple a "type" of Tabernacle. This notion, which has clear ideological motivations, has caused the Chronicler to create 1 Chr 7:1–3. The history which these verses present is concerned with the Chronicler's present, rather than the Israelite past.

H. G. M. Williamson has shown that the accession of Solomon in Chronicles is modeled after Joshua's succession of Moses.[111] His arguments are extensive, overlapping and well-documented, and will not be repeated in detail here. He notes a wide range of similarities between the two accounts, especially in cases where the Chronicler diverges from his *Vorlage*, and either thematically, structurally or in word choice, agrees with the account in Deuteronomy concerning the transference of power to Joshua. For example, he shows that the phrase "be strong and mighty,"[112] which is found in relation to Joshua's succession of Moses at the end of Deuteronomy and again at the beginning of Joshua, is used in the Chronicler's passages depicting the transition between David and Solomon. Together, these extensive similarities show beyond a doubt that the

Chronicler modeled the transition between David and Solomon after that between Moses and Joshua.

Williamson assumes that this patterning served two related purposes: it emphasized the continuity of the period of David and Solomon, which the Chronicler presents "as a single, unified 'event' in the history of his people,"[113] and it helped the Chronicler in depicting the relationship between the two kings as "*complementary*,"[114] where Solomon frequently finishes what David had begun. There is an additional reason why the Chronicler had to change his source's transition story, and why the use of the Moses–Joshua transition was particularly appropriate. As noted above, the Chronicler omits most of the material considered to be part of the succession narrative, such as the account of the battle over the succession when David is old (1 Kings 1–2), and the nearly successful attempt by Absalom to wrest the kingship from his father (2 Samuel 15–19). He combats these traditions to some extent by stating (1 Chr 29:24): "All of the officers, warriors and all of the sons of King David supported Solomon the king."[115] However, a single verse cannot make a reader "forget" several chapters of Samuel. A longer counter-story needs to be presented, and this is what the Chronicler has accomplished through extensive literary patterning: by depicting the transition from David to Solomon like that from Moses to Joshua, he is strongly suggesting, in several places and in various ways, that the change of kings was as smooth, complete and authoritative as the transition from Moses to Joshua. By viewing Chronicles as a work that revises earlier authoritative texts, the purpose of the patterning becomes clear. The Chronicler is using a Torah text, which might have been better known to his community than Samuel and Kings, to create a new, strong image of a proper transition between David and Solomon. Noticing and understanding the typology is thus a necessary part of understanding this unit in Chronicles.

In *Israel in the Books of Chronicles*, Williamson, to some extent following the suggestions of others, has shown how the reign of Hezekiah is patterned after that of Solomon.[116] The same pattern may be responsible for Proverbs 25:1, which connects Hezekiah to Solomon's proverbs. The evidence is quite compelling and often explicit; Williamson cites 2 Chr 30:26, concerning Hezekiah's *maṣṣôt* festival: "There was great joy in Jerusalem, for there had been nothing like this in Jerusalem since the days of Solomon son of David." Even the length of the celebration is fourteen days (2 Chr 30:23), patterned after Solomon's celebration in 1 Kgs 8:65 (// 2 Chr 7:9). Williamson adduces five other places which seem to reflect the projection of Solomonic descriptions onto Hezekiah; these include similarities in the Temple and priestly arrangements.[117] Though the parallels are not as strong as those adduced between the David–Solomon and Moses–Joshua pericopae, the case is still compelling.

Williamson suggests that the Chronicler created the parallelism because

Hezekiah was the first king after Solomon to reign over both Judah and the north.[118] This is an incomplete explanation of the motivation for the Chronicler's historical creativity. The Chronicler, reading through Kings, probably noted a much larger set of similarities between Hezekiah and Solomon: Hezekiah is Solomon-like in that he reigned over both Judah and Israel, established proper cultic worship in Jerusalem (2 Kgs 18:3–6), petitioned YHWH and was answered (2 Kgs 20:2–6; cf. 1 Kgs 3:5–15), and was excessively wealthy (2 Kgs 20:13).[119] These multiple correspondences, some of which concerned issues of great significance to the Chronicler,[120] allowed the Chronicler to believe that Hezekiah was patterned after Solomon. Once deducing this principle, he added additional illustrative details when he rewrote his history.

All of the similarities between Solomon and Hezekiah adduced by Williamson reflect material moved from the Solomon pericope to the Hezekiah pericope, or material written by the Chronicler which he sets in both of their reigns. However, an additional way of depicting Hezekiah as a new Solomon is to move material to Solomon to anticipate Hezekiah. This is precisely what is done in 1 Chr 29:25b: "He [YHWH] placed upon him [Solomon] royal splendor which no king of Israel before him had ever had." Williamson uses this verse to show that Solomon was "not inferior to" David.[121] It is surprising, however, to speak of the "best" king so soon after the monarchy is established.[122] This verse should be compared to 2 Kgs 18:5, concerning Hezekiah: "He [Hezekiah] trusted YHWH the God of Israel; after him there was none like him among all the kings of Judah, nor were there any [like that][123] before him."[124] This type of comparison is certainly appropriate for a king reigning three centuries after the establishment of the monarchy. The Chronicler has taken the end of this verse concerning Hezekiah, and has (less appropriately) used it of Solomon, the second Judean king, because the comparability of Hezekiah to Solomon allows material to be moved from Hezekiah to Solomon. This reflects a less usual pattern, where material has been moved from a later to an earlier figure, rather than vice versa. This is similar to 1 Chronicles 15, where material was moved from the story of Solomon to the story of David.

Earlier material reused by the Chronicler is like "clay in the hands of the potter"[125]; just as the potter creatively uses lumps of clay to fashion different types of vessels, so the Chronicler reuses earlier texts for different purposes. This process is usually discussed under the rubric of "literary patterning," and is seen as serving an aesthetic function. Since the Bible should not be considered literature in our modern sense, we must wonder: Why does the Chronicler use this device? What purposes does it serve in his hands?

The cases studied illustrate several different reasons for using patterning. The use of the term "full price" in 1 Chr 21:22, 24, which the Chronicler knew from Gen 23:9, is a case of an echo, where the Chronicler used thematically appropriate terms that he knew from his extensive familiarity with the Torah, though he was not making an obvious ideological or historical point. The patterning of Hezekiah after Solomon is based on several significant parallels already found in Kings. The Chronicler, as a very careful reader of texts, has noted them, and has elaborated upon them. He believed that the text itself suggested that Hezekiah was a new Solomon; he merely filled in additional details. In this case, the patterning is caused by certain characteristics already noted in his source, and is not (primarily) ideological in nature.

The other cases of patterning have an ideological basis. The notion of "all Israel" was central to the Chronicler, and could be represented by the reign of the kings David and Solomon. For this reason, he unified their reigns still further, by copying events from Solomon's reign and claiming that they also transpired with David. The Chronicler was very concerned with the Second Temple, and he devotes many new chapters to details concerning its proper functioning. The Chronicler has used patterning to bolster the status of the Temple, by claiming in 2 Chronicles 7 that the Temple received the same signs of the divine presence as the Tabernacle. He applies texts from Exodus and Leviticus to Kings' account of the Temple to further his theological aims. Political forces were the primary motivation for the patterning of the transition from David to Solomon after that from Moses to Joshua. The Chronicler was aware that his readers knew the succession narrative, which depicts the struggles over who would succeed David as king. The Chronicler lived after the rise of the notion of a Davidic messiah, and half a millennium after the establishment of the Davidic dynasty; he therefore wanted to de-emphasize the story of the succession narrative. By depicting the David–Solomon transition like that of Moses–Joshua, and by omitting most of the succession narrative and adding 1 Chr 29:24, he was stating that the transition from David to Solomon was smooth. Thus, this case served the political aim of furthering the reputation of David and the house of David.

Sometimes patterning allowed the Chronicler to rewrite history, to create new traditions. He did this by moving events from earlier texts and periods to later ones and from later figures to earlier ones. He has revised his source's depiction of Hezekiah; he has changed some of the depiction of David so that it more closely matches that of Solomon; he has refashioned the transition from David to Solomon. In the case of Hezekiah, earlier biblical texts probably suggested to him that his depiction was accurate. The other cases are more difficult to evaluate. It is possible that in depicting Solomon, he might have honestly believed that 2 Samuel and 1 Kings are wrong, and that the transition from David to Solomon must have been as smooth as that from Moses to Joshua. Alternatively, he may have known that he was depicting events that did not transpire. This can be understood in two ways. Perhaps he believed that the lessons that these events offer to the community, such as stability of the Temple and of the Davidic monarchy, were so important that they justified the "creation" of history by falsifying earlier sources. Alternatively, perhaps he understood himself as writing a type of didactic history, like the medieval Jewish story of the four captives,[126] where the author and audience knew that what was essential was what might be learned from the event or pattern, and not the historicity of the event itself. If this is the case, we misread the Chronicler when we suppose that all of his narrative intended to reflect past events. Instead, we must read him only for the meaning that his events convey.[127] This issue of the Chronicler's purpose for writing a new history will be considered further at this chapter's conclusion.

NEW CHRONOLOGIES[128]

Chronology is often seen as the backbone of history.[129] If this were the decisive factor in determining whether a narrative should be considered history, then the Chronicler should not be considered a historian. The Chronicler, like the rabbis, may have noted that Torah texts are sometimes not in chronological order. The rabbis developed a principle to classify this phenomenon: "there is nothing early or late in the Torah," in other words, chronological order may differ from narrative order.[130] This principle is based on the observation that the narrative of Numbers is not presented in chronological order, specifically that the narrative of Num 9:1, according to its date formula, transpires before the events described in Num 1:1. Rather than seeing this textual ordering as anomalous (or the result of "improper" editing), they derived a generalization from it. The Chronicler may have made the same observation. Furthermore, H. G. M. Williamson has noted that the prophetic books had an immense influence on the Chronicler.[131] The books of Isaiah and Jeremiah are not arranged in chronological order, and the Chronicler may have analogized from these works to sections of the historical corpus that served as his source. Given the Chronicler's immense knowledge of earlier texts, it is quite possible that these Torah and prophetic patterns might have affected his rearrangement of events.

In some cases, the Chronicler has rearranged material to conform to certain patterns or beliefs. For example, it is well known that the Chronicler favors the tribe of Judah. He lived in the post-exilic period, when most Israelites considered themselves descendants of Judah, and he had a favorable attitude towards the kingship of David, who was from the tribe of Judah. When he outlines the tribes of Israel in 1 Chr 2:1-2, he puts Judah in his standard place, as fourth son. However, when he follows this list with more detailed genealogies, that of Judah comes first (2:3–4:43). This rearrangement reflects Judah's primary role, which is later justified in 5:1-2.[132] Although moving up Judah's genealogy is not a case of rearranged chronology, it shows how the Chronicler restructures material to reflect his ideological program.

Sometimes the Chronicler rearranged material in Samuel and Kings to conform to patterns found in the Torah. This may be seen by examining the episode already explored above concerning the point at which YHWH, through a divine manifestation, indicated to Solomon that the Temple is a desirable dwelling place. In Kings, the cloud and glory fill the house (1 Kgs 8:10–11) before Solomon's prayer. The Chronicler, however, sets the descent of the cloud and glory both before (2 Chr 5:13–14) and after (2 Chr 7:1–3) the prayer. Here, a Torah text, which we saw influenced the Chronicler's reformulation of Kings, also affected his placement of the verses. Lev 9:22–4 explicitly state that the fire descended only after Moses and Aaron completed blessing the nation. Indeed, Lev 9:22–3 twice contains the word "to bless,"[133] which is found in Solomon's prayer in 2 Chr 6:3, 13 as well. The authoritative Torah pattern in Leviticus 9 of blessing/prayer followed by divine manifestation encouraged the Chronicler to rearrange the account he found in Kings so that it would also conform to Leviticus.[134]

One ideological issue that was of great concern to the Chronicler was the reward that one received for observing the Torah.[135] Thus, sin causes punishment (after prophetic forewarning), and proper behavior is rewarded by blessing. This may be reversed as well: if someone is blessed, he has acted properly, and as a result we may deduce that the more blessed the individual, the more proper his or her behavior. As a result of this principle, the Chronicler inferred that David and Hezekiah, who were exceedingly blessed, were exceedingly righteous, and he rearranged the material he found in Samuel and Kings to reflect this.

The Chronicler's revision of the chronology of these reigns has been studied most recently by Mordechai Cogan, who uses the term "pseudo-dating" to describe what the Chronicler has done.[136] According to Cogan, the claim of 2 Chr 29:3 that Hezekiah restored the Temple at the very beginning of his reign reflects a "pseudo-date," which helps to justify his salvation by YHWH from the Assyrians: "This was simply the Chronicler's way of saying: The pious Hezekiah concerned himself with Temple affairs from his very first day on the throne."[137] The case with Josiah is similar; the Chronicler has divided the reform into three stages, and has moved it up to an early point in the reign, so his image as pious king is enhanced.[138] Cogan argues convincingly that the ideological framework of the Chronicler has caused him to restructure these narratives. Put differently, the Chronicler's notion of "historical probability" led him to believe that the chronology suggested by the earlier sources was inaccurate or incomplete, and he revised them accordingly.

The early reign of Solomon is described in 2 Chronicles 1, but this does not reflect the same order of material as 1 Kings. In both chapters, Solomon converses with YHWH in a dream, requests wisdom, and YHWH promises him both wisdom and wealth (2 Chr 1:12 [//1 Kgs 3:13]: "I will give you exceedingly great wealth, unlike any king who preceded you, or will follow you"). The Chronicler immediately follows this promise with a description of Solomon's wealth, much of which has 1 Kings 10 as its source. Material is moved forward several chapters to convey the notion, central to the Chronicler, that God speaks and fulfills his promises in a quick and reliable fashion.[139] This idea is surely a projection of the hopes of the post-exilic community.

The Chronicler has similarly rearranged the material concerning Solomon and Tyre so that it follows an order that he felt was more logical. There is a significant break between the text in 1 Kings which describes Solomon's initial contacts with Hiram, king of Tyre, who supplied many of the Temple's building materials (1 Kgs 5:16–25//2 Chr 2:1–11, 14–15), and the text that narrates that Hiram sent Solomon an artisan to aid in the Temple's construction (1 Kgs 7:13–14). Such an artisan would be needed early in the project, especially if his responsibilities were general in nature.[140] For this reason, the Chronicler has moved the passage up to where he felt it more appropriately belonged (2 Chr 2:12–13).

Knowledge of business practices seems to have motivated the Chronicler to shift the place of 1 Kgs 5:25 (//2 Chr 2:9[141]). That verse deals with the terms of payment for the goods which Hiram is supplying to Solomon for constructing the Temple. In Chronicles, these terms are moved up to the initial negotiations, where they logically fit into the context better.[142]

Bigger blocks were sometimes transferred as well. For example, the Chronicler, like modern scholars, must have recognized that the material at the end of 2 Samuel is not in its chronologically appropriate place.[143] He has moved the list of David's warriors (2 Sam 23:8–39) to the very beginning of the narrative describing David (1 Chr 11:10–47). The Chronicler felt free to move this big block of material to where it chronologically belonged.

A more complicated case involves the reorganization of 2 Samuel 5–6.[144] Previously, we looked at 1 Chronicles 15, which is partially based on the second half of 2 Samuel 6. The first section of 2 Samuel 6 is the source for 1 Chronicles 13. 1 Chronicles 14, however, has its source in 2 Sam 5:11–25, an earlier section in Samuel. A chart will clarify the relationship between these chapters in Chronicles and Samuel, and their rearrangement by the Chronicler:

(1) 1 Chronicles 13 (2) 2 Sam 6:1–11   Uzza Episode – Unsuccessful Conveyance of the Ark

(2) 1 Chronicles 14 (1) 2 Sam 5:11–25 David's House, War and Victory

(3) 1 Chronicles 15 (3) 2 Sam 6:12ff. David's Temple preparations – Successful Conveyance of the Ark

Why has the Chronicler changed the order of his *Vorlage*?[145]

The new order imposed by the Chronicler has a compelling logic. All three chapters have as a central theme, God "breaking out,"[146] that is, acting destructively against someone or some nation.[147] Chapter 13 deals with a case where God has "broken out" against Israel, while chapter 14 deals with a case where he "breaks out" against Israel's enemies. Thus, chapter 14 serves as a more fitting introduction for the narrative of chapter 15, which reflects positively on David. This, however, is not the main cause of the Chronicler's restructuring of his *Vorlage*.

A more important factor for the Chronicler's new arrangement may be seen by studying the verse which leads into chapter 15, namely 14:17: "David's name became known in all the lands, and YHWH put the fear of him upon all nations."[148] This verse, which does not reflect a text in Samuel, and was thus likely composed by the Chronicler, is probably dependent on Deut 11:25, "No person shall stand before you; YHWH will place your fear and your dread on the whole land on which you tread, just as he has promised you."[149] The topic of the following chapter in Deuteronomy is the construction of the "place which YHWH will choose," namely the Temple. The explicit reference to Deuteronomy 11 suggests that the Chronicler may be patterning David's activities after Deuteronomy 11–12; David conquers, is at peace and then may concern himself with Temple building (cf. e.g. Deut 12:10). The Chronicler patterns his hero, David, after the actions of Deuteronomy 11–12.

An additional element facilitated the rearrangement of the chapters. Based on 2 Sam 7:1, 1 Chr 17:1 states, "After David had settled in his home, David said to Nathan the Prophet, 'Here I am sitting in a cedar house, while the ark of the covenant of YHWH is under the curtains.' " A close reading of this text suggests that the completion of David's royal palace immediately preceded David's desire to build God a house. The Chronicler makes this connection more explicit by moving the texts around, so that 14:1 (based on 2 Sam 5:11), which describes David building his house, more closely precedes David's preparations to build a house for God (in 1 Chr 15:1).

The new sequence also helps to improve David's image, a major concern of the Chronicler.[150] According to 2 Sam 6:11, the ark resided in the house of Obed-Edom for three months, and only after David heard that Obed-Edom was blessed by God, did David attempt to move it (v. 12a). This reflects poorly on David, who is depicted in Samuel as an opportunist, looking for God's blessing. Chronicles provides a much more favorable depiction of David than Samuel does; for example, it omits David's affair with Bathsheba and the rebellions against David that followed. It is then no surprise that Chronicles does not here reflect 2 Sam 6:12a, which may be seen as depicting David in a somewhat negative light. The omission of 2 Sam 6:12a left the Chronicler with a problem: what was David doing during the ark's three-month stay with Obed-Edom that was important enough to justify his delay in moving the ark? By rearranging his *Vorlage*, the Chronicler places David's construction of the palace, and especially his wars against the Philistines, within that three-month period.[151] This creates a very different impression of David: David was too busy with state affairs to prepare a place for the ark, but (following Deuteronomy 11–12), as soon as he was at peace with his neighbors, he began to prepare for the Temple.[152] So in this case, the Chronicler's rearrangement of material is based on the confluence of logical and textual factors. The multiplicity of factors responsible for these changes makes the Chronicler similar to the modern historian, who is influenced by a range of factors in constructing history.

Two main reasons contributed to the Chronicler's re-editing: common sense and ideology. Both of these can be subsumed under "historical probability," Bickerman's notion that sources may be revised to fit the way the Chronicler believed the world functioned. Logic suggested to him that Solomon described the terms of payment in his initial contacts with Hiram and that the warriors listed at the end of 2 Samuel were actually those who served with David at the beginning of his career. Ideology forced him to restructure a number of events narrated in his sources: the divine response to the building of the Temple is restructured to conform to Leviticus 9; the reigns of David and Solomon are restructured so that kings who were rewarded greatly are portrayed as truly righteous; the Solomon material is restructured so that YHWH fulfills his promises immediately; and the genealogies are restructured so that Judah's prominence is highlighted. These ideological changes reflect issues crucial to the post-exilic community: the role of Judah and its king, and the new prominence of a particular doctrine of retribution.

The final, reorganized text does not always betray the fact that it has been substantially edited and reshaped. In some cases, where obvious patterns are used, like the ideal king performing a righteous act at the beginning of his reign, we might have guessed that these are patterns imposed by the Chronicler on earlier events or sources. Other cases are less transparent. Without their sources, we would not have known that the descent of YHWH's glory after Solomon completed the Temple is the Chronicler's creation, or that the list of David's warriors is in a secondary position, or that some of the material in 2 Chronicles 1 has been restructured, or that 1 Chronicles 13–15 reflects a reorganization of its source. This observation is of fundamental importance for modern historians of ancient Israel, for it shows that a reworked text need not have explicit signs that it is a revision of an earlier source. We therefore cannot tell, simply by looking at a text, how removed it might be from the event that it is narrating.

IDEOLOGY OR SYMBOL?

What was the Chronicler? Some have suggested that he was a theologian.[153] Others have claimed that he was an author of midrash or Targum, or that he was an exegete.[154] Others have seen him as a historian in the sense of Ranke,[155] accurately recording the past.[156] This last position is difficult to uphold, given that most historians now recognize that all history reflects bias, and that scholars have isolated clear cases where the Chronicler is inaccurate, or is anachronistically patterning the past after the present.[157] Although the Chronicler cannot be seen as a historian in Ranke's sense, he certainly was a historian in our sense of an individual depicting a past. His past is portrayed with a particular eye to the present, but as many scholars of history and memory have pointed out, this is not at all unusual for historians.[158]

The two factors which the Chronicler had to balance, which confront all historians, are the sway of previous traditions, and the relationship of these traditions to the community and its ideology.[159] In accordance with the ideology of his period, the Chronicler has emphasized the authority of the Torah, both explicitly and in various contexts which apply Torah legislation to the historical narratives of the monarchy. He has also changed his sources by introducing certain patterns of history for ideological reasons: his new history emphasizes issues of collective significance, such as the continuity between the Second Temple, the First Temple and the Tabernacle, and the legitimacy of David. Other scholars have noted that he incorporated a theme of exile, return and complete restoration, which was aimed at encouraging his contemporaries; this is most obvious in his restructuring of the Manasseh story (2 Chronicles 33, esp. vv. 10–13).[160] In addition, he has rearranged blocks of material from his sources to illustrate his theology of retribution. Throughout, he is extremely aware of the impact that depictions of the past make on the present,[161] and using "a shocking amount of freedom,"[162] he restructures the past with this in mind.

Ivan G. Marcus has written concerning medieval Jewish chronicles, "The occasion for writing down a narrative about the past is not idle curiosity or even family pride or community self-respect but a perceived change or loss."[163] This observation is equally true of the Chronicler, who was very conscious of the destruction of the First Temple, and felt that the new Temple was but a shadow of the old, which could not be truly replaced.[164] The way in which Samuel–Kings claims the world had functioned in the past often conflicted sharply with the ideology of this new community in crisis, so the Chronicler reshaped that past to conform to the ideologies of his present. The survival of Chronicles within the community is the most important biblical evidence we have for the relationship between community and history, and how ideologies reshaped communal memory. Even at this late point in biblical Israel, an individual could radically revise the accepted depiction of the past, and his work could become accepted and ultimately canonized, since it conformed to and reinforced general communal beliefs.

This position presumes that the ancients believed that historical texts are meant to accurately depict the past. This is the position, for example, put forward by W. Den Boer:

> Modern man cannot swallow the historicity of stories like that of the building of the Tower of Babel or of Romulus and Remus. But the pious historian of old believed that what he communicated truly happened.... It is impermissible to impose *our* skepticism and *our* allegories on these writers.[165]

An alternative view is adumbrated by Dennis Nineham, who claims that pre-modern history was written as an

> edifying tale which would promote deeper faith and true morals... for earlier ages edification was frequently a value in history writing which stood alongside, and very often high above, accuracy. This is something which will be recognized alike by students of the books of Chronicles, or, say, eighteenth-century British historians; and it is not a matter for moral disapproval, but just a difference of outlook.[166]

This second view suggests that the Chronicler was not intending to write a depiction of the actual past, but was writing a type of fiction with a historical substratum to illustrate certain values.[167] The historical language would then be similar to mythical language, which is not meant to be taken literally.[168] Other scholars have called this type of history writing "figurative" or "allegorical."[169] This model is possible within biblical history writing, but to my mind, it is not an accurate description of the Chronicler. There are no internal clues that the work does not intend to depict a real past;[170] in fact the Chronicler's numerous source citations suggest just the opposite. The Chronicler in many ways was like the official newspapers that are published by some non-democratic regimes – the people writing them are often so convinced of a particular doctrine that dissenting sources have little impact on their reporting. Everything that they see and report is shaped by the ideological lens through which they view the world. Similarly, the Chronicler, along with members of his community, was so sure of certain political and religious ideologies that he rewrote the accepted version of history to conform to (and to confirm) what he truly believed happened. It is only because we no longer subscribe to the Chronicler's ideologies that we so clearly perceive the Chronicler's bias, and suspect that his history diverges significantly from the actual past.

3

THE TYPOLOGIES OF GENESIS

Absolutely everything that occurred to the father happened to the children.

Nachmanides, *ad* Gen 12:10

TYPOLOGIES IN BIBLICAL AND POST-BIBLICAL LITERATURE

There is little consensus about the ancient Israelite understanding of "time." Some scholars have contrasted cyclical time in Greek historical texts to Israelite time, which is purported to be linear and teleological, pointing toward an eschatological age.[1] Both aspects of this contrast have been questioned. James Barr and Arnaldo Momigliano have noted that the notion of cyclical time is hardly representative of Greek historical writing.[2] Others have pointed out that sometimes cycles appear in Israelite historiographical works, and that Israelite eschatology is not represented in major historical works such as the Deuteronomistic History; thus linear time pointing to the *telos* of the *eschaton* cannot be seen as central to Israelite historiography.[3] A consensus is beginning to emerge that no single idea dominates either the Hebrew or the Greek historical corpus; many major classical and ancient Israelite historians mix linear and cyclical depictions of historical events.[4]

Cyclical depictions of history, namely narratives in which at least three common features are repeated several times,[5] may be found in the Hebrew Bible. The clearest example is in the Book of Judges, which presents in chapter 3 a pattern of the Israelites committing evil, being oppressed by foreigners, crying out for help and being sent a "judge." This pattern is re-enacted several times in chapters 3–16.[6] It is used in Judges as a nostalgic depiction of the ancient past as a period of divine grace and unconditional divine commitment to Israel;[7] however, such explicit cyclical patterning is rare.

More typical is a depiction of the re-enactment or pre-enactment of a single, seminal event. This is frequently discussed in New Testament scholarship under the rubric of "typology,"[8] an "advanced presentation,"[9] where (the depiction of) an event is seen to anticipate or symbolize a later, similar event. For example, Luke 4:16–21 records Jesus" reading of Isa 61:1–2 (and 58:6b), which in its original context, referred to the Israelite prophet. However, according to the Gospel, Jesus claims (v. 21) that the text has only now "come true" or "been fulfilled" (πεπλήρωται).[10] This notion is also spoken of as "prefiguration." For example, from the Christian perspective, Moses "prefigures" Christ. A more neutral, less theologically laden term, which I will typically use, is "re-enactment"[11]; thus the life of Jesus was seen by certain early Christians as a re-enactment of Old Testament figures.

Typology is certainly at home in classical Jewish texts. Typological exegesis is a fundamental feature of the *pesher* literature from Qumran; indeed, the word *pesher*, "prophetic meaning,"[12] suggests that a text from the biblical period anticipates events that would transpire half a millennium later.[13] Prefiguration is ubiquitous in the pseudepigraphic book of Jubilees, where religious practices are given additional legitimacy by retrojecting their origin into the patriarchal period.[14] Many typologies are also found in the midrash,[15] especially in Genesis Rabbah. In a study of these, Jacob Neusner notes, "Scripture, the book of Genesis in this case, is turned into future-history, and events of the day – the fourth century – are reshaped into a historical pattern by reading in their light the book of Genesis ... "[16] For example, Genesis Rabbah often reads Genesis by understanding Esau as a "type" referring to Rome and/or Christianity.[17] That midrashic work explicates the struggling of the twins in Rebecca's womb (Gen 25:22):

> When she [Rebecca] went by houses of idolatry, Esau would kick, trying to get out: "The wicked are estranged from the womb" (Ps 58:4). When she went by synagogues and study-houses, Jacob would kick, trying to get out: "Before I formed you in the womb, I knew you" (Jer 1:5).[18]

The biblical Esau represents idolatrous Rome, while Jacob represents the righteous nation Israel. The experiences of the brothers *in utero* are symbolic of what would transpire millennia later. This use of typologies in the rabbinic and Qumran corpora shows that typological thinking should not be seen as exclusively Christian. A survey of biblical texts suggests that it played a role in the understanding and composition of history in the earlier biblical period as well.

Several typologies within the Hebrew Bible have been noted by others.[19] In Chapter Two, on Chronicles, I cited several instances of historical patterning, many of which fall under the rubric of typology. For example, Hezekiah may be seen as a new Solomon, or David may be seen as a new Moses. Chronicles is typical of the biblical corpus in that its typologies do not serve a literary-aesthetic role; instead, they are used to convey meaning.

It is generally acknowledged that the exodus had a fundamental influence on the depiction of other historical events.[20] For example, the crossing of the Jordan River led by Joshua in Joshua 3–5 is patterned after the crossing of the Re(e)d Sea.[21] Deutero-Isaiah depicts the anticipated journey from Babylon to Israel as a second exodus.[22] Isa 52:11–12 reads:

> (11) Depart, depart, leave there, touch nothing impure, leave its midst, purify yourselves, those who carry the vessels of YHWH.
> (12) For you will not go out in haste, and will not go fleeing, because YHWH is walking ahead of you, and the God of Israel is the one who gathers you up.

The use of a word such as "in haste,"[23] which is rare in the Bible but is firmly anchored in the exodus tradition (e.g. Exod 12:11), makes it virtually certain that the prophet is recalling that specific tradition. All typologies, however, are not exact copies of other contexts;[24] in this case, the prophet reverses the tradition by stating that due to YHWH's great power, the Israelites leaving Babylon need not flee like their ancestors. The verbal similarities between the Deutero-Isaiah and Exodus texts suggest that at some point in Israelite history, the exodus as described in tradition was seen as the primary event of liberation; it could therefore have influenced the shape in which other events were recorded.

Sometimes, as in the case of Joshua crossing the Jordan, the typology connects two events which from the author's perspective are both in the past. Another sort of typology connects the perceived past with the present. This is found, for example, when Deutero-Isaiah, who lived in Babylon at the end of the exilic period, compared the expected exodus from Babylon to the liberation of the Israelites from Egypt. A comparable use of typology was noted in Chronicles (see Chapter Two), where the pattern of exile, prayer and complete restoration in the episode of Manasseh is used by the Chronicler to anticipate events in his own period of exile and partial restoration.[25] The use of this pattern expresses his hope that the restoration will soon be complete as well. This type of biblical typology is similar to the rabbinic typologies concerning Esau and Rome, or to the typologies in the *pesharim*, where a biblical text is read as referring to events in the lifetime of its author, and the past is reread, or rewritten, as a reflection of the present.

This chapter will explore two examples in Genesis which exhibit typological thinking. As in Chronicles, the patterns should not be viewed as decorative, but their purposes must be explored.[26] Given the early place of Genesis within the canon, the events are not "types" or re-enactments of earlier occurrences, but foreshadow later events; for this reason, I refer to them as "pre-enactments."

A PRE-ENACTED EXODUS: GENESIS 12:10–20

As noted by a small number of modern scholars, a clear example of pre-enacted history may be found in Gen 12:10–20, the first of the so-called wife–sister tales[27] in that book. It reads:

(10) There was a famine in the land, and Abram went down to Egypt to stay there because the famine was severe in the land. (11) When he approached Egypt, he said to Sarai his wife, "Look here – I know that you are a beautiful woman. (12) When the Egyptians see you and say, 'She is his wife,' they will kill me, and will allow you to live. (13) Come on, say that you are my sister, so that all will go well for me for your sake, and I will live because of you." (14) When Abram came toward Egypt, the Egyptians saw how very beautiful the woman was. (15) The officers of Pharaoh saw her and praised her to Pharaoh, and she was taken to Pharaoh's palace. (16) He made things go well for Abram because of her; he had small and large cattle, asses, servants and maidservants, donkeys and camels. (17) YHWH afflicted Pharaoh with great plagues, along with his household, because of the matter of Sarai, Abram's wife. (18) Pharaoh called for Abram and said, "What have you done to me? Why did you not tell me that she is your wife? (19) Why did you say, 'She is my sister,' so that I took her as my wife? Now, here is your wife – take her and leave." (20) Pharaoh assigned some men to him, and they kicked him out, along with his wife and all that he had.

As is well known, this story appears in two other versions, in Gen 20:1–18, of Abraham and Sarah, and in 26:1–11, of Isaac and Rebecca.[28] Stories which appear in such variant forms are especially fertile grounds for investigation and have been used to sort out the ideological stances of the authors of classical and rabbinic texts.[29] Biblical scholarship has studied these three stories in great detail, generally with the goal of finding the historical kernel which stands behind all three versions and/or deciding which of the three is original.[30] For example, E. A. Speiser felt that all three stories reflected a misunderstanding of a socio-legal institution which allowed a favored wife to be considered by her husband as his sister.[31] However, this interpretation should now be discarded since the Mesopotamian legal institution which Speiser reconstructed as an analogy to these chapters is based on a faulty understanding of Akkadian texts, and probably never existed.[32] The search for historical kernels dating from the "patriarchal period" has been largely abandoned after the studies of John van Seters[33] and Thomas L. Thompson.[34] Klaus Koch attempted to use form-critical methods to reconstruct an earlier story, closely related to the one in Genesis 12, but having Isaac as its original protagonist.[35] However, stories can develop in many unexpected ways, and the criteria used by

Koch to decide which plot elements are original are subjective. As Susan Niditch points out, folklorists who study parallel versions of the same story "would suggest that such searches for originals are fruitless."[36] Instead, it is best to treat each story on its own terms, using the other variants to help highlight significant elements that might otherwise escape notice.

Several issues arise when we look at the structure and content of the story in Genesis 12, especially in comparison with Genesis 20 and 26. In Genesis 20 and 26, the patriarch wanders to Gerar, and in chapter 20 no reason is given for the migration, while in chapter 12, Abram goes down to Egypt because of a famine. In addition, only in Genesis 12 does Pharaoh play a prominent role. When the king is warned or punished, the phrase "great plagues"[37] is used only in Genesis 12 (in v. 17). Chapter 12 presents several problems:[38] why is Pharaoh's entire house afflicted if only he is primarily guilty? Why is it that even after Pharaoh expels Abram in v. 19, Pharaoh sends people with Abram to ensure that he leaves? The ending of Genesis 12 is not logical – why would the Pharaoh allow Abram to leave with all his property, if Abram is guilty of the trickery? Chapter 26 has no such payment to Isaac, while 20:16 considers the payment a type of compensation due Sarah for the wrong committed.[39] Finally, the placement of the story in Genesis 12, at the very beginning of the Abraham cycle, is odd, since a story of famine and emigration immediately follows the divine promise of land.

All of these issues are resolved if we consider the story to be a pre-enactment of the exodus, or as Peter D. Miscall has called it, "A Mini-Exodus."[40] This solution is first found in Genesis Rabbah 40:6:[41]

> Rabbi Phinehas in the name of Rabbi Hoshayah[42] says, "God said to Abraham our father, 'Go and prepare the path for your children.' Indeed, you find that everything that is written about Abraham our father is written about his children. About Abraham it is written: 'There was a famine in the land'; about Israel it is written, 'Because the famine has gone on for two years' (Gen 45:6); about Abraham it says: 'Abraham descended to Egypt'; about Israel it is written: 'Our ancestors descended to Egypt' (Num 20:15); about Abraham it is written: 'to stay there'; about Israel it says, 'We have arrived to stay in the land' (Gen 47:4)."

This analysis is picked up by the medieval Jewish commentator Nachmanides, who lived from 1194 to 1270. He glosses Gen 12:10:

> Abraham descended to Egypt to live there because of the famine, to sustain himself in the time of drought, and the Egyptians oppressed him for nought to take his wife, and God exacted his revenge by sending great plagues and liberated him [Abraham] from there with silver and gold, and even commanded Pharaoh's officers to kick him

out. This hints that his descendants would go down to Egypt to sojourn there because of a famine, and the Egyptians would oppress them and take their wives ... and God exacted his revenge with great plagues until the Egyptians let them out with silver and gold, and much big and small cattle, and they [the Egyptians] forced them [the Israelites] out of the land. Absolutely everything that occurred to the father happened to the children. This entire matter is explained (similarly) in Genesis Rabbah.

It is not surprising that Nachmanides has made this comment, since of all the medieval Jewish interpreters, he was most willing to offer typological interpretations of biblical texts, quite possibly under Christian influence.[43] His formulation of the relationship between Gen 12:10–20 and Exodus is more explicitly typological than that of Genesis Rabbah; that midrash concentrates on verbal similarities, as is typical of the classical rabbinic way of reading texts, while Nachmanides notes similarities between events, which typifies the Christian understanding of typology.[44] In any case, the confluence of verbal and general similarities strongly suggests that Gen 12:10–20 was structured after the exodus. Given the fundamental role that the exodus, as a "paradigmatic event,"[45] had in shaping typologies in various biblical books, it is not surprising that it has left its imprint on Genesis as well. This strong power of the exodus as a paradigmatic event would continue through the rabbinic period.[46]

The suggestion that the first of the brother–sister stories is typological answers several of the problems that were raised above concerning Gen 12:10–20 and its variants. It explains the setting of the chapter in Egypt after a drought, Pharaoh's prominent role, and why Abram is permitted to leave with his property. The word "plague" is found in the plague narrative in Exodus (11:1); furthermore, the "overkill" of "great plagues," which affect not only Pharaoh but his entire household, reflects the great extent of the plagues in Exodus, rather than the more limited punishment expected for unwitting adultery. The verb of v. 20, "to expel,"[47] is a central verb of the plague narratives, while the unexpected detail in v. 20, that Abram was escorted out by Egyptians, probably reflects the Egyptians' chase of the Israelites out of the land, before their ultimate demise in the Re(e)d Sea. In addition, a motif of Gen 12:10–20 is trickery; this might reflect Exod 12:35–6, where the Israelites tricked the Egyptians into lending them silver and gold vessels and clothing. In Gen 12:16 Abram is given various animals and servants in exchange for Sarai; this may be related to the Israelites' despoiling of the Egyptians (Exod 11:2; 12:35–6). Finally, the prominent placement of this story at the beginning of the Abraham pericope reflects its importance; its location makes little sense if the story is about a famine and trickery in the patriarchal period, but makes good sense if it is a typological story dealing with the exodus, which is a major biblical theme.[48]

From the perspective of the rabbis quoted in Genesis Rabbah and of Nachmanides, the similarities between the actual events in Genesis 12 and the exodus event are real, and reflect a theology of history where the exodus is intrinsically related to Abraham's actions.[49] (This is similar to the non-critical understanding of typology in the New Testament.) From the critical perspective, the issue is quite different – a historian has created a tradition concerning Abram to parallel a later seminal event. Usually in typologies, "The new is like the old,"[50] but here the earlier event is rewritten to conform to the more recent one. This is similar to the case noted in Chapter Two, where the reign of Solomon was partially revised by the Chronicler to conform to, and thus to prefigure, Hezekiah's reign. Here, the author of Gen 12:10–20 either refashioned a common story to reflect the events of the exodus or wrote this story deliberately for that purpose.[51] Why?[52]

Umberto Cassuto, who noted many of the parallels between the stories, suggests that the similarities are intended to teach that the bondage in Egypt is part of the divine plan and that God always protects Israel.[53] This suggestion partially explains the function of the typology. In addition, we must realize that the exodus was such a seminal event in ancient Israelite memory that it imposed itself on earlier events as well. The pre-enactment of the exodus in Gen 12:10–20 becomes another way of fulfilling the injunction (Deut 16:3): "so that you will remember the day that you left Egypt all the days of your life."[54] Furthermore, as noted by Zakovitch, the periodicity of history is quite comforting for those who live within it, at least when it is a positive event that is being repeated.[55] By creating an exodus–liberation pattern in Genesis that then gets repeated in Exodus (and still later again in Deutero-Isaiah), the community, even when in a state of subjugation, will feel that the cycle is about to turn, that liberation is again around the corner.

Gen 12:10–20 involves many of the same general interpretive problems discussed at the end of Chapter Two concerning the revisionist Book of Chronicles. It is therefore very difficult to discern how Gen 12:10–20 might have been read in ancient Israel. Perhaps the author of Gen 12:10–20 meant his unit to be read symbolically, as history only in the sense of "a narrative that presents a past," but in no way intending to suggest that this event, or some similar one, transpired in the past. This is similar to the position of M. D. Goulder, who notes that typologies in Acts are symbolic, rather than historical: "St Luke is both a fundamentalist and a poet, and . . . he did not realize that there was a contradiction between the two."[56] If we accept this approach to typologies, only later, certainly by the time of Genesis Rabbah, was the unit (mis)understood as a depiction of a real past.[57] Alternatively, the author of Gen 12:10–20 truly believed in a cyclical pattern of events, and supposed that these events transpired this way with Abram to insure that they would transpire again and again, leading time after time to the redemption of Israel. Deciding between these two options concerning the author's intention seems impossible,[58] so we are left uncertain whether the unit should be read symbolically, or as a depiction of what its author believed was an actual event.

SIBLING RIVALRY AND TRIBAL HIERARCHIES: THE JOSEPH STORY

It is relatively certain that Gen 12:10–20 was written as a typology because a typological understanding of that text explains certain problems within it, and because there are many verbal correspondences between that story and various phrases and words in Exodus. The second factor is decisive; although typology is based on events and traditions, it can often only be definitively recognized when the typological text uses the vocabulary of another text.[59] However, when the event that the text typologizes is not a paradigmatic event like the exodus, which has a set, extensive vocabulary associated with it, it is more difficult to determine with certainty that a typology is present.

One such case where typological thinking is probably partially responsible for the creation or shaping of biblical traditions is in the relationship between Judah, Reuben and Joseph in the Joseph cycle (Genesis 37–50). Viewed typologically, the drama between these brothers at the end of Genesis reflects the relationship among the later tribes that carry the brothers" names.[60] The use of personal names to reflect wider ethnic groupings is well attested in the Bible. For example, it is unquestionably present in the Table of Nations in Genesis 10. Earlier in this century, Hugo Gressmann viewed sections of the Joseph story as typological,[61] but more recently, even among scholars who feel that reading the Joseph story "as history is quite wrongheaded,"[62] this type of reading has been ignored or dismissed with contempt.[63]

A major stumbling block toward understanding this text as a typology is our lack of knowledge of the early history of Israel, specifically that of the tribe of Reuben.[64] In all of the genealogical lists, he is the first-born son; comparative anthropological studies of the structure of genealogies suggest that this represents not family history, but the tribe's powerful position.[65] Judg 5:15b–16, which is one of the earliest biblical texts, probably also presents Reuben as strong. However, in texts such as Gen 49:3–4 and Deut 33:6, which are later than Judges 5, Reuben is without question portrayed as weak. It is difficult to date any of these poems exactly enough to know when the tribe's status changed. Some additional evidence may bear on the status of this tribe: certain clans which are ascribed to Reuben in some texts are elsewhere considered to be from the tribe of Judah[66]; this may reflect the absorption of Reubenites into stronger Judean clans. Finally, even those scholars who do not consider the tribal names in the Joseph story to be typological consider the episode in Gen 35:22a, where Reuben sleeps with Jacob's concubine Bilhah, to be an explanation for why that tribe lost power.[67] The comment related to this verse in 1 Chr 5:1, 2b is especially pertinent: "the descendants of Reuben, the first-born of Israel, for he was the first-born, but when he desecrated the bed of his father his right of first-born was given to the descendants of Joseph son of Israel . . . and the right of first-born belongs to Joseph." In sum, there is a general consensus that a variety of biblical evidence suggests that the tribe of Reuben at one point became weakened to the profit of Judah.

It is possible to read certain elements of the Joseph story in reference to this likely historical reconstruction. Twice in that story, Reuben and Judah appear in close proximity. The first time is early in the narrative, in chapter 37, in a doublet involving Reuben and Judah. In the first version (vv. 21–2), Reuben saves Joseph from death, with the hope that he will be able to return Joseph to Jacob. This hope is not realized. In the continuation of the text, Judah's plan, that Joseph should be sold to foreigners (vv. 26–7), is heeded by his brothers. The second time is later in the story, when Jacob's family runs out of food after their first trip to Egypt. The brothers attempt to convince Jacob that they must return for more food. Jacob resists because the Egyptian ruler had insisted that the youngest brother, Benjamin, must return with them. When Reuben attempts to persuade his father by offering to leave his two sons as surety, Jacob refuses (42:37–8). However, soon afterwards, when Judah takes responsibility for Benjamin, Jacob accedes (43:8–14). Both of these doublets dismiss the authority of Reuben to the profit of Judah.[68]

The elevation of Judah among the brothers (except for Joseph) continues. In 44:16, after the hidden goblet is found in Benjamin's sack, it is Judah who responds to Joseph. In vv. 18–34, when it is time to plead on behalf of Benjamin, it is Judah who takes the initiative, and, in an impassioned speech, succeeds in winning back Benjamin. Finally, in 46:28, when the entire family of Jacob is travelling to Egypt, Jacob sends Judah ahead of his brothers. These actions reflect Judah's status as the prime brother; in the words of 1 Chr 5:2a, which appear in the introduction of *Reuben*'s genealogy: "for Judah grew stronger than his brothers, and the king[69] is from him."

The status of Judah in relationship to Reuben in the Joseph story is modeled on the importance of Judah, the strong southern tribe, which produced King David and his dynasty. The plausibility of a royal reading of this unit is fostered by internal indications that its author was familiar with the Judean court.[70] The Joseph story twice describes Reuben's rejection, which historically represents the weakening of that tribe. It projects history backward by representing Judah as the central, non-Joseph tribe already in the period of Joseph. This type of typological depiction obviously serves the interests of Judah and David. It combats the notion that Judah became powerful only in the early monarchic period, suggesting instead that its exalted status dates from antiquity, from the time of the tribe's eponymous leader. The more ancient exalted status adds prestige, and fosters Judean kingship.

This interpretation of the story fits a wide range of dates and theories for the composition of the Joseph story. There is a consensus that the story incorporates earlier written or oral traditions, but the particular sources found earlier in Genesis (J, E and P) do not appear here, and cannot explain the redundancies and terminological variation in Genesis 37–50.[71] Thus, it is the story's editor who fashioned the story into its current shape, to reflect Judean interests. According to Redford, however, the story originally concerned only Reuben and Jacob (as opposed to Judah and Israel), and was later expanded to incorporate Judah.[72] The same editor who added Judah used the name Israel rather than Jacob for the patriarch. If this model is correct, then the original form of the story may have reflected, like the genealogies where Reuben is always first-born, the dominant role of Reuben, while a later editor, interested in pro-Judean, pro-Davidic ideologies, revised the story by adding sections in which Judah usurps Reuben's role. That editor's interest in later history may also be reflected in his use of the name Israel, which more transparently refers to post-patriarchal history. The Joseph story clearly has a long history and its final form is difficult to date.[73] Although we cannot determine when either its supposed early Reuben version or its later Judah revision was composed, we do know that the theme of Judah as proto-king fits a wide range of dates through the exile and beyond.

The more elements in a text that can be interpreted typologically, the more certain we are that the text is typological.[74] Thus, the typological interpretation of these elements in the Joseph story is bolstered by the presence of other elements that likely refer to events in later Israelite history, some of which may also be related to the monarchy. However, it must be admitted that the following elements are not as central or as certain as the ones adduced above. Gressmann suggested that the exchange of place of Ephraim and Manasseh (Gen 48:17–21), where Ephraim is made into the first-born, is related to a historical change in the two tribes" status.[75] This may reflect the fact that the first king of the north in the divided monarchy, Jeroboam son of Nebat, was from the tribe of Ephraim (1 Kgs 11:26) or the general prominence of Ephraim, which is seen in the use of that term for the northern kingdom as a whole.[76] An author might have projected backward Ephraim's central role to hoary antiquity.

Finally, it is interesting that prominent sections of the Joseph narrative focus on the conflict between Joseph and Judah. Joseph, like Ephraim, is used in prophetic literature to symbolize the northern kingdom[77]; it is thus possible to read these sections as representing the strife between the northern and southern kingdoms.[78] In 1 Chr 5:1–2, a later historian recognizes Judah and Joseph as the two strong tribes. The general outlines of the story of Joseph may reflect historical events; he is born late, a possible reference to the establishment of the northern kingdom after that of David. He is the predominant, favored son, representing the geographical and military importance of the north. However, the north was exiled first; perhaps this is reflected in Exod 1:8, which refers to "a new king who did not know Joseph." The Joseph story as a whole, from the end of Genesis to the very beginning of Exodus would then sanction the conflict between the north and the south.

It is difficult to know when and where the typologies of Joseph and Ephraim have entered the story. If this tradition originated in the north, it reflects the domination of the Joseph tribes, especially Ephraim, and the role of the north as a military power superior to the south. If it is written by a Judean, it may reflect the complicated attitude of the south toward the north. The Book of Kings suggests that Judean scribes felt an ambivalence toward northern kingship. Some saw it as a treacherous rebellion against the Davidic dynasty (1 Kgs 12:19), while others legitimized northern kingship by telling the story of Ahijah of Shiloh, who offered the kingship to Jeroboam only after Solomon sinned (1 Kgs 11:29–39). The Joseph story can be read as incorporating a set of anti-northern reflections by a Judean. Joseph was not the first-born, but became the most powerful, suggesting that kingship did not originally belong to the north. Joseph later becomes a powerful, even a royal figure, representing the rise of a powerful independent north with its own dynasties. Joseph competes against Judah, and is superior to him. However, in the end, Judah wins and "Joseph" is forgotten – a new king arises who does not remember Joseph (Exod 1:8); this conclusion to the Joseph story may reflect the early destruction of "Joseph" in 722, one and a half centuries before Judah's exile to Babylon.

The negative portrayals of Joseph in Genesis 37, which motivate the brothers' plotting, may then reflect the Judeans' attitude toward their northern brothers, who act as if they are superior. Like the brothers of Joseph, the south envied its politically powerful neighbor; the Joseph story projects this envy backward.

In sum, there are several correspondences between the family relationships described in the Joseph story and the later political history of Israel and Judah. A careful reading of the story might uncover additional elements that could be interpreted in a similar vein. It is possible that the correspondences between the Joseph story and the later history of Israel and Judah are coincidental; we do not find the same strong vocabulary links binding the units together that we saw in Gen 12:10–20 in relationship to Exodus. However, their absence cannot be determinative, because we have no central texts relating to the fates of Judah and Reuben or Judah and Joseph, to which the author of the Joseph story might be referring. Rather than seeing these similarities as accidental, I am suggesting that here too we have pre-enacted history. Certain plot elements within Genesis are fostering the Judean Davidic monarchy and suggesting that the strife between Judah and Israel is an intrinsic element of the relationship between the two tribes.[79] This reading is supported by noting the existence of other some texts in which the "defence of David"[80] is of paramount importance, including some texts like Genesis that do not explicitly deal with the monarchy.[81]

I am not claiming that the Joseph story was composed to legitimate the relationship between Reuben and Judah and the north and the south. There are too many story elements which cannot be explained in that way. The Joseph story has an unusually long and complex history, and is quite exceptional for biblical narratives in its length and in what we perceive as its literary-aesthetic grace.[82] The absence of clear signs of the Pentateuchal sources J or E in the story suggests that it may have been composed or transmitted in different circles from the rest of Genesis. In any case, at some point(s), an author or various authors who were interested in contemporary politics had a hand in the story's transmission, and (re)formulated it so that it (also) became a typological tale, reflecting the interests of the Judean ruling class.

TYPOLOGY AND HISTORY

Von Rad has claimed that typology "is an elementary function of all human thought and interpretation."[83] He may have overgeneralized; however, it is crucial to understand that typology is in fact frequently used by the ancient biblical historians,[84] and does not have its origin in the New Testament. Its frequent use in the Hebrew Bible does not imply that the ancient Israelites believed only in "cyclical time" and always viewed the world as a set of recurring events; rather, *certain events* were depicted as if they had transpired more than once.[85] These typologies sometimes create symmetries within the biblical text, but these symmetries should not be seen as primarily literary-aesthetic. Rather, they emphasize the fundamental importance of central political and religious events.

In many pre-exilic texts, it is difficult to know for certain that an event is being depicted typologically. In Chronicles and in the New Testament, it is relatively easy to isolate typological passages because they are re-enactments of earlier narratives. Cases of pre-enactment are more difficult to isolate, especially when we do not have the traditions that might be referred to in such pre-enactments. The multiple vocabulary links between Gen 12:10–20 and the exodus narratives, as well as the existence of biblical stories parallel to Gen 12:10–20, suggest that it was written as a "mini-exodus." The case with the Joseph story is less certain because it is a more highly developed narrative, it is not *primarily* typological in nature and the events which it typologizes do not have a set vocabulary associated with it. Still, a set of substantial similarities suggests that at some point one of the tradents shaped the Joseph story using typological thinking.

These two typologies have a similar function: to create a certain continuum in history that emphasizes key events. The typology in Gen 12: 10–20 concerns religious history and emphasizes the importance of the exodus; it reinforces the nature of that "event"[86] as paradigmatic by making it one of the first events described in the patriarchal history. The Joseph story helps sanction certain political realities, such as Judean kingship and the competing dynasties in the north and south. These realities probably raised certain problems for the average Judean, because David could easily be seen as usurping Saul's dynastic prerogatives,[87] and because many Judeans were probably quite ambivalent concerning northern kingship. By pre-depicting these events in a much earlier period, the sole legitimacy of Davidic kingship is sanctioned, and the anxiety surrounding the existence of northern sovereignty is to some extent dissipated.

These are only two examples of typological thinking in Genesis. A careful reading of the book will uncover other typologies.[88] There are probably many events and traditions which are referred to typologically in Genesis and elsewhere, but since we do not know what these events are and how they were told, we can no longer see the typologies. This is especially unfortunate because missing typologies causes readers to under-read or to misread texts.[89]

Furthermore, it is almost impossible to date and to assign geographical proveniences to specific Torah texts,[90] and thus to perceive the presence and the meaning of certain typologies. For example, there is a wide disparity of opinion concerning the date of individual Pentateuchal sources and the redaction of the Torah. Yet, we should not succumb to the temptation of over-typologizing, of seeing all of Israel's past as told in the Hebrew Bible as a projection of the author's period.[91] It is difficult to evaluate David J. A. Clines' provocative statements, "In the patriarchal narratives, exilic Israel reads not only the life of its ancestors but its own life-story" and "The significance of such a[n exilic setting for the redaction] is that the Pentateuch functions as an address to exiles, or perhaps it would be better to say, the self-expression of exiles who find themselves at the same point as that reached by the Israelite tribes at the end of Deuteronomy."[92] Certainly Clines is correct that the exiles must have felt a certain kinship with these texts and gained a sense of comfort from them, and in that sense these texts were probably *read* typologically. However, we do not know when the outline of the story, which is already found in J,[93] was written, nor do we know when the Torah was redacted. For these reasons, we cannot say whether or not the story was originally *written* or *shaped* as a typological narrative. Similarly, the position of Keith W. Whitelam, that "The exodus and conquest traditions of the Hebrew Bible need to be understood in terms of the complex processes which contributed to the formation of the canon prior to and particularly during the second temple period,"[94] is uncertain, since it suggests as a given the late date of the composition and redaction of the Torah.

Unfortunately, we are unlikely to become more certain concerning either the events of pre-exilic history or the dating of much of the Torah. Thus, many cases which we suspect to be typological creations of history will remain in the realm of possibility rather than certainty. This does not, however, negate the importance of typology, which is one of the many ways a historian allows the present to bear upon the past.

4

DEUTERONOMY AS
INTERPRETATION

Do not add anything from what I have commanded you, and
do not take away from it.

Deut 4:2

REVISIONIST HISTORY

In *The First Historians: The Hebrew Bible and History*, Baruch Halpern[1]
claims that the Deuteronomist is a historian; one reason that the Deuteronomist deserves this attribute, according to Halpern, is that he used sources.
Though the specific cases adduced by Halpern may not be convincing,[2]
the general principle they reflect is certainly correct: some ancient Israelite
historians did hear, read, repeat, rephrase and rewrite earlier works and
traditions.

Most scholars agree with Halpern's general point, that biblical authors
often used written and oral sources. There is less agreement on, or even
discussion of, how we may know that a particular unit is based on extant
written sources. I would suggest that in order to demonstrate that historian
A has reworked a composition of historian B, two things must be shown:
that A is later than B and that A knew the work of B. The first can be
demonstrated using the standard canons of biblical scholarship; the second
depends on noting sufficient unusual terminology that is common to
the two texts. Both of these criteria are fulfilled in certain texts in the
introductory chapters of Deuteronomy which reflect a reworking of narrative material of JE.[3]

I will treat two short episodes in Deuteronomy: the establishment of the
Israelite judicial system (1:9–18) and the conquest of Transjordan (2:26–3:7).
These episodes, like most of the first three chapters of Deuteronomy, have
clear sources in earlier Pentateuchal literature; this chapter will show the
various ways in which these sources have been used. The study of
additional texts would reveal how almost all of the first three chapters
should be read as an interpretation of traditions preserved in JE, which
were blended with other traditions and updated by a Deuteronomic author.

The Book of Chronicles has already provided us with models for how a later historian might rework earlier texts.[4] He can omit episodes which are unfavorable to his ideology (e.g. David and Bathsheba), he can blend together divergent texts (e.g. the Passover legislation of Exodus and Deuteronomy), he can update stories to reflect more recent legislative changes (e.g. Solomon celebrating the eighth day of Sukkot), he can move around material for chronological or thematic reasons (e.g. David and the Temple preparations) and he can create new themes through close (over-) interpretation of earlier sources (e.g. David laying the groundwork for the Temple). These characteristics are in no way unique to the Chronicler; many of them typify midrash,[5] and may be found in the classical Jewish midrashim and in the pseudepigraphic genre of rewritten biblical texts.

The inclusion of Deuteronomy within pseudepigraphic literature follows Morton Smith, who has shown that pseudepigraphy is a characteristic biblical phenomenon, and that Deuteronomy is a classic example of it.[6] A brief examination of some aspects of an Israelite pseudepigraphic work will allow a model to emerge which is helpful for understanding how Deuteronomy might relate to its sources.

I have chosen the Testament of Job, a work usually dated to between 100 BCE and CE 100.[7] Its author used as his primary source (the LXX of) the Book of Job. He combined this with other biblical works and was influenced by the religious beliefs and the stylistic norms of his period. These encouraged him to introduce some notions which were quite foreign to the biblical Job, such as Merkabah mysticism.[8] This rewritten Job differs from its *Vorlage* as much as modern rewritings of Job, such as *J.B.*, by Archibald MacLeish or Neil Simon's *God's Favorite*. The main differences between the pseudepigraphic work and its biblical source are summarized by Nahum Glatzer:

> The Biblical Job fears the distant, silent, God; Job of the Testament can love him: "I shall from the love of God endure until the end." Thus Satan, who in the Biblical Job is but the initiator of the tension between Job and God, remains in the Testament a fighting antagonist throughout the drama, and his spirit imbues Elihu, the youngest of Job's "friends." Against the mighty but perishable realm of the Evil One, Job represents the eternal kingdom of God.[9]

There are additional changes; for example, in comparison to the biblical text, women have a very prominent role in the Testament, and the biblical book, which is a short prose narrative with an extensive poetic center, has become a long prose narrative containing short poems.[10] Other changes typify midrashic exegesis; these include giving names to figures who are unnamed in the biblical text and increasing the numbers found in the text.[11] As a result of these changes, little of the original structure or message of the biblical Book of Job remains in the Testament.

The Testament, however, unlike modern rewritings of Job, does not totally create its new Job by moving the biblical book into line with its contemporaneous modes of thought or stylistic preferences. Several of the changes are the result of interpretation or of blending various biblical episodes together. Some of these blendings reflect the combination of disparate episodes from different sections of the biblical book. Modern scholarship has distinguished between the passive Job of the prose and the feisty Job of the poetry;[12] the Testament, like other pre-critical readings, has combined these two Jobs. For example, the Testament states (20:7–8), "In great trouble and distress I left the city, and I sat on a dung heap wormridden in body." This represents a conflation of Job 2:8 (prose), "He [Job] took a potsherd to scratch himself while he was sitting in the dungheap,"[13] with the poetic 7:5a, "My flesh is clothed with worms." A different type of conflation may be seen in 3:1–2, where God reveals himself to Job(ab)[14] "saying, 'Jobab, Jobab!' And I said, 'Yes, here I am.' " Here a verse from Gen 22:11, the binding of Isaac, is combined with Job. The author of the Testament, following various hints that place the biblical Job in the patriarchal period,[15] has gone one step further, and has made Job into a type resembling Abraham.[16] Although the second example is more extreme than the first, in both various biblical texts are combined, resulting in a new text which differs decisively from its sources. Furthermore, as may be seen from both examples, the author of the Testament felt comfortable enough speaking for Job, changing the Bible's third-person narrative into a first-person "testament."[17]

This evidence from late biblical works such as Chronicles, and from still later pseudepigraphic writings such as the Testament of Job, suggests that post-exilic biblical and later Jewish works used sources, but were not enslaved to them. At times the source was quoted verbatim, while elsewhere it was paraphrased or even radically revised. These various ways in which sources can be used, ranging from quotation to polemical rebuttal, are fundamental to the historical venture, and there is no reason why they should not have been used in a variety of fashions before Chronicles.[18] Though it is easiest to isolate their use in post-exilic texts, Michael Fishbane has shown in *Biblical Interpretation in Ancient Israel* that there is a great deal of continuity in the interpretive methods of pre-exilic, exilic, post-exilic and rabbinic texts.[19] In addition to showing how the Deuteronomic historians wrote history by interpreting earlier texts, this chapter will also show how they injected contemporary notions into older sources. We saw this above with Chronicles,[20] and this was responsible for the introduction of Merkabah mysticism into the Testament of Job. The use of the present to interpret or to rewrite the past is a fundamental feature of history writing.[21] In the words of Ben Halpern, "[M]emory and history, as constructions of the past, are often more clearly adjusted to what serves present intentions than to what may 'really' have happened and cannot in fact be altered."[22]

The starting point of this chapter, that much of the introduction of Deuteronomy is a revision of narrative texts in JE, receives further support from a recent study of Bernard Levinson, "The Hermeneutics of Innovation: The Impact of Centralization upon the Structure, Sequence, and Reformulation of Legal Material in Deuteronomy." This work shows in great detail how various laws in Deuteronomy have reworked earlier laws from the Book of the Covenant in Exodus. At times, D quotes; elsewhere it revises or interprets radically, often using some of the same principles later found in rabbinic literature. Though Levinson has not treated the narrative material in Deuteronomy, there is every reason to expect the relationship of the Deuteronomists[23] to be the same toward legal and narrative material; indeed, close to a century ago, S. R. Driver noted, "The author's method in treating the history of JE is analogous to that followed by him in dealing with the laws."[24] Some modern scholars have developed Driver's points,[25] but in general, the exploration of the transformation of narrative material has lagged behind that of legal material.

THE JUDICIAL SYSTEM

Both Deut 1:9–18 and Exod 18:13–26 (E) narrate the establishment of a judicial system to aid the overburdened Moses.[26] According to Exodus, Moses" father-in-law sees that Moses is overburdened with judicial responsibilities, and recommends that Moses appoint individuals with the appropriate religious qualities to serve as judges of first recourse.[27] In Deuteronomy, however, Moses complains that he is overburdened, and suggests, with the people's approval, that various wise people be appointed as judges of first recourse.[28] The thematic and verbal connections between these texts were evident already in antiquity; these seem to have motivated an ancient editor outside of the proto-masoretic tradition to integrate the Deuteronomy text into the Exodus pericope. This change may be seen in the Samaritan Pentateuch,[29] which is based on the tradition preserved in the Qumran text 4QpaleoExod[M].[30]

Scholars typically recognize that the episode dealing with judges in Deuteronomy is based on Exodus and other texts.[31] Weinfeld, for example, in his recent commentary notes that the Deuteronomy pericope "is dependent in many ways on the sources in Exod 18:13–23 and Num 11:11–17. There are phrases in our passage that even look like quotations from these sources. . . . But there are also significant differences among various accounts, which merit examination."[32]

The genetic connection between Exodus and Deuteronomy in this case is virtually assured by the great verbal similarity of Deut 1:15, "and I appointed them as chiefs over you: officers over one thousand, officers over one hundred, officers over fifty and officers over ten," to Exod 18:25 (cf. v. 21), "and he [Moses] appointed them as chiefs over the nation: officers over one thousand, officers over one hundred, officers over fifty and officers over ten." The term "officers over fifty"[33] is not used elsewhere in the Torah and is rare in the Bible, and none of the other terms are used elsewhere in a judicial (rather than military) context. This strongly suggests that the texts are genetically connected; in this particular case, given what we know about the general relationship between JE and D, Deuteronomy must depend on Exodus.[34]

This type of literary dependence is expected; what is more unusual is the way in which other sections of the Deuteronomy pericope diverge markedly from Exodus 18.[35] Some of these differences are the result of the influence on our author of other source texts, such as Numbers 11; others result from our author's creative impulses as a writer of history. Instead of offering a comprehensive list of differences between Deut 1:9–18 and its sources, I will emphasize those changes which highlight how this Deuteronomic author functions as a historian reworking his sources.

Two changes may be directly attributed to the world-view of the Deuteronomic author: the greater concentration on Moses relative to Exodus, and the substitution of the religious qualifications of the judges as narrated in Exodus with ones related to wisdom. Deuteronomy is a pseudepigraph, with Moses as its central figure. The centrality of Moses in Deuteronomy may be illustrated from several passages where his role as a paradigmatic prophet and covenant mediator is exalted (e.g. Deut 5:5; 18:9–22).[36] In contrast, Moses" father-in-law[37] plays no role in Deuteronomy. It is thus natural to shift the idea of initiating the judicial system to Moses; this lends prestige to Moses and to the system he establishes.

The other change, from religious to wise judges, was already attributed by Weinfeld in his early work on Deuteronomy to the wisdom milieu of Deuteronomy.[38] Given the preponderance of wisdom ideology in Deuteronomy, this change is quite natural and expected, and has parallels elsewhere in related passages between the two books.[39]

Before seeing more technical types of changes which involve interpretation[40] or the blending of biblical texts, it is important to establish a likely relative chronology between Deut 1:9–18 and the texts it might be blending. Deut 1:9–18 three times uses the phrase "at that time;"[41] this phrase typifies late, usually exegetical additions in Deuteronomy 1–5.[42] Furthermore, many scholars view the first introduction to Deuteronomy, 1–3 (or 4), as exilic.[43] Even those who do not see all of these chapters as exilic, view Deut 1:9–18 as later than the first redaction of Deuteronomy.[44] This suggests that the historian responsible for Deut 1:9–18 might have known earlier Deuteronomic texts as well as JE.

Many scholars have noted that the historian in Deut 1:9–18 has used Num 11:11–17, which deals with the establishment of the institution of seventy elders, to supplement Exod 18:13–26. I will return to that text shortly; I will begin with Deut 16:18–20, which most scholars have not adequately addressed, though its influence on Deut 1:9–18 is greater than that of Numbers. 11.[45]

The influence of Deut 16:18–20 on our unit is so extensive that it is worth quoting in full:

> (18) You should establish judges and officials in all of your cities which YHWH your God is giving you according to your tribes; they should judge the people justly. (19) Do not pervert justice, do not favor anyone and do not take bribes, for bribes blind the eyes of wise people and pervert the words of righteous people. (20) Rather you should earnestly pursue righteousness so that you will live to possess the land which YHWH your God is giving to you.

Some of the technical administrative terminology of Deut 16:18 has been moved to Deut 1:15. It is on that basis that the judicial officers in Deut 1:15 are called "officials."[46] In fact, Deut 1:15aβb may be seen as a conflation of Exod 18:25aβb and part of Deut 16:18, as may be seen below:

> Deut 1:15aβb: "and I appointed them as chiefs over you: officers over one thousand, officers over one hundred, officers over fifty and officers over ten and officials according to your tribes";
> Exod 18:25aβb: "and he [Moses] appointed them as chiefs over the nation: officers over one thousand, officers over one hundred, officers over fifty and officers over ten";
> Deut 16:18a: "judges and officials . . . according to your tribes."

It is possible that our interpreter in Deuteronomy 1 understood the second person masculine subject of Deut 16:18 ("*You* should establish") as referring to Moses, especially since Moses was the individual who received the law according to the ideology of Deuteronomy; this may be another reason why Moses" father-in-law is absent in Deuteronomy 1. Though the referent in v. 18 was understood as Moses, the context does not allow vv. 19–20 to refer to him; Moses certainly does not need to be reminded to be fair (v. 19), and the end of v. 20, which suggests that whoever judges fairly will possess the land, is inappropriate for Moses, who does not enter the land. Thus, a natural reading of Deut 16:18–20 presumes that vv. 19–20 are a description of the "just ruling" which the judges appointed by Moses must apply.[47] It is as if a statement saying "and this is what you must tell these judges and officers" implicitly stands between vv. 18 and 19, and this is precisely how the historian in Deut 1:15–17 read the verses.

Deut 1:16, which reads "I commanded your judges at that time saying, 'adjudicate between your fellow people and you shall rule justly between fellow people and strangers,' " picks up on the theme and the terminology of 16:18–20. It transposes the nominal phrase "just ruling"[48] into "and you shall rule justly"[49] and it explicitly states what is implicit in chapter 16: that Moses, upon hearing this legislation, told the judges how to behave (1:16, "I commanded your judges at that time, saying . . . "). A clear indication that these verses in Deuteronomy 16 are used and reworked by the author of Deuteronomy 1 is from Deut 1:17a, where Moses commands the judges "do not favor anyone in judgement," most likely a paraphrase of 16:19a, "Do not pervert justice, do not favor anyone."[50]

Finally, it is possible that the motive clause in Deut 1:17, "for judgement is God's," is based on the motive clause in Deut 16:20, "so that you will live to possess the land which YHWH your God is giving to you." Deuteronomy 1, probably written during the exile, cannot comfortably assert that proper judicial systems will assure land tenure; it therefore transforms its source, stating in general terms that God is the ultimate judge and by implication that he will punish you for judicial abuses and will reward you for proper judicial behavior.[51]

The final verse of our pericope (1:18), "and I commanded you at that time concerning all the deeds which you should do," is based on Exod 18:20b, "and you should make known to them the path in which they should walk and the deed that they should do."[52] Our historian has changed the perspective of the verse, so that the people are referred to in the second rather than third person; this fits the fiction of Deuteronomy as Moses' valedictory address. The verse has been moved to the end of the pericope in Deuteronomy to give it a neater structure of Moses' complaint and its answer (vv. 9–14), enactment of the solution by appointing and instructing judges (vv. 15–17), and commanding the entire nation concerning proper behavior (v. 18).[53] This is reminiscent of the types of narrative restructuring seen above (Chapter Two) in the Chronicler.[54] Deuteronomy adds a favorite phrase, "at that time,"[55] to its source in two places (vv. 9, 16), to bind the unit together. Finally, the Deuteronomic historian has changed non-Deuteronomic phraseology to phrases which are more typical of his vocabulary and more in line with his world-view; this explains the changes of "the laws and ordinances" to "all the deeds"[56] and of "and I made known" to "I commanded."[57]

Deut 1:9–12 form a separate subunit, which is framed by the phrase "to bear alone."[58] These verses are only loosely connected to what follows; they narrate in general terms Moses" complaint of being overburdened by the nation. There is little to suggest that the problem is specifically juridical, with the exception of the final Hebrew word of v. 12,[59] which may be understood as either a general term for strife or as a specific term for judicial cases.[60] This ambiguity integrates vv. 9–12 with what follows. As noted above, many scholars claim that these four verses have their source primarily in Num 11:11–17, the story of the choosing of the elders. Two factors influenced our historian to look towards Num 11:11–17 as a potential source that might bear on Exod 18:13–27 + Deut 16:18–20. The first is verbal, the second thematic: (1) the mention of officials there (11:16)[61] ties the unit to Deut 16:18 and thus to our unit; and (2) like our unit, Num 11:11–17 deals with relieving Moses of his administrative burden.

The influence of Numbers 11 on our passage may be seen in several different ways. First of all, Deut 1:9 and 12 (twice) use words from the root *nś*, "to bear"; this is a *Leitwort* of Numbers 11.[62] Second, in contrast to Exodus 18, where the judges are appointed as a result of the initiative of Moses" father-in-law, Numbers suggests that administrative relief is necessary because Moses himself realizes that he alone cannot handle the entire population. Additionally, Numbers 11, which is currently embedded in a complaint narrative, does not deal specifically with judges; this explains why Deut 1:9–12 uses general, non-judicial terms such as "your trouble" and "your burden."[63] Finally, even though Deut 1:12 ("How can I bear alone your trouble, your burden, your disputes") is addressed to the Israelites, it sounds like a lament.[64] Once we realize that its source is Num 11:11–14, a lament to YHWH, we can appreciate why Deut 1:12 has this tone.

Our historian, however, does not slavishly incorporate the Numbers text, but transforms it dramatically. In Numbers, the attitude of Moses toward the Israelites is highly negative; Moses is so fed up with them that he wants to die (v. 15). In a sense, Moses" complaint could be taken as a wish that the people would be less populous, thus less burdensome. His complaint allows an alternative solution rather than a new administrative system: a drastic reduction in the population so that they can be handled more easily.[65] Our historian in Deuteronomy seems to be sensitive to this option, which he finds too upsetting, so he combats it with two verses (10–11) written in Deuteronomic style, and thus clearly his own composition, which state that the nation should grow a thousand-fold, like the stars, and that they should be blessed, as God promised.[66] If this passage is exilic, following the devastating Babylonian conquest,[67] it is easy to see why our author would have taken Moses' attitude of despair toward the nation and overturned it into a description of a nation deserving of blessing.[68]

I would like to return to several other elements of near quotation and interpretation in Deuteronomy 1 which depend solely on Exodus 18, rather than the combination of Exodus 18 with Deuteronomy 16 or Numbers 11. Deut 1:16 states that the judgements are between Israelites or between Israelites and strangers. This reflects the language of Exod 18:16, "I will judge between a person and his neighbor," but has been "Deuteronomized" through the addition of the stranger in accordance with Deuteronomy's concern for the underclass, including the stranger.[69] Finally, Deut 1:17b, "and the issue that is too difficult for you, you should bring to me so I may hear it" is a paraphrase of Exod 18:22, "and every serious matter they should bring to you." The language of Deuteronomy differs from its source in several ways. It uses a different verb, "to bring near" rather than "to bring;"[70] this is likely a stylistic variant, reflecting the fact that later authors felt free to paraphrase their sources.[71] The other variants may reflect midrash-like interpretation. The word used in Exodus for cases that the judges must bring to Moses often means "big" or "great," and the phrase containing the term might even be understood as "the judicial matter relating to an important person."[72] Deuteronomy has clarified the sense of "great" as a matter that it is too difficult for the judges to adjudicate.[73] Finally, Deuteronomy adds to its source the word "so I may hear it," making explicit what is implicit, namely, that the cases will not merely be brought to Moses, but that Moses himself will adjudicate them.[74]

I have attempted to show how three passages, now found in Exodus, Numbers and Deuteronomy, have been melded together to form Deut 1:9–18, which is inserted between vv. 8 and 19.[75] Why has the historian chosen to insert this episode here rather than to follow the example of his *Vorlage*, Exodus 18, and place the unit immediately preceding the decalogue, in Deuteronomy 5?

Contextual reasons might have motivated our author. Deut 16:18–20 suggests that the administration of a judicial system will assure land possession – v. 20b, "so that you will live to possess the land which YHWH your God is giving to you." Deut 1:8, the verse immediately preceding our unit, reads: "See, I have placed the land before you; come and possess the land which YHWH has sworn to your ancestors, Abraham, Isaac and Jacob, to give to them and to their descendants after them." It is quite possible that our historian reasoned that if the establishment of a judicial system allows land tenure, it must be established immediately before the Israelites are ready to possess the land. Additionally, the establishment of a properly functioning judicial system is one of the most fundamental social institutions; indeed, it must precede the giving of individual laws. This too may have influenced our author's placement of the unit at the beginning of Deuteronomy.[76]

In sum, our historian has blended together three sources. Exod 18:13–26 is his main source, whose story he rewrites on the basis of Deut 16:18–20, and Num 11:11–17, which he used only for vv. 9–12. Thematic and vocabulary links make these two episodes relevant to Exodus 18. The historian, however, was not enslaved to these sources; they are used creatively, and their phraseology is often changed to reflect the author's Deuteronomic language and ideology. The changes were not merely linguistic or stylistic; for example, the changes in the role of Moses" father-in-law and in Moses" attitude toward Israel should be considered as ideological. The final product flows well, but some tension remains between vv. 9–12, which reflect a general lament, and vv. 13–18, the establishment of the judicial system.[77]

THE CONQUEST OF TRANSJORDAN

The conquest of Sihon, king of Heshbon and of Og, king of Bashan is narrated in Deut 2:26–3:7, a section which heavily depends on sources.[78] It immediately follows a narrative which details how the Israelites circumvented the Edomites ("the descendants of Seir") and the Moabites. That section is probably based on Numbers, though it shows significant differences from it. For example, according to Deut 2:8, the Edomites allowed the Israelites to pass through their territory, while Num 20:21 claims that Israel went around Edom. Some scholars see this as evidence that the author in Deuteronomy used a different account[79] or that Numbers and Deuteronomy shared a similar account, but that Deuteronomy is not directly dependent on Numbers.[80] Other scholars, however, claim direct dependence, and this is likely.[81] The radical difference between Numbers and Deuteronomy could be the creation of the historian[82] and is no more radical than the changes seen in Chronicles in relationship to its sources. It does not differ, for example, from the Chroniclers' omission of the Bathsheba episode in order to create David's new, totally positive image. This tendency toward extensive revision of sources may also be seen later in rabbinic literature, which had the Hebrew Bible, including Samuel, as its source, but could nevertheless claim that David did not sin with Bathsheba.[83]

Given the very substantial differences between Numbers and Deuteronomy concerning the treatment of Edom and Moab, it is not fruitful to investigate in detail how Deut 2:1–25 interprets its sources. I will turn instead to the accounts concerning Sihon, king of the Amorites/Heshbon (2:26–37) and Og, king of Bashan (3:1–7), where the differences are more modest and the interpretive techniques are easier to identify.

The defeat of Sihon as narrated in Num 21:21–5 is quite short and unremarkable; Israel sends messengers to Sihon, asking for safe passage through his territory. Sihon refuses, attacks Israel, is beaten and killed,[84] and his cities are taken by the Israelites.

The same story is expanded considerably in Deut 2:26–37. According to that account, Moses sent messengers to Sihon, asking for safe passage through his territory. Sihon refused because YHWH hardened his heart. As a result, Sihon was utterly defeated, and his population was subject to the *ḥerem* or ban. The general story line is similar, but there are substantial differences of detail. Four general principles are responsible for the transformation of Num 21:21–5:

1 The author of Deuteronomy was disturbed by a logical problem of the original story – why would Sihon turn down Israel's offer?
2 Num 21:34, concerning Og, states, "You shall do to him [=Og] what you did to Sihon the king of the Amorites who resides in Heshbon." This implies that the conquests of Sihon and Og are similar in detail,

even where the same details are not narrated of both of them in the Numbers text. This gave the Deuteronomic author license to move material from the Og account to the Sihon account.

3 In general, readers tend to make contiguous units bear on each other. In the Bible too narrative material often shifts between adjacent and near-adjacent units, especially when they are thematically related.[85]

4 The brief statement in Num 21:24, "Israel smote him by sword," which might suggest that only Sihon was killed, conflicts with Deuteronomy's notion of "historical probability," which mandates that the entire native population be killed.[86]

These four principles acting together are responsible for most of the transformation of Numbers 21 into Deuteronomy 2. Before seeing how this was accomplished, it is necessary to focus on Deut 20:10–18, a pericope which also influenced the author of the Og episode in Deuteronomy. The relationship of Deut 20:10–18 to our passage is similar to that of Deut 16:18–20 to Deuteronomy 1. Both Deut 20:10–18 and Deut 16:18–20 are Deuteronomic legislation from an early stage of the Book of Deuteronomy, which influenced the later narrative introduction of Deuteronomy, including chapters 2–3.

Deut 20:10–18 and Deut 2:26ff. are clearly related. There are close verbal similarities between these passages; these include "words of peace" (Deut 2:26), which is similar to "you shall offer it terms of peace" (Deut 20:10), and Deut 2:35, "we only took as spoils the animals and the booty" which is similar to "only . . . and the animals . . . you may despoil . . . and you may eat the booty" (Deut 20:14).[87] It is likely that the author of Deuteronomy 2 knew a form of Deuteronomy 20.[88] This is supported by the general inclination to date Deuteronomy 1–3 later than the original lawbook, which would have included Deuteronomy 20.[89] In addition, literary evidence suggests that Deuteronomy 2 is later than chapter 20. The phrase, "you shall offer terms of peace" (Deut 20:10) is well integrated to Deuteronomy 20, while the comparable "words of peace" (Deut 2:26) is problematic in Deuteronomy 2 because the text later indicates that the Israelites' intentions were not truly peaceful (vv. 30–1) and suggests Israelite hostility towards the Moabites (v. 24).[90] This suggests that the phrase in Deuteronomy 2 is borrowed from chapter 20, and thus Deuteronomy 2 is the later text.

Deut 20:10–18, however, is generally acknowledged to be a composite text; a core of vv. 10–14, which suggests that conquered people may be used for corvée, is modified by vv. 15–18, which draw a distinction between the nations native to Canaan, who must be killed, and the far-away, non-Canaanite cities, whose residents need not be massacred.[91] However, in modifying vv. 13–14, "you shall smite all of its males by sword. You shall only despoil the women and the children and the animals and all that is in the city" to (v. 16) "you shall not allow any *nĕšāmâ* to live," a certain ambiguity remains: how should the animals be treated? Although no answer is explicit, several factors within the complex Deut 20:10–18 allow the conclusion that animals should be spared:

1 The word *nĕšāmâ* in biblical Hebrew refers to humans and not to animals.[92]
2 The reason for mandating the *ḥerem*, as described in v. 18, is to prevent the Israelites from learning the abominations of the nearby residents of Canaan. Although the Bible suggests that animals may be held accountable for crimes which they have committed or in which they have been involved,[93] it does not generally suppose that animals lead people to sin.[94]
3 The law in Deut 20:19–20, which immediately follows the *ḥerem* law, prohibits chopping down fruit-bearing trees during a prolonged siege. An analogy might suggest that domesticated animals, which are used for food, should similarly be spared during war.

To summarize: the author of Deut 2:26–3:7 believed that the *ḥerem* law as reflected in Deut 20:10–18 was authoritative. Although Deut 20:10–18 does not clearly state that animals may escape the *ḥerem*, and the traditions recorded in Josh 6:21 concerning Jericho and in 1 Sam 15:3 concerning Amalek imply that certain traditions included animals under the *ḥerem*, the three factors previously mentioned combine to suggest that Deut 20:10–18 might be interpreted to imply that animals should be spared. With this Deuteronomic understanding of the *ḥerem* law in mind, it is now possible to see how Deuteronomy reshaped the Og episode of Numbers 21.

Four changes are evident in the transformation of Num 21:21 to Deut 2:26: "Israel sent" became "I [Moses] sent"; the place has been specified as "the wilderness of Kedemoth"; "king of the Amorites" has been changed to "king of Heshbon"; the phrase "with an offer of peace" has been inserted. The change to "I sent" is part of Deuteronomy's general tendency to give Moses greater authority, which we explored earlier in reference to Moses rather than Jethro initiating the judicial system according to Deuteronomy. The change is especially easy to effect here since "Israel sent" in Numbers is ambiguous. Israel as a whole could not have sent a messenger; therefore the action is attributable to their leader, Moses. Alternatively, the nearby text of Num 20:14, which deals with a similar topic and opens "Moses sent messengers," might have influenced our text.[95] This would then be a case where nearby units influence each other. The tendency to clarify the unclear or ambiguous words, such as "Israel" in this unit, typifies inner-biblical and post-biblical interpretation. Num 21:21 does not specify the place from which the messengers originated; since Num 21:23 says "he marched out towards Israel, to the wilderness," it is clear that

Israel was in the wilderness. This interpretive detail is copied into the text of Deut 2:26, where it is further modified by Kedemoth, either based on another tradition[96] or the author's general geographical knowledge.[97] The change to "king of Heshbon," a place name, from "king of the Amorites," a gentilic, reflects the author's tendency toward the blending of adjacent units. That is, since the following unit refers to Og, king of Bashan, Sihon's modifier is converted into a city name so that his account would more clearly parallel what follows. Additionally, "Amorites" no longer existed as an ethnic group in Deuteronomy's time, and the phrase "king of Heshbon," referring to a city standing in the time of the Deuteronomist, made the episode more contemporary.[98] Finally, the phrase "words of of peace" is, as noted above, a citation of Deut 20:10, the introduction of the *herem* law. The introduction of this phrase is thus similar to that of "and officials according to your tribes" in Deut 1:15 on the basis of 16:18.[99]

Deut 2:27–9 are a revision of Num 21:22. While these verses show some similarities to Num 21:22[100] and share some similar themes (not straying, water use),[101] there are substantial differences between the two texts. In v. 28a, the Deuteronomic historian has modified his source with a preferred formula, which is also found in Deut 2:6. V. 29, which states that the Edomites and Moabites allowed free passage to Israel, is a dramatic revision of the source in Numbers. This verse, which opens "as the descendants of Esau did," may have the language of Num 21:34, "as you did to Sihon" as a model, but the specific application of "as ... did" to Edom and Moab is our author's innovation, probably the result of a change in attitude toward Moab and Edom. The phrases "turning off neither to the right nor to the left" (Deut 2:27) and "let me just pass through (on foot)" (v. 28) are probably introduced from Num 20:17–19, which uses similar language of Moses sending messengers to Edom. The Edom passage has influenced our author's depiction of Sihon; the justification for this is found in Deut 2:29, "[You, Sihon, should do] just as the children of Esau [the Edomites] did to me." According to this author's conception, the Esau/Edom episode is just like the Sihon episode, so specific details may be transferred from Edom to Sihon.

Deut 2:30a, "Sihon, king of Heshbon did not desire to let us pass through it" is a paraphrase of Num 21:23a, "Sihon did not let Israel pass through its boundary." The continuation of the verse in Deuteronomy, which suggests that God made Sihon stubborn so that Israel would conquer his territory, has no source in Numbers 21, and is Deuteronomy's answer to why Sihon could refuse such a reasonable offer from the Israelites. It is based on a parallel situation, where a king is confronted with a proposal and refuses – Pharaoh, king of Egypt. Earlier Torah sources presumably known to our author describe YHWH hardening Pharaoh's heart.[102] These have been generalized, and reapplied to Sihon.

After stating that Sihon did not want Israel to pass through, Numbers continues by narrating Sihon's preparations for war (21:23aβb). Before noting this, Deuteronomy adds a verse (2:31) in which YHWH speaks to Moses, telling him to conquer Sihon. This verse begins with "see," commonly used in Deuteronomy in divine discourse.[103] It is probably based on Deut 1:8, which it resembles. That verse, which also begins with "see," tells in general terms that the Israelites should conquer the land. Our author has taken that verse and has particularized it to the conquest of Sihon. This is quite sensible and unremarkable; what is significant, however, is that through this transformation, our historian felt comfortable putting new words into YHWH's mouth, which were not attested to in his source – it is not only history that is created and interpreted, but divine speeches are made up. Our author here is functioning like Thucydides, who records speeches that he did not actually hear, but that are appropriate for the situation.[104]

The following verses, Deut 2:32–5, are a blending of a description of Sihon's conquest as it happened according to Num 21:23–5, and of Deut 20:13ff. (the ḥerem law), a description of the conquest as it should have been. The Numbers text is paraphrased and somewhat reformulated; for example, Num 21:24, "Israel smote him," is transformed into (Deut 2:33) "YHWH our God delivered him before us." Deuteronomy rephrases its source to make it clear that victory was only accomplished with the help of YHWH; this is a central Deuteronomic theological idea.[105] The major change concerns the death of Sihon. Num 21:24 states only "he smote him," while Deut 2:33 expands this to "we smote him, his children and his whole nation." This phrase is thematically linked to the ḥerem law in Deut 20:13, which mandates killing all the males. In addition, Deut 2:33 is a quotation from Num 21:35, referring to Og, "they killed him, his children and his whole nation," and is therefore another realization of the principle of Num 21:34, "You shall do to him [Og] what you did to Sihon." The verbal correspondences between Deut 2:34b–35 and Deut 20:14–18 have already been noted; it is worthwhile just reemphasizing that the text in Deut 2:33–5 is a result of the blending of Num 21:24 and Deut 20:14–18.

In contrast to the previous unit, which shows much divergence from its source, the initial verses concerning Og in Deut 3:1–3 are nearly identical to Num 21:33–4, with the exception that Deuteronomy prefers first-person narration, as seen for example by comparing Num 21:34, "YHWH spoke to Moses," with Deut 3:2, "YHWH spoke to me." Otherwise, a Deuteronomist seems to have copied over nearly verbatim an earlier tradition.[106] The similarities between the two texts are so extensive that some scholars have suggested that the passage in Numbers was copied over from Deuteronomy.[107] However, the passage in Numbers is not characterized by Deuteronomic phraseology, which would be expected if it originated from Deuteronomy. Deut 3:1–3 would then reflect a case where a later tradent felt no need to interpret an earlier source in line with contemporary needs, and copied over that text almost verbatim. This introduction to the Og episode, remarkable for its uninterpretive nature, serves as a striking contrast to the preceding episode, concerning the defeat of Sihon. Though it may seem very surprising by our standards of consistency, this mixing of material copied over exactly with material which is highly rewritten, is very common in Chronicles (e.g. 1 Kgs 8:1–11//2 Chr 5:2–14).

The continuation of the Og episode in Deut 3:4–7 begins with a parallel to the Sihon episode; 3:4a, "we captured all of his cities at that time; there was no city which we did not take from them" parallels 2:34aα, "we captured all of his cities at that time" and 36aβ, "here was no city which was too high for us." As we saw earlier, Num 21:34, "You shall do to him [=Og] what you did to Sihon," allows material to be moved between the pericopae. Indeed, this verse from Numbers is found in our unit as well, in Deut 3:6aβ, though its "tense" has been changed, transforming it from a prediction to an accomplished fact.

The geographical information in Deut 3:4b-5 is not found in Numbers; either our author had an additional source for this material, or wrote on the basis of his own knowledge.[108] Finally, the rest of the unit, vv. 6–7, narrates the application of the law of the *ḥerem* to Og. It closely parallels vv. 34b-35 of the previous chapter, the *ḥerem* of Sihon, though there seem to be several attempts to vary the terminology slightly to avoid monotony.[109]

In sum, the author of Deut 2:26–3:7 had Num 21:21–35 as his main source. He omitted several sections, such as the poem preserved in Num 21:27–30. He read his source carefully, adducing several facts that are not explicit within it. He brought it into line with his own terminology and ideology, especially regarding the *ḥerem* laws as reflected in the *ḥerem* text now found in Deuteronomy 20. In some cases, the base text in Numbers was adhered to closely (e.g. Deut 3:1–3), while elsewhere it was freely changed and interpreted. This mixture of conservatism and radical change matches the patterns of rewriting seen in the Deuteronomic historian who rewrote the episode from Exodus 18 concerning the establishment of the judicial system.

DEUTERONOMY'S "ATTITUDE TOWARDS THE MATERIAL IN THE TRADITIONS"[110]

Martin Noth has remained one of the most central figures of biblical scholarship, especially in relationship to Deuteronomy and the Deuteronomistic History.[111] His understanding of the Deuteronomist as a historian was a major influence on Baruch Halpern's recent synthetic work on biblical history, *The First Historians*,[112] as well as on Steven L. McKenzie's *The Trouble with Kings*. For this reason, it is worth exploring Noth's view of the Deuteronomist as a historian in comparison with the analysis suggested above for Deut 1:9–18 and 2:31–3:7.

Noth opens the twelfth chapter of *The Deuteronomistic History*, on Deuteronomy's "Attitude Towards the Material in the Traditions," by stating:

> Dtr. had no intention of fabricating the history of the Israelite people. He wished to present it objectively and base it upon the material to which he had access. Like an honest broker he began by taking, in principle, a favourable view of the material in the traditions. In describing the various historical events he spoke in his own person only at exceptional points, letting the old traditions speak for themselves instead. He did so even when these old traditions told of events which did not fit in with his central ideas.... Dtr. was not a redactor trying to make corrections, but a compiler of historical traditions and a narrator of the history of his people.[113]

Noth further claims that the Deuteronomistic Historian valued all his sources equally as historical documents and it therefore did not occur to him to examine them critically; he had simply to add together the information at his disposal and, as a result, he used one source to supply what seemed to be lacking in another.[114] Noth does, however, concede with hesitancy that the Deuteronomistic Historian (Dtr.) does not always preserve his traditions exactly: "Finally, Dtr. has occasionally corrected the traditions he has utilised. These corrections are mostly unintentional but unmistakable."[115]

The analysis of selected passages in Deuteronomy 1–3 suggests that Noth's understanding is fundamentally flawed. No historian is fully objective; the Deuteronomists, who were highly ideological, certainly were not. Furthermore, the voice of the Deuteronomist(s) comes through loud and clear throughout the two units surveyed. The vocabulary of the sources is rewritten in his language, and more significantly, episodes are refashioned in a significant way to accommodate his beliefs.[116] For this reason, it is difficult to see how Noth can claim that Dtr.'s changes are "occasional" and "unintentional." For example, Moses rather than Jethro establishes the judicial system, and the *herem* is superimposed on the older stories narrating the conquest of Transjordan; these are not accidental changes. When old traditions did not fit, the Deuteronomist typically omitted them or changed them, though occasionally they are preserved. Further, like all historians, the Deuteronomist could not assume that all sources were of equal value; he might not have evaluated them critically in our sense, but, like the Chronicler, applied to them his own canons of "historical probability."[117] Finally, Noth has not emphasized the role of the Deuteronomist as a careful reader of texts, who not only preserved and retold them, but attempted to tease out implicit information through interpretation.

True, Noth has incorrectly emphasized the conservative nature of historians, while almost totally ignoring their radically creative role. But can we contradict Noth's opening statement, and suggest that the author of our passages did "fabricate" history?[118] This question returns us to our discussion of the Chronicler,[119] who, like the historian responsible for the passages I have analyzed in Deuteronomy 1–3, sometimes quotes earlier sources, but often radically reshapes them.[120] The Deuteronomist's belief in how the world works was more important than what his sources claimed. This belief encouraged him to restructure his sources, to fill them out, and, if necessary, to modify them radically. It is ironic that this is all accomplished within a work that emphasizes that the Israelite community should neither add to nor subtract from YHWH's teaching (Deut 4:2; 13:1).[121] The same irony may be seen in Josephus" *Antiquities*, I.17, where the Jewish historian claims, "The precise details of our Scripture records will, then, be set forth, each in its place as my narrative proceeds, that being the procedure that I have promised to follow throughout this work, neither adding nor omitting anything."[122] In fact, however, Josephus rearranged biblical events, omitted and added material, all for apologetic, didactic or literary reasons.[123] Josephus, who reuses the quote from Deuteronomy, offers a clear example of how the author of Deuteronomy diverged in a very striking way from his sources, and could be viewed as "fabricating" history. However, to the extent that the Deuteronomist honestly believed his ideology, and like all of us, was simply viewing the past from the perspective of his present, he was writing history like all other historians.

5

THE EHUD STORY AS SATIRE

All satire is not only an attack; it is an attack upon discernible, historically authentic particulars.

Edward R. Rosenheim, "The Satiric Spectrum," *Satire: Modern Essays in Criticism*, ed. Ronald Paulson (Englewood Cliffs, NJ: Prentice-Hall, 1971), 317–18.

JUDGES 3:12–30

I begin with a translation of the Hebrew text of the Ehud story in Judg 3:12–30.[1] The translation depends upon my comprehension of the text's genre and tone. Thus, it anticipates my understanding of the pericope's genre and purpose.[2]

(12) The Israelites again did what was evil[3] in the eyes of YHWH;[4] YHWH empowered Eglon, king of Moab against Israel because they did what was evil in the eyes of YHWH. (13) He mobilized the Ammonites and the Amalekites under him; when he went and attacked Israel, they[5] conquered the City of Datepalms. (14) The Israelites were vassals of Eglon, king of Moab for eighteen years. (15) The Israelites cried out to YHWH, and YHWH established a savior for them, Ehud son of Gera, a Benjaminite,[6] a left-handed[7] man; the Israelites sent tribute in his hand to Eglon king of Moab. (16) Ehud made himself a sword – it was double-edged and short;[8] he girded it under his garments on his right hip. (17) He "sacrificed" the tribute-offering[9] to Eglon, king of Moab. Incidentally, Eglon was a very corpulent man. (18) As he finished "sacrificing" his tribute-offering, he dismissed [his] retainers, the tribute bearers. (19) He had just returned from Pesilim,[10] which is near Gilgal. He said, "I have a secret matter concerning you, O king." He said, "Quiet!" All of his retainers left him. (20) Ehud had come to him while he was sitting in the throne room,[11] which was his private room. When Ehud said, "I have a divine oracle concerning you," he arose from the throne.

79

(21) Ehud moved his left hand, took the sword from his right thigh and stuck it into his belly.[12] (22) The hilt followed the blade, and fat surrounded the blade because he did not remove the sword from his belly; and the excrement[13] came out. (23) Ehud left toward the portico(?);[14] he closed the doors of the throne room behind himself, and locked them.[15] (24) Just as he had left, [Eglon's] servants came, and they noticed – the doors of the throne room were locked. They said, "He must be 'covering his legs'[16] in the throne room." (25) They waited until the point of embarrassment, but he still did not open the doors of the throne room. They took the key, and opened it, and there was their master sprawled on the ground, dead. (26) Meanwhile, Ehud had fled while they were waiting. He had passed Pesilim, on his way to Seir. (27) When he arrived, he blew a shofar on Mount Ephraim. The Israelites descended the mountain with him, with him in the lead. (28) He said to them, "Follow[17] me, for YHWH has given your enemies, the Moabites into your hands"; they followed him, and captured the Jordan crossings that belonged to Moab, and let no one pass. (29) They smote the Moabites at that time, about two thousand men, every fat man and every warrior; not one fled. (30) Moab was subjugated on that day under the hand of the Israelites; the land was then at peace for eighty years.

"LITERARY" PATTERNS IN THE TEXT

Scholars have previously outlined several literary features of the story. For example, Alonso-Schökel in his study of "*Erzählkunst*" (narrative art) notes devices such as the repetition of words and phrases, including the story's use of "hand"[18] as a *Leitwort*, and the rhythmic nature of much of the story.[19] Alter's analysis of the Ehud story emphasizes its mimetic nature, its use of punning, name symbolism (especially Eglon, "a play on ᶜegel, calf... [who] turns out to be a fatted calf ready for slaughter"), prefiguration (*tqᶜ* in vv. 21, 27, used of thrusting the dagger and blowing the shofar to rally the troops), and scatological and sexual references (the bathroom incident, dagger thrusts, locked doors).[20] Alter alludes to a similarity between the Ehud story and "satire in time of war."[21] He concludes his discussion by noting of the story:[22]

> In all this, as I have said, it is quite possible that the writer faithfully represents the historical data without addition or substantive embellishment. The organization of the narrative, however... produce[s] an imaginative reenactment of the historical event, conferring upon it a strong attitudinal definition and discovering in it a pattern of meaning. It is perhaps less historicized fiction than fictionalized his-

tory – history in which the feeling and the meaning of events are concretely realized through the technical resources of prose fiction.

The analyses of Alonso-Schökel and of Alter highlight the problem of understanding the Ehud story as literature. While I do not doubt that the text gives pleasure to contemporary readers, and should be considered literature from that vantage point, I am most interested in historical-critical readings, which contextualize the work in ancient Israel. Is "fictionalized history" a useful term for describing how the ancient audience understood the narrative? Does "literature" best describe the function of this narrative in ancient Israel?

Another problem with these literary analyses is that it is difficult to know which of the devices noted by each scholar were actually perceived in ancient Israel. Literary devices depend on conventions which vary widely between cultures and within individual cultures at different times. For example, v. 21 contains three words which we would consider to rhyme: *śĕmōʾlô, yĕmînô, bĕbiṭnô*,[23] yet as far as we know, rhyme was not a characteristic device of Hebrew poetry, so the Israelite ear probably did not hear it as we do, nor did it function in ancient Israel in a way similar to rhyme in contemporary society.[24] We can list particular devices and phonological features, but their perception is culturally and historically bound. I would suggest, however, that when devices are found consistently throughout a text, or sets of unusual phrases are used, these were likely perceived in antiquity. However, we should not immediately call texts showing such patterns "literary," which typically implies an aesthetic judgement. Rather, we should inquire after the purpose of the unusual patterning or word choice.

One pattern that runs throughout the unit is the use of sacrificial terminology. This was noted by Alonso-Schökel, Alter and Yairah Amit, who comment on the sacrificial overtones in Eglon's name, from *ʿēgel*, "a calf."[25] This observation, however, requires additional strengthening, since animal names are not infrequently used of biblical characters,[26] and only further contextual evidence can make us confident that the sacrificial motif is present and is significant. In this case, further careful stylistic analysis provides additional sacrificial terminology. Vv. 17 and 18, in saying that Ehud offered tribute, employ an expression typically used of offering a sacrifice.[27] This exceptional and inappropriate use of animal sacrifice terminology would have likely led the ancient Israelite reader or listener to conclude that sacrifice is an underlying theme of the passage.[28] This is why I translated v. 17 as, "He 'sacrificed' the tribute-offering." The author's choice of this idiom suggests that the name Eglon is symbolic, and is chosen because of its sacrificial overtones.[29] The story as a whole plays on the notion of sacrifice: while pretending to bring tribute/"offering" to Eglon, it is actually Eglon, "the calf," who becomes the offering. Indeed, the sacrificial knife and the partial disembowelment of the "animal" are depicted in graphic detail. The function of this motif may be seen after we observe how this sacrificial image functions in conjunction with other motifs in the story.

Alter noted certain aspects of the narrative's scatology and "deliberate sexual nuance."[30] The text explicitly refers to Eglon's excrement (v. 22) and his servants' assumption that he is relieving himself (v. 24). In addition, as Alter notes, the thrust of the dagger may be viewed sexually. These observations may be further extended through a closer reading of the story and an analysis of the terms that its author chose to use.

We know relatively little about ancient Israelite sexual terminology, particularly sexual slang. The Ehud story, however, contains several phrases which are elsewhere found in explicitly sexual contexts. For example, disproportionate space is given to the opening and closing of doors (vv. 23–5). This certainly develops the story, but also introduces a set of words that are well anchored in metaphors for sexuality in ancient Israel. These include the use of "to open," and "locked," which are used sexually in Song of Songs 5:2 and 4:12.[31] The possible sexual significance of Ehud's sword in v. 16, as short and double-edged, namely as a short straight sword, gains credence once we realize that the typical sword of the period had a curved side with which one hacks away at enemies,[32] and thus was much less appropriate as a phallic symbol. It is possible that the unique phrase "waiting until embarrassment" in v. 25 plays with the notion of a person impatiently waiting for the toilet,[33] thus heightening the scatological nature of the chapter. Furthermore, in v. 20, the author uses the expression "come to" to express Ehud's approach toward Eglon; this term may also be used of sexual intercourse.[34] Finally, the "formulaic" ending in v. 30 is slightly different from the similar formulae in Judges in that it contains the word "hand."[35] Certainly, in this context its primary meaning is "hand," but elsewhere, it is used euphemistically for the penis.[36] It is quite possible that the choice to break with the typical pattern and to insert "hand" was informed by an awareness that the chapter is depicting the subjugation of the Moabites to the Israelites in sexual terms. If this is so, an editor of Judges appreciated the sexual aspect of Eglon's subjugation, and slightly modified the usual concluding formula so it would fit that image.

The sexual reading of the passage suggested by Alter should not be seen as a product of modern, post-Freudian sensibilities. An explicitly sexual poem of Todros Abulafiah ends, "Oh how I wish – may she come to me and the hilt will penetrate after the blade."[37] The reuse of Judg 3:22 in this poem shows that the sexual imagery that stands behind this chapter was already appreciated in the thirteenth century.

Judg 3:12–30, almost from the beginning, sets up the Moabite enemy as a sacrificial victim. It is full of scatological and sexual references at the enemy's expense. Recognition of these features certainly makes the chapter more pleasurable for us to read. But to the extent that a reader is committed to a historical-critical understanding of the chapter, he or she must wonder about the purpose of these devices within a context that describes a battle between Moab and Israel.

ISRAELITES AND MOABITES

Ideally, we should present the relationship between the two nations during the period of the story's composition. This is impossible, however, because we do not know when it was written, though it is noteworthy that according to some scholars, there was no real Moabite kingdom before the rise of the Israelite monarchy,[38] so the story's setting in the period of the judges is certainly anachronistic. Most scholars would agree that the Book of Judges was redacted at the latest in the early exilic period, incorporating earlier traditions, some of which originated as tribal stories.[39] Therefore, in order to understand the story's stylistic features in relation to its author's historical background, it is relevant to sketch the evidence concerning the relations between Moab and Israel in the pre-exilic period.[40] Given the nature of the story in Judges, it is not necessary to outline the history in detail, but only to offer in general terms the relationship between Israel and Moab.

The vast majority of evidence suggests hostility between the neighbors. This is reflected in many types of stories. For example, the story of Moab's birth (Gen 19:37) reflects negatively on the Moabites, as do the oracles of Balaam in Num 21:29 and 24:17, and the legislation of Deut 23:4. According to "historical texts," the Moabites were vassals already at the time of David (2 Sam 8:2), and battles between Moab and Israel are narrated in 2 Kgs 1:1, 3:4–27, 13:20 and 24:2. The Moabites are condemned in collections of oracles against the nations from the beginning through the end of classical prophecy (Amos 2:1–3, Isaiah 15–16, Jeremiah 48 and Ezek 25:8–11). Antipathy is also reflected in Ps 60:10 (=108:10) and 83:7. It is difficult to date most of these texts, but they likely point to the existence of antagonism between Moab and Judah and Israel for much of the pre-exilic period. This perspective is also confirmed by the Moabite Mesha Stele, which mentions Israelite oppression of Moab for "many days" (line 5), and follows this with a depiction of Moabite conquest of Israelite territory.[41]

Positive relations between Moab and Israel might be suggested by Deut 2:9, which notes that Israel should not harass Moab when entering Eretz Israel, and by 1 Sam 22:3–4, where David leaves his parents with the king of Moab for safekeeping.[42] It is likely that these two texts reflect some period of peaceful co-existence between Israel and Moab, but it is unclear when this might have been. In any case, these two texts are in the minority, and probably reflect a relatively brief period of friendship.[43]

MODERN LABELS, ANCIENT TEXTS: THE GENRE OF THE STORY

The story in Judg 3:12–30 should be understood against this historical sketch as a humorous story mocking the Israelites' enemy, the Moabites; more specifically, it should be read as a satire. Various studies of this genre can be productively used to understand its meaning and purpose.

The contention that the story is humorous is actually quite challenging to prove. Although scholars have claimed that "the holy book we call the Bible revels in profound laughter,"[44] it is difficult to determine what ancient Israelites actually found funny, since the biblical text rarely contains clues to the reactions of the audience. Certainly conceptions of what makes contemporary stories funny may not be automatically projected backward on to biblical Israel. It is therefore desirable to understand Israelite humor by using models that do not depend on contemporary Western humor. The discussion of humor in Franz Rosenthal, *Humor in Early Islam*[45] is especially useful in this regard. Many of the stories which according to Moslem tradition are humorous, are no longer humorous to us, and this forces Rosenthal to form generalizations about humor that cover both modern and ancient societies. He notes:[46]

> The definition [of humor] which would appear to be the most plausible one because of its general applicability connects humor with the relief felt at the momentary lifting of one of the many restrictions which the physical and social environment imposes upon man. . . . The humor in puns . . . has its origin in the fact that human linguistic expression moves in quite narrow and circumscribed and usually logical channels. Any deviation from those channels is keenly felt as a release from conventional restrictions and, therefore, is humorous. A great variety of dealings among human beings is immediately classified as humor if there is any suggestion of a deviation from ordinary reality and the conventions of human society.

Some biblical evidence suggests that Rosenthal's conventions are applicable to ancient Israel as well. For example, one of the rare cases when the narrator tells us that someone laughs concerns the laughter of Abraham or Sarah at the impending birth of a son (Gen 17:17; 18:12, 15). They laugh because their old age makes the event highly unlikely; this fits Rosenthal's observations, that laughter reflects one type of "deviation from ordinary reality."

Following Rosenthal's suggestions, it is clear that the Ehud story is humorous.[47] Its explicit, extensive use of scatology and its sexual innuendo is a "momentary lifting of one of the many restrictions which the . . . social environment imposes upon man." The episode described, with a single commoner defeating the enemy king and outsmarting the royal courtiers, is certainly "a deviation from ordinary reality." Furthermore, if this story was written during one of the periods when Israel was a vassal of Moab, by portraying Israel as the victor it presents a substantial release from everyday life. Thus, although humor is to a large extent culturally bound, what we do know of Israelite culture suggests that this story was appreciated as humorous in antiquity. It was seen as poking fun at Eglon and the Moabites in general, who, as noted above, were typically viewed as an outgroup from the Israelites" perspective. This type of humor which disparages an outgroup typically functions, "(1) To increase the morale and solidify the ingroup [and] (2) To introduce or foster a hostile disposition toward that outgroup."[48]

I suggested above that this humorous story should more specifically be characterized as satire, as was briefly noted by Alter.[49] This raises the question of whether it is appropriate to apply to the Bible such genre labels as "satire," which originate in the classical world. This concern has been raised by Yair Zakovitch regarding the application of the Greek genre terms "tragedy" and "comedy" to biblical literature.[50] It has in some ways been anticipated by the earlier discussion in this book of using the labels "history" and "literature" of biblical texts. I will first examine the general notion of applying non-native genres to (ancient) texts; I will anchor my general discussion with a brief examination of the usefulness of the term "biblical poetry," and of the genre designations developed by Hermann Gunkel in his study of the Psalms.[51]

The application of non-native genre labels to ancient texts has been recently discussed in detail by Tremper Longman III in connection to his isolation of the genre "Fictional Akkadian autobiography."[52] He notes that genre labels perform an invaluable function by guiding the reader in interpreting a work, since interpretation is largely genre-determined.[53] Other scholars would concur; for example, Tsvetan Todorov claims that genres offer readers "horizons of expectation."[54] Ralph Cohen, in a defense of the concept "genre," notes that this function is true for literature of any period, oral as well as written.[55] For example, a person who reads a work written to be a parody as a historical account would be misunderstanding that work's ancient function, and would misinterpret it.[56] Given the importance of genre as a guide for reading, Longman claims that it is appropriate to impose genre labels not known to be native to a culture.[57] Following Gunkel, various criteria, such as mood, vocabulary and social setting might help determine a work's genre.[58] Finally, Longman suggests that texts of similar genres should be studied together because of the light that they may shed on each other.[59]

The position that non-native genres should be avoided is argued by James L. Kugel, *The Idea of Biblical Poetry: Parallelism and Its History*.[60] He notes that there is no biblical Hebrew word for poetry,[61] and states, "Thus, to speak of 'poetry' at all in the Bible will be in some measure to impose a concept foreign to the biblical world."[62] However, as noted by Kugel's critics, even though "poetry" is a Greek term, it is appropriate in reference to biblical texts because calling a text "poetry" offers us clues as to how to read it.[63] If we read (the "poetic") Isaiah 1 in the same way that we read (the "prosaic") Exodus 1, we would seriously misunderstand Isaiah. We would be stumped by certain syntactic features (such as the frequent omission of the verb in the B line), we might interpret some figurative language literally, and we would not know how to process verses which are constructed using parallelism. By offering the label "poetry" to Isaiah, we help to classify it as not prose, and as similar *in certain significant respects* to varieties of poetry known from our Western civilization. As modern readers of the biblical texts, we need some term to designate this group of texts and to indicate that they should not be read in the same way as different types of other ("prose") texts, and hence we choose the most helpful of our own terms, "poetry."[64]

Kugel's desire to avoid designating biblical texts as "poetry" is partially motivated by a legitimate concern that we might incorrectly impose all of the typical characteristics of non-biblical poetry on to the Bible. However, genres are relatively open-ended and flexible categories,[65] so all works of the same genre need not share all the same characteristics. Defining ancient genres aids us in seeing certain characteristics of a work that were not previously highlighted and sometimes allows us to presume a likely social setting or role for literary texts.

The psalms of the Bible have been divided on the basis of form-critical features into such genres as laments of the individual, laments of the community, hymns, etc. Hermann Gunkel played a central role in this division,[66] and his categories or genres, which do not reflect biblical terminology, have remained influential.[67] These categories have been recently called into question in H. J. Kraus" Psalms commentary, where designations actually found in the psalms themselves are preferred.[68] His suggestion has not been generally accepted because Gunkel's model (in a modified form) offers a more useful interpretive tool than Kraus" terms, since its categories help to group together certain psalms with certain terms and characteristics (e.g. the phrase "YHWH is/has become king" or the "confidence motif"), allowing them to be viewed together and to bear on one another.[69]

In sum, the application of genre titles which are not known from the biblical period remains useful if the modern and ancient texts share significant features. It is quite possible that these genre groupings did not explicitly exist in antiquity; still, it is possible to write a particular type of literature with certain characteristics and forms even when there is no name used to define their concurrent use. The genre designations "poetry" and "lament of the individual" are therefore appropriate to biblical literature, since they help to designate a group of texts that share a common body of characteristics and might have a similar *Sitz im Leben*.[70] Similarly, it is legitimate to isolate a group of biblical texts that share the typical characteristics usually attributed to satire. Judg 3:12–30 is one such text, as is Isa 14:4–23, which is typically seen as a mocking or satirical lament about a "Babylonian" ruler, most likely Sargon of Ashur.[71]

The definition of satire by Northrop Frye suggests that it is typified by "wit or humor founded on fantasy or a sense of the grotesque or absurd [and] . . . an object of attack."[72] The Ehud story fulfills this definition. Furthermore, once we realize that the Ehud story is satire, the chapter's prominent use of sexual and scatological themes falls into place; as noted by scholars of literature in such essays as "Bowl Games: Satire in the Toilet"[73] and "Decadent Sexuality and Satire,"[74] these elements frequently characterize satire. In addition, scholars of satire have noted that political satire is characterized by the use of animal imagery;[75] this might help to explain the use of the calf-related name, Eglon.[76]

"All satire is not only an attack; it is an attack upon discernible, histori-cally authentic particulars."[77] This statement emphasizes that the *literary* category of satire has a particular *social-historical* setting, and that the satire in Judg 3:12–30 must be understood within the background of the actual relationship between Israel and Moab. It functioned as literature of attack, mocking the enemy neighbor Moab, reinforcing its identity as an outgroup. It was important to do so because the Moabites were geographically proxi-mate to Israel and according to the tradition in Gen 19:29–38, they were related to Israel via Lot, Abraham's nephew. Furthermore, there were several traditions circulating in ancient Israel that indicated a positive attitude toward Moabites; to the extent that this was a vocal minority opinion, it was necessary to combat it with means such as the satirical story in Judges 3.

In applying the label "satire" to an ancient Israelite text, it is noteworthy that satire as a genre transcends cultural and chronological boundaries, as noted by Paul Frye: "The satiric spirit as it is manifested in verse seems to appear (whether as mockery, raillery, ridicule, or formalized invective) in the literature or folklore of all peoples, early and late, pre-literate and civilized."[78] Leonard Feinberg has outlined the many satirical elements that can be found in non-Western literature,[79] including "use of grotesque material, scatological details, and allusions to sex"[80] and puns.[81] In analyzing the function of satire in both East and West, he notes the importance of satire in making the satirist's audience feel superior to the person or group being satirized,[82] and claims, "For many people this feeling of superiority, illusory though it may be, offers one of the few sources of delight they are likely to experience. Humor . . . is often unkind, but by providing a release from psychic tensions it serves a useful purpose."[83] All of these observations concerning ancient and non-Western satire are relevant to the Ehud story.

This analysis has an important corollary. Any interpreter who misses the satirical nature of the story is bound to misinterpret and to misuse it.[84] This has especially important implications for the modern biblical historian. Composers of satire typically exaggerate or misrepresent the object that they satirize; satire involves a range of "distortions, analogies, or "pure" fabrications."[85] Thus, much of the story might be an "invented tradition"[86] set in the past, which was composed for political purposes, namely to mock the enemy Moabites. Its author did not intend to write a straightforward representation of historical events. Thus, the identification of the story's genre as "satire" implies that Halpern's understanding of it as "history" is misguided. The historical enmity between Israel and Moab stands behind the story, but given the nature of satire, there is no reason to assume that any of the specifics of the Ehud story are based in reality.

Halpern is not unique in "misgenrifying" the story, namely assigning it to the wrong genre. Many of the histories of Israel treat the story of Judg 3:12–30 as history in the sense of a source for what actually transpired in the so-called period of judges. Most do not see all of its details as accurate, but search for some historical kernel.[87] For example, Noth uses the story to determine the boundaries between Israel and Moab in the period of the judges;[88] Bright claims that, "It is probable that Ehud's victory over Moab (Judg 3:12–30) likewise fell during the twelfth century,"[89] and Mayes, on the basis of a comparison of this story with other events depicted in Judges, concludes, "The indications are, therefore, that the position of the story [Judg 3:12–30] as first of the series accurately reflected its reference to an event which took place early in the period of the judges."[90] The newer history of Miller and Hayes,[91] which expresses general skepticism concerning the information found in Judges,[92] nevertheless uses the Ehud story to help reconstruct the tribal relationships in the period of the judges.[93] Only a small minority of historians, such as Soggin[94] and Ahlström,[95] claim that because of its genre the Ehud story is inappropriate for use in reconstructing the history of the pre-monarchic period. Certainly, they are correct, for the story is political satire, which is anchored in the historical period in which it was composed rather than in the historical period which it pretends to narrate.[96]

IS THE EHUD PERICOPE LITERATURE OR HISTORY?

Judg 3:12–30 is history only in the sense that it is a narrative that presents a past. The specifics of this past likely have little to do with the real Moab; instead, an author has fashioned a creative work of political satire, predominantly reflecting not the history of the period it purports to describe, but the period and conflicts of its author. In defining the story as satire, I do not make any claims about how it was appreciated from an aesthetic perspective in antiquity. Rather, I mean to show how certain motifs, such as the enemy as a sacrificial victim, and scatological and sexual references, had a social function of mocking the real (not the literary) Moabites, who were perceived by the writer as Israel's enemies.

Although this pericope does not narrate factual history, the literary representations it conveys did play a historical role within ancient Israel, expressing the Israelite belief in their superiority over their neighbors, the Moabites.[97] It is a story of national pride, which serves to illustrate the special way in which Israel perceived itself as God's chosen nation, small, but greater than others.[98] Certainly in its final form, in which Ehud is sent as a savior after Israel is subjugated (but before it repents),[99] the story illustrates the principle articulated in Deut 7:7–8aα: "It is not because you are more populous than the other nations that YHWH has desired you and has chosen you, for you are the smallest of all the nations. Rather it is because of YHWH's love for you . . ." The Ehud story would help the average Israelite appreciate Moab's (real or hoped for) humiliation, countering any feeling of empathy that may have been felt toward the Moabites either because of their geographical proximity or their status as (supposed) relatives.

Not all of the rhetorical elements isolated by various scholars, such as Alonso-Schökel or Alter, within the Ehud episode may be accounted for by understanding the story as satire. Biblical texts, like many writings, are not typically composed for a single purpose. As noted by David Gunn, "Literature that reads like a theological tract or political pamphlet typically has a short life as entertainment."[100] Thus, it is natural for texts which depict a past to appeal to the aesthetic sensibilities of its audience. This is acknowledged, though sometimes hesitantly, by most biblical scholars. For example, Peter R. Ackroyd, in his "Introduction" to his commentary *The First Book of Samuel*, asks "Why are [biblical] books written?" He replies:

> A book may be written for the sheer joy of telling a story. But though this could be a factor in the preservation of many ancient traditions in Israel, the books which we have in the Old Testament must all be regarded as religious books in the sense that they offer an interpretation in religious terms of what they relate. This does not make them any less artistic as stories.[101]

Ackroyd's position is reasonable, though his "religious books" should be replaced with the broader "ideological books." In any case, few biblical works were written primarily as aesthetic masterpieces,[102] though this may be their end result. Aesthetic features of biblical texts may be connected to their genre, as in the satirical elements in the Ehud story, or they made be related to the authors" or tradents" interest in the story's preservation and perpetuation.

We can follow other scholars and point out certain devices that make the Ehud story interesting, fun or aesthetic *to us*. These might include the use of irony, especially concerning the left-handed Righthander [Benjaminite],[103] which raises a chuckle to many current readers, and might have had a similar effect in the past. The linking of various sections with the root tq^c used of "thrusting" the dagger (in v. 21), and of "blowing" the shofar (in v. 27), ties the unit together in a way which is pleasing to most *contemporary* readers of Hebrew.[104] The rhyme between the proximate obscure words *happaršĕdonâ*, "the excrement" (v. 22b), and *hammisdĕrônâ*, "the portico" (v. 23a), is pleasing *to us*, though textual difficulties make the rhyme uncertain, and in any case, it is clear that ancient Hebrew authors did not employ rhyme, and thus these words would have been perceived differently by people in ancient Israel who read or heard the story.[105]

The last point is fundamental. James L. Kugel has suggested that readers imagine biblical poetry in the image of poetry that they know; thus Josephus speaks of the biblical metrical poetry written in "hexameters."[106] Josephus is not unique; we tend to project our notion of the Bible's literariness on to the biblical period, despite clear evidence that literary sensibilities change in such fundamental ways over time. We can each tell in what way a biblical verse or unit is literary *to us*, but that should not be confused with ancient "literary competence,"[107] what Diana Vikander Edelman calls to "read like an ancient Judahite."[108]

My position that the Ehud story is not literature, but is satire, seems self-contradictory, but is based on the notion that unlike "literature," the genre of satire is known in a relatively stable form across many cultures and epochs and is useful in interpreting the pericope because it helps to explain a clustering of unusual features within the text. The story survived because in antiquity it had a purpose – political satire is a utilitarian genre, which helps you to define yourself *vis-à-vis* another group. For these reasons, I have focussed on "literary" elements that are connected to this genre, rather than on those which might have been connected to the story's preservation or its other aesthetic qualities; though these latter elements were likely important in antiquity, I do not believe that they may be recovered by us.

6

IDEOLOGY IN THE BOOK OF SAMUEL[1]

Without doubt the motivation for the author of this narrative was ... (a) to legitimate David's succession to the throne which rightly belonged to the house of Saul, and (b) to acquit David of charges brought against him for complicity in the disaster which ruined Saul's family.

Niels Peter Lemche, "David's Rise," *JSOT* 10 (1978), 2

THE KING DAVID REPORT

The best starting point for understanding the ideological nature of the biblical Book of Samuel is the novel by the (former) East German writer Stefan Heym, *The King David Report*.[2] Heym, much like an ancient Israelite author, did not live under a regime which encouraged a free press and complete access to information. Both East Germany and ancient monarchical Israel were highly centralized, and in terms of powers given to the king and his bureaucracy, the Judean king could be seen as parallel to the East German premier.[3] We know little about patterns of censorship in ancient Israel, but analogies from other ancient Near Eastern societies suggest that official versions of stories could be propagated through the monarchy, which could also attempt to suppress alternative versions.

According to *The King David Report*, Solomon commissions Ethan to write a history after David dies because

> Israel abounds with stories about him [David], most of them useless, some even harmful. ... so we must have one authoritative report, to the exclusion of all others, on the life and great works and heroic battles of my father, King David, who chose me to sit upon his throne.[4]

Before Ethan starts his work, the court recorder describes the guidelines that Ethan must follow:[5]

Members of the Royal Commission on the Preparation of *The One and Only True and Authoritative, Historically Correct and Officially Approved Report on the Amazing Rise, God-fearing Life, Heroic Deeds, and Wonderful Achievements of David the Son of Jesse, King of Judah for Seven Years and of Both Judah and Israel for Thirty-three, Chosen of God, and Father of King Solomon*: Jehoshaphat the son of Ahilud, recorder; Zadok, priest; Nathan, prophet; Elihoreph and Ahiah, the sons of Shisha, scribes; Benaiah the son of Jehoiada, who is over the host. Redactor, but without vote: Ethan, son of Hoshaiah, of the town of Ezrah, author and historian. . . . Said report to establish for this and all time to come *One Truth*, thus ending *All Contradiction and Controversy*, eliminating *All Disbelief of the Choice by our Lord Yahveh of David ben Jesse*, and allaying *All Doubt* of the *Glorious Promises* made to him by our Lord Yahveh.

Ethan quickly learns that he must be selective. Michal, Saul's daughter and David's widow, tells him:[6]

Later on, it was said for appearance's sake that Jesse [David's father] had many herds, and a great house, that his voice was prominent in the councils of Judah, and that his ancestry might be traced back to the founders of the tribe. In truth, Jesse was an obscure, poverty-stricken peasant with more sons than he could feed.

Such eye-witness testimony, however, would not be incorporated within the official history.

In contrast, other events get recorded, even though they do not have an accurate written historical pedigree, because various voting members of the commission favor them. So, for example, the story of David and Goliath is incorporated, despite its dubious historicity, because according to Benaiah the warrior, "The armed forces . . . especially the Cheritites and Pelithites [David's foreign mercenary troops], have the greatest interest in inculcating the children of Israel with the spirit which induced young David to his valiant deed."[7] The lesson justifies the story's inclusion. Elsewhere, Nathan the court prophet says:[8]

once we are agreed that David is the Chosen of the Lord, then everything he does is for the good of Israel. But as knowledge of the facts may lead a person to dangerous thoughts, the facts must be presented so as to direct the mind into the proper channels.

This becomes a central principle – the facts are secondary to the beliefs that they may inculcate.

Ethan's history, however, does not ultimately survive; he contacts unauthorized individuals, and is convicted of displeasing the king. He is sentenced to death, but that sentence is commuted; instead, he is to be remembered only through his ascription by name to a mediocre psalm. One may presume that according to Heym, the current version of the story of David in Samuel incorporates many elements of Ethan's account, but has been properly cleaned up.

The parallels between Samuel and *The King David Report* have been teased out most successfully by Peter Hutchinson, Professor of German Literature at Cambridge.[9] Hutchinson notes that single-party states frequently breed despots who "desire to produce a definitive history of the recent past."[10] Thus, "one of the earliest examples of modifying the records in order to give a sense of 'sanction' to a new regime is to be found in the composition of the biblical Books of Kings [*sic*; he means Samuel], and one of the most recent is evident in the historiography of the Communist countries."[11] Although Israel was not a communist nation, nor was its government totalitarian, the fundamental observations of Heym seem applicable to Israel as a strongly centralized, pre-modern society.

Hutchinson's point, that the Book of Samuel is a highly ideological work, that is, it develops "a system of representations existing and playing a historical role within a given society,"[12] is appreciated by many contemporary biblical scholars. Already in 1926 Leonhard Rost noted that sections of Samuel are ideological.[13] This was later de-emphasized by Gerhard von Rad, who, in an immensely influential treatment of the story, first published in 1944, discusses these portions in terms of literature, psychology and theology, but is not at all interested in the political aspects of the story and how these might have shaped its storyteller.[14] With some minor exceptions, von Rad's position, which emphasized the accuracy of the history of David as told in Samuel and its chronological proximity to the events it described, was immensely influential within biblical scholarship until the late 1970s.[15]

The early 1980s witnessed a renewed interest in Samuel, perhaps connected to the rise of literary study of the Bible. However, unlike Rost and von Rad, who emphasized the literary greatness of various sections of Samuel and allowed other aspects of the story to recede into the background, in the 1980s, scholars often discussed the stories in terms of literature and ideology.[16] Few descriptions of the composition of Samuel agree with the fully totalitarian picture offered by Heym, though it is typical now to see the second part of Samuel[17] discussed in terms such as "Court Apologetic"[18] or "The Defence of David."[19] Thus, Keith Whitelam, writing in 1984, concluded that

> Rather than being read as a historical source in the usually accepted sense, as a reflection of historical reality, it becomes rather evidence for the highly subjective *self-perception* of the Davidic monarchy as portrayed by the royal bureaucracy, heirs to the scribal traditions and training of the ancient Near East.[20]

This type of approach suggested by Whitelam has been accepted by many biblical scholars.[21]

It is very difficult to prove the ideological nature of particular historical works in ancient Israel. In general, it is easy to discover ideologies when we have multiple depictions of the same event from different sources; this is not the case with much of Samuel. Alternatively, biases are easy to isolate when we know something about a work's author, or when we have explicitly articulated ideological positions by those involved in writing the history; these are missing from the Bible. We know nothing about who wrote the history now found in Samuel and when it was written. Heym, following a predominant school of biblical scholarship influential until the 1970s, assumed that it was written by someone in the royal court in the period of (David or) Solomon.[22] More recently, this contention has been seriously eroded.[23] Additionally, the functions of the members of the royal court continue to be debated, and it is not clear whether or not there was an official court historian in ancient Israel.[24] Given these difficulties, the rest of this chapter should really be seen as an exploration of the ideological nature of various texts in Samuel. The plausibility of my readings should be balanced against other readings which attempt to explain the same evidence.

The likelihood of an ideological reading of Samuel is reinforced by evidence elsewhere in the ancient Near East of compositions about kings written under the influence of royal (scribal) ideologies. These analogies cannot be exact, because no other ancient Near Eastern civilization has produced (an extant) long royal history focussed on a relatively short period of the type found in Samuel. I will concentrate on several examples from Assyria, a civilization from the same time-period as ancient Israel, whose language and literature had a sway on Israelite writing.[25] Modern biblical scholarship, however, has also emphasized that cultures not contiguous to Israel can aid our understanding of the biblical world.[26] For this reason, I will also briefly adduce further analogies from civilizations later than Israel.

ROYAL IDEOLOGY IN HISTORICAL LITERATURE

The best-known genre of the Mesopotamian historical inscriptions is the Assyrian annal,[27] which is the product of a highly ideological culture.[28] These were typically revised annually. As a result of various explorations of the sources of the annals, as well as extensive study of their revisions, we have an impression of how they were composed. In the words of Mordechai Cogan:

> Now it is an almost universal working hypothesis that behind the annal inscriptions is the raw data collected by the scribes in the field

who accompanied the army on its campaigns. Military scribes are depicted on wall-reliefs, often in pairs, one with a tablet and stylus in hand writing cuneiform, the other with a scroll and pen writing Aramaic; they are shown recording the number of dead and captured as well as the booty carried off. It seems a fair assumption that the campaign itinerary, the outcome of the battles and other items of interest were noted in the scribes" "diaries." (Though there are no extant examples of campaign notebooks, a "diary style" has been detected within the annals.) Upon their return to the capital, the scribes took to writing up the season's undertakings; in some instances, if not in all, an official report was filed in the main temple. These reports, known in scholarly jargon as "Letters to the Gods," are addressed to Ashur, the national god, and to the temple and city dignitaries; they are styled in high poetic language and contain the fullest and most detailed accounts of the campaign. At the same time, summaries of varying lengths were prepared for whatever needs might arise, for annals, summary inscriptions, dedicatory texts, epigraphs.[29]

The ideological nature of the Assyrian scribes" compositions may be disclosed either by internal study of the final product or by comparing various texts which deal with the same episode. The first method is used by Frederick Mario Fales to study Sargon's letter to the god Ashur.[30] Fales notes how this text functions with "the deliberate aim of propaganda of the qualities of Assyrian kingship."[31] It accomplishes this, among other ways, by opposing the righteous king against the treacherous enemy, by using contrasting laudatory epithets for Sargon versus derogatory epithets for the enemy, and by presenting the Assyrian king's total destruction of abundant enemy goods. Indeed, the first section of the letter is explicitly ideological, focussing on "the feats of Sargon himself as righteous and heroic king." It uses what some would consider literary devices for an ideological purpose, carefully selecting and reworking its source material to glorify the Assyrian king before the population and the gods.

The alternative method, of studying various recensions of annals or various texts bearing on a single event in order to see diverging ideologies, also yields significant results.[32] Scholars have emphasized the freedom with which scribes treated older events of a king's reign when they updated the annals; sometimes they condensed an earlier version, while at other times they harmonized various sources.[33] Much more significant is the type of ideological revision of history that has been explored by J. A. Brinkman.[34] We know from multiple sources that Sennacherib destroyed Babylon in 689. However, ten years after this event, a scribe in the court of his son, Esarhaddon, wrote a text which attributed the destruction of that city to a severe flood. That text was widely copied; it is found in seven versions in over fifteen manuscripts. The rewriting of history it presents is drastic;

to drive this point home, Brinkman notes, "This is roughly comparable to an historical account of the final days of World War II in the Pacific neglecting to mention use of atomic weaponry."[35] Significantly, this rewriting transpired within the time-period of people who knew the real events; yet, the revisionist text was written and, if we may judge by the number of extant copies, circulated extensively. Brinkman speculates that this new version of history could survive and thrive because it helped to bolster the image of Esarhaddon, who rebuilt Babylon, and that the new version fits in with the elite's theological perspective.[36] Because we have other sources which document the military destruction of Babylon, we can in this case realize this account's deeply tendentious nature. We can only wonder whether the *extreme* selectivity and reinterpretation it represents typified Assyrian historiography in this period.

Another source for the dissemination of royal ideology by the Assyrian monarchy may be found in the Assyrian royal palace reliefs.[37] According to Irene J. Winter's fundamental study of these reliefs

> there is an ideological "end" to the apparent historicity of the rep-
> resentations. In fact, content is carefully manipulated, and the spec-
> tator is enjoined to participate in a foregone conclusion: only the
> enemy fall; the Assyrians never lose and, given the strength of the king
> and the benevolence of the gods, are never even wounded.[38]

The strength and centrality of the king is constantly reinforced through reliefs that show him with sacred trees and winged protective genies, successfully hunting the mighty lion, massacring his enemies or reviewing booty. These reliefs, which are certainly not interested in depicting a balanced biography of the kings, are the pictorial equivalents of the public historical inscriptions such as the annals.[39]

This evidence suggests that much of the writing and depiction of history in Mesopotamia was controlled by the court scribes, who wrote ideological history that would satisfy the ruling king.[40] Though the details of this process are not fully known, it is clear that such history was not typically interested in the actual past, but has been variously described as ideological, propagandistic or apologetic. Sometimes, the creation of a particular historical account was accomplished by emphasizing or de-emphasizing particular events; at other times, the shape of the event depicted differed so dramatically from the actual event, that it would be best to speak of the *creation* of an event by the royal scribe.

Bernard Lewis has noted that a fundamental "function of [accounts of] the past is to legitimize authority."[41] This may be seen in detail with the use of oral materials as political propaganda in traditional African societies, which suggests that traditions were malleable.[42] The Middle Ages also offer a well-known example of this type of ideological rewriting of history – the "Donation of Constantine," a forgery dating from the eighth century

CE which "documented" how Constantine I, in return for Pope Sylvester's having cured him of leprosy, ceded all secular power in the western empire to the pope."[43] This document has been suspected as a forgery since the middle of the fifteenth century CE, and it is now universally agreed that the document was created to legitimize the papal stand which demanded control over certain lands. There are other similar forgeries outside of ecclesiastical circles;[44] they offer additional examples of how history may be created to advocate a particular viewpoint.

Other examples are more subtle, but are nevertheless instructive. The ninth-century CE *Histories* of Nithard is a central work concerning the Carolingian Empire.[45] It was commissioned by Charles the Bald, and generally reflects favorably on its patron. It speaks of Charles becoming king through divine intervention, significantly on Easter Sunday, "by God's grace and with his approval."[46] Sections of the text are clearly *apologia*, polemical or ideological, written for propagandistic purposes. At one point, Nithard says he is writing his history "in case someone, tricked by some means or other, should dare to give an account of recent events otherwise than as they really happened."[47] That line sounds as if it could come out of Heym's *The King David Report*. This suggests that the type of closely supervised writing of history within central governmental circles that Heym suggests on the basis of an East German analogy is far from confined to modern totalitarian regimes, and might typify a wide range of pre-modern history.

THE STRUCTURE OF SAMUEL

An immediate objection may be raised against the proposal that Samuel is a work permeated throughout with a pro-Davidic ideology[48] – several sections of the book portray David in a negative light. The best-known of these is the story of David and Bathsheba in 2 Samuel 11–12, where David is depicted as an adulterer and as a murderer. The section reflects negatively on David from its very beginning; already in its first verses David is described as ignoring his royal responsibilities, strolling on his palace roof looking for beautiful women while his army is off fighting a battle against Ammon.[49] Though David's depiction may be viewed somewhat positively in that his sins are immediately forgiven once he confesses (2 Sam 12:13), a strong pro-Davidic ideologue would have left out the sins altogether. That this was possible may be seen from Chronicles, which contains the frame of the story narrating the capture of Ammon (1 Chr 20:1–3), but omits the David–Bathsheba–Uriah episode. An even more revisionist author could have claimed that David was off fighting the battle while Uriah, fighting by his side, got killed accidentally, after which David returned gallantly to Jerusalem to marry the grieving widow Bathsheba. The example of the rearrangement of events in the Book of Chronicles or of Esarhaddon omitting his father's devastation of Babylon should remind us of the power of ancient historians to ignore or rewrite events which disagreed with the ideology they wished to convey.

Thus, the material found in 2 Samuel 11–12 cannot be seen as pro-Davidic. The same may be said for much of the material in the following chapters, narrating the rape of Tamar, Absalom's rebellion and the rebellion of the Benjaminite, Sheba ben Bichri. The anti-Davidic stance of these chapters was seen clearly by R. A. Carlson, who labelled them "David under the Curse."[50]

As pointed out by Carlson, this section actually begins in chapter 9. Carlson has returned to a position advocated by scholars such as Budde and Nowack at the turn of the century.[51] This position was, however, often abandoned under the influence of Rost's seminal discussion of what has been called the Succession Narrative, a document whose concern was seen as "Who shall rule after David," which extends from 2 Samuel 6 or 7 through 1 Kings 2.[52]

The boundaries of this document are of substantial importance. It is very difficult to create objective arguments for the boundaries of biblical units, especially if one allows for the possibility of secondary retouching or for original elements that were lost through late redaction.[53] Furthermore, there is a clear relationship between the interpretation of a unit which a scholar proffers and the boundaries that he or she finds.[54] A structural argument is the most important type of argument that can be adduced for a unit's construction. If we can show that several verses have been repeated unnecessarily, especially if they are cumbersome and seem misplaced chronologically, it is likely that the verses were placed in their current spot for formal reasons, to demarcate the boundaries of a unit.[55]

A structural argument for the extent of the Succession Narrative has been adduced briefly by James W. Flanagan, who notes the significance of the repetition of the "list of David's court officers in 8:16–18 ... [and] in 20:23–6."[56] The first list, which claims that Benaiah served as an officer early in David's reign, is very unlikely, since he is not mentioned in connection with the revolts of Absalom and Sheba son of Bichri.[57] This suggests that the list does not reflect the early years of the reign of David but was put in its current place for other reasons. Thus, the lack of chronological accuracy strengthens Flanagan's observation that this repetition serves to demarcate the intervening material as an editorial unit.[58]

The suggestion that 2 Samuel 9 begins a new unit is fostered by several other observations. The verse immediately preceding the list of David's officers, 2 Sam 8:15, "David ruled over all of Israel; David executed justice and righteousness to all his people," sounds like a concluding formula.[59] Additionally, that verse shows a sign of late biblical Hebrew, and may thus be from a later, redactional layer of the book.[60] Finally, all the material in chapters 9 and 10 thematically belongs with what follows.[61] Structural and contextual factors therefore combine to confirm that 2 Sam 8:16–18 are a dividing point between two units.

I would suggest that these verses separate two sections with fundamentally different interests. 2 Samuel 9 and following is a theological unit, interested in showing the severe ramifications of serious sins, even when committed by David. Murder and rape beget murder, rape and almost the loss of the kingdom. The chapters illustrate the fundamental principle of measure for measure,[62] though of course it is David who rapes, and his daughter (ch. 13) and concubines (16:22) who are raped.[63] These chapters narrate fundamental theological rules using David as their protagonist, but these principles are presented to all Israel.[64]

In contrast, the previous material offers no such religiously ideological lessons; instead, it is interested in secular, political ideology, namely fostering Davidic kingship. The material in 2 Samuel 9–20 is created, selected and redacted to reflect badly on David, as a warning to all Israel to act properly; the editor of the previous chapters, in contrast, created, selected and redacted traditions to foster the legitimacy of David and his dynasty. Thus, Samuel, like the *Histories* of Nithard, which I used for an analogy above, has two histories. In Nithard, one is private, one is public.[65] In Samuel, one is interested in secular ideology, namely politics, while the other focusses on religious ideology, namely theology.

To the extent that the central figure of this first unit is David, most scholars would begin it with 1 Samuel 16, the prophetic story of the anointing of David by Samuel, though some scholars see this unit as secondary, and would begin the story still later.[66] The chapters incorporated in this unit are typically named "The History of David's Rise," a reflection of the German term "*Aufstieg Davids*."[67] The name suggests that David must be present in the narrative at its inception. However, there are no formal markers of a unit at either chapters 16 or 17. Furthermore, the issue of David's rise is difficult to separate from Saul's downfall. I would therefore like to suggest that 1 Sam 14:52 through 2 Sam 8:15 comprise a unit, which has been formed by a redactor, largely by collecting and revising earlier traditions with a particular purpose in mind. I call this section "David as Proper King."

Several factors coincide to suggest that 1 Sam 14:46–51 demarcate the end of a large unit.[68] First, the previous chapters, with few exceptions,[69] are favorable to Saul, depicting him as a victorious king. This contrasts sharply with what follows. 1 Sam 14:47–8 sound like a summary for a section concerning Saul, the victorious king.[70] That section reads:

> Saul seized kingship over Israel,[71] and he fought against his enemies on every side – against Moab, Ammon, Edom, the kings of Zobah and the Philistines; wherever he turned, he was successful.[72] He was strong and smote Amalek; he saved Israel from its plunderers.

These verses are quite remarkable; they narrate events which are mostly not recorded in Samuel, but which are very favorable to this first king. They begin and end with a general statement of Saul's great success, while in the middle, important specific supporting information is added: the nations encircling Israel on all four of its sides are listed (v. 47), and the claim is made that Saul saved Israel from its archenemy, Amalek (v. 48). He was, according to these verses, successful indeed. This contrasts sharply with the neutral 1 Sam 14:52, which says, "There was a severe war against the Philistines all of the days of Saul; when Saul saw any strong man and warrior, he recruited him," which suggests that Saul was not entirely successful in fighting his most significant enemies.[73] Given the central role of king as warrior in ancient Israel, this is a serious short-coming.

The intervening verses, 1 Sam 14:49–51, contain a list, which details Saul's family and notes (v. 50b): "and the name of his army commander was Abiner son of Ner, the uncle of Saul."[74] There is no other list of Saul's cabinet officers in Samuel. It is likely that 1 Sam 14:49–51 is the material most similar to the lists of David's cabinet officers that our editor could find. In that case, 1 Sam 14:49–51 serve in a function similar to that of 2 Sam 8:16–18 and 20:23–6 – they demarcate a unit.

The argument that 1 Sam 14:47–51, whose structure is military victory and royal cabinet, are a dividing point between units is furthered when that unit is compared with the end of 2 Samuel 8, which has a similar structure and also functions as a dividing line between two units. It is especially noteworthy that vv. 12–14 list the booty brought from Aram,[75] Moab, Ammon, Philistines, Amalek, Zobah and Edom; this list is nearly identical to 1 Sam 14:47–8 of Saul.

Scholars have not previously understood the structural significance of 1 Sam 14:47–51. McCarter, for example, has suggested that 14:47–52 (not 51) are a unit, and has called it "Further Notices About Saul's Kingship."[76] However, the correspondences between this unit and the end of 2 Samuel 8, both in the structure of "victory plus cabinet," and in the similarity of countries conquered, suggests that a redactor was attempting to organize the material with a particular purpose in mind. The intervening material, 1 Sam 14:52 through 2 Sam 8:15, "David as Proper King," starts by delegitimating Saul and ends by legitimating David. At its beginning, Saul is embattled (1 Sam 14:52) and sinful (1 Samuel 15);[77] at its conclusion, David is strong (2 Samuel 8) and righteous (2 Sam 8:15). This unit is distinct thematically from the surrounding material;[78] as noted, the material preceding it is favorable to Saul, while that which follows points to David's sins and (the resulting) military weakness. Thus, structural and thematic evidence converge to suggest that 1 Sam 14:52 through 2 Sam 8:15 was structured in antiquity as a unit.[79]

DAVID AS PROPER KING

Before it is possible to show how this unit demonstrates that David is fit for kingship, it is necessary to outline the royal Davidic ideology, which suggests the functions of the proper king. According to Ben C. Ollenburger, the Davidic tradition "has three characteristic concerns: legitimacy, succession and hegemony."[80] It would be circular to develop these concerns from an examination of Samuel, and then to see how Samuel furthers these concerns. Instead, I will use the royal psalms[81] to illustrate their significance. These psalms develop the legitimacy of the Davidic king by noting the divine selection of David and by using adoption imagery regarding him.[82] Royal succession is a central issue of Psalm 89:29–30 and Psalm 132:11–12. As is well known, there are different conceptions concerning succession; some texts suggest an unconditional dynasty, while for others the continuation of the dynasty is dependent upon the king's obedience of the law.[83] Thus, there were different royal Davidic ideologies in ancient Israel reflecting various notions concerning the perpetuity of the Davidic dynasty, but succession itself was a central issue. Finally, the centrality of hegemony may be seen in the frequent references to military conquest by the Davidic kings in the royal psalms.[84]

This ideology and its components cannot be dated precisely.[85] The problems of dating Samuel and the traditions it incorporates are similar; until recently, it was assumed that most of the traditions concerning David were pre-Deuteronomistic, but this has now been questioned.[86] I follow the majority of scholars, who suggest that some form of Davidic ideology, which concerned itself with the three issues of legitimation, succession and hegemony, did exist during the time of the editing of Samuel, though neither the date of the editing of Samuel, nor of the development of this ideology, is known.

I recognize that Samuel incorporates a variety of material and contains several doublets.[87] However, we cannot unravel and date these sources with certainty, nor can we be sure when particular Deuteronomistic additions were inserted. My interpretation of the book as a whole suggests that an editor gathered the material together to show that David was the proper king, and that various Deuteronomistic editors, who were familiar with and sympathetic to the goals of this editor, added material in a similar vein.[88] Roger Lemuel Ward describes the editor in this way: "The writer is an historian who has combined his 'sources' into a remarkably powerful and coherent narrative. He is an author in the full sense of the word."[89] For this reason, I feel comfortable speaking of the *Tendenz* of the unit as a whole, while acknowledging that it contains diverse material and has a complicated pre-history.

The argument that this unit, "David as Proper King," is constructed according to ideological rather than historical criteria is generally acknowledged. For example, Vanderkam notes:

> The story of David's Rise is, of course, hardly historiography in the moderns" sense of that term; it is rather a literary unit that has undergone heavily pro-davidic editing. The fundamental themes of the finished account are theological: the Lord chose David and protected him, but he rejected and abandoned Saul; these themes serve the basic purpose of the entire story, viz. to legitimate David's acquisition of the throne that was once occupied by Saul. For this purpose the editor(s) gathered, arranged, and supplemented a number of stories and fashioned them into a compelling, attractive whole.[90]

Many scholars have pointed out chronological improbabilities in the material incorporated in our unit as it is currently organized. For example, geographical considerations suggest that 1 Samuel 28–30 are not in chronological order.[91] Finally, in contrast to the Succession Narrative, which was typically seen until very recently as a historically accurate account written in the period of David and/or Solomon,[92] the material concerning David and Saul has always been somewhat suspect because the author, who is interested in justifying David at the expense of Saul, has made his *Tendenz* too obvious.

A major vehicle for asserting the legitimacy of David is emphasizing the illegitimacy of Saul. This took some effort to accomplish, because according to the tradition, Saul was anointed by Samuel according to the request of YHWH.[93] Thus, the redactor of this section had to find or create various traditions that would explain why Saul did not deserve to retain his kingship. He accomplishes this by depicting the reign of Saul as "a tale of error,"[94] particularly by emphasizing that Saul is a military failure and a murderer who disobeys YHWH's word and behaves in a way which does not befit a king. Any of these traits would be a serious flaw in a king; working together, they delegitimate Saul, and assure the reader that the kingship was justly transferred to David.

The large unit which precedes ours, which narrates Saul's accession to the throne, emphasizes his military ability: he becomes king because he defeats the Ammonites (1 Samuel 11),[95] and together with his son Jonathan, he successfully contends against the Philistines (13–14). As noted, the previous unit concludes with an almost formulaic declaration of Saul's victories (14:47–8). In contrast, the unit fostering David's legitimacy opens with the implication that Saul was unable to overcome his Philistine enemies (14:52). This is strengthened in chapter 17, which depicts the confrontation between David and Goliath. Early in the chapter, our author narrates (v. 11), "Saul and all Israel heard these words of the Philistine, and they were extremely fearful." The continuation of the chapter focusses on David and Goliath – Saul is nearly absent. It is especially noteworthy that according to the tradition contained in the Book of Samuel, Saul was the tallest of the Israelites (1 Sam 9:2; 10:23), while David is called "the little/short one" (1 Sam 17:14).[96] Thus, the little David replaces the tall Saul, the king who should have confronted Goliath. Three times within our unit we find the victory song "Saul has killed thousands, but David tens of thousands" (1 Sam 18:7; 21:12; 29:5), emphasizing the military superiority of David over Saul. Saul's military weakness is of course confirmed in chapter 31, when he is unable successfully to lead the Israelites against the Philistines; he is killed and his Israelite army is trounced.

In 1 Samuel 18–26, Saul is depicted as a murderer and an attempted murderer. His victims and intended victims are always, according to the narrator, innocent. So, for example, he kills the priests of Nob (1 Sam 22:16–19), under the incorrect belief that their priest had given David access to a divine oracle. His massacre of them is complete – indeed, he acts as if they were under the ḥerem, killing men, women, children and animals (v. 19). This deliberately contrasts with Saul's non-compliance with the ḥerem against the Amalekites in chapter 15 – he spares those he should kill under the ḥerem, while he carries out the ḥerem against the innocent. He tries to kill David several times (1 Sam 18:10–11; 19:1–2, 9–10, 11–24, throughout chapters 23–6), and once even tries to kill his own son Jonathan (20:33). Murder was viewed very seriously in ancient Israel; it was expressly prohibited in the Decalogue (Exod 20:13; Deut 5:17) and was one of the sins projected upon the archetypally evil king of Judah, Manasseh (2 Kgs 21:16).

The function of 1 Samuel 15, which introduces our unit, is to show how Saul has abandoned YHWH. Saul has rejected YHWH's word by not killing Agag and all of the Amalekite sheep; the command was clear and his infraction of it is unambiguous.[97] Saul does not later attempt to compensate for his initial failure by killing Agag; this is accomplished by Samuel (v. 33). As a result of Saul's rejection of the divine word, he is rejected as king. The word used to reflect this measure-for-measure pattern (v. 26) is a very strong term.[98] This rejection is further symbolized by the rending of a garment (vv. 27–8); this theme is repeated later in our unit (1 Sam 24:5, 12), and becomes a powerful symbol for the rending of the kingdom away from Saul.[99] Chapter 28, placed soon before Samuel's death, provides another example of Saul disobeying YHWH. This chapter opens with a wonderful irony – Saul, in his earlier righteous days, had banned necromancers from the land (28:3), but now must consult one himself, breaking both the Deuteronomic law (Deut 18:10–11)[100] and the royal edict.

According to the text of Samuel, Saul's abandonment of YHWH is mirrored by YHWH's abandonment of Saul. This is explicitly stated in 1 Sam 16:14, which describes the divine spirit leaving Saul. It also serves as the background for chapter 28, the story of Saul and the necromancer at En-Dor, which opens with a description of Saul attempting to consult

YHWH through the standardly accepted means – dreams, Urim and prophets (v. 6) – but with no success. From the time our unit opens until his death, Saul is depicted as having abandoned YHWH. For this reason, YHWH abandons him, making him unsuitable for kingship. This contrasts strongly, for example, with Psalm 110:1, which depicts the Davidic king as sitting to the right of YHWH.

Finally, at various places throughout the unit, Saul acts in an unroyal fashion. Kings are supposed to be the strong head of society. It is therefore surprising, for example, when Saul thanks the people of Zif for having pity upon him (23:21).[101] The depiction of King Saul in chapter 28 is especially astonishing. He is very fearful (v. 5b), and faints as a result of his encounter with Samuel (v. 20). Much of this section portrays Saul as paranoid, rather than as strong and confident.[102] Such an individual does not deserve kingship.

The depiction of David in this unit explicitly contrasts with that of Saul.[103] David is successful militarily,[104] he is not a murderer, he obeys God and is protected by him, and is considered a royal figure even before he is fully recognized as king by all Israel. In addition, the accounts narrating his anointing and the dynastic promise, which are close to the boundaries of the unit, emphasize David's legitimacy.

A major theme of the second part of our unit is that David had ample opportunities and reasons to commit murder, but he restrained himself.[105] 1 Samuel chapters 24 and 26 are often seen as doublets;[106] in both, David has an opportunity to kill Saul, but instead performs a symbolic action to show Saul that he has not used the opportunity to fight back. In fact, in chapter 24, David even regrets having gone so far as to rip off part of Saul's garment (v. 6).[107] Chapters 24 and 26 frame an incident which clears David of the death of Nabal.[108] It is quite conceivable that a version of the story of David's marriage to Abigail which paralleled that of David and Bathsheba circulated in ancient Israel; 1 Samuel 25 counters that story, showing how Nabal dies a natural death and that David thanks Abigail for preventing him from killing Nabal (vv. 33–4). The beginning chapters of 2 Samuel go out of their way to "prove" that David was not involved in the death of Saul, Abner and Saul's son, Ish-bosheth.[109] David's actions upon hearing of these deaths might seem exaggerated (2 Sam 1:11–16; 3:28–9, 33–7; 4:9–12), but these are meant to clear David of any accusations that he was implicated in any way in these deaths. The text forcefully and continually suggests that David, in contrast to Saul, does not murder. The contrast between Saul and David in 2 Samuel 1 is made quite clear by narrating an interesting set of intersecting "coincidences": an Amalekite kills Saul, the same Saul who was too weak to kill the Amalekite, Agag, while David appropriately inflicts capital punishment upon the Amalekite who inappropriately killed Saul.

In contrast to Saul, who abandons YHWH and is abandoned by him, a major theme of this section is that YHWH is with David.[110] Upon his anointing, the spirit of YHWH rests upon David (16:13). Our narrator emphasizes the absolute truth of YHWH being with David by putting it in the mouths of so many different individuals. It is stated by the narrator (1 Sam 18:12, 14), by one of Saul's attendants (1 Sam 16:18) and even by Saul (18:28). The various victories of David, especially that over Goliath (1 Sam 17:37), illustrate that YHWH is with David. Toward the end of the unit, this idea appears in an expanded form (2 Sam 5:10): "David became greater and greater, and YHWH the God of Hosts was with him."

YHWH was not with Saul, so he had no access to divine oracles. In contrast, David has easy and frequent access to YHWH through oracles throughout this unit (1 Sam 23:2, 4, 11; 30:7–8; 2 Sam 2:1; 5:19, 23). The contrast between Saul going to the necromancer in 1 Samuel 28 and David easily consulting YHWH in 1 Samuel 30 is heightened through the proximity of these two narratives.

In contrast to Saul, who is non-royal even when he is king, David is recognized as king even before he is officially anointed ruler over all of Israel. It is surely significant that the servants of the Philistine, Achish, call David "king of the land" (1 Sam 21:12).[111] In contrast to Saul, who is cowardly, David engenders fear in others (1 Sam 21:2). This, however, could open David to the accusation that he was acting like king while Saul was still alive. This is countered, however, by depicting David's behavior towards Saul as following the appropriate subject–king norms. In the two key narratives where David does not avail himself of the easy opportunity of killing Saul, David uses the respectful title "YHWH's anointed"[112] in reference to Saul (1 Sam 24:7, 11; 26:9, 23; 2 Sam 1:14, 16). David calls himself a flea or a dead dog in respect to the king of Israel (1 Sam 24:15). David considers his father Jesse to be a servant of Saul (17:58) and properly addresses the king "my master, the king" (26:17). Thus, the narrator shows us that David, unlike Saul, is truly royal, but at the same time rebuts the insinuation that David acted royally while Saul was still alive.

Though the Judean royal ritual was complex and had many components,[113] anointing was its central element. David is first anointed near the unit's beginning, at 1 Sam 16:13.[114] He is anointed a second time by the Judeans (2 Sam 2:4) and finally, toward the unit's conclusion, by all of Israel (5:3). This triple anointing, along with other components of the royal ritual articulated by each of these passages, legitimates David.

The most important element in our unit which legitimates David as king is the dynastic oracle in 2 Samuel 7, which has been termed "[t]he climax of pro-Davidic propaganda."[115] The chapter likely has a complex history, but this need not concern us; in its final form, it promises David a perpetual dynasty (vv. 13, 16, cf. 29), which is the foundation of royal legitimation. The dynastic oracle is in an emphatic position at the end of our unit, and is referred to earlier in 1 Sam 25:28, where Abigail says that YHWH will give David "an enduring house" (cf. 2 Sam 7:16). In addition, a less specific dynastic promise is alluded to in the image of the conveyance of kingship from Saul to David. This suggests that kingship, with its attendant expectation of dynastic succession, has been transferred. This conveyance of kingship is narrated first in 1 Samuel 15–16, but is also repeated by the "ghost" of Samuel in 2 Sam 28:16–17, and is put in the mouth of Abner, Saul's army commander, in 2 Sam 3:9–10. The repetition of the promise from all of these perspectives significantly fosters the legitimacy of David's rule.

I have just noted that according to the conception of our author, kingship has been transferred by YHWH from Saul to David, making David the legitimate successor of Saul. This raises the second issue which according to Ollenburger was central to the Davidic ideology – succession. The importance of succession within the narrative was especially appreciated by Sigmund Mowinckel, who noted that "it was part of the policy of David to appear as the legitimate heir of the Saulides."[116] What Mowinckel takes as the policy of David, I would suggest was initiated by later, pro-Davidic authors, who inserted various statements of abdication in the mouths of Saul and Jonathan and used several means to create a father–son relationship between Saul and David.

For David to reign, both Saul, the king, and Jonathan, the oldest son and thus crown-prince,[117] need to cede their kingship to him. This is done first by Jonathan, who makes a pact with David, stating (1 Sam 23:17): "you will reign over Israel, and I will be second-in-command to you; even my father Saul acknowledges that."[118] Saul soon echoes the same sentiment, when he emphatically states (24:21): "now I really know that you will surely reign, and kingship over Israel will be established through you."[119] This is stated again in more general terms in 1 Sam 26:25, where shortly before his death, Saul says to David: "You are blessed, my son David, you will indeed succeed whatever you do." In its context, this is an admission by Saul that David will succeed as king. Furthermore, it is possible that the term "to love," which is used in relation to Jonathan and David (1 Sam 18:1, 3; 20:17), has a technical sense of treaty partner, suggesting that David should assume kingship upon Jonathan's death.[120]

It is certainly significant that in chapters 24 and 26, Saul calls David "my son" (24:17; 26:17, 21, 25), while David calls Saul "my father" (24:12).[121] While these can be seen merely as hierarchical terms,[122] it is more likely that they are meant to create a father–son relationship between Saul and David, suggesting that David is Saul's legitimate successor. The three-fold repetition of "my son David" in chapter 26 emphatically suggests that Saul accepts this relationship.[123]

A person may be symbolized by the clothing that he or she wears.[124] It is thus significant that in the David and Goliath story, Saul offers David his armor. David tries it on, but in a comic touch, the narrator notes that small David was too weak to walk in the heavy armor of King Saul (1 Sam 17:38–9). This symbolizes David's refusal to usurp Saul's royal place. In contrast, however, in the next chapter, Jonathan, the crown-prince, gives his clothing to David. The verse's structure is emphatic (18:4): "Jonathan stripped off the cloak he was wearing and gave it to David; and his tunic from his sword to his bow to his belt," repeating the word "to"[125] three times. David becomes Jonathan, the crown-prince. It is especially significant that Jonathan initiates the action; David is not tricking him out of his kingship. Chapters 17 and 18 probably originate from different hands, but they were likely juxtaposed here to show that David refused to usurp power from Saul, but became a type of surrogate son to Saul when Jonathan dressed David in his clothes. David, then, very early in this narrative, becomes the true crown-prince.

Finally, David is depicted as Saul's son-in-law through his marriage to Michal (1 Sam 18:17–27). This might have opened David up to the charge of opportunism, much like the man who marries the boss's daughter so that he can take over the business. The narrator of that text, however, shows that the initiative for the marriage was Saul's, and in fact, the suggestion that David marry into the royal family was a ruse, since Saul set the brideprice at one hundred Philistine foreskins with the hope that David would die while collecting them (v. 17, 25). The trick failed, David became the son-in-law, and thus part of the royal family and qualified for kingship – all as a result of Saul's initiative. This is why Saul's daughter and David's wife Michal is highlighted again much later in the narrative, in 2 Sam 3:14–16, when David demands from Ish-bosheth that Michal be returned to him.[126]

Incidentally, this theme of David advancing at court through the initiative of others, and not through his own opportunism, is fundamental to the unit. So, for example, it is through Saul's initiative that David entered the court (1 Sam 16:17–23), David's important friendship with Jonathan was initiated by Jonathan (18:3) and Saul encouraged David to become a warrior (18:5). Additional examples with this clearly apologetic bent could be cited.[127] They suggest that in ancient Israel, a group felt that David was a conniving individual, who took advantage of Saul; these stories were collected or composed as propaganda to counter these rumors.

In sum, the author of "David as Proper King" could not change the genealogy of David and Saul; traditions were well enough known that Saul could not become a Judahite, and David could certainly not be depicted as a Benjaminite. Therefore, it is clear that David and Saul could not be genetically related, and the kingship of David could not be legitimated genealogically. However, working within these parameters, the narrator used as many means as possible to depict Saul and David as father and son; these create a strong pseudo-genealogical relationship between them.

The final element of the Davidic ideology is hegemony. The narratives incorporated within "David as Proper King" emphasize this by describing David's military strength and by noting his conquest of land even before he was king. Early in the narrative, he defeats the Philistine giant Goliath (1 Samuel 17). As noted earlier, the women sing of the tens and thousands that he has slain (1 Sam 18:7; 21:12; 29:5). He becomes an army leader (1 Sam 18:16), and the text twice says of him in reference to the arch-enemy, the Philistines, "he smote them greatly" (19:8 and 23:5). He controls a band of 400 armed bandits (22:2). David is so strong that the Moabites, typically depicted as enemies of Israel, agree to watch his parents while he is away fleeing from Saul (22:3–4). David successfully raids various migrant tribes (27:8–9) and defeats in a lopsided victory the Amalekites who had raided his city of Ziklag (30). According to 1 Sam 27:6, he possesses Ziklag even before he officially becomes king.

David's power increases once he is anointed as king. His conquest of Jerusalem, which would be central to the Judean monarchy, is narrated in 2 Samuel 5. It is likely that its placement so soon after David's anointment reflects ideological desires rather than chronological realities.[128] Furthermore, he vanquishes the Philistines, who had been the enemies of Saul (5:17–25). The last chapter of our unit, chapter 8, is a compilation, probably not in chronological order, of David's victories. These are extensive and fully convince the reader of David's military power and hegemonic accomplishments.

As already stated, David's attainments contrast sharply with those of Saul in our narrative. King Saul can engage the Philistines (1 Sam 23:28), but cannot, like David, smite them so that they flee (19:8). The contrast between David and Saul is very sharp in the juxtaposed chapters 30 and 31 – David vanquishes the Amalekites, returning with much booty, while Saul and his family fall before the Philistines. Additionally, David's military successes in this unit contrast sharply with his defeats and humiliations in the following unit, which incorporates various rebellions against David. In fact, the difference between 2 Samuel 8, David's victories, and chapter 10, the humiliation of David's servants by Hanun of Ammon, is an important argument for claiming that these two episodes reflect different ideologies.

To summarize, 1 Sam 14:52 to 2 Sam 8:15 is a unit whose main goal is to describe David as proper king. Although a multiplicity of goals stand behind any work,[129] propagandistic motives predominate in the unit; there is no escaping that "[t]he complex is strongly coloured by a pro-Davidic and anti-Saulide bias."[130] But it is very serious propaganda; its aim is to help create a people Judah centered upon the royal Davidic dynasty.[131] Almost every chapter of the long unit can be seen as fitting into the ideological program of legitimating David at Saul's expense. This was accomplished by a set of narrators who compiled, shaped and wrote texts to foster their position. In this process, the narrators used for ideological purposes what some would call literary devices, such as contrasts or antitheses between Saul and David.[132] These are used, however, for ideological rather than literary-aesthetic purposes. In some senses, the narrative that they produced engages in overkill – David looks so good, we almost start to feel sorry for Saul.[133] That, however, is an anachronistic reading of the material. Rather, the authors and editors of Samuel lived in a era of competing royal ideologies in ancient Israel, and it was necessary for them to combat propaganda with counter-propaganda. A brief exposition of the continued life of the pro-Saul ideology in ancient Israel will clarify the necessity for the type of ideological writing found in "David as Proper King."

THE AFTERLIFE OF THE SAULIDE IDEOLOGY

Many scholars have placed the pro-Davidic narratives within Samuel at the beginning of the Davidic dynasty or at a time when the dynasty was under threat.[134] The Davidic kingdom was, according to the biblical account, threatened frequently during the existence of the northern kingdom, and the justification of David in 1 Sam 14:52–2 Sam 8:15 could be seen as a response to that threat. Saul could then be viewed as a symbol of non-Judean, non-Davidic kingship.[135] Though that might have been a factor, I would like to suggest that a careful reading of the biblical text suggests that a pro-Saul ideology continued long after the death of Saul, and that the unit "David as Proper King" should be understood as part of the ideological battle of David versus Saul, which began with the rise of David and continued into the post-exilic period.

The predominant source of the pro-Saul ideology is the first fourteen chapters of Samuel. These narrate Saul's accession to power in terms of both divine legitimation (sections of chs 9–10) and military prowess (ch. 11). Even these chapters, however, have been subject to some pro-Davidic editing. For example, 14:47, which in the MT states of Saul, "He was wicked in whatever he did," is a tendentious change by a late, anti-Saul redactor.[136] Similarly, the story of the extraordinary birth of Samuel in chapter 1 is almost certainly originally a story concerning Saul, as is made clear through the numerous etymological connections between the root *š'l*, *"to ask," which is central to that chapter, and Saul's name (*š'wl*).[137] The change of the protagonist to Samuel reflects a diminution of Saul's status. It is not coincidental that these changes which alter a pro-Saul narrative into a pro-Samuel narrative in one case, and a pro-Saul to an anti-Saul narrative on the other, were perpetrated at the boundaries of the pro-Saul material, since it is these beginning and concluding texts which are most central for forming the reader's impressions.[138]

Evidence embedded within Samuel suggests that a pro-Saul ideology must have outlived the king.[139] It is stated in 2 Sam 3:1 that a long (MT) or difficult (versions) struggle was battled between the house of David and the house of Saul. This is not surprising; why should the royal ideology favoring Saul all of sudden die with the rise of David? Two late biblical sources confirm the continuation of a pro-Saul ideology. 1 Chr 8:33–40 is a genealogy of Saul's descendants, extending twelve generations beyond Saul. The presence of this genealogy in Chronicles, a post-exilic composition which is pro-Davidic, is very striking. It is likely that the list was kept through the exile by descendants of Saul who saw themselves as potential royalty. Furthermore, according to that genealogy (v. 35), one of Saul's descendants is named Melek, "king";[140] this probably reflects the continued royal aspirations of the family.[141] The significance of the genealogical information in Chronicles is appreciated by James W. Flanagan, who claims, "The survival of Saul's memory... suggests a continuing prominence [of the Saulide dynasty], perhaps based upon a hope of returning to power."[142]

An additional post-exilic source reflecting positively on Saul is the Book of Esther.[143] The protagonist of the work is "Mordecai, son of Jair, son of Shimei, son of Kish, a Benjaminite" (2:5). "Son" is being used in this genealogy in the sense of descendant, a typical use in genealogical texts,[144] and Kish is none other than the father of Saul (1 Sam 9:1).[145] The exilic author of Esther who composed this work of doubtful historicity[146] used a descendant of Saul as his hero. Texts like Isa 55:3, and indeed Deutero-Isaiah as a whole, should remind us that not everyone in exilic and post-exilic Israel had messianic expectations of the house of David.[147] The fact is that the hero of Esther, a work supposedly transpiring in the fifth century, is a descendant of Saul, who was killed (according to the standard biblical chronology) over five hundred years earlier. This is eloquent testimony to the tenacity of the pro-Saul ideology.

It is even possible that rabbinic material from the post-biblical period has retained a memory of the pro-Saul ideology that existed in the period of the monarchy. We would have expected rabbinic texts, written in a milieu which typically favored a Davidic messiah,[148] to follow the biblical example of denigrating Saul, David's predecessor. In contrast to our expectations, one third-century Palestinian Amora characterizes Saul as "faultless" (b. Yoma 22b). A tradition in the same source ignores the explicit condemnation of Saul in 1 Samuel 15 for not killing all of the Amalekites and their cattle, and instead claims that Saul was dethroned because he "was willing to forgo the honor due him." Other reversals of the biblical Saul are found in Midrash Shmuel, a collection of Palestinian traditions on the Book of Samuel from diverse time-periods.[149] For example, this midrash incorporates a retelling of the story of Saul and the necromancer at En-Dor (1 Sam 28:3–25), in which Samuel offers Saul the opportunity to be saved by fleeing from the battle, but Saul refuses and marches off to fight, gladly accepting his divine punishment. God is so impressed by Saul's choice that he tells the ministering angels, "Look at the person that I have created . . . he is so happy that he is being punished by the divine attribute of judgement."[150] Several rabbinic sources blame David for the death of Saul and his sons.[151] Although it is very difficult to know when rabbinic stories preserve old traditions and when they are creating new ones for their own ideological reasons,[152] these stories, which reflect so very positively on Saul at David's expense, may be old traditions which were disregarded by the editors of Samuel as a result of their largely pro-Davidic bias. Similar traditions may have been known to Josephus, who has reshaped the biblical Saul, portraying him more positively.[153]

The likely vitality of this pro-Saul ideology explains why "David as Proper King" was so extensive and needed to make its arguments repeatedly with such tenacity – it was fighting a continuing ideological battle. The same battle might have very well been fought by the Chronicler, whose strident pro-Davidic revisionism we have already seen. Unfortunately, we can catch only glimpses of the pro-Saul side, but these suggest that there might have been a forceful pro-Saul tradition or document, which the biblical editors, with their predominant pro-Davidic bias, have not preserved. This prevents us from seeing directly the full range of dynamics of ideological battles in ancient Israel, but it certainly confirms their existence.

Exactly who wrote and read these ideological texts remains unknown. Some have assumed that they were read and heard only by the court and the elite,[154] but given the importance of the king in ancient Israel,[155] it is likely that interest in these stories was more extensive. Medieval evidence suggests that Nithard's *Histories* was read beyond the royal court;[156] if this offers a valid analogy, it is likely that the Book of Samuel was known by a broader Israelite audience. Certainly, as the dynasty of David continued to reign through the centuries, and especially once the idea of David as messiah became popular in ancient Israel, interest in the story of David as proper king would have extended beyond the royal court.

7

TEXT IN A *TEL*

2 Kings 17 as history

When the Israelites sinned against YHWH their God . . .

2 Kgs 17:7

ARCHEOLOGICAL AND TEXTUAL *TELS*

Few events are as traumatic to a community as exile. The exile of Judah in 586[1] left its imprint on many sections of the Hebrew Bible; that event is described in 2 Kings 25, is lamented in the Book of Lamentations and is reflected upon in various prophetic works, most especially in parts of Jeremiah[2] and in the final section of Ezekiel (33:21ff.). The destruction of the northern kingdom in the late eighth century by Assyria,[3] and the accompanying large-scale forced population exchanges that typified the Assyrian policy,[4] must have similarly been a traumatic event. The northern literature that reflected upon it is no longer extant,[5] but we do have a set of Judean meditations that attempt to understand why their northern "brothers" have suffered such a terrible fate. One can imagine the mixed emotions felt by many Judeans: on the one hand, they felt a close ethnic affiliation to the northern Israelites, to whom they were closely related. On the other hand, for many years, the northern kingdom was geographically more extensive than Judah and politically more powerful, so it is easy to imagine that Judah could have been jealous of its accomplishments and happy at its demise. Various groups in Judah probably felt differently about the north's destruction, and attitudes must have continued to shift following the destruction of the northern kingdom. 2 Kings 17 is a collection of some of these attitudes.

In our contemporary society, when an author disagrees with a prevailing theory, he or she writes a work to dispute it. That was the model we saw in Chronicles; the Chronicler disagreed with the authoritative version of history that was circulating in his period, and he wrote a new work that he hoped would cause the old history to be read in a new way. However, when the disagreement was less programmatic than that seen in Chronicles,

112

short corrective texts could be written, much like the contemporary genre of letters to the editor. These short pieces could not be published as separate documents such as "an opinion concerning the exile of the northern kingdom,"[6] but they could sometimes become incorporated as glosses to the main text.

Editors played a major role in deciding whether particular versions should be included or not; we may presume that some stories concerning the exile of the north circulated which were not incorporated into the Bible. For example, it is unlikely that a Judean editor would have incorporated a tradition that suggested that it was a shame that the north was exiled, because its inhabitants were pious. Thus, 2 Kings 17 is a limited collection of reflections concerning the exile, representing a circumscribed band of ideologies.

The multiple meditations contained in this chapter make it resemble an archeological *tel*, a layered collection of settlements. It presents many of the same problems as archeological *tels*: just as it is not always easy to distinguish definitively between archeological layers, so it is often difficult to isolate groups of verses that belong together. Similar criteria may be used in archeology and texts: artifacts or verses that share certain key elements and differ significantly from surrounding material are usually assigned to the same period or author, and the researcher must discover formal indications (e.g. burn layers, formal structural devices) that suggest the boundaries between levels. Archeological *tels* are not always neatly layered, with the oldest layer on the bottom; frequently, older materials are reused by subsequent generations. The same is even more true of texts: we cannot presume that the textual layers are neatly stacked. This kind of multi-layered text, difficult to disentangle, is foreign to us; we are more used to the model found in Chronicles, where an author who disagrees with the prevailing opinion composes a completely new text. However, the model provided in 2 Kings 17 is found in other biblical texts.[7]

However, 2 Kings 17 does not typify the biblical corpus. It has an unusually large number of sources, because the event that it depicts was unusually momentous and therefore evoked a wide variety of responses.[8] Most events did not cause a similar amount of reflection, and thus their *tels* are much less complex. However, 2 Kings 17 is not unique; the completion of the Temple by Solomon in 1 Kings 8 and Sennacherib's invasion of Judah in 701 (1 Kings 18–20) were also seen as extraordinary events. Such events acted as magnets, attracting a multiplicity of traditions and reflections.[9] The multiplicity of reflections concerning the revelation of the Torah on Sinai is comparable.[10] An ideal final text to examine within the context of the creation of history in ancient Israel is 2 Kings 17 since it offers many reflections by different historians on the same event. This text illustrates in a nutshell almost the full range of attitudes held by biblical historians, from those who seem to be interested in recording the outlines of the actual political history, to those who ponder events and let the present extensively modify the depiction of the past. It also shows how the four central factors responsible for the production of ancient Israelite biblical historical text, which were surveyed in the previous chapters, function together in a single large unit.

A PREVIEW

My examination of 2 Kings 17 has three main goals: it attempts a source-critical analysis of the chapter, it develops a set of criteria that may be used for this venture and it tries to understand each of the sources as history in the sense used throughout this book. Due to the excessive complexity of chapter 17, it is best first to outline the chapter's structure:[11]

A. Vv. 1–2: The standard Deuteronomistic introduction of a king.

B. Vv. 3–4: Shalmaneser and Hoshea.

C. Vv. 5–6: The exile of Hoshea by the king of Assyria.

D. Vv. 7–12 (except for the anticipatory gloss in 8b): A (misplaced) condemnation of the Children of Israel, that is, Judah, for cultic sins.

E. Vv. 13–18a (except for the anticipatory gloss of "Judah" in 13), 23, 34–40: A condemnation of Israel, namely, the northern kingdom, for covenant infractions, and a description of their exile to Assyria and of the Israelites" continued religious apostasy there.

F. 18b–20: A reference to Judah's exile, written as an attempt to update the chapter.

G. 21–2: A condemnation of the North for breaking away from the Davidic line and for following Jeroboam's sins.

H. 24–33, 41: A source concerning the non-Israelite settlers of the North which has been shaped into a polemic against the northerners, claiming that their behaviour is worse than that of the non-Israelites who replaced them.

The rest of this chapter will offer a detailed defense of this structure.[12] I will not attempt to cover every single problem that arises in this chapter, and I will sidestep many issues relating to the reconstruction of the events in the 720s; my focus is on the texts and the historians who produced them, and not on the events that they narrate. I will concentrate on providing a context for the various perspectives within the chapter. To avoid working with a 41-verse chapter as a whole, I will follow the standard tripartite division of the chapter (vv. 1–6, 7–23 and 24–41), even though this division is simplistic and problematic.

2 KINGS 17:1-6

Vv. 1–2, attributed to a Deuteronomistic redactor, are mostly formulaic. They contain the typical synchronic note concerning the king's (Hoshea) accession to the throne (1abα), the length of his reign (1bβ) and the notice that he was evil (2a). However, this notice does not appear in its usual full form; there is no mention of the sins of Jeroboam, which is found with most other northern kings.[13] This lack is consistent with v. 2b, "but [he was] not [evil] to the extent of the kings of Israel who preceded him," which is quite terse and enigmatic.[14] It is likely that the Deuteronomistic author who wrote v. 2b knew some tradition concerning Hoshea which he did not include in Kings. Thus, 2 Kgs 17:2b is probably a case which illustrates Halpern's thesis concerning sources: an editor knew a source or tradition concerning Hoshea's religious behavior, and included it even though it inconveniently suggests that the king under whom Israel was exiled was less evil than previous kings.[15]

Content initially suggests that vv. 3–6 should be considered as the next unit, dealing with political history, which serves as an introduction to vv. 7–23, which contain a theological reflection upon that political history. However, a careful examination of vv. 3–6 suggests that they actually incorporate two sources. One indication of the multiplicity of sources is the observation that vv. 5–6 are parallel to 2 Kgs 18:9b–11, while vv. 3–4 have no parallel in that chapter. This suggests that vv. 5–6 and 2 Kgs 18:9b–11 are based on a single source, while vv. 3–4 are from a separate source.[16] This external evidence is supplemented by internal evidence, adduced below, that vv. 3–4 and 5–6 are different compositions.

Vv. 3–6 present several thorny problems. They open with the phrase "[Shalmaneser, king of Assyria] went up [in battle] against him." This phrase[17] is found nowhere else at the beginning of a verse in the Deuteronomistic History; it is found only in 2 Chr 36:6, "Nebuchadnezzar, king of Babylon went up [in battle] against him [=Zedekiah]." In contrast, several episodes in the Deuteronomistic History open with the phrase "In his days X went up [in battle],"[18] which might be a formula for a citation from archival material.[19] The likely source of 2 Chr 36:6, 2 Kgs 24:1, uses the phrase "In his days [of Zedekiah, Nebuchadnezzar] went up [in battle]." This raises the possibility that "In his days X went up [in battle]" is the exilic and post-exilic equivalent of the pre-exilic term "X went up [in battle] against him."

Previous scholars have noted several internal indications that vv. 3–6 are not from a single source.[20] Most compelling is the double introduction of the king of Assyria going up in vv. 3 and 5. In addition, the text as it now stands suggests that the north withstood a three-year siege (v. 5) after its king was exiled (v. 4); this is unlikely.

The similarity between the phrases that open vv. 3 and 5 suggest that this might be a case of a *Wiederaufnahme*, a repetitive resumption, a compositional or editorial device used to bracket material. This device was noted by some of the medieval Jewish exegetes, and later by Harold M. Wiener and Curt Kuhl,[21] and has been used by various scholars to disentangle sources.[22] Leviticus 23 presents a case which is formally very similar to the one here. That chapter's theme is the appointed times[23] or festivals. It contains in vv. 2 and 4 two introductions which are nearly identical. The material framed by the introductions, v. 3, describes the Sabbath, which elsewhere does not fall under the category of an "appointed time," and is thus intrusive. This suggests that the chapter originally started in v. 4, and a later editor added the Sabbath to the pericope. But because the text's form already had semi-authoritative status, the Sabbath could not be added after the introduction. Instead, it was added at the beginning of the chapter, and the introduction, in a slightly modified form, was recopied at the beginning.[24] Graphically, this may be represented in the following way:

A': Lev 23:1–2: Secondary introduction, based on Lev 23:4. Addition: Lev 23:3: The Sabbath law, which is thematically inappropriate.

A: Lev 23:4: Original introduction.

B: Lev 23:5ff.: The appointed times.[25]

The structure of 2 Kgs 17:3–6 is similar:

A': 2 Kgs 17:3a: Secondary introduction, based on 2 Kgs 17:5a. Addition: 2 Kgs 17:3b–4: Supplementary material concerning the exile of Hoshea.

A: 2 Kgs 17:5a: The original introduction.

B: 2 Kgs 17:5b–6: The original account of the exile of the north.

This reconstruction of the textual history of 2 Kgs 17:3–6, with vv. 4–5 coming from a different source, resolves the problem of Samaria enduring a three-year siege without a king. The repeated notices in 3a and 5a are the result of redactional activity. Finally, the king who conquered Samaria according to the earlier source is anonymous, and need not be Shalmaneser, as Nadav Na'aman has recently argued.[26]

A later editor found or created an additional fragment which offered background information concerning the political history of events that led up to the conquest of Samaria: Hoshea's conspiracy with Egypt[27] and his rebellion against the king of Assyria. Since it described events which chronologically precede the capture and exile of the city, he added it as an introduction to what are now vv. 5–6.[28] Following good biblical style, he marked his insertion with a *Wiederaufnahme*, now found in v. 3a. Two elements of that *Wiederaufnahme* are significant: it names Shalmaneser, perhaps incorrectly,[29] as the king of Assyria involved in Samaria's capture, and it contains the phrase, "[Shalmaneser, king of Assyria] went up [in battle] against him," which is only attested in late biblical Hebrew. The use of this phrase might suggest that vv. 3–4 are an exilic addition, which incorporates information which became available at a later period, or were composed by an exilic editor. If this is the case, the addition of these verses post-dates the events they describe by at least a century and a half, and should be used as a historical source with caution.[30]

It is natural to speculate further concerning the nature of the sources in 2 Kgs 17:3–6. It is quite possible that vv. 5–6, the earlier sources, are based on an Assyrian text; this is suggested both by the progression of the verbs in these verses, which follows that of the Assyrian annals, and by the type of list of cities in v. 6 to which the northerners were exiled, also a feature of the annals. The verbs in vv. 5–6 form a pattern of the king of Assyria going up against the country in general, coming to Samaria, besieging it, capturing it, exiling the northerners, and settling them in foreign cities. A similar pattern is found in the Assyrian annals. A clear example is found in the long Ashur-Naṣir-Apli II (=Ashurnasirpal) inscription from the Ninurta Temple at Kalach:

> After crossing the Tigris I marched to the land of Bit-Adni and approached the city Kaprabu, their fortified city . . . I besieged the city and conquered it . . . I massacred many of them, I slew 800 of their men-at-arms, (and) carried off captives (and) property from them. I uprooted 2,500 of their troops (and) settled them in Kalach.[31]

This is a quotation from the middle of the inscription, and thus does not mention the name of the Assyrian king involved; this might also explain the use of the general title "the king of Assyria" in the account of 2 Kgs 17:5. In fact, a partial correspondence may be found in the Annals of Sargon II, in the description of his third year, "I besieged and conquered the city of Samaria. I took as booty 27,290 people . . ."[32] The pattern "besieged" (*alme*), "conquered" (*akšud*), "took people as booty" (*ašlula*) corresponds to 2 Kgs 17:5b–6a.[33] The names of the cities to which people were exiled are frequently found in royal inscriptions,[34] and are very common in the Annals of Sargon II,[35] even though they are absent in reference to Samaria in the version of his annals that has been preserved. Finally, the description of scattering the exiles among several cities reflects actual ancient practice as recorded in Assyrian texts.[36]

Furthermore, it is likely that v. 6 originally opened, "He captured," without the introductory words, "In the ninth year of Hoshea." The syntax of that verse is found only in texts which likely date from the exile and after.[37] The insertion of this note would also explain why the verb breaks the narrative sequence and is not in the converted imperfect.[38] It is thus likely that the phrase, "In the ninth year of Hoshea" was added in light of v. 1, which notes that Hoshea reigned for nine years. If vv. 5–6 are from an Assyrian source, that source would not have been dated to the regnal year of Hoshea; this observation adds to the plausibility that v. 6aα is an addition. Furthermore, it is likely that the end of v. 5, "three years," is an error by an Israelite scribe.[39] The light treatment of Samaria after the rebellion suggests that it did not fiercely resist the king of Assyria for three years. It is possible that a Judean scribe or copyist accidentally turned the fact that this event transpired in the third year of Sargon into a three-year siege.

The origins of vv. 3–4 are less clear.[40] Many of the elements found in it, such as paying tribute, conspiring, ceasing to pay tribute and being fettered, are found in various Assyrian royal inscriptions; it is thus possible that this account is also based on an Assyrian account. However, in most Assyrian texts, the rebellious king is exiled to Assyria, rather than imprisoned.[41] Furthermore, in contrast to the list of cities to which the northerners were exiled in 2 Kgs 17:6b, there is no specific information in vv. 3–4 that would require access to Assyrian material. Indeed, the only specific information given, the names of the Assyrian king Shalmaneser, and of especially So, king of Egypt, is highly suspect. This raises the possibility that vv. 3–4 were created to offer background information concerning the exile. It may be based on two central accounts: 2 Kings 18–19, which describes Hezekiah's alliance with Egypt and implies that he had stopped paying tribute to Assyria, and 2 Kgs 25:7, which describes the fettering of Zedekiah as he was brought to Babylon. It is thus feasible that 2 Kgs 17:3–4 were not from an old source at all, but were created by an editor by analogy to other adjacent and/or central biblical texts.

In other cases, internal evidence suggests that the author of Kings used sources, and hints at their nature. For example, the set of notices in 1 Kgs 14:26, 15:18 and elsewhere all seem to be connected to the Temple treasury, and likely reflect access to some type of Temple accounting book.[42] However, 2 Kgs 17:3–4 and 5–6 do not offer us clear clues concerning their origin. Perhaps the unlikelihood of a Judean knowing the cities to which the northerners had been exiled, coupled with the typical Assyrian phraseology of v. 6, suggest that vv. 5–6 are based on an Assyrian source. Exactly how this source would have been known to a Judean is not certain, though there are other cases where Assyrian literary influence on biblical texts has been suggested.[43] Some of the elite of the royal Judean scribes might have known Akkadian, especially in periods of Mesopotamian domination over Judah.[44] Perhaps the borrowing was mediated via Aramaic, which was becoming the lingua franca of the ancient Near East in the seventh and sixth centuries, and was clearly known by both Assyrian and Judean officials.[45] Vv. 3–4 are not as clearly connected to a Mesopotamian source, and quite possibly contain two historical errors: the beginning stages of the exile are attributed to Shalmaneser,[46] and the problematic "So, king of Egypt" is referred to (v. 4). Perhaps these verses are based on a source; alternatively, they might have been structured to conform to the biblical patterns of being reliant on Egypt, and being sent in fetters to Mesopotamia.[47] This would follow patterns we have observed in Chronicles and Judges regarding how historical traditions come into being.

2 KINGS 17:7–23

This section is typically seen as a unit.[48] While what precedes concentrates on political history, these verses present a theology of history. Tadmor and Cogan call vv. 7–23 "A Homily on the Fall of the Northern Kingdom" and name the end of the chapter (vv. 24–41) "Samaria Resettled."[49] This is typical of other scholars as well. I will show below that this division is misleading; vv. 24–41 are just as homiletic as vv. 7–23, and actually have as their focus the northern Israelites, rather than the (proto-)Samaritans. However, it is easier to present separate analyses of two 17-verse units rather than one analysis of a 34-verse unit, so I will adhere to the traditional division.

Even scholars who de-emphasize the source-criticism of Kings are forced to note the multiplicity of perspectives within this unit.[50] The standard criteria may be used to disentangle the sources: duplications and *Wiederaufnahme*, awkward juxtapositions and changes in vocabulary. Throughout, I will use source-criticism as a tool toward understanding the perspectives, dates and proveniences of the chapter's building blocks. Finally, I will attempt to show how and why they were joined together in their current form.

Several repetitions help to suggest the division of the section into its component sources. Three times the text tells us what Israel has done wrong: 7b–12 lists sins related to idolatry, 13–17 lists infractions in general terms (cf. vv. 13 and 15 and such words as "commandments," 'torah/instruction," and "covenant") as well as idolatry and sundry other offences, while vv. 21–2 cite Jeroboam and his sins. There is no obvious narrative reason for the chapter to contain these three different descriptions of sins. Furthermore, the differences in content to some extent correlate with the varied terminology used to refer to the residents of the north: in vv. 7, 8 and 9 they are "the children of Israel,"[51] in vv. 13, 18 and 21 they are "Israel,"[52] and in v. 20, they are "all the descendants of Israel."[53] Thus, the combined criteria of repetitions and different names begin to suggest the outlines of four sources: (1) vv. 7–12, which use the term "the children of Israel" and are concerned with general idolatry; (2) vv. 13–18a, which use the term "Israel" and are concerned with general infractions and several specific sins; (3) v. 20, which concerns "all the descendants of Israel"; (4) vv. 21–2, which use the term "Israel," and are concerned with the sin of Jeroboam.

Several verses are unaccounted for in this initial division. In assigning v. 23 to a source, it is noteworthy that it begins with the phrase "until YHWH cast Israel from before his face," which is very similar to the end of v. 20, "until he [YHWH] cast them from before him." This suggests that the phrases form a *Wiederaufnahme*, and v. 23 was the original conclusion of the source which contains v. 20.[54] This observation would indicate that vv. 21–2 were inserted between 20 and 23; this is consistent with the fact that only vv. 21–2 are explicitly concerned with Jeroboam.

The only section which has not yet been assigned is vv. 18b–19. Unlike the rest of the chapter, these verses deal with the sins of Judah and its exile. Though this differs in perspective from the previous sections which concern the north, vv. 18b–19 serve as a good introduction to v. 20, which contains the very general term "all the descendants of Israel." For this reason, vv. 18b–20 should be seen as a unit.[55]

A careful rereading of 2 Kgs 17:7–23 offers other clues that support the proposed source division. The sections reflect different conceptions of the pre-Israelite residents of Canaan, who later became Israel's neighbors. In v. 8 they are called "the nations which YHWH dispossessed before the Children of Israel," and in v. 11 they are called "the nations which YHWH exiled before them." This is only a slight terminological difference, which does not reflect different conceptions of the nations; thus both verses may stem from the same author. In contrast, v. 15 calls the Canaanites "the nations which were around them." Vv. 8 and 11 reflect the notion (found, for example, in Josh 11:10–23) that the conquest of Canaan was complete, while v. 15 (like Exod 23:29–30 and Judg 2:20–3:6) implies an incomplete conquest, where Israel was influenced by the surrounding nations.[56] Vv. 8 and 11 suggest the paradoxical situation where the Children of Israel learn idolatry from their non-existent "dispossessed" (v. 8) or "exiled" (v. 11) neighbors,[57] while the neutral claim of v. 15 ("the nations which were around them") avoids this problem. A further difference should be seen between v. 10, which accuses the Children of Israel of "setting up"[58] *asherim* in the plural, while v. 16 states a similar idea using the word "made"[59] and referring to an *asherah*[60] in the singular. The distribution of these differences matches the source distinctions drawn above.

It is now possible to study each unit separately, and to see the viewpoint that each is professing. Vv. 7–12 (unit D) are a condemnation of "the Children of Israel." The unit's central theme is idolatry or the improper worship of YHWH. As is typical of Deuteronomic literature, it confuses worship of other deities with "improper" worship of YHWH. It contains a central list of illegitimate practices (9b–10aα), which is flanked by general condemnations in 9a and 11b. This central list in 9b–11 reads:

> They built for themselves shrines[61] in all of their cities, from watch-towers to fortified cities, and they set up for themselves pillars and *asherim* on every high hill and under every leafy tree and they offered incense at all high places like the nations whom YHWH had driven out before them.

This list of infractions does not, in fact, typify the sins listed elsewhere of the northern kingdom. Instead, as may be seen below, a substantial section of it matches 1 Kgs 14:23 almost exactly. The identical words are indicated in bold: 2 Kgs 17:10–11aα: "and they set up for themselves **pillars and asherim on every high hill and under every leafy tree** and they burnt food offerings[62] at all **shrines**"; 1 Kgs 14:23: "They indeed built for themselves **shrines and pillars and asherim on every high hill and under every leafy tree.**" There is further agreement between these two contexts. 2 Kgs 17:8a reads "they followed the ways of **the nations whom YHWH dispossessed before the Children of Israel**," which is almost identical to 1 Kgs 14:24, "the abominations of **the nations whom YHWH dispossessed before the Children of Israel.**" These correspondences are too specific to be coincidental.[63] The discovery that 2 Kings 17 is quoting from 1 Kings 14, which deals with Rehoboam, the first Judean king of the divided monarchy, highlights the problem of the identity of "the Children of Israel" in 2 Kgs 17:7–12.[64]

The term, "the Children of Israel" was used to refer to three political entities in ancient Israel: (1) the northern kingdom (e.g. 1 Kgs 19:10, 14; 20:27, 29; 2 Kgs 13:5); (2) the Judeans after the exile of the north (frequently, especially in Ezekiel, Ezra–Nehemiah and [the Deuteronomistic sections of] Jeremiah); and (3) the collective entity of both the south and the north (frequently).[65] Commentators have generally assumed that the children of Israel in 2 Kgs 17:7 refers to the north. This is suggested by context, and by the mention of Israel in vv. 13–18, which clearly refer to the northerners, who "fashioned for themselves two molten calves" (v. 16). However, given the composite nature of this chapter, this argument is of no value.

I would suggest that 2 Kgs 17:7–12 are a misplaced fragment of a speech which justified the exile of Judah. The lack of such a speech in 2 Kings 25, where it would have been expected, has been noted.[66] Such a speech probably did exist, and has been misplaced to 2 Kings 17. In its original context, that speech blamed the exile of Judah on Rehoboam, the first Judean king of the divided monarchy. This created a symmetry between the exile of Judah and that of the North, which was similarly blamed on the cultic sins of its first king, Jeroboam (e.g. 2 Kgs 17:16). It also formed a frame for the history of the divided monarchy, from Rehoboam in 1 Kings 14, to the exile of Judah for the sins of Rehoboam, originally in 2 Kings 25.

There are other examples in Kings of historical material no longer being in its original place. Cogan and Tadmor have suggested that 2 Kgs 15:29 has been moved.[67] I have proposed that 2 Kgs 24:13–14, which now describe the exile of 597, probably originally referred to the exile of 586.[68] The reason for this particular case of displacement in 2 Kings 17 is not obvious. The common usage of "the Children of Israel" for the northern kingdom facilitated its transferal. It is possible that an editor understood 1 Kgs

14:23, said of Rehoboam, as "and they also[69] built," suggesting that Rehoboam followed the ways of Jeroboam and the northern kingdom, narrated
in the immediately preceding pericope.[70] If this is correct, the material has
been moved from 2 Kings 25 to 2 Kings 17 on the basis of interpretation.
This would be similar to the interpretation of the conquest narrative in
Numbers by the Deuteronomist, who used the tradition (Num 12:34) "You
shall do to him [Og] as you did to Sihon, king of the Amorites" to create
more historical details.[71] In sum, although the reasons for the movement
of vv. 7–12 to 2 Kings 17 are not certain, it is likely that they originally
referred to the cultic sins responsible for the exile of the south, and are
incorporated in our chapter secondarily, aided by the incorrect equation
of "the children of Israel" = "Israel" = the northern kingdom.

On thematic grounds, unit E, that is, vv. 13–18a+23, may be divided into
three units: (1) 13–16aα: the covenant infractions by Israel;[72] (2) 16aβ–17:
infractions for which the royal house is (implicitly) responsible; (3) 18a+23:
YHWH's anger and his punishment of Israel through exile.[73] These subunits do not represent separate sources. The first subunit is characterized
by its repetitive style, as seen in 13aα, "every prophet, every seer,"[74] 13aβ,
"and observe my commandments, my laws according to all the instruction," and 15, "his laws and his covenant which he made with their
ancestors and his testimonies with which he charged them." These repetitions in section E1 differ in content and style from D: while D lists
specific misdeeds, E1 refers to covenant violation in general terms, and is
thus similar to certain sections in the prologue and epilogue of Deuteronomy (e.g. 6:17; 10:13; 26:17; 28:15). Furthermore, in section D the Israelites
are portrayed as ingrates, who have forsaken their liberator God (vv. 7–8),[75]
while in section E1, they are condemned in judicial terms for covenant
infractions.

A common biblical notion presumes that the king is the religious leader
of the nation; for this reason, kings are often condemned for non-standard
cultic activities which from the Bible's perspective lead the nation astray.[76]
This is why section E2 lists several practices which may be attributed to
specific northern kings. In v. 16, "a molten image, two calves" refers to the
calves fashioned by Jeroboam, first king of the north (1 Kgs 12:28, 32;
14:9; 2 Kgs 10:29). The fashioning of an *asherah* and worshipping of the
Ba'al may refer to actions committed by many northern kings (1 Kgs
14:15; 15:13; 16:31, 33; 18:18; 22:54; 2 Kgs 13:6). The vocabulary of 2
Kgs 17:17 recalls Ahab. It uses the rare verb *htmkr*, which is found only
four times in the Hebrew Bible; of these, one is in 2 Kgs 17:17, while two
are found in 1 Kgs 21:20 and 25, in reference to Ahab.[77] Thus, in recalling
the sins responsible for the exile of the north, the northern kings Jeroboam
I and Ahab are implicitly singled out. This is consistent with Jeroboam's
depiction elsewhere in the Book of Kings, which frequently refers to "the
sins of Jeroboam," and with 1 Kings 21, the story of Ahab's appropriation

of Naboth's vineyard, which depicts Ahab as a paradigm of evil royal behavior.

However, there are three elements in E2 which are not citations of offences recorded elsewhere of northern kings: (1) v. 16, "they bowed down to all the host of heaven"; (2) v. 17aα, "they passed their sons and daughters through the fire"; and (3) v. 17aβ, "they practiced divination."[78] It is always possible that an author drew upon a tradition concerning the sins of the northern kings which is no longer extant. However, as has been noted by Walter Dietrich,[79] the correspondence between this list and the list of the sins of Manasseh in 2 Kgs 21:5–6 is striking. I juxtapose the two below: 2 Kgs 17:16b–17a: "they bowed down to the **hosts of heaven**[80] . . . **and passed** their **sons** and daughters **through fire and they practiced divination**[81]; 2 Kgs 21:5–6aα: "he built altars to the **hosts of heaven . . . and passed** his **son through fire, and practiced divination**."

The association between the sins of the north and those of Manasseh is also seen by studying the ending formula of E2 (2 Kgs 17:17): "they gave themselves over to do that which is evil in the eyes of YHWH, thereby angering him." This may be seen as a conflation of the Ahab formula of 1 Kgs 21:25 (cf. v. 20): "he gave himself to do evil in the eyes of YHWH" and the Manasseh formula of 2 Kgs 21:6: "he exceeded to do that which was evil in the eyes of YHWH, thereby angering [him]." This raises the strong possibility that some of E2 originates from the list of sins attributed to Manasseh, the Judean king who followed the exile of the north by approximately half a century. But how have the sins of Manasseh found their way into a list recounting the sins responsible for the exile of the north?

There are several elements in the text of Manasseh's sins that could be read as suggesting that they were also perpetrated by the north as well. The text notes explicitly that Manasseh followed in the way of Ahab (2 Kgs 21:3), a northern king. Furthermore, it notes that Manasseh followed (v. 2) "the abominations of the nations whom YHWH dispossessed before the Children of Israel." This is the same notion stated in 2 Kgs 17:8, 11, 15 in relation to the northern kingdom. An author might have reasoned: If the north committed the same sins as the "Canaanite" nations, and Manasseh committed the same sins as the "Canaanite" nations, then the sins of the north are identical to those of Manasseh. Thus, the projection of Manasseh's sins on to the north is likely based on the careful reading of the biblical text.

Blaming the demise of the north on the sins committed by Manasseh is actually quite logical. After all, according to Kings those sins are responsible for the destruction of Judah; it can naturally be assumed that they had the same function for the north. Finally, by noting these sins in 2 Kings 17, in relationship to the north, Manasseh's sins are anticipated, and thus do not seem as innovative or as horrifying when they are later committed again by the Judean Manasseh. This would certainly be consistent with the aims of a Judean author who wrote this section of 2 Kings 17.

Vv. 18b–22, enclosed by the *Wiederaufnahme* in E, are not a single unit. Vv. 18b–20 are explicitly concerned with Judah,[82] while vv. 21–2 explicitly refer to Jeroboam I, the first king of the northern kingdom. V. 21 is difficult; it begins with the word "because," but it lacks the expected protasis. Some scholars have assumed that a protasis which originally preceded this verse was lost.[83] It is preferable, however, to see vv. 21–2 as a gloss that originally followed v. 18a.[84] This produces a smooth text: (18a) "YHWH was very angry with Israel and cast them out from before him (21) because Israel tore away [85] from the Davidic dynasty . . ." If this observation is correct, then vv. 21–2 (unit G) would have been added to 2 Kings 17 before vv. 18b–20 (unit F). As we shall see, this is consistent with the content of the units.

Most of unit G is straightforward: it accuses Israel of being misled[86] by Jeroboam's cultive "reforms."[87] The term "great sin" (v. 21bβ) is used only four other times in the Bible, three of them in reference to the golden calf (Exod 32:21, 30, 31).[88] This makes it clear that Jeroboam's sin of fashioning and worshipping the calves is being singled out in 2 Kgs 17:21b–22. The author of this gloss concluded with "they did not leave it [the sin]," which provides an effective bridge to the following verse, into which this verse was inserted (v. 23): "until YHWH made [them] leave." This is, then, a good illustration of a glossator or editor who is not a hack, but successfully integrates his addition into the main text by using the common biblical pattern of "measure for measure."[89]

The only section in unit G that does not dwell on the sin of the calves is 21a, which is usually translated, "When he [YHWH] had torn Israel from the house of David, they made Jeroboam, the son of Nebat, king."[90] This understanding is supported by a cursory comparison to similar texts, such as 1 Kgs 11:11, concerning the removal of kingship from Solomon, which was symbolized through torn clothing. However, a close examination of the stylistic resemblances between 2 Kgs 17:21a and its supposed parallels suggests an alternative rendering.

Five other contexts refer to the divestiture of kingship through the verb "to rend or tear":[91]

1 Sam 15:28: "Samuel said to him, 'YHWH has torn the kingship of Israel from you today and has given it . . .' "

1 Sam 28:17: "YHWH has done to him just as he had spoken through me; YHWH has torn the kingdom from your hand and has given it . . ."

1 Kgs 11:11–13: "I will certainly tear the kingdom from you and I will give it to your servant; but I will not do this in your lifetime for the

sake of David your father. I will tear it away from your son; however, I will not tear away the entire kingdom . . ."

1 Kgs 11:31: "He said to Jeroboam, 'Take for yourself ten torn pieces, for thus says YHWH, the God of Israel, I am about to tear the kingdom from Solomon, and I will give you ten tribes.' "

1 Kgs 14:8: "I tore the kingdom from the Davidic house and I gave it to you."

All of these contexts explicitly have YHWH as the subject of "to tear." All follow "to tear" with the marker of the defined direct object.[92] All have words for "kingdom,"[93] rather than the noun Israel, as its direct object. In contrast, 2 Kgs 17:21a lacks the direct object marker, lacks a word for "kingdom" and does not have YHWH as the verb's unambiguous subject. These syntactic and semantic differences suggest an alternative rendering for our verse and imply that 2 Kgs 17:21a may not be referring to the same events as 1 Kings 11:11–13, 31 and 14:8.[94]

The correct translation: of 2 Kgs 17:21a is found in the new Jewish Publication Society translation:[95] "For Israel broke away from the house of David, and they made Jeroboam son of Nebat king." Israel is the subject, not the object, of "to tear." This understanding is already suggested by the Targum's rendering,[96] "because the house of Israel separated itself from the house of David," and in the Peshitta's,[97] "because the house of Israel broke away from David." These versions presuppose that *qārac* in the *qal* has the middle-voice sense "to tear oneself away from."[98] This interpretation is also advocated in the commentary by David Altschuler, printed in the Rabbinic Bible as Metzudat David, who glosses the verse, "this means that this happened because all of Israel participated in sin, because they themselves tore away and separated themselves from the house of David, and did not inquire of the LORD."[99] Thus, strong reasons, based on parallel texts and on grammar, indicate why Israel should be read in v. 21 as the subject of "to tear," and not as its object. In contrast, the "traditional" rendering is based on a false analogy to 1 Kgs 11:11 and understands the text in a syntactically unlikely way, ignoring the fact that Israel, the supposed defined direct object of "to tear," is not preceded by the defined direct object marker, as would have been expected. This lack is noteworthy because v. 21 twice elsewhere uses the defined direct object marker, as expected.

I have spent so much time on the correct translation of 2 Kgs 17:21 because its correct meaning reveals an important religio-political concept: the northern kingdom deserved its fate for breaking away from the Davidic monarchy. According to this view, non-Davidic kingship is illegitimate from its inception. This is similar to the ideology of the Books of Judges and Samuel. However, it is in striking contrast to the prophecy of Ahijah (1 Kgs 11:29–39), which offers divine legitimation to the northern kingdom.

In fact, it is very likely that the use of the verb "to tear" in 2 Kings 17 is a deliberate allusion to 1 Kings 11,[100] where it is used of tearing clothes, which is symbolic of the removal of kingship from Solomon. This allusion in 2 Kings 17 polemically subverts the original context in which it was used: in 1 Kings 11 tearing legitimizes the northern kingship, while in 2 Kgs 17:21 it condemns it.

The view that the kingship of the north is illegitimate is stated strongly once earlier in Kings as well: 1 Kgs 12:19 states, "and Israel has rebelled against the house of David until this very day." The use of the verb "to rebel"[101] is significant: it is a treaty term, and indicates that the northern kingdom has rebelled against its overlord, Judah.[102] Although the Book of Kings was edited by a Judean, it typically does not emphasize the illegitimacy of the institution of northern kingship; 1 Kgs 12:19 and 2 Kgs 17:21, which stand strategically at the introduction and termination of northern kingship, are important exceptions to that view.

The view of these two verses is to some extent seconded by the Chronicler. Our conception of the Chronicler's view of the north has been rethought recently, especially by Williamson and Japhet;[103] the Chronicler is no longer seen as polemicizing against the Samaritans of the Second Temple period, whom earlier scholars felt were represented by the northern kingdom. However, a strong anti-northern polemic is found in the speech of Abijah, king of Judah, in 2 Chr 13:4–7:

> Abijah got up on the top of Mount Zemaraim in the hill country of Ephraim, and said, "Listen to me, Jeroboam and all of Israel: You should verily know that YHWH, the God of Israel, has given eternal kingship over Israel to David, to him and his sons as a covenant of salt. However, Jeroboam the son of Nebat, the servant of Solomon son of David, arose and rebelled against his master. He gathered to himself worthless, base people, and they pressed hard against Rehoboam, son of Solomon; Rehoboam was just a youth and fainthearted, and he did not persevere against them."

This text is quite similar in ideology to 2 Kgs 17:21; 2 Chr 13:6b, "he rebelled against his master," is parallel to 2 Kgs 17:21, "because Israel tore away from the house of David." There is nothing in this view of the Chronicler that is dependent on a post-exilic setting; such an ideology of extreme loyalty to David, which recognizes neither the conditional nature of the Davidic covenant nor the prophecy of Ahijah to Jeroboam,[104] is exceptional in Kings, but certainly existed in ancient Israel. It is likely that Kings" predominant attitude of relative tolerance toward a separate northern kingdom did not represent the feelings of many highly loyal Judean courtiers.

The latest section of 2 Kgs 17:7–23 is found in vv. 18b–20.[105] The date of this section is suggested by several factors. Its content, which deals with the exile of Judah, implies that it must have been written after 586. The anthological style of vv. 18b–20, which quote several other biblical texts, is consistent with this later date. For example, v. 19, "did not observe the commandments of YHWH their God," is a conflation of verses found earlier in this chapter, specifically of v. 13, "and observe my commandments," and of v. 16, "and they abandoned all of the commandments of YHWH their God." Furthermore the very awkward syntax of v. 19, "and they followed the norms of Israel [=the north] which they did," is based on the (slightly) less awkward v. 22, "and the Children of Israel followed all of the sins of Jeroboam which he did."[106] Material outside of our chapter is probably used as well; v. 20, "and he despised all of the descendants of Israel," is nearly identical with Jer 31:37, "I too shall despise all of the descendants of Israel because of what they did."[107] In 2 Kgs 17:20, "and he handed them over to people who despoiled them" is found elsewhere only in the cyclical introduction to Judges (2:14), "[YHWH was angry with Israel] and handed them over to those who despoiled them." The exile of Judah is expressed at the end of 2 Kgs 17:20 as, "until he cast them from before him"; similar phrases are used in 2 Kgs 24:20 and Jer 7:15. At the very least, the author of 2 Kgs 17:18b–20 was living in a period when Jeremiah and the latest Deuteronomistic material was written; it is even possible that the person who added these two and a half verses to 2 Kings 17 lived after these texts were authoritative, and borrowed their language.

The reason why this section was added is clear: to the Judean community living after 586, the exile of the north was a relatively unimportant event in comparison with the exile of Judah by Nebuchadnezzar. 2 Kings 17, which referred to the north, was therefore no longer as significant, so someone updated it by making it refer to Judah as well. The language used in this addition in v. 19, "Judah too did not follow the commandments of YHWH their God, and they followed the norms of Israel [=the north] which they did," explicitly compared Judah to the north, enabling the whole chapter to become relevant to the Judean reader. The short addition quite radically reshapes the chapter and its relevance: it is no longer a dry "historical" description of the exile of a close neighbor, but is important for understanding why Judah was exiled in 586.[108]

The historian who added this section also touched up earlier parts of the chapter to anticipate his addition. He added the phrase found in v. 8b, "and the kings of Israel which they did,"[109] as well as "and against Judah" in v. 13. The purpose of the gloss in v. 8b is the same as that of vv. 18b–20 – to suggest that Judah, called "the Children of Israel" in v. 8, followed the ways of the northern kingdom. Such extensive touching up of a chapter by an editor is not the norm in the Book of Kings; in this case, the destruction of Judah was sufficiently traumatic to embolden someone to make these additions.

The glosses added by this editor all create confusion: v. 8b is awkward, the addition of "and against Judah" (v. 13) is unexpected in its context, and vv. 18b–20 destroy the original connection between vv. 18a and 23. But the editor had little choice; it is often difficult to put an addition neatly into a text. The importance of the contents of these additions to the exilic community justified their insertion. This is in some ways analogous to the insertion in Jer 25:26b, "and the king of Sheshakh shall drink after them [= all the other nations]."[110] As is well known, Sheshakh is a cipher for Babylon. Jer 25:26b creates a problem within its chapter, whose subject is a cup of poison passing from country to country, which represents the conquest of much of the ancient world by Babylon. Babylon is the cup; the other nations drink from it. However, at some point, Israel's animosity toward Babylon grew to such an extent that Babylon was added as one of the nations who drank from the cup.[111] Even though the addition of Babylon created an illogical image within the chapter, the anti-Babylon feelings were great enough to foster it. In the same way, the exile of Judah was a significant enough event to cause a major recasting of 2 Kings 17, even though it disrupted the general chronological flow of Kings.

VERSES 24–41

These verses presented a serious problem to many previous interpreters who could not understand how the settlers whom the Assyrians exiled to Samaria could have been condemned for failure to observe the teachings "which YHWH commanded to the children of Jacob, whose name he had changed to Israel" (v. 34). As a result, this unit as a whole was read as an anti-Samaritan polemic, and was frequently attributed to the late exilic or the post-exilic period.[112] A major breakthrough in this unit's interpretation was accomplished when Mordechai Cogan suggested that the words opening v. 34, "until this day" form a *Wiederaufnahme* with the identical words at the end of v. 23.[113] Thus, the reference in v. 34 to non-observance of the law refers to the Israelites in exile, and not to the Samaritans. Consequently, it is no longer necessary to see either v. 34, or the section as a whole, as a post-exilic addition to the chapter.[114]

On formal and thematic grounds, vv. 24–41 should be divided into three sections: (1) vv. 24–33, a description of the non-Israelite settlers in Samaria; (2) vv. 34–40, a description of the Israelites (=northerners) in exile, outside of Samaria; (3) v. 41, a concluding summary.[115] The unit as a whole has one theme which binds the various sections together; who properly observes the norms of the deity? The answer is definitive: the non-Israelites in Samaria do a better job of following these norms than the Israelites who have been exiled from Samaria.

The theme of vv. 24–33 is that the non-Israelite worship in Samaria is a syncretism that at least includes YHWH.[116] These verses contain a progression from v. 25 where "when they at first resided there, they did not fear YHWH" to v. 33, where they are described as "they feared YHWH, and also worshipped their gods." The idea behind this section is that YHWH demands that he be worshipped by all who live in the land of Israel, whether or not they belong to the people of Israel. This is connected to various other texts such as 1 Kgs 8:41–3 and 2 Kings 5, which emphasize the importance and sanctity of the land of Israel, even for non-Israelites. The story in 2 Kings 17 begins quite logically: the people exiled in Samaria did not know the proper norms of worship. As a result, YHWH was angry and punished them with lions.[117] The story suggests that foreign settlers, of their own initiative, realized what the problem was, and arranged instruction in "the norms of the deity of the land" (v. 27). They heeded the words of instruction; the narrative twice narrates that they feared YHWH (vv. 32, 33), and this point is again emphasized in the chapter's concluding summary verse (v. 41).[118]

In contrast, the northern Israelites in exile are characterized by (v. 40) "they did not obey; rather they continued following their old norms." The phrase "to fear YHWH," which was central to the previous section, reappears in vv. 38b–39a: the northerners were told, "Do not fear other deities, rather, you must fear YHWH your God." In contrast to the people resettled in Samaria, the northerners did not uphold this injunction.

Vv. 34–40, which are demarcated as a unit through the inclusion "in accordance with (their) former norm(s),"[119] have certain characteristics which are reminiscent of earlier sections of the chapter. The opening of v. 40, "and they did not heed," is identical to the beginnings of v. 14. Furthermore, the style of the verses is highly repetitive. For example, v. 34 mentions "according to their law and their norm, and their teaching and commandment." V. 37a, "and the laws and norms and the teaching and the commandment which he wrote for you that you should observe to fulfill all the days" is similar in style. This was a style which we earlier saw in vv. 13–17.[120] These shared features further Cogan's suggestion that v. 34 is a continuation of v. 23, since, as we saw earlier, v. 23 was the concluding verse of a unit comprising 13–18a, 23.

A final issue remains concerning the composition of this unit: are vv. 24–33 and 34–40 from the same hand or are they the product of different authors? The two possibilities are allowed by the two different functions that a *Wiederaufnahme* may serve. The first function, which we saw above, is editorial. If the *Wiederaufnahme* of vv. 23 and 34 is redactional, then vv. 24–33 would be later than the surrounding material, and were inserted by an editor who marked the points of insertion with the *Wiederaufnahme*. A second function of the *Wiederaufnahme*, however, is compositional rather than redactional, and is typically used to show that two events are simultaneous.[121] A clear example of this is in Exod 14:22, 29, where the Israelite flight and Egyptian chase are framed by the phrase: "and the waters served as a wall for them at their right and at their left," indicating that the two events were transpiring simultaneously. Similarly, the phrase "until this day" could be seen as suggesting that the foreigners" partial worship of YHWH and the Israelites" improper worship of YHWH were simultaneous actions.

The evidence does not conclusively prove either of these two possibilities, but it is likely that two authors are involved here.[122] On the one hand, there are several phrases that link the two units together. "Norm"[123] is found in vv. 26 (twice), 27, 33, 34 (twice) and 40. "Fearing YHWH" is found in vv. 25, 32, 33 and 35, 36, 37, 38, 39. On the other hand, there are substantial differences between the two units as well. Vv. 34–40, as noted above, are highly repetitive, and also filled with Deuteronomistic language;[124] these features are not as prevalent in vv. 24–33.[125] Furthermore, vv. 24–34 are characterized by an exceptional use of the verb ʿśy, in the sense of "to worship" (vv. 30–2), which is quite possibly an Akkadianism.[126] No similar unusual features are attested to in vv. 34–40. Finally, vv. 24–33 have specific historical information, such as the cities from which the settlers of Samaria originated (v. 24),[127] their deities and some details concerning their worship (vv. 30–1). Even if some of this information is highly corrupt or simply wrong,[128] the mention of specifics contrasts sharply with the generalizations in vv. 34–40.

The evidence thus suggests that vv. 24–33 and 34–40 were likely not written by the same person, though it is possible that the author of vv. 34–40 had a source which described the events narrated in vv. 24–33, and used that source for his own purposes by inserting phrases concerning "norms" and fearing YHWH. This process would explain why the two units share several features, but are not very similar. It is more likely, however, that vv. 24–33 were written later than vv. 34–40, perhaps based on a common source.[129] The list of countries of origin of the people exiled to Samaria might have been known from Assyrian sources.[130] In addition, vv. 24–33 show certain signs of late Hebrew.[131] This makes it likely that vv. 24–33 are later than vv. 34–40, and were written to further denigrate the northerners, by showing that even after the exile, they refused to heed the prophets. If these verses are exilic in origin,[132] they are addressed to the Judeans as well, warning them that it is never too late to repent, and that they must cease behaving like their ancestors. If that is the case, this unit is similar to Jeremiah 44, which reminds the Judeans exiled in Egypt that their ancestors were killed or exiled because they did not heed the prophets (v. 5, "and they did not heed"), and warns them that even in exile, the Judeans who sin may be punished.

The theme of 2 Kings 17:24–41 is then "like father, like son," or to use a biblical image (Ezek 16:44), "like mother, like daughter." Before the exile, the prophets had warned the northerners to heed the teachings and the prophets; but they had not heeded (v. 14). The descendants of this rebellious group continued this failure to heed (v. 40). In contrast, the group exiled to the north did take notice, and added to their national observances the partial observance of YHWH (vv. 24–33). The concluding summary to our chapter states (v. 41) that this partial observance continues – "as their ancestors did, so do they, until this very day." The author of this conclusion has picked up the phrase "until this very day," which was used previously to denigrate the north (vv. 23, 34), and has used it to show the partial religiosity of the non-Israelite settlers in Samaria. Thus, this phrase too, like the words "norms" and the idea "fear of YHWH," becomes a means of comparison, through which the worship of the exiles from the north is deprecated.

THE HISTORIAN AND THE ARCHEOLOGICAL LAYERS

Chapter 2 Kings 17 is so complex that it is necessary to conclude any study of it with a summary of its composition:

A: Vv. 1–2. The standard Deuteronomistic introduction, which incorporates a source that noted that Hoshea was less evil than the northern kings who preceded him. The date of this notice will depend on whether one is inclined to see a single Deuteronomistic redaction of Kings, in which case it derives from the exile, or whether some form of a multiple redaction is likely, in which case it derives from the period of Josiah.

B: Vv. 3–4. A unit of questionable historical accuracy, which describes in stereotypic terms the exile of the north. It contains terms that may be late, and may have been composed in the exile. It is either based on sources or has used standard biblical patterns to fill out the events.

C: Vv. 5–6. A unit depicting the exile of the north by an unnamed Assyrian king. The style of this source as well as the specific information it contains raises the possibility that its author had access to Assyrian royal material.

D: Vv. 7–12. A unit written after 586, which depicts the exile of Judah. Although we cannot be certain, it is possible that several texts which suggest that Judah and the north share the same sins influenced the movement of this unit from the story of Judah's exile (2 Kings 25) to that of the north (2 Kings 17).

E: Vv. 13–18a + 23 + 34–40. The integrity of this unit is suggested by a pair of *Wiederaufnahmen*: the repetition of "and he cast them out from before him" and "until YHWH cast Israel from before his face" in vv. 18a and 23, and of "until this day" in vv. 23 and 34. This unit first describes the covenant infractions of the north in general terms (vv. 13–16aα), and then states specific sins for which the northern kings were responsible (vv. 16aβ–17). These sins share the vocabulary of the description of Manasseh's sins, suggesting that the author has projected Manasseh's sins on to the north. This may be based on suggestions within the biblical text, and makes Judah look less guilty for the sins of its apostate king. The unit then follows the northerners into exile, and notes that even there they continue their abominable behavior. The date of the unit cannot be determined precisely, though it clearly was written after the reign of Manasseh. Although Judeans continued to presume that Israel, in the sense of the north, still existed as a people as late as the exilic prophet Ezekiel,[133] and it is possible that some northerners exiled by the Assyrians actually returned with the Judeans after the conquest of Babylon by Cyrus the Great,[134] this section seems to have the attitude that the north deserved its fate. Therefore, it was likely written before 586, when a similar fate befell Judah.

F: Vv. 18b–20. An addition by an editor who wanted to update the chapter by narrating the destruction of Judah in 586. By claiming that Judah was also guilty of the sins of the north (v. 19b), the chapter was recast, so it would be significant to its Judean, exilic audience. The editor who added these two and a half verses smoothed his additions by adding anticipatory glosses in v. 8b ("and the kings of Israel that they did") and v. 13 ("and against Judah").

G: Vv. 21–2. A unit which originally followed v. 18a, as indicated by its abrupt opening "because." It blames the exile of the north on their establishment of a dynasty which rivals that of David. This ideological argument has both pre- and post-exilic parallels. This passage is later than E, to which it was attached, but is earlier than F.

H: Vv. 24–33, 41. A unit added to highlight the evil behavior of the north. Its author may have had access to some sources concerning the people exiled to Samaria. He recast this material to contrast the non-Israelite people with the northerners: the northerners continue to sin, while the non-Israelite people have heeded the divine word and at least partially adhere to minimal Yahwistic religious practices.

It is impossible to put the units that comprise this chapter into a precise chronological order that would offer a clear history of its development. Among vv. 7–41, which contain reflections on the exile of the north, it is likely that unit E is the earliest. It is probably pre-exilic, though post-Manasseh.[135] This was supplemented with various sections for different reasons. Of these, unit G, vv. 21–2, which suggests that the north was exiled for political reasons, may be pre-exilic. The other units are likely exilic. This is certainly the case for unit D, vv. 7–12, which originally referred to the exile of Judah in 586, and for unit F, vv. 18b–20, which updated and refracted the chapter to focus on the exile of 586. The date of unit H, vv. 24–33, 41, is unclear. It mentions the exile of Babylon (vv. 24, 30), so it must be later than 689;[136] its use of a late biblical Hebrew syntagma may suggest that it is exilic.

In sum, it is likely that five people are responsible for the reflections concerning the exile of the north: two of these (responsible for E and G) probably lived before the exile of 586, while three (responsible for D, F and perhaps H) probably lived during the exile. The dates of the introductory sections A, B and C are uncertain, and depend to some extent on the general dates suggested for the composition of various editions of Kings. If Halpern and Vanderhooft are correct that a first edition of Kings was completed under Hezekiah,[137] and if elements of our chapter date from that time, these reflections encompass a time-period of over a century and a half.

I reiterate that because the reason that the north was exiled was of tremendous ideological importance for the Judeans, the story of the exile of the north acted as a magnet, collecting an unusually large number of traditions and reflections. For some, the exile was connected to religious ideologies, such as improper worship, while according to others, political factors were responsible.[138] Even in political terms, different explanations were offered; vv. 3–4 are interested in the political relationship between Israel and Assyria, while v. 21 concerns that between Israel and the Davidic kings. Different historians, with different agendas, continued to reshape the chapter.

So 2 Kings 17 did not remain a chapter that merely narrated the history of the north. As philosophers of history have emphasized, the present often bears on, or shapes, the past; this is clearly illustrated by the updating of 2 Kings 17 to incorporate the Judean exile, one and half centuries after the northern one. This was deliberately done by adding glosses in vv. 8 and 13, and by composing vv. 18b–20; the attraction of vv. 7–12, which originally dealt with the exile of Judah, may have also been facilitated by the shift of interest to Judah. In addition, it is possible that the final section, vv. 24–41, which emphasizes the partial adherence of the new settlers in the north to Yahwistic norms, and the (implied) abeyance of the lion attacks, could also be read as an encouragement to Judeans to repent.[139] In its final form, the chapter is very concerned with the post-586 Judean community, who felt that the exile of the north was intimately and perhaps typologically connected to their own exile. In the words of Burke O. Long, "the fate of Judah is never very far from [this historian's] consciousness."[140]

Because the text that was being revised was in some sense authoritative, it could not easily be rewritten to create a smooth, unified whole. The process of updating left several seams which allow us to trace the chapter's history. Yet, despite their presence, the chapter is "broadly coherent."[141] The glossator who inserted vv. 21–2 was especially skillful, creating a measure-for-measure pattern between vv. 22 and 23. In contrast, the person who added vv. 18b–20 was less skillful, breaking up the effect-and-cause relationship between vv. 18a and 21. Many literary studies of the Bible have emphasized only the artfully crafted text; a careful study of this chapter's redaction history provides a correction to that model, by showing that in some cases additions created a text that is grammatically and, to most modern readers, aesthetically deficient.

One outcome of this study is to show that much of the material in this chapter was written a good deal later than the events it purports to describe. For example, the religious behavior of the north depicted in vv. 10–11aα, 16b–17a is really a projection of Judean practices, and does not reflect the northern reality at all. This is true not only of vv. 1–2, 7–41, but of vv. 3–6 as well.[142] As a result, the modern historian of ancient Israel should not use 2 Kings 17 in the reconstruction of the political or institutional history of the north.[143] However, the chapter as a whole is a wonderful source that has been vastly underutilized for understanding a different historical issue: the variety of Judean attitudes toward the north.[144] Chapter 2 Kings 17 is a significant ideological document, and should play a major role in the history of Israelite ideologies.

I have just alluded to two features of this chapter which fit into the patterns discussed earlier in this book as central to biblical historical texts: the rhetorical style of the final product and the centrality of ideology. The other two features, typology and interpretation, may also be seen in 2 Kings 17. In vv. 10–11, the sins of the inhabitants of the north are patterned after those of Rehoboam, the first king of Judah; this is a case of re-enactment. In vv. 16b–17, the sins of Manasseh are projected on to the north; this is a case of pre-enactment. This typology serves to diminish the guilt of the Judean Manasseh, and by extension, the people of Judah. In addition, at several junctures, the chapter typologically develops the connections between the exile of the northern kingdom and the later exile of Judah. Finally, through interpretation, the word "also" of 1 Kgs 14:23 might have allowed an attentive historian to attribute the sins of Rehoboam to the northern kingdom. It is possible that interpretation may have suggested that the sins of Manasseh were also committed by the people in the north. Thus, 2 Kings 17 illustrates the major devices used by the ancient Israelite historian to create history.

Finally, the chapter highlights the various senses in which history was "created." Vv. 5–6 create history only in the sense that they select events which likely did occur, and commit them to writing. In contrast, the events in vv. 16b–17, which falsely attribute to the Israelites sins that they never committed, have no basis in reality. Other sections of the chapter fit somewhere in between; we can no longer determine whether they contain relatively accurate depictions of the past, or are invented for ideological or other purposes.

CONCLUSION
The creation of biblical history

Let us learn to live with ambiguity.
> Donald B. Redford, *Egypt, Canaan, and Israel in Ancient Times* (Princeton: Princeton University Press, 1992), 311

The historian Edward Hallett Carr notes, "Study the historian before you begin to study the facts."[1] He continues with an analogy:

> The facts are really not at all like fish on the fishmonger's slab. They are like fish swimming about in a vast and sometimes inaccessible ocean; and what the historian catches will depend, partly on chance, but mainly on what part of the ocean he chooses to fish in and what tackle he chooses to use – these two factors being, of course, determined by the kind of fish he wants to catch.

This is a good description of the modern author of history, who is "swimming" in facts, and whose biases may be discerned.[2] The authors of modern historical works are typically known: we know when they wrote, with whom they have studied, where they taught, and with which political or ideological groups they aligned themselves. This is even true to an extent of some ancient historians – we know that Herodotus wrote *The Histories* and that Thucydides wrote *History of the Peloponnesian War*, there is a scholarly consensus on when these two great historians lived and wrote, and these two classical historians refer to earlier historians whose works they knew. Though we do not have full biographies of Herodotus or Thucydides, we have information that serves as a significant guide toward understanding their works. Furthermore, each work contains an important statement of purpose. Though like any statements outlining an author's goal, these are somewhat suspect, they still may help to guide the reader. In contrast, the biblical historical books are written anonymously and the date of their final composition and of the sources that they have integrated is extensively debated. In addition, no biblical historical book contains a statement of purpose, like that found in Herodotus or Thucydides.

135

For these reasons, many fundamental questions about biblical historical texts remain unresolved. The relationships of biblical historical texts to actual Israelite historical events are certainly quite complex, probably more complex than is suggested by most biblical scholars. Some texts are probably written very close to the events they describe, and reflect authors who did not have a heavy ideological bias or great creative flair, but were interested in what actually transpired. At the opposite end of the spectrum, certain ancient historians lived many centuries after the "events" that they described, and they constructed or created events without recourse to sources.[3] David Damrosch's description of the Deuteronomistic Historian's range of creativity is applicable to ancient Israelite historians in general: "[he] took advantage of 'found' themes, developed implicit connections explicitly, and created themes of his own."[4] To return to Carr's analogy – some ancient biblical historians did not fish in the ocean, but bought fish at the fishmonger's and told others that they themselves had caught it. The Chronicler is a good example of this; as I have shown in Chapter Two, his dominant ideological slant convinced him that the past as recorded in Samuel and Kings was largely incorrect. It is impossible to enter into the mind of these more creative historians – we shall never know whether the Chronicler honestly believed that he was correcting an error in earlier sources, or whether he is more similar to the modern historian writing in a totalitarian regime, attempting to control the ideology of the population, even if it means intentionally distorting what is known to have transpired. In either case, the Chronicler, my starting point, provides an incontrovertible example of the flexibility of the past in the hands of one biblical historian. It is this range of flexibility that I attempt to capture by using the word "creation" in reference to biblical history.[5]

Another issue concerning the Chronicler, however, can be resolved quite confidently, namely why he felt the need to revise the earlier sources. As many scholars have pointed out, the Bible contains several commands to "remember" particular events; in that sense, ancient Israel held history in great esteem.[6] Too many people have been misled by that notion, and have confused it with the belief that the historical records of the Bible are predominantly interested in the actual past and therefore contain an accurate description of it.[7] This issue has been discussed extensively within biblical theology, which has attempted to reconcile the biblical "God who acts" with the critical suggestion that many central actions which the Bible claims of YHWH did not transpire.[8] Yet it is not historical accuracy that the Bible means to emphasize, but what may be learned from the "events" which "transpired" in the past. This point has been perceived with great perspicacity by Yosef Hayim Yerushalmi, who entitled his work on Jewish history and memory *Zakhor*, "remember!" which is taken from the biblical injunctions to remember particular events, such as the enslavement of the Israelites in Egypt (Deut 5:15 and often elsewhere) or the attack of the Amalekites upon the Israelites (Deut 25:17).[9] One passage, "Remember the days of old" (Deut 32:7), even seems to suggest the importance of remembering the past in general. Concerning these passages, Yerushalmi wittily remarks,

> The biblical appeal to remember thus has little to do with curiosity about the past. Israel is told that it must be a kingdom of priests and a holy people; nowhere is it suggested that it become a nation of historians.[10]

This emphasis on recalling and remembering the past, even if it is typically for "theologically-didactic"[11] reasons, makes the Israelite attitude toward the past unique within the ancient Near Eastern world.[12] This was perceived by Bertil Albrektson, whose ground-breaking work *History and the Gods: An Essay on the Idea of Historical Events as Divine Manifestations in the Ancient Near East and in Israel*[13] showed that the Bible was in most of its aspects a typical Near Eastern historical text. Yet, he discerned a fundamental difference concerning "[t]he important rôle that the commemoration of Yhwh's deeds in history plays in Hebrew worship."[14]

There is a danger in a civilization assigning such great importance to the past. Modern works on the nature of historical writing, such as J. H. Plumb's *The Death of the Past*, have noted that the past is often used to serve the present or the future.[15] In the words of Ben Halpern, "memory and history, as constructions of the past, are often more clearly adjusted to what really serves the present than to what may 'really' have happened and cannot in fact be altered."[16] Texts are typically written or reshaped to foster or to overthrow particular perspectives or ideologies. This tendency is especially acute in civilizations or subcultures where historical texts are of fundamental importance, such as ancient Israel or the royal court in Assyria.

A useful analogy to this process may be found in the study of a subcategory of biblical history – genealogies. In some cases, no doubt, genealogies reflect the actual lineage of individuals. However, genealogies also had important social functions in the ancient world, functions which they still serve in many non-Western societies, such as legitimating a particular powerful group or ruler.[17] Within the Bible, for example, we can see how a later author has created a genealogy of the priest Zadok, who according to the Book of Samuel, first served under David. Early sources do not connect Zadok to the line of Aaron the priest; this has allowed for the speculation that he was originally a Jebusite priest in Jerusalem.[18] The Chronicler, however, in an effort to legitimate the Zadokites" role as priests, has made them linear descendants of Aaron, the first high priest (1 Chr 5:29–34). Though it does not reflect historical reality, this genealogy is indistinguishable in form from genealogies which are thought to accurately reflect family relationships.

My analogy again is from Chronicles; perhaps I placed undue emphasis upon that book when I used it as a model for understanding Israelite history in general. This is a fair criticism, but I must point out that there was little choice – there is no other biblical historical text whose method of composition is as well understood. Furthermore, the tendencies seen in Chronicles have their analogues in other ancient historical texts, which often have similar revisionist tendencies. In addition to citing the Chronicler, I have offered analogies from pre-modern history writings outside of Israel to show that the model I am suggesting for ancient Israel is plausible. Certainly other models, such as that of the twentieth-century academic historian, could be used,[19] but the models I have chosen are closer historically and geographically to texts such as Genesis or Kings.[20]

Chronicles does not consistently betray its author's strong ideological imprint. For example, the Chronicler mentions the prophecy of Ahijah of Shiloh addressed to Jeroboam, which legitimates the northern kingship (2 Chr 10:15); this conflicts with the Chronicler's typical lack of interest in the north, and the assertion of many scholars that the Chronicler did not view the northern kings as legitimate. The mention of Ahijah's prophecy in Chronicles should not be terribly surprising, for ancient authors or editors, who used earlier sources, were often not as successful in producing a consistent final product as their best modern counterparts. What is crucial, however, is that Chronicles contains some material from earlier sources, which scholars consider to be historically reliable, mixed in with a substantial amount of material which reflects its author's ideological biases. To the extent that Chronicles is a suitable model, we would expect the same to be true of earlier biblical authors as well, though the proportion of ideologically motivated material versus historically reliable material may differ between various biblical books.

The central problem for the contemporary scholars of biblical history is to distinguish between material which is historically reliable and that which is not. A fundamental difficulty impedes this venture – there is no distinction in form between a work which accurately depicts the past and a work depicting the past that has no historicity. They frequently both look identical, just as the genealogy of Zadok in Chronicles, which is considered specious, is similar in form to that of the kings of Judah, which most scholars accept as accurate. Phrased differently, an ancient author interested in inventing a story showing how David had no involvement in the death of Saul would have used historical language identical to that of an author who was an eyewitness to the "events" of 2 Samuel 1. Thus, the term "history" or "historical/historiographical narrative" should be dropped from the form-critical lexicon, since the form of a text has little bearing on its historicity.[21]

Biblical historical texts reflect a combination of genuine interest in the past, strong ideological beliefs and refined rhetorical devices. Texts such as

2 Kgs 17:4–5 seem to be interested in actual political history, and scholars could use them with some confidence to help reconstruct the political history of the end of the northern kingdom. In contrast, other texts within that same chapter certainly may not be used for reconstructing the history of the northern kingdom. Most texts, however, cannot be so easily pigeon-holed; the extent of the ideological involvement of various authors and editors is difficult to discern with full confidence, and many biblical texts have reached us in heavily edited forms, which may have obscured their earlier relationship to events. Texts may have a historical kernel, but there is no easy way to decide where it may be located and how large it may be – is it the size of a grape seed or an avocado pit? Additionally, it is difficult to know the distance between any event and its literary description in the Bible, although the author's proximity to an event is not a guarantee of his text's facticity.[22]

In certain cases, rhetorical tropes are an intrinsic element in the story's structure, such as the various devices which suggest that the Ehud story in Judges is a work of political satire mocking the Moabites, Irony, scatological reference and animal symbolism typify the work's genre of political satire. In other cases, rhetorical devices do not define a biblical text's genre, but function as embellishments, which likely added to the listeners' pleasure and the text's preservation.

We know little about how and when most biblical historical texts were actually read, though we can be quite certain that the picture presented by Hermann Gunkel of "In the leisure of a winter evening the family sits about the hearth; the grown people, but especially the children, listen to the beautiful old stories"[23] is a naive, incorrect recreation of ancient Israelite life. However, we do know that some historical texts were intended for recitation in cultic settings (e.g. Deut 26:1–15) and within the family (e.g. Deut 6:21), and it is likely that authors who feel that their stories are important will have the good sense to offer them in a pleasing form, so that they will be listened to, remembered and transmitted further. Thus, at a certain point, historical stories may have been shaped for reasons which some scholars have termed literary, a term that I prefer to avoid in reference to the Hebrew Bible.

Additionally, we know little about the forms of textual transmission in ancient Israel and how these may have changed a work through time. There are significant scholarly debates on whether the texts in their current form reflect oral or written transmision.[24] In fact, scholars now speak of a variety of methods for the transmission of oral literature, so even when we speak of a stage of oral transmission, the extent to which this involves changing a work's content or adjusting it to new social and political contexts remains unclear.[25] Finally, as even a cursory study of the Septuagint and the Dead Sea Scrolls reveals, biblical texts continued to be transformed, sometimes in a radical fashion, even after they began to be transmitted in written form, as various copyists took on the role of editors, partaking in the continual creative transformation of the text.

Another issue deserves serious consideration: it is often difficult to know on the basis of a story's form or context whether an author was interested in depicting the actual past or if he was writing a symbolic or typological narrative. The recent administration of Ronald Reagan provides an instructive example: one of President Reagan's press secretaries was named Larry Speakes. One could imagine an overly cautious historian living in the twenty-second century suggesting that this individual never existed, and that he was created by a historian living after Reagan, when the actual name of the press secretary was forgotten. The press secretary was therefore given the symbolic name "Speakes." That historian might even posit that the "e" of Speakes is an archaism, through which the historian betrays a lack of knowledge of twentieth-century spelling conventions. In other words, actual events sometimes look symbolic, or may sometimes approximate earlier events, and thus in reality may look typological. We must therefore remember that, by themselves, typologies or perceived name symbolisms, such as Eglon, the "fatted calf" of Judges 3 who just happens to become a sacrificial victim, are not a *certain* indication that a text may not be used to reconstruct the event that it is purporting to tell. Yet, they are likely pointers in this direction, which can be further corroborated with additional evidence.

So what is the modern historian of ancient Israel to do? One option, of course, is to forget the biblical text, and to base a history of Israel on non-biblical evidence, such as archeology, the Hebrew epigraphic corpus and references to Israel in the texts of its neighbors.[26] Though this has not yet been done, several recent works, including Robert B. Coote's and Keith W. Whitelam's *The Emergence of Early Israel in Historical Perspective*,[27] Niels Peter Lemche's *Ancient Israel: A New History of Israelite Society*[28] and Thomas L. Thompson's *Early History of the Israelite People From the Written and Archaeological Sources*, have moved in this direction. This approach also has its problems, for archeology is rarely unambiguous and typically demands the same types of interpretation as written sources.[29] An important post-biblical example concerns the so-called scriptorium found at Qumran, which was connected to the community which produced the Dead Sea Scrolls, but is now considered by some to be a large dining or reception room of a private villa.[30] While it is true that "*historical* Israel" must be distinguished from "*biblical* Israel,"[31] the biblical text will remain fundamental in reconstructing ancient Israelite history. But given the problems of that text, how should the historian proceed? Before considering that question, it is important to ask why someone is interested in reconstructing the history of Israel.

Modern scholarly histories of Israel are written for two main purposes: in order to understand the place of Israel within the actual history of the ancient Near East or in order to understand better the Hebrew Bible. The second reason has predominated, and it is no accident that many authors of the standard histories of Israel have also written biblical commentaries.[32] Large-scale histories of Israel are not typically written by individuals whose primary training is in general historical method or in ancient Near Eastern history.[33] It should not be surprising, then, that biblical histories show so little agreement with the canons of modern historiography, especially concerning the use of evidence, specifically the evaluation of source material before using it for reconstructing the past.[34] Indeed, the problems of writing ancient Israelite history are fundamentally different from writing the history of much of the rest of the ancient Near East, where we have a wide variety of sources whose dates are clear and whose biases are known. J. A. Brinkman's *A Political History of Post-Kassite Babylonia 1158–722 B.C.*[35] offers a striking contrast to the work of the biblical historian. Brinkman, working on a period covering less than half of that covered in modern biblical histories, has a plethora of sources to deal with – indeed, over thirty pages are needed to enumerate and to briefly evaluate them.[36] If this author had attempted to cover religious and social history as well, like most biblical historians, the available sources would have increased exponentially. The historian of more recent periods, of course, has even more material to work with.[37] In contrast, the biblical historian is working with one major source, the Bible, which is a compilation of texts whose dates of composition are debated, and which is supplemented by few outside sources.[38]

Though the modern historian, applying the standard canons of historical research, may despair of reconstructing the actual Israelite past in the same way that he or she might reconstruct the Egyptian or Mesopotamian past,[39] most biblical exegetes are simply unwilling to give up on the past. Matitiahu Tsevat, in his essay "Israelite History and the Historical Books of the Old Testament," has outlined several reasons why the actual history of Israel is important for the exegete:[40] an understanding of the actual historical background lets us see how the Bible uses its raw historical material, lets us determine whether a unit is fact or fiction and lets us see the constraints within which an author composed a story. These are all issues with which the interpreter would want to engage.

The suggestions of Tsevat are methodologically sound, but often impossible to implement. For example, we cannot know enough about the real David or Saul to see how the biblical authors' accounts relate to the facts. Only in rare circumstances, where we have a multiplicity of biblical and ancient Near Eastern sources which bear on the same event, might the past be reconstructed with some degree of certainty.[41] The obvious example should be the conquest of Judah by Sennacherib and the siege of Jerusalem in 701, which is attested to in several biblical accounts in Kings, Isaiah and Chronicles, as well as several Assyrian inscriptions and reliefs. In such cases, it ought to be possible to triangulate, reaching a likely reconstruction of the event based on careful internal analysis of each source and then balancing these sources against each other. However, even in this case, or phrased more accurately, especially in this case, there have been extensive debates concerning the reconstruction of the events, especially whether there were one or two campaigns by Sennacherib against Judah.[42] Though I am firmly convinced that there was a single campaign, and that scholars who advocate for two campaigns have misrepresented the evidence of biblical and of ancient Near Eastern texts because they are attempting to maintain the historicity of each piece of biblical literature, the debate concerning this issue is very instructive. Most historians would agree that it is best to reconstruct actual history when we have multiple sources bearing on the same event. If biblical scholarship cannot agree concerning the western campaigns of Sennacherib, on which there are multiple sources of various types from each side, and some of these sources may be dated with certainty close to the events that they narrate, it should be no surprise that no consensus has been reached concerning most other events, where there is a much greater paucity of historical material.

As noted above, since the actual history of Israel is important for understanding biblical texts and for biblical theologians, it is unlikely that scholars will despair of reconstructing that history. However, when they reconstruct the history of Israel or Judah, they must be more cautious, and must remember the tentative nature of their reconstructions. In *The Idea of History*, R. G. Collingwood has developed at length the analogy of the historian as detective and jurist.[43] Both historian and jurist evaluate evidence; one fundamental difference is that the court needs a speedy verdict, while the historian may produce a verdict at his or her leisure. I would like to extend the juridical side of Collingwood's metaphor, which I will move from British to American law. Within United States federal (and most state) law, two different types of tests may be used by the jury. Criminal cases are typically decided by unanimity, using the test of "beyond a reasonable doubt," a criterion which is not identical with absolute certainty. In contrast, most civil cases are decided by a majority of jurors, using a less stringent test of "a preponderance of evidence."[44] In some small number of cases, we can reconstruct elements of biblical history "beyond a reasonable doubt." We know, for example, "beyond a reasonable doubt" that Jehoiachin, according to the Bible, the next-to-last king of Judah, was exiled to Babylon in 597, and continued to live there. Our confidence is based on the multiplicity of evidence in various historical and prophetic biblical texts, a reference to the exile in the Babylonian Chronicle and mention of Jehoiachin in a list of Babylonian grain rations.[45] This set of events is exceptional – we cannot reconstruct much biblical history using the more stringent test of "beyond a reasonable doubt." Some non-political events may also be reconstructed "beyond a reasonable doubt"; so, for example, the evidence adduced in Chapter Five concerning the existence of a royal Davidic ideology, which may be bolstered through an analysis of the structure and contents of the Book of Judges,[46] suggests that a royal Davidic ideology did actually exist in ancient Israel. Indeed, given the evidence, we can be more certain of the existence of that ideology than of the existence of David as ruler of a Judean state![47]

More often, however, the evidence from the Bible is not complete enough, or is ambiguous, or has come down to us in a highly reworked form, so we cannot reconstruct the past "beyond a reasonable doubt." We can, however, often reconstruct a possible past by carefully reading the text and balancing various reconstructions against one another using the criterion of "a preponderance of evidence."[48] Often, such an examination will yield different conclusions to different biblical historians who are acting as jurors. For example, two reasonable reconstructions of David's complicity in Saul's death may be justified: one follows the basic outlines of the biblical text, while the other suggests that the biblical story is highly ideological and polemical, and was composed to counter the truth, that David was somehow involved in, or at least approved of, the death of Saul. Each of these reconstructions, which is based on evidence and a different set of premises, may be used as a possible background for understanding the end of 1 Samuel and the beginning of 2 Samuel. The two resulting readings of these chapters, however, would be quite different. The first would speak of the narrative development of the righteous David following the historical reality, while the second would speak of propaganda produced within the royal court that subverted the truth. Given my personal leanings toward skepticism and my interpretation of available evidence, I am sympathetic to the second position. I do, however, recognize that the evidence allows for other conclusions, and does not suggest that my claim may be made "beyond a reasonable doubt." Phrased differently, the evidence which suggests that the exile of Jehoiachin took place in 597 is much more certain that the evidence which suggests that the beginning of 2 Samuel does not narrate events that actually happened in antiquity.

Much of this discussion might seem to depend on the central issue of whether historical objectivity is possible. The issue continues to be debated in almost every journal which concerns itself with the philosophy of history.[49] I am most disposed to the recent position advocated in Lionel Gossman's essay, "The Rationality of History."[50] Gossman has moved away from his earlier position, which was sympathetic to Hayden White, emphasizing the narrative nature of history and the problems that this presents for an objective recreation of the past. Gossman now argues that history cannot be objective in the sense of "ontologically founded," but can be "something like rationally justifiable or defensible, not arbitrary, open to criticism."[51] We cannot, according to this position, be certain that we have recreated the actual past, but at the same time, the past is not totally unrecoverable, and we can bring rational arguments that support or topple particular historical recreations.

This cursory examination concerning the status of biblical historical texts as evidence suggests that biblical exegetes and historians should be more sensitive to the problems of recreating the history of ancient Israel. They should develop more tentative, open-ended readings of biblical texts which take into account various possible historical situations which stand behind a text. This is difficult to accomplish; biblical scholarship has often considered itself to be a science, which aims to be objective. This is now typically disputed. In this post-structuralist, post-modernist scholarly world, few would consider biblical scholarship to be an objective science; indeed, some scholars now question the objectivity of the natural sciences.[52] The analysis of Chronicles with which I began, and the exploration of various biblical historical texts which shows that they are very much like Chronicles, suggests that most biblical texts present serious problems to the historian interested in objectivity.

Because of the special blend of devices used by biblical historians, such as typologies, creative reinterpretations of earlier texts, rhetorical devices and strong ideological shaping of historical texts, the reconstruction of the ancient Israelite past is especially difficult. Some of the devices, like typology, mold events to re-enact or to pre-enact other events, while other devices, such as rhetorical or ideological shaping, may bend earlier texts or traditions to accomplish certain goals. In some cases we do not even know whether the history is meant to be taken literally or is symbolic or didactic. Though modern historians cannot always know whether the biblical historical texts are even attempting to describe the actual past, they must not give up, and must continue to apply the general criteria used by historians to decide which of the alternative reconstructions of the Israelite past best fits the evidence.[53] The evidence is not always univocal; this explains, for example, why the current debate concerning competing reconstructions of such fundamental past events as the sojourn of the Israelites in Egypt or the settlement/conquest of Canaan will continue.[54] On some issues, we may reach a conclusion "beyond a reasonable doubt." More typically, scholars reach a conclusion based on "the preponderance of evidence." Like the civil courts, we must learn to be comfortable with this test for truth, but we must also remember not to overstate our case by confusing such reconstructions, which are often the best we can do, with the certain knowledge of what actually transpired in the past. To repeat the opening words of the chapter, "let us learn to live with ambiguity."

NOTES

INTRODUCTION: THE NEW BIBLICAL HISTORIOGRAPHY

1 This has been recognized in more recent works on biblical historical texts; see Ernst Axel Knauf, "From History to Interpretation," *The Fabric of History: Text, Artifact and Israel's Past*, ed. Diana Vikander Edelman, JSOTSup 127 (Sheffield: Sheffield Academic Press, 1991), 26–64, Gösta W. Ahlström, *The History of Ancient Palestine from the Paleolithic Period to Alexander's Conquest*, JSOTSup 146 (Sheffield: Sheffield Academic Press, 1993), 19–55 ("Introduction"), esp. 53 and Philip R. Davies, *In Search of "Ancient Israel,"* JSOTSup 148 (Sheffield: JSOT Press, 1992), 13, "All story is fiction, and that must include historiography."

2 For a similar approach concerning a different text, see Thomas L. Thompson, *Early History of the Israelite People From the Written and Archaeological Sources*, Studies in the History of the Ancient Near East, 4 (Leiden: E. J. Brill, 1992).

3 K. Lawson Younger, Jr, *Ancient Conquest Accounts: A Study in Ancient Near Eastern and Biblical History Writing*, JSOTSup 98 (Sheffield: Sheffield Academic Press, 1990), 63.

4 Marilyn Robinson Waldman, *Toward a Theory of Historical Narrative: A Case Study in Perso-Islamicate Historiography* (Columbus: Ohio State University Press, 1980), 3–4.

5 For an additional critique of this typical view, see Jacob Neusner, "The Role of History in Judaism: The Initial Definition," *The Christian and Judaic Invention of History*, American Academy of Religion Studies in Religion, 55, ed. Jacob Neusner (Atlanta: Scholars Press, 1990), 233–48, esp. 247.

6 Moshe David Herr, "The Conception of History among the Sages," *Proceedings of the Sixth World Congress of Jewish Studies*, vol. 3 (Jerusalem: World Union of Jewish Studies, 1977), 129–42 (Hebrew). I would like to thank Professor Isaiah Gafni of the Hebrew University in Jerusalem for calling this article to my attention. The older position concerning the centrality of history to the rabbis is defended by Ephraim E. Urbach, "Halakhah and History," *Jews, Greeks and Christians: Religious Cultures in Late Antiquity. Essays in Honor of William David Davies*, ed. Robert Hamerton-Kelly and Robin Scroggs (Leiden: E. J. Brill, 1976), 112–28.

7 It may be found, for example, in *b. Yoma* 5b (מאי דהוה הוה). On the idiom, see Herr, "The Conception of History among the Sages," 140–1, and my forthcoming "Response to Joseph Blenkinsopp, 'Memory, Tradition and the Construction of the Past in Ancient Israel,'" *History and Memory in Jewish*

and Christian Traditions (Notre Dame: University of Notre Dame Press, forthcoming).

8 Herr, "The Conception of History among the Sages," 142. All translations from modern Hebrew are my own.

9 See the schematic study of James Barr, *Judaism – Its Continuity with the Bible*, The Seventh Montefiore Memorial Lecture (Southampton: University of Southampton, 1968).

10 Herr's observations have been applied to biblical studies already by Yair Zakovitch, "Story Versus History," *Proceedings of the Eighth World Congress of Jewish Studies Panel Sessions: Bible Studies and Hebrew Language* (Jerusalem: World Union of Jewish Studies, 1983), 48–9.

11 This term, a reflection of the German *geschichtliche*, was popularized by Hans Frei, *The Eclipse of Biblical Narrative: A Study in Eighteenth and Nineteenth Century Hermeneutics* (New Haven: Yale University Press, 1974).

12 For a different description of the shift from history to historiography, see Thomas L. Thompson, *The Origin Tradition of Ancient Israel: I. The Literary Formation of Genesis and Exodus 1–23*, JSOTSup 55 (Sheffield: Sheffield Academic Press, 1987), esp. 11–24.

13 Thompson, *Early History of the Israelite People*, 1–76.

14 W. L. Wardle, Theodore H. Robinson and H. H. Rowley, "The History of Israel," *Record and Revelation*, ed. H. Wheeler Robinson (Oxford: Oxford University Press, 1938), 110–86.

15 N. H. Snaith, "The Historical Books," *The Old Testament and Modern Studies: A Generation of Discovery and Research*, ed. H. H. Rowley (Oxford: Oxford University Press, 1951), 84–114.

16 J. R. Porter, "Old Testament Historiography," *Tradition and Interpretation*, ed. G. W. Anderson (Oxford: Oxford University Press, 1979), 125–62.

17 Roland de Vaux, *The Bible and the Ancient Near East*, trans. Damian McHugh (Garden City, New York: Doubleday, 1971), 238–51; this article first appeared in French in 1941.

18 Albrecht Alt, *Essays of Old Testament History and Religion*, trans. R. A. Wilson (Garden City, New York: Doubleday, 1967), 311–35; this article was first published in German in 1951.

19 W. Lee Humphrey, "From Tragic Hero to Villain: A Study of the Figure of Saul and the Development of 1 Samuel," *JSOT* 22 (1982), 95–117.

20 Lillian R. Klein, *The Triumph of Irony in the Book of Judges*, JSOTSup 68 (Sheffield: Almond Press, 1989).

21 J. Maxwell Miller and John Hayes, *A History of Ancient Israel and Judah*, Philadelphia: Westminster.

22 *JSOT* 39 (1987), 3–63. The importance of this book and these reviews is also highlighted by Thompson, *Early History of the Israelite People*, 104.

23 *JSOT* 39 (1987), 53–7.

24 Davies, *In Search of "Ancient Israel,"* 11.

25 Gerhard von Rad, "The Beginning of History Writing in Ancient Israel," *The Problem of the Hexateuch and Other Essays* (London: SCM, 1984), 166–204.

26 Von Rad, "The Beginning of History Writing," 176.

27 Von Rad, "The Beginning of History Writing," 166.

28 Walter Brueggemann, *David's Truth in Israel's Imagination and Memory*, Philadelphia: Fortress, 1985, pp. 13–14. Brueggemann's work is not the first to shy away from von Rad's position; cf. Lienhard Deleket, "Tendenz und Theologie der David–Salomo–Erzählung," *Das ferne und das nahe Wort: Festschrift Rost*, BZAW 105 (Berlin: Töpelman, 1967), 26–36, esp. 29 and Ernst Würthwein,

Die Erzählung von der Thronfolge Davids – theologische oder politische Geschichtsschreibung, ThStud 115 (Zürich: Theologischer Verlag, 1974). More recently, see esp. Keith Whitelam, "The Defence of David," *JSOT* 29 (1984), 61–87.

29 On the current interest in ideology, which has replaced recent literary perspectives, see David J. A. Clines, "Possibilities and Priorities of Biblical Interpretation in an International Perspective," *BI* 1 (1993), 82–6.

30 See, for example, A. T. Chapman, *An Introduction to the Pentateuch*, CBC (Cambridge: Cambridge University Press, 1911), which, despite its title, actually concerns itself with the Hexateuch.

31 Reprinted Tübingen: Max Niemeyer, 1967. The first half of this work was translated by various scholars as *The Deuteronomistic History*, JSOTSup 15 (Sheffield: Scholars Press, 1981). The second half of Noth's study concerns the Chronicler, who until recently has played a much less significant role in biblical studies than the Deuteronomistic History. That half appears in English as *The Chronicler's History*, trans. H. G. M. Williamson, JSOTSup 50 (Sheffield: JSOT Press, 1987).

32 Note the work's subtitle: *Die sammelnden und bearbeitenden Geschichtswerke im Alten Testament.*

33 This debate continues. See, for example, the debate concerning the authorship of the last four verses of Kings: Jon D. Levenson, "The Last Four Verses in Kings," *JBL* 103 (1984), 353–61, Christopher Begg, "The Significance of Jehoiachin's Release: A New Proposal," *JSOT* 36 (1986), 49–56 and Bob Becking, "Jehojachin's Amnesty, Salvation for Israel? Notes on 2 Kings 25, 27–30," *Pentateuchal and Deuteronomistic Studies: Papers Read at the XIIIth IOSOT Congress Leuven 1989*, ed. C. Brekelmans and J. Lust (Leuven: Leuven University Press, 1990), 283–93.

34 See the summaries of Richard D. Nelson, *The Double Redaction of the Deuteronomistic History*, JSOTSup 18 (Sheffield: JSOT Press, 1981), Mark A. O'Brien, *The Deuteronomistic History Hypothesis: A Reassessment*, OBO 92 (Freiburg: Universitätsverlag, 1989), Steven L. McKenzie, *The Trouble with Kings: The Composition of the Book of Kings in the Deuteronomistic History*, SVT 42 (Leiden: E. J. Brill, 1991), 1–19, and most recently, Baruch Halpern and David S. Vanderhooft, "The Editions of Kings in the 7th–6th Centuries B.C.E.," *HUCA* 62 (1991), 179–224.

35 For a discussion of additional aspects of Noth's significance in the creation of the new biblical historiography, see Thompson, *Early History of the Israelite People*, 81–2. Stephen Geller (letter of August 1, 1991) has suggested to me that this debate concerning the Deuteronomistic History is symptomatic of the general state of biblical studies in the early 1960s, when the consensus position that was developed and refined in Germany began to fall apart. The dissolution of this consensus opened the field to newer methodologies, such as the literary study of the Bible. For an essay which expresses the attitude toward the disintegration of the standard views, see John Bright, "Modern Study of the Old Testament Literature," *The Bible and the Ancient Near East: Essays in Honor of William Foxwell Albright*, ed. G. Ernest Wright (Winona Lake, IN: Eisenbrauns, 1979 [f.p. 1961]), 13–31. More recently, see Rolf Rendtorff, "Between Historical Criticism and Holistic Interpretation," SVT 40 (Leiden: E. J. Brill 1988), 289–303.

36 *BA* 25 (1962), 66–87, reprinted in *BAReader* 3 (1970), 100–20.

37 See esp. *Palestine in Transition: The Emergence of Ancient Israel*, SWBA 2, ed. David Noel Freedman and David Frank Graf (Sheffield: Almond, 1983),

Niels Peter Lemche, *Early Israel: Anthropological and Historical Studies on the Israelite Society Before the Monarchy*, SVT 37 (Leiden: E. J. Brill, 1985) and Robert B. Coote and Keith Whitelam, *The Emergence of Early Israel in Historical Perspective*, SWBA 5 (Sheffield: Almond Press, 1987). For a summary, see Lowell K. Handy, "The Reconstruction of Jewish History and Jewish-Christian Relations," *SJOT* 1991/1, 11–16.

38 Israel Finkelstein, *Archaeological Discoveries and Biblical Research* (Seattle: University of Washington, 1990), 37–84 and Amihai Mazar, *Archaeology of the Land of the Bible 10,000–586 B.C.E.*, AB (Garden City, New York: Doubleday, 1990), 328–38.

39 *Early History of the Israelite People*, 115.

40 Thompson, *Early History of the Israelite People*, 132.

41 See his *In Search of "Ancient Israel."*

42 For a summary of the "new history" and other contemporary approaches to writing history, see Georg G. Iggers, *New Directions in European Historiography*, revised edition (Middletown, CT: Wesleyan University Press, 1984) and *New Perspectives on Historical Writing*, ed. Peter Burke (University Park, PA: Pennsylvania State University Press, 1992).

43 See, for example, the critique of Miller and Hayes by Fredric R. Brandfon, "Kingship, Culture and '*Longue Durée*,' " *JSOT* 39 (1987), 30–8, and note the new series entitled The Social World of Biblical Antiquity, appearing from Almond.

44 Earlier, history and theology were closely connected, esp. under the influence of Gerhard von Rad. For an American example, see G. Ernest Wright, *God Who Acts: Biblical Theology as Recital*, SBT 8 (London: SCM, 1952). For a general discussion, see Gerhard Hasel, *Old Testament Theology: Basic Issues in the Current Debate* (Grand Rapids, MI: Eerdmans, 1979), 57–75 ("The Question of History, History of Tradition, and Salvation History") and the important comments of Matitiahu Tsevat, "Israelite History and the Historical Books of the Old Testament," *The Meaning of the Book of Job and Other Biblical Studies: Essays on the Literature and Religion of the Hebrew Bible* (New York: Ktav, 1980), 177–83. On the status of the Bible in contemporary American universities, see Bruce Zuckerman, "Choosing Among the Schools: Teaching Old Testament Survey to Undergraduates at a Secular University," *Methodology in the American Teaching of Judaism*, ed. Zev Garber (Lanham, MD: University Press of America, 1986), 91–115 and the essays in *Hebrew Bible or Old Testament? Studying the Bible in Judaism and Christianity*, ed. Roger Brooks and John J. Collins (Notre Dame: University of Notre Dame Press, 1990). The earlier, predominantly theological, approach is captured by Gösta W. Ahlström's *The History of Ancient Palestine from the Paleolithic Period to Alexander's Conquest*, 52:

> The intention of this book has not been to write a theological history of Bible lands. There are already too many of these. My goal has been to try to write a history of ancient Palestine in the same way that the history of any other nation country and all of its people is normally written.

45 Hayden White, *Tropics of Discourse: Essays in Cultural Criticism* (Baltimore: John Hopkins University Press 1978), 121–34.

46 Paul Veyne, *Writing History*, trans. Mina Moore-Rinvolucri (Middletown, CT: Wesleyan University Press, 1984), 31–46.

47 I do not mean to imply, however, that the issues facing modern biblical historians are identical to those encountered by historians of the more recent

past. In studying the history of ancient Israel, the nature of the sources has caused disagreements concerning the basic outlines of the events. The facticity of events such as the exodus, the conquest of Canaan and the reforms of Hezekiah and Josiah have been extensively debated. In contrast, major debates concerning the facticity of major recent events are much less common. On these issues, see the Conclusions below.

48 For a brief summary, see Luis Alonso Schökel, "Some Recent Developments in Old Testament Studies: Trends: The Plurality of Methods, the Priority of Issues," SVT 40 (Leiden: E. J. Brill, 1988), 286–8. Many important articles in this field have been collected in *Beyond Form Criticism: Essays in Old Testament Literary Criticism*, Sources for Biblical and Theological Study 2, ed. Paul R. House (Winona Lake, IN: Eisenbrauns, 1992).

49 *The Bible from Within: The Method of Total Interpretation* (Jerusalem: Magnes, 1984); the first Hebrew edition appeared in 1962.

50 A recent summary of his approach is *A Manual of Hebrew Poetics*, AnBib 11 (Rome: Pontifical Biblical Institute, 1988).

51 See his selected essays: *Hearing and Speaking the Word: Selections from the Works of James Muilenburg*, ed. Thomas F. Best (Chico, CA: Scholars Press, 1984).

52 J. P. Fokkelman, *Narrative Art in Genesis: Specimens of Stylistic and Structural Analysis* (Assen: Van Gorcum, 1975).

53 David Gunn, *King David: Genre and Interpretation*, JSOTSup 6 (Sheffield: JSOT Press, 1978) and *The Fate of King Saul: An Interpretation of a Biblical Story*, JSOTSup 14 (Sheffield: JSOT Press, 1980).

54 Robert Alter, *The Art of Biblical Narrative* (New York: Basic, 1981).

55 To some extent, literary scholars are also beginning to move away from new-critical models and are beginning to explore newer ("post-modernist") approaches to biblical texts, including biblical historical texts; see the collection of essays in J. Cheryl Exum and David J. A. Clines, eds, *The New Literary Criticism and the Hebrew Bible*, JSOTSup 143, (Sheffield: JSOT Press, 1993).

56 Note the summary of Albright's position by his student, David Noel Freedman: "W. F. Albright as an Historian," *The Scholarship of William Foxwell Albright: An Appraisal*, HSS 33, ed. Gus W. Van Beek (Atlanta: Scholars Press, 1989), 30, "In any case, he [Albright] opted for an older and simpler solution: the essential historicity of the biblical narrative going all the way back to patriarchal times." Cf. Handy, "The Reconstruction of Jewish History," 4–6 and the summary and critique of Albright in Thompson, *Early History of the Israelite People*, 11–26. Most recently, see the essays on Albright in *BA* 56 (1993), *Celebrating and Examining W. F. Albright*, esp. Burke O. Long, "Mythic Trope in the Autobiography of William Foxwell Albright," 36–45, which relies heavily on the Albright papers.

57 Other factors might also be considered, especially the role of etiology in biblical historical consciousness. However, it is noteworthy that etiologies have played a diminished role in recent biblical scholarship on historical texts; cf. P. J. van Dyk, "The Function of So-Called Etiological Elements in Narratives," *ZAW* 102 (1990), 19–33 and John van Seters, *Prologue to History: The Yahwist as Historian in Genesis* (Louisville, KY: Westminster/John Knox, 1992), 28–30. An important earlier study which they fail to mention is I. L. Seeligmann, "Aetiological Elements in Biblical Historiography," *Zion* 26 (1961), 141–69 (Hebrew with English summary).

58 John van Seters, *In Search of History: Historiography in the Ancient World*

and the Origins of Biblical History (New Haven: Yale University Press, 1983), 249–353.

59 Charles William Fornara, *The Nature of History in Ancient Greece and Rome* (Berkeley: University of California Press, 1983).

60 T. P. Wiseman, *Clio's Cosmetics: Three Studies in Greco-Roman Literature* (Leicester: Leicester University Press, 1979).

1 DEFINING HISTORY, IDEOLOGY AND LITERATURE

1 Rolf Knierim and Gene M. Tucker, eds, *The Forms of Old Testament Literature* (Grand Rapids, MI: Eerdmans, 1981–).

2 George W. Coats, *Genesis*, FOTL I (Grand Rapids, MI: Eerdmans, 1983), 318. This chapter on definitions was completed before K. Lawson Younger, Jr, *Ancient Conquest Accounts* appeared; it is noteworthy that he too uses Coats" definition as a foil (pp. 31–2).

3 Burke O. Long, *1 Kings*, FOTL IX (Grand Rapids, MI: Eerdmans, 1984), 250–1.

4 Lucien Febvre, *A New Kind of History and Other Essays*, ed. Peter Burke, trans. K. Folca (New York: Harper & Row, 1973), 31, following Marc Bloch.

5 G. J. Renier, *History: Its Purpose and Method* (London: George Allen and Unwin, 1950), 33.

6 Cf. in reference to defining "literature," Murray Krieger, "Literature as Illusion, as Metaphor, as Vision," *What is Literature?*, ed. Paul Hernardi (Bloomington: Indiana University Press, 1978), 182, "In the humanities, after all, definitions should be beginnings only, pointing toward opportunities rather than conclusions which would preclude further work and further uncertainty."

7 Johan Huizinga, "A Definition of the Concept of History," *Philosophy and History: Essays Presented to Ernst Cassirer*, ed. Raymond Klibansky and H. J. Paton (Gloucester, MA: Peter Smith, 1975 [f.p. 1936]), 1–4.

8 For such a discussion, see Gerald A. Press, *The Development of the Idea of History in Antiquity* (Kingston: McGill–Queen's University Press, 1982); for a short survey, see *idem*, "History and the Development of the Idea of History in Antiquity," *H and T* 16 (1977), 280–96.

9 John Barton, *Reading the Old Testament: Method in Biblical Study* (Philadelphia: Westminster, 1984), 205.

10 Contrast the following comment by Edward L. Greenstein, "Biblical Studies in a State," *The State of Jewish Studies*, ed. Shaye J. D. Cohen and Edward L. Greenstein (Detroit: Wayne State University Press, 1990), 37, "The effect of recognizing that all scholarship relies on theories and methods that come and go, and that modern critical approaches are no more or less than our own midrash, places us, if we are informed and responsible, on the same footing as our predecessors."

11 Jon D. Levenson, "Response [to Edward Greenstein]," *The State of Jewish Studies*, ed. Shaye J. D. Cohen and Edward L. Greenstein (Detroit: Wayne State University Press, 1990), 53.

12 Quoted from Fritz Stern, ed., *The Varieties of History from Voltaire to the Present* (New York: Vantage, 1973 [f.p. 1956]), 198.

13 For a survey of these and other new methods, see Geoffrey Barraclough, *Main Trends in History* (New York: Holmes and Meier, 1978) and the works cited above, p. 148, n. 42.

14 For a survey of some of the more important definitions, see Paul Veyne,

Writing History: Essay on Epistemology, trans. Mina Moore-Rinvolucri (Middletown, CT: Wesleyan University Press, 1984 [f.p. 1971]), 58–9.

15 R. G. Collingwood, *The Idea of History* (Oxford: Oxford University Press, 1956), 9–10.

16 Collingwood, *The Idea of History*, 17–20.

17 Collingwood, *The Idea of History*, 11–17. His discussion of Mesopotamian texts is especially problematic, since he uses the *Enuma Elish*, commonly called the Mesopotamian Creation Epic, as his main text (15–16). This is usually characterized as a myth or as an epic. A discussion of the Assyrian annals or the various Babylonian chronicles would have been much more apposite. Collingwood is not alone in treating the Greeks as the first historians, while ignoring Semitic and Chinese historiography; for a more recent example, see Ernst Breisach, *Historiography: Ancient, Medieval, and Modern* (Chicago: University of Chicago Press, 1983). Some scholars such as Herbert Butterfield, *The Origins of History* (New York: Basic, 1981) are more inclusive.

18 Thomas E. J. Wiedemann, "Review of Charles William Fornara, *The Nature of History in Ancient Greece and Rome*," *Journal of Roman Studies* 75 (1985), 308, "The crucial difference between modern and ancient historiography, the existence of salaried professionals in universities and research institutes, is not discussed." See M. I. Finley, *Ancient History: Evidence and Models* (New York: Viking, 1986), 14, "We start from the wrong premise by assuming that Greeks and Romans looked upon the study and writing of history essentially as we do."

19 Finley, *Ancient History*, 9. Cf. C. R. Ligota, " 'This Story is not True.' Fact and Fiction in Antiquity," *Journal of the Warburg and Courtauld Institutes* 45 (1982), 1–13.

20 J. A. S. Evans, "Father of History or Father of Lies; The Reputation of Herodotus," *The Classical Journal* 64 (1968), 11.

21 See most recently Donald Lateiner, *The Historical Method of Herodotus* (Toronto: University of Toronto Press, 1989); for a study of the varying reputation of Herodotus, see Arnaldo Momigliano, "The Place of Herodotus in the History of Historiography," *History* 43 (1958), 1–13 and Evans, "Father of History or Father of Lies," 11–17.

22 For a summary, see W. R. Cronner, "A Post Modernist Thucydides?" *Classical Journal* 72 (1977), 289–98, and more recently, *idem*, "Narrative Discourse in Thucydides," *The Greek Historian: Literature and History. Papers Presented to A. E. Raubitschek* (Stanford: Anma Libri, 1985), 2–3.

23 Virginia J. Hunter, *Thucydides the Artful Reporter* (Toronto: Hakkert, 1973), 177.

24 *Past and Process in Herodotus and Thucydides* (Princeton: Princeton University Press, 1982), 103.

25 Emilio Gabba, "True History and False History in Classical Antiquity," *Journal of Roman Studies* 71 (1981), 50 notes that Thucydides and Polybius were "untypical and exceptional."

26 A similar point is made with reference to medieval historiography by Yosef Hayim Yerushalmi, "Clio and the Jews: Reflections on Jewish Historiography in the Sixteenth Century," *PAAJR* 46–7 [Jubilee Volume] (1979–80), 608–9. Note esp. 609, "Clearly, however, such approaches merely enable one to dismiss almost any medieval historical work, and thus preclude any discussion at the very outset."

27 John van Seters, *In Search of History: Historiography in the Ancient World and the Origins of Biblical History* (New Haven: Yale University Press, 1983).

28 Contrast other general surveys of history writing, such as James Westfall Thompson, *A History of Historical Writing*, vol. 1 (New York: Macmillan, 1942), which remarkably lack a clear definition of the genre that they are describing.

29 "A Definition of the Concept of History," 1–10; the complete definition is on p. 9.

30 Indeed, some reviewers have noted that van Seters does not fully adhere to the definition of Huizinga; see for example J. W. Rogerson in *JTS* 37 (1986) 453 and K. Lawson Younger, Jr, *Ancient Conquest Accounts: A Study in Ancient Near Eastern and Biblical History Writing*, JSOTSup 98 (Sheffield: Sheffield Academic Press, 1990), 26–31.

31 "A Definition of the Concept of History," 6.

32 For a similar reason, I object to the definition of Younger, *Ancient Conquest Accounts*, 35–46, who sees history as "a committedly true account which imposes form on the actions of men in the past" (36). See Alan Cooper, "On Reading the Bible Critically and Otherwise," *The Future of Biblical Studies: The Hebrew Scriptures*, ed. Richard Elliott Friedman and H. G. M. Williamson (Atlanta: Scholars Press, 1987), 66, who censures biblical scholars" obsession with historicity: "the idea that either the meaning of the Bible or its truth depends on its historical accuracy is probably the silliest manifestation of historical criticism."

33 William W. Hallo, "Biblical History and Its Near Eastern Studies: The Contextual Approach," *Scripture in Context: Essays on the Comparative Method*, Pittsburgh Theological Monograph Series 34, ed. Carl D. Evans, William W. Hallo and John B. White (Pittsburgh: Pickwick Press, 1980), 1–26, also uses Huizinga's definition, but he slants it by over-emphasizing the words "to itself," thus exaggerating Huizinga's understanding of the subjectivity in history.

34 Baruch Halpern, *The First Historians: The Hebrew Bible and History* (San Francisco: Harper & Row, 1988).

35 Halpern, *The First Historians*, 8.

36 Halpern, *The First Historians*, 8.

37 Halpern, *The First Historians, passim.*

38 Halpern, *The First Historians*, 12.

39 Halpern, *The First Historians*, 12.

40 H. G. M. Williamson, *1 and 2 Chronicles*, NCBC (London: Marshall Morgan and Scott, 1982), 17–24.

41 Richard H. Moye, "Thucydides' 'Great War': The Fiction in Scientific History," *Clio* 19 (1990), 162, "the novelist intends to present a story that, however fully based on a historical reality, nevertheless proclaims itself a fiction – a product of an individual imagination – while the historian intends to present a story based solely on a historical past. But authorial intentions are, finally, impossible to prove, if not ultimately irrelevant to the reader's understanding."

42 W. K. Wimsatt and Monroe C. Beardsley, "Genesis: A Fallacy Revisited," *On Literary Intention*, ed. D. Newton-de Molina (Edinburgh: Edinburgh University Press, 1976), 136. This represents a modification of their classical statement in "The Intentional Fallacy," *The Verbal Icon: Studies in the Meaning of Poetry* (Kentucky: University of Kentucky Press, 1954), 3–18. The entire volume edited by Newton-de Molina contains useful perspectives on the problems of literary intentionality. A summary may be found in Annabel Patterson, "Intention," *Critical Terms for Literary Study*, ed. Frank Lentricchia and Thomas McLaughlin (Chicago: University of Chicago Press, 1990), 135–46.

43 This is a modification of the definition proposed by Herbert Chanan Brichto, *Toward a Grammar of Biblical Poetics: Tales of the Prophets* (Oxford: Oxford University Press, 1992), 23, "a narrative about the past." See his discussion on 22–5. Brichto's formulation might be misconstrued as referring to narratives that tell something about the real past, implying a certain degree of facticity for historical narratives. In this study, I generally avoid the term "historiography," preferring instead to use "history" or "historical narratives." I concur with the scholars such as R. J. Shafer, *A Guide to Historical Method* (Homewood, IL: Dorsey, 1969), 2–3, Harry Ritter, *Dictionary of Concepts in History* (New York: Greenwood, 1986), 193 and Jacques Barzun and Henry F. Graf, *The Modern Researcher*, fourth edition (San Diego: Harcourt Brace Jovanovich, 1985), 46–9, who use "history" to refer to both the events of the past and the record of these events. Using "history" and "historiography" as distinct terms may incorrectly imply that the actual events are perceived in some objective way that "historiographers" either consciously or subconsciously bend or pervert. But this is not the case; as noted by Oscar Handlin, *Truth in History* (Cambridge, MA: Belknap, 1979), 405–6: "History is not the past, any more than biology is life, or physics, matter. History is the distillation of evidence surviving from the past."

44 Matitiahu Tsevat, "Israelite History and the Historical Books of the Old Testament," *The Meaning of the Book of Job and Other Biblical Studies: Essays on the Literature and Religion of the Hebrew Bible* (New York: Ktar, 1980), 184. This raises the question concerning the relationship between myth and history. For various opinions see William H. McNeill, "Mythistory, or Truth, Myth, History, and Historians," *American Historical Review* 91 (1961), 1–10, M. I. Finley, *The Use and Abuse of History* (London: Chatto and Windus, 1975), 11–33 ("Myth, Memory and History"), J. J. M. Roberts, "Myth *Versus* History," *CBQ* 38 (1976), 1–13, Peter Muntz, *The Shapes of Time: A New Look at the Philosophy of History* (Middletown, CT: Wesleyan University Press, 1977), esp. 113–50, Hayden White, "The Historical Text as Literary Artifact," *The Writing of History: Literary Form and Historical Understanding*, ed. Robert H. Canary and Henry Kozicki (Madison, WI: University of Wisconsin Press, 1978), 45–6, Jonathan D. Hill, ed., *Rethinking History and Myth: Indigenous South American Perspectives on the Past* (Urbana, IL: University of Illinois Press, 1988), Lionel Gossman, *Between History and Literature* (Cambridge, MA: Harvard University Press, 1990), 250–3 (on Barthes), Jeremy Hughes, *Secrets of the Times: Myth and History in Biblical Chronology*, JSOT-Sup 66 (Sheffield: Sheffield Academic Press, 1990), Richard Moye, "In the Beginning: Myth and History in Genesis and Exodus," *JBL* 109 (1990), 577–98, Joseph Mali, "Jacob Burckhardt: Myth, History and Mythistory," *History & Memory* 3 (1991), 86–118 and John van Seters, *Prologue to History: The Yahwist as Historian in Genesis* (Louisville, KY: Westminster/John Knox, 1992), esp. 20–5. The comments of Eric Voegelin, *Order and History, Vol. 1: Israel and Revelation* (Baton Rouge: Louisiana State University Press, 1986), 124 are especially insightful: "the paradigmatic narrative is, in the historical form, the equivalent of myth in the cosmological form."

45 Susan Rubin Suleiman, *Authoritarian Fictions: The Ideological Novel As a Literary Genre* (New York: Columbia University Press, 1983), 1. Cf. Walter Carlsnaes, *The Concept of Ideology and Political Analysis: A Critical Examination of Its Usage by Marx, Lenin and Mannheim*, Contribution in Philosophy, 17 (Westport, CT: Greenwood, 1981), 235, "It is obvious that historically the meaning of 'ideology' has had a troublesome journey, one during which

the only constant factor seems to have been its chameleonlike change of coloration."

46 Clifford Geertz, *The Interpretation of Cultures* (New York: Basic, 1973), 193 (from "Ideology as a Cultural System").

47 See, for example, Joseph S. Roucek, "A History of the Concept of Ideology," *JHI* 5 (1944), 479 and Ben Halpern, " 'Myth' and 'Ideology' in Modern Usage," *H and T* 1 (1960–1), 131. In relation to biblical texts, see David M. Gunn and Danna Nolan Fewell, *Narrative in the Hebrew Bible* (Oxford: Oxford University Press, 1993), 190.

48 Raymond Williams, *Marxism and Literature* (Oxford: Oxford University Press, 1977), 55. This derogatory use helps to explain the end of ideology debate in the 1960s; see Chaim I. Waxman, ed., *The End of Ideology Debate* (New York: Funk and Wagnalls, 1968) and M. Rejai, ed., *Decline of Ideology?* (Chicago: Aldine, 1971).

49 See Williams, *Marxism and Literature*; for a short summary, see Mostafa Rejai, "Ideology," *Dictionary of the History of Ideas* (New York: Scribners, 1973), 554. For antecedents for this usage by Marx, see the discussions in Arne Naess, Jens A. Christopherson and Kjell Kvalø, *Democracy, Ideology and Objectivity: Studies in the Semantics and Cognitive Analysis of Ideological Controversy* (Oslo: Oslo University Press, 1956), 151–2 and Paul Ricoeur, *Lectures on Ideology and Utopia*, ed. George H. Taylor (New York: Columbia University Press, 1986), 3–4.

50 For brief summaries of the early use of the term, see Arne Naess *et al.*, *Democracy, Ideology and Objectivity*, 148–53, Martin Seliger, *The Marxist Conception of Ideology: A Critical Essay* (Cambridge: Cambridge University Press, 1977), 13–19 and *Ideology and Modern Culture* (Stanford: Stanford University Press, 1990), 29–33.

51 See similarly, Karl Mannheim, *Ideology and Utopia: An Introduction to the Sociology of Knowledge*, trans. Louis Wirth and Edward Shils (New York: Harcourt, Brace and World, n.d. [1936]), 55. For an exception, see John B. Thompson, *Studies in the Theory of Ideology* (Berkeley: University of California Press, 1984) and *Ideology and Modern Culture: A Critical Social Theory in the Era of Mass Communication* (Cambridge: Polity, 1990), who believes that it is desirable to use ideology in what he calls its "critical" (rather than its "neutral") sense. For general surveys of the term's use through the early 1960s, see George Lichtheim, "The Concept of Ideology," *H and T* 4 (1964–5), 164–95; see more recently Jorge Larrain, *The Concept of Ideology* (Athens, GA: University of Georgia Press, 1979); he makes the important point that scholars had actually studied ideology in a time prior to the use of the term (pp. 17–28).

52 See, for example, Edward Shils, *The Constitution of Society* (Chicago: University of Chicago Press, 1982), 202. He would use the term "outlook" to refer to what others call "ideology." Similarly, see the definition of Talcott Parsons, *The Social System* (Glencoe, IL: Free Press of Glencoe, 1951), 349.

53 See for example Edward Shils, "Ideology," 202–3, and "Ideology," *International Encyclopedia of the Social Sciences*, ed. David L. Sills (New York: Macmillan and Free Press, 1968), vol. 7, 66, Talcott Parsons, *The Social System* (Glencoe, IL: Free Press of Glencoe, 1951), 349 and Martin Seliger, *Ideology and Politics* (New York: Free Press, 1976), 119–20.

54 Eric Carlton, *Ideology and Social Order* (London: Routledge & Kegan Paul, 1977).

55 "Ideology," *A Dictionary of the Social Science*, ed. Julius Gould and William L. Kolb (Glencoe, IL: Free Press of Glencoe, 1964), 315.

56 *Ancient Conquest Accounts*, 51; cf. his discussion of ideology on 47–52.

57 George Duby, "Ideologies in Social History," *Constructing the Past: Essays in Historical Methodology*, ed. Jacques Le Goff and Pierre Nora, trans. David Denby *et al.* (Cambridge: Cambridge University Press, 1974), 151–65; the definition appears on 152. See Louis Althusser, *For Marx*, trans. Ben Brewster (New York: Pantheon, 1969), 231. For a discussion of Althusser's use of ideology, see Steven B. Smith, *Reading Althusser: An Essay on Structural Marxism* (Ithaca: Cornell University Press, 1984), 129–40.

58 See, for example, *Assyrian Royal Inscriptions: New Horizons in Literary, Ideological, and Historical Analysis*, ed. F. M. Fales (Rome: Instituto Per L'Oriente, 1981).

59 See, for example, the use of the term throughout Keith Whitelam, "The Defence of David," *JSOT* 29 (1984), 61–87 and more recently, *idem*, "Israelite Kingship: The Royal Ideology and its Opponents," *The World of Ancient Israel: Sociological, Anthropological and Political Perspectives*, ed. R. E. Clements (Cambridge: Cambridge University Press, 1989), 119–39.

60 For the use of the term in conjunction with politics, cf. Colwyn Williamson, "Ideology and the Problem of Knowledge," *Inquiry* 10 (1967), 134, Seliger, *Ideology and Politics*, esp. 15, 103–4 and J. P. Stern, "Literature and Ideology," *Comparative Criticism* 3 (1981), 59. For its use with religion, esp. with Catholicism, note Richard V. Burks, "A Conception of Ideology for Historians," *JHI* 10 (1949), 183–98 and Joseph LaPalombara, "Decline of Ideology: A Dissent and an Interpretation," *The End of Ideology Debate*, ed. Chaim I. Waxman (New York: Funk and Wagnalls, 1968), 320; note the general comments of Carlton, *Ideology and Social Order*, on pp. 36–7, esp. 37, "In short, all religions are ideologies, but not all ideologies are religion." For theology as religious ideology, see Philip Davies, "Do Old Testament Studies Need a Dictionary?" *The Bible in Three Dimensions: Essays in Celebration of Forty Years of Biblical Studies in the University of Sheffield*, JSOTSup 82, ed. David J. A. Clines *et al.* (Sheffield: Sheffield Academic Press, 1990), 53–64, 333. Max Mark, *Modern Ideologies* (New York: St Martin's Press, 1973) treats both political and religious ideologies.

61 See, for example, the definition of Leonard W. Doob, *Public Opinion and Propaganda* (New York: Henry Holt and Co., 1948), 240, "the attempt to affect the personalities and to control the behavior of individuals toward ends considered unscientific or of doubtful value in the society at a particular time."

62 For a brief historical survey, see Oliver Thomson, *Mass Persuasion in History: An Historical Analysis of the Development of Propaganda Techniques* (Edinburgh: Paul Harris, 1977). More detailed material is found in the three-volume set *Propaganda and Communication in World History*, ed. Harold D. Lasswell, Daniel Lerner and Hans Speier (Honolulu: University Press of Hawaii, 1979–80). On the general avoidance of the term "propaganda" in reference to religious texts, see Elisabeth Schüssler Fiorenza, "Miracles, Mission and Apologetics: An Introduction," *Aspects of Religious Propaganda in Judaism and Early Christianity*, ed. Elisabeth Schüssler Fiorenza (Notre Dame: University of Notre Dame Press, 1976), 1–25. The term is used, however, in the major study of Harold D. Lasswell, "The Study and Practice of Propaganda," *Propaganda and Promotional Activities: An Annotated Bibliography*, ed. Harold D. Lasswell, Ralph D. Casey and Bruce Lannes Smith (Chicago: University of Chicago Press, 1969), 6–7 and 20–1 in reference to both religions

and antiquity, and in the context of New Testament studies by Dietr Georgi, "Forms of Religious Propaganda," *Jesus and His Time*, ed. Hans Jürgen Schultz, trans. Brian Watchorn (Philadelphia: Fortress, 1971), 124–31. It is used in a descriptive sense in S. G. F. Brandon, "The Propaganda Factor in Some Ancient Near Eastern Cosmogonies," *Promise and Fulfilment: Essays Presented to S. H. Hooke*, ed. F. F. Bruce (Edinburgh: T & T Clark, 1963), 20–35. A relatively recent study that uses the term non-judgementally about Mesopotamia is *Power and Propaganda: A Symposium on Ancient Empires*, Mesopotamia 7, ed. Mogens Trolle Larsen (Copenhagen: Akademisk Forlag, 1979). It is used neutrally in biblical scholarship by Keith Whitelam, "The Defence of David," and "The Symbols of Power: Aspects of Royal Propaganda in the United Monarchy," *BA* 49 (1986), 166–73.

63 See J. A. C. Brown, *Techniques of Persuasion: From Propaganda to Brainwashing* (Harmondsworth: Penguin, 1963), 10–11 and Harold D. Lasswell, "The Study and Practice of Propaganda," *Propaganda and Promotional Activities: An Annotated Bibliography*, ed. Harold D. Lasswell, Ralph D. Casey and Bruce Lannes Smith (Chicago: University of Chicago Press, 1969), 6; the Catholic Church has had a "College of Propaganda" since 1622.

64 A. P. Foulkes, *Literature and Propaganda* (London: Methuen, 1983), 8.

65 Oliver Thomson, *Mass Persuasion in History*, 4, "In reality, it is hard to find any piece of communication which is totally devoid of propaganda content or intention."

66 Jacques Ellul, *Propaganda: The Formation of Men's Attitudes*, trans. Konrad Kellen and Jean Lerner (New York: Knopf, 1965), 138; the quotation is from p. 166.

67 Harold D. Lasswell, *Propaganda Technique in World War I* (Cambridge, MA: M.I.T. Press, 1971 [f.p. 1927]), 14, 219.

68 This definition is my own, but is based on several studies of propaganda in antiquity, including George N. Gordon, "Aristotle as a Modern Propagandist," *Communication Arts in the Ancient World*, ed. Eric A. Havelock and Jackson P. Hershbell (New York: Hastings House, 1978), 56, Michael Balfour, *Propaganda in War 1939–1945: Organisations, Policies and Publics in Britain and Germany* (London: Routledge & Kegan Paul, 1979) and Harold D. Lasswell in the introduction to *Propaganda and Communication in World History: Vol 1: The Symbolic Instrument in Early Times*, ed. Harold D. Lasswell, Daniel Lerner and Hans Speier, 4.

69 "Symbols of Power," 166, "Propaganda is defined here as the process by which a particular worldview (ideology) is disseminated to a specific audience." See his "The Defence of David," *passim*.

70 "History and Ideology in Talmudic Narrative," *Approaches to Ancient Judaism, Vol IV: Studies in Liturgy, Exegesis, and Talmudic Narrative*, ed. William Scott Green (Chico, CA: Scholars Press, 1983), 159–71, esp. 159, "I wish instead to examine these stories as ideological propaganda."

71 Irene Winter, "Royal Rhetoric and the Development of Historical Narrative in Neo-Assyrian Reliefs," *Studies in Visual Communication* 7/2 (Spring 1981), 22.

72 *Propaganda*, esp. 63,

> Propaganda as it is traditionally known implies an attempt to spread an ideology through the mass media of communication in order to lead the public to accept some political or economic structure or to participate in some action. . . . Ideology is disseminated for the purpose of making various politica! acts acceptable to the people.

Note also 194, "Propaganda appears – spontaneously or in an organized fashion – as a means of spreading an ideology beyond the borders of a group or of fortifying it within the group."

73 The connection is made explicitly in the title of B. S. Murty, *Propaganda and World Public Order: The Legal Regulation of the Ideological Instrument of Coercion* (New Haven: Yale University Press, 1968).

74 The full title is *The Literary Study of The Bible: An Account of the Leading Forms of Literature Represented in the Sacred Writings Intended for English Readers* (Boston: A. C. Heath, 1899 [f.p. 1895]).

75 For a summary, see *What Remains of the Old Testament*, trans. A. K. Dallas (New York: Macmillan, 1928), 59–68 ("Fundamental Problems of Hebrew Literary History"). For an interesting set of essays which show the early literary study of Samuel, a historical book, see David M. Gunn, ed., *Narrative and Novella in Samuel: Studies by Hugo Gressmann and Other Scholars 1906–1923*, trans. David E. Orton, JSOTSup 116 (Sheffield: Almond Press, 1991).

76 *The Art of Biblical Narrative* (New York: Basic, 1981), *The Art of Biblical Poetry* (New York: Basic, 1985) and *The World of Biblical Literature* (New York: Basic, 1992). In addition, *The Pleasures of Reading in an Ideological Age* (New York: Simon and Shuster, 1989) provides many illustrative examples from the Bible.

77 *The Great Code: The Bible and Literature* (New York: Harcourt Brace Jovanovich, 1982) and *Words with Power: Being a Second Study of "The Bible and Literature"* (New York: Harcourt Brace Jovanovich, 1990).

78 *The Poetics of Biblical Narrative: Ideological Literature and the Drama of Reading* (Bloomington, IN: Indiana University Press, 1985).

79 Note the extensive reviews of his *Narrative* book in *JSOT* 27 (1983), 75–117.

80 A good summary may be found in Gunn and Fewell, *Narrative in the Hebrew Bible*.

81 These include Barry Webb, *The Book of Judges: An Integrated Reading*, JSOTSup 46 (Sheffield: JSOT Press, 1987), Lillian R. Klein, *The Triumph of Irony in the Book of Judges*, JSOTSup 68 (Sheffield: Almond Press, 1988), J. P. Fokkelman, *Narrative Art and Poetry in the Books of Samuel* (Assen: Van Gorcum, 1981–), Robert Polzin, *Samuel and the Deuteronomist: A Literary Study of the Deuteronomic History: 1 Samuel* (San Francisco: Harper & Row, 1989), *David and the Deuteronomist: 2 Samuel* (Bloomington, IN: Indiana University Press, 1993), Lyle Eslinger, *Kingship of God in Crisis: A Close Reading of 1 Samuel 1–12* (Sheffield: Almond Press, 1985), Peter Miscall, *1 Samuel: A Literary Reading* (Bloomington, IN: Indiana University Press, 1986) and David Gunn, *The Fate of King Saul: An Interpretation of a Biblical Story*, JSOTSup 14 (Sheffield: JSOT Press, 1980) and *The Story of King David: Genre and Interpretation*, JSOTSup 6 (Sheffield: JSOT Press, 1978).

82 It is unclear why Germany and France remain more committed to the historical-critical method at the expense of literary study. Compare, for example, the literary studies of Judges in the note above to Uwe Becker, *Richterzeit und Königtum: Redaktionsgeschichtliche Studien zum Richterbuch*, BZAW 192 (Berlin: Walter de Gruyter, 1990).

83 James L. Kugel, "On the Bible and Literary Criticism," *Prooftexts* 1 (1981), 217–36 and "Controversy: James Kugel Responds," *Prooftexts* 2 (1982), 328–32.

84 Cf. René Wellek, "Literature and its Cognates," *Dictionary of the History of Ideas*, ed. Philip P. Wiener (New York: Charles Scribner's Sons, 1973), 81–9, which remains the standard survey of the term's history.

85 Wellek, "Literature and its Cognates," 82.

86 Wellek, "Literature and its Cognates," 85.

87 Elias L. Rivers, "Prolegomena Grammatologia: Literature as the Disembodiment of Speech," *What is Literature?* ed. Paul Hernadi (Bloomington, IN: Indiana University Press, 1978), 79–88.

88 Tzvetan Todorov, "The Notion of Literature," *NLH* 5 (1973), 16. Todorov is not alone here; Robert Scholes, *Textual Power: Literary Theory and the Teaching of English* (New Haven, CT: Yale University Press, 1985) considers the distinction between literature and non-literature to be "invidious" (5).

89 The first two approaches are outlined in John M. Ellis, *The Theory of Literary Criticism: A Logical Analysis* (Berkeley: University of California Press, 1974), 26–7.

90 Others consider this type of definition analytic (Charles Altieri, "A Procedural Definition of Literature," *What is Literature?* 68); these definitions are called "Differentiation in Terms of the Internal Organization of the Text" by Jurij Lotman, "The Content and Structure of the Concept of 'Literature,' " *PTL: A Journal for Descriptive Poetics and Theory of Literature* 1 (1976), 341–2.

91 For this distinction, see Todorov, "The Notion of Literature," 6.

92 On the Russian formalists in general, see Victor Erlich, *Russian Formalism: History–Doctrine*, second, revised edition (The Hague: Mouton & Co., 1965). A brief summary is in Ann Jefferson, "Russian Formalism," *Modern Literary Theory: A Comparative Introduction*, ed. Ann Jefferson and David Robey (Totowa, NJ: Barnes & Noble Books, 1982), 16–37. An example of the Prague School approach to our problem may be seen in Paul L. Garvin, ed., *A Prague School Reader on Esthetics, Literary Structure, and Style* (Washington, DC: Georgetown University Press, 1964), esp. 17–30.

93 On the concern of this school predominantly with poetry, see Terry Eagleton, *Literary Theory: An Introduction* (Minneapolis: University of Minnesota Press, 1983), 5–7.

94 Ellis, *Theory of Literary Criticism*, 27–9, Joseph Strelka, "The Literary Work: Its Structure, Unity, and Distinction from Forms of Non-Literary Expression," *What is Literature?* 115–26, esp. 116–20.

95 See, for example, Monroe C. Beardsley, "The Concept of Literature," *Literary Theory and Structure: Essays in Honor of William K. Wimsatt*, ed. Frank Brady et al. (New Haven: Yale University Press, 1973), 23–39.

96 Note the classic article by Morris Weitz, "The Role of Theory in Aesthetics," *Journal of Aesthetics and Art Criticism* 15 (1956), 27–35; see esp. p. 30, "aesthetic theory is a logically vain attempt to define what cannot be defined, to state the necessary and sufficient properties, to conceive the concept of art as closed when its very use reveals and demands its openness." A similar point is made by Stanley E. Fish, "How Ordinary is Ordinary Language?" *NLH* 5 (1973), 52, in relationship to definitions of literature that depend on aesthetics: "All aesthetics, then, are local and conventional rather than universal, reflecting a collective decision as to what will count as literature, a decision that will be in force only so long as a community of readers or believers (it is very much an act of faith) continues to abide by it."

97 René Wellek and Austin Warren, *Theory of Literature* (Harmondsworth: Penguin, 1973), 22.

98 Wellek and Warren, *Theory of Literature*, 22–4.

99 Wellek and Warren, *Theory of Literature*, 27.

100 Cf. Christopher Butler, "What is a Literary Work?" *NLH* 5 (1973), 25, which offers a similar critique of Northrop Frye's definition of literature.

101 Robert Alter, *The Pleasures of Reading in an Ideological Age* (New York: Simon and Shuster, 1989).

102 Alter, *The Pleasures of Reading in an Ideological Age*, 28.

103 Alter, *The Pleasures of Reading in an Ideological Age*, 38.

104 Alter, *The Pleasures of Reading in an Ideological Age*, 48.

105 *Literary Theory*, esp. 1–16. Note also 22, "Literature, in the meaning of the word we have inherited, *is* an ideology. It has the most intimate relations to questions of social powers."

106 *Marxism and Literature*. Cf. Etienne Balibar and Pierre Machery, "On Literature as an Ideological Form," *Untying the Text: A Post-Structuralist Reader*, ed. Robert Young (Boston: Routledge & Kegan Paul, 1981), 70–99; note their reference to "the material function of literature" (p. 86).

107 Williams, *Marxism and Literature*, 48.

108 Ellis, *The Theory of Literary Criticism*, 44; emphasis in original.

109 Cf., for example, Benjamin Harshaw (Hrushovski), "Fictionality and Fields of Reference," *Poetics Today* 5 (1984), 238–9. Note Hayden White, *Tropics of Discourse: Essays in Cultural Criticism* (Baltimore: Johns Hopkins University Press, 1978), 118, "When a great work of historiography or philosophy of history has become outdated, it is *reborn* into art."

110 Ellis, *The Theory of Literary Criticism*, 46.

111 Ellis, *The Theory of Literary Criticism*, 35–42.

112 The importance of audience is especially emphasized by Christopher Butler, "What is a Literary Work?" *NLH* 5 (1973), 17–29 and George McFaden, " 'Literature': A Many-Sided Process," *What is Literature?*, 49–61. Note p. 56, "literature is a canon which consists of those works in language by which a community defines itself through the course of its history," and Richard Ohmann, "The Social Definition of Literature," *What is Literature?* 89–101, esp. p. 90, "In short, the definition of Literature, capital L, is a social process." (This is emphasized to some extent in his earlier, "Speech Acts and the Definition of Literature," *Philosophy and Rhetoric* 4 [1971], 1–19.) Note also Morse Peckham, " 'Literature': Disjunction and Redundancy," *What is Literature?*, 219–30 and Ross Chambers, *Story and Situation: Narrative Seduction and the Power of Fiction*, Theory and History of Literature, 12 (Minneapolis: University of Minnesota Press, 1984), 24,

> My assumption is that the "literary", as a quality of certain texts, is not a characteristic of the texts *as such* but that it is a contextual phenomenon in the sense that it is produced either by the situation in which the texts are read or by the situation that the texts themselves produce as being their appropriate reading situation or – of course – by both.

113 See W. W. Robson, "The Definition of Literature," *The Definition of Literature and Other Essays* (Cambridge: Cambridge University Press, 1982), 12–19 and Norman N. Holland, "Literature as Transaction," *What is Literature?* 206–7. This usage has been noted and criticized by the Marxist critics; cf. Eagleton, *Literary Theory*, and especially Jurij Lotman, "The Content and Structure of the Concept of 'Literature,' " 339–56, esp. 348–54.

114 See, for example, F. E. Sparhott, "On the Possibility of Saying What Literature Is," *What is Literature?* 13–14, E. D. Hirsch, Jr, "What Isn't Literature?" 24–34, esp. 34, "Literature includes any text worthy to be taught to students by teachers of literature, when these texts are not being taught to students in other departments of a school or university."

115 Contrast the attempt of Norman N. Holland, "Literature as Transaction,"

206–18 to define literature on the personal level; cf. esp. 212, "Literature is transacting literarily, that is, through linguistic hypotheses and cultural conventions (such as evaluating and not acting in response) *personally defined.*"

116 This is why, for example, *Gone with the Wind* is not considered literature, as noted by Alvin B. Kernan, "The Idea of Literature," *NLH* 5 (1973), 38.

117 Gerald Graf, *Professing Literature: An Institutional History*, (Chicago: University of Chicago Press, 1987).

118 Indeed, discussions of the definitions of literature frequently discuss the Bible's status as literature; cf., for example, E. D. Hirsch, Jr, "What Isn't Literature?" 27, "Need I call to your attention the fact that a great many persons consider the Bible to be great literature? But I do not think we would find unanimity in the criteria on which this judgement is based." Cf. W. W. Robson, "The Definition of Literature," 7–8.

119 Other scholars, who do not accept the social definition of literature, would contest this point; cf., for example, Monroe Beardsley, "Aesthetic Intentions and Fictive Illocutions," *What is Literature?* 161–77, esp. 161, where he notes that the entity "brontosaurus" existed before the term "brontosaurus" was known. It is significant that Alter, *The Pleasures of Reading in an Ideological Age*, 25–8, who sees the Bible as literature, rejects the social definition, at least as it is developed in its social-ideological form by Eagleton.

120 See, for example, Chapter Five.

121 "Between History and Literature: The Social Production of Israel's Traditions of Origin." *SJOT* 1991/2, 63–6.

122 Many examples of this may be found in Chapter Six.

123 Roland Barthes, "Historical Discourse," *Introduction to Structuralism*, ed. Michael Lane (New York: Basic, 1970), 145–55; Hayden White, *Meta-History: The Historical Imagination in Nineteenth-Century Europe* (Baltimore: Johns Hopkins University Press, 1973), 22–9; Bernard Lewis, *History Remembered, Recovered, Invented* (New York: Simon and Shuster, 1975), esp. 44, 61, 69; J. H. Plumb, *The Death of the Past* (Harmondsworth: Penguin, 1973), 17–50 ("The Sanction of the Past").

124 There is an immense literature on this topic. On the narrative nature of history, see the collected essays of Hayden White, *Tropics of Discourse* and *The Content of the Form: Narrative Discourse and Historical Representation* (Baltimore: Johns Hopkins University Press, 1987), and his *Meta-History*. For a summary of his work, see Lloyd S. Kramer, "Literature, Criticism, and Historical Imagination: The Literary Challenge of Hayden White and Dominick LaCapra," *The New Cultural History*, ed. Lynn Hunt (Berkeley: University of California Press, 1989), 97–128. For a critique of his major book, see *Metahistory: Six Critiques*, H and T Beiheft 19 (Middleton, CT: Wesleyan University Press, 1980); on *The Content of the Form*, see Ann Rigney, "Narrativity and Historical Representation," *Poetics Today* 12 (1991), 591–605. For other scholars' thoughts on the connection between history and narrative, see W. H. Dray, "On the Nature and Role of Narrative in Historiography," *H and T* 10 (1971), 153–71, esp. 153, Dorrit Cohn, "Fictional *versus* Historical Lives: Borderlines and Borderline Cases," *Journal of Narrative Technique* 19 (1989), 3–24, Robert H. Canary and Henry Kozicki, eds, *The Writing of History: Literary Form and Historical Understanding*; John Clive, *Not by Fact Alone: Essays on the Writing and Reading of History* (Boston: Houghton Mifflin, 1989); Lionel Gossman, *Between History and Literature* (Cambridge, MA: Harvard University Press, 1990). Additional studies are found in almost every issue of the journals *H and T* and *Clio*. Most recently, see Bruce Mazlisch,

"The Question of *The Question of Hu*," *H and T* 31 (1992), 143–52, Cushing Strout, "Border Crossing: History, Fiction, and *Dead Certainties*," *H and T* 31 (1992), 153–62. The connection between narrative and history is even recognized by Ranke; see Peter Gay, *Style in History* (New York: Basic, 1974), 63, who notes concerning Ranke, "the shaping hand of the literary artist is never far from the constructive effort of the historian." Maurice Mandelbaum, *The Anatomy of Historical Knowledge* (Baltimore: Johns Hopkins University Press, 1977), esp. 25, is exceptional among modern philosophers of history in downplaying the relationship between history and literature.

125 *Style in History*, 156.

126 *Style in History*, 7.

127 The literature on this is very extensive; for a set of examples, see *The Greek Historians: Literature and History* (Stanford: Anma Libri, 1985).

128 Hunter R. Rawlings III, *The Structure of Thucydides" History* (Princeton: Princeton University Press, 1981), 63.

129 June W. Allison, *Power and Preparedness in Thucydides* (Baltimore: Johns Hopkins University Press, 1989), 8.

130 John T. Kirby, "Narrative Structure and Technique in Thucydides VI-VII," *Classical Antiquity* 2 (1983), 183–211; the quote is from 208.

131 Robert Anchor, "Narrativity and the Transformation of Historical Consciousness," *Clio* 16 (1987), 133–4. This is also a major theme of David Lowenthal, *The Past is a Foreign Country* (Cambridge: Cambridge University Press, 1985), though he subsumes much of this discussion under the rubric of "memory."

132 Finley, *Ancient History*, 4.

133 Charles William Fornara, *The Nature of History in Ancient Greece and Rome* (Berkeley: University of California Press, 1983), 105.

134 The possible continuities between biblical and post-biblical Jewish texts is noted above, p. 146, n. 9, and below, p. 18, n. 19.

135 "History, Story and Collective Memory: Narrativity in Early Ashkenazic Culture," *Prooftexts* 10 (1990), 365–88.

136 *Approaches to Ancient Judaism, Vol. IV: Studies in Liturgy, Exegesis, and Talmudic Narrative*, ed. William Scott Green (Chico, CA: Scholars Press, 1983), 159–71. The quotation is from p. 159.

137 "The Akiban Opposition," *HUCA* 50 (1979), 179–197, "Rabbi Judah I and his Opponents," *JSJ* 12 (1981), 135–72 and "The Politics of Reconciliation: The Education of R. Judah the Prince," *Jewish and Christian Self-Definition, Vol. 2: Aspects of Judaism in the Graeco-Roman Period*, ed. E. P. Sanders, A. I. Baumgarten and Alan Mendelson (Philadelphia: Fortress, 1981), 213–25, 382–91.

138 In Jacob Neusner, ed., *The Christian and Judaic Invention of History* (Atlanta: Scholars Press, 1990), 143–56.

139 The studies cited above are far from comprehensive; on the explicit combination of history, ideology and narrative see additionally, for example, Graham Holderness, *D. H. Lawrence: History, Ideology and Fiction* (Dublin: Gill and Macmillan Humanities Press, 1982).

140 James Barr, "Story and History in Biblical Theology," *JR* 56 (1976), 1–17, John Collins, "The 'Historical Character' of the Old Testament in Recent Biblical Theology," *CBQ* 41 (1979), 185–204, R. J. Coggins, "History and Story in Old Testament Study," *JSOT* 11 (1979), 36–46 and Yair Zakovitch, "Story versus History," *Proceedings of the Eighth World Congress of Jewish Studies: Panel Sessions: Bible Studies and Hebrew Language* (Jerusalem: World Union of Jewish Studies, 1983), 47–60. Cf. Albert Cook, " 'Fiction' and His-

tory in Samuel and Kings," *JSOT* 36 (1986), 27–48. See more recently, Sarah Japhet, " 'History' and 'Literature' in the Persian Period: The Restoration of the Temple," *ScrHier* 33 (1991), 174–88.

141 Harold Fisch, *Poetry with a Purpose: Biblical Poetics and Interpretation* (Bloomington, IN: Indiana University Press, 1988).

142 Sternberg, *The Poetics of Biblical Narrative*, 44.

143 Sternberg, *The Poetics of Biblical Narrative*, 44–8.

144 See the critiques of Sternberg by David M. Gunn, "Reading Right: Reliable and Omniscient Narrator, Omniscient God, and Foolproof Composition in the Hebrew Bible," *The Bible in Three Dimensions*, ed. David J. A. Clines *et al.*, JSOTSup 87 (Sheffield: Sheffield Academic Press, 1990), 53–64, Danna Nolan Fewell and David M. Gunn, "Tipping the Balance: Sternberg's Reader and the Rape of Dinah," *JBL* 110 (1991), 193–211 (with a response by Sternberg, "Biblical Poetics and Sexual Politics: From Reading to Counterreading," *JBL* 111 [1992], 463–88) and esp. Bernard Levinson, "From the Poetics of Biblical Narrative to the Hermeneutics of the Hebrew Bible," *"Not in Heaven": Contemporary Criticism of the Bible*, ed. J. Rosenblatt and J. Sitterson (Bloomington, IN: Indiana University Press, 1991), 129–53.

145 Keith Whitelam, "Between History and Literature," 68.

146 For a sketch of precise correspondences, see my "From the Deuteronomist(s) to the Chronicler: Continuities and Innovations," *Proceedings of the Eleventh World Congress for Jewish Studies: Division A: The Bible and Its World* (Jerusalem: World Union of Jewish Studies, 1994), 83–90.

2 CHRONICLES AS A MODEL FOR BIBLICAL HISTORY

1 The first edition of the Deuteronomistic History was probably written during Josiah's reign, and was completed in Babylon, between 561 and 538. For a survey of opinions, see Richard D. Nelson, *The Double Redaction of the Deuteronomistic History*, JSOTSup 18 (Sheffield: JSOT Press, 1981), 13–28 and Mark A. O'Brien, *The Deuteronomistic History Hypothesis: A Reassessment*, OBO 92 (Göttingen: Vandenhoeck & Ruprecht, 1989), 3–23. An important new study which only covers Kings is Baruch Halpern and David S. Vanderhooft, "The Editions of Kings in the 7th-6th Centuries B.C.E.," *HUCA* 62 (1991), 179–244.

2 Julius Wellhausen, *Prolegomena to the History of Ancient Israel* (Gloucester, MA: Peter Smith, 1973), 171. More recently, Burke O. Long, *1 Kings*, FOTL IX (Grand Rapids, MI: Eerdmans, 1984), 18, tentatively uses Chronicles to elucidate the Deuteronomistic History.

3 I have used Chronicles rather than Ezra–Nehemiah, which is a fundamentally different type of historical work, and does not provide a useful model for understanding the majority of the historical works in the canon. On the different natures of Chronicles and Ezra–Nehemiah, see Shemaryahu Talmon, "Esra–Nehemiah: Historiographie oder Theologie?" *Ernten, was man sät: Festschrift für Klaus Koch zu seinem 65. Geburtstag*, ed. Dwight R. Daniel *et al.* (Neukirchen: Neukirchener Verlag, 1991), 329–56.

4 Wellhausen, *Prolegomena*, 227, in reference to midrash and Chronicles. See Lou H. Silberman, "Wellhausen and Judaism," *Sem* 25 (1982), 75–82, Jon D. Levenson, *The Hebrew Bible, the Old Testament and Historical Criticism: Jews and Christians in Biblical Studies* (Louisville: Westminster/John Knox, 1993), esp. 10–15, 41–2, and Moshe Weinfeld, *Getting at the Roots of Wellhausen's Understanding of the Law of Israel on the 100th Anniversary of the*

Prolegomena (Jerusalem: Institute for Advanced Studies, 1981), 3–15, 25–7. For a valuable survey of this notion and its function among various scholars, see Rolf Rendtorff, "The Image of Postexilic Israel in German Bible Scholarship," *"Sh'arei Talmon": Studies in the Bible, Qumran, and the Ancient Near East Presented to Shemaryahu Talmon*, ed. Michael Fishbane and Emanuel Tov (Winona Lake, IN: Eisenbrauns, 1992), 165–73.

5 A set of extended examples that bears directly on this continuity may be found in Michael Fishbane, *Biblical Interpretation in Ancient Israel* (Oxford: Oxford University Press, 1985), which illustrates aspects of midrashic technique that were previously associated only with rabbinic and post-exilic texts but are also well established in the pre-exilic period.

6 For a summary, see Peter Ackroyd, *Exile and Restoration*, OTL (Philadelphia: Westminster, 1968) and Ralph Klein, *Israel in Exile: A Theological Interpretation*, OBT (Philadelphia: Fortress, 1979).

7 The exact date of the Chronicler has been debated, with scholars variously dating the work from the sixth to the second century, with the clearest evidence pointing to the fourth. For a summary of the evidence, see H. G. M. Williamson, *1 and 2 Chronicles*, NCBC (London: Marshall Morgan & Scott, 1982), 15–17. For a list of opinions, see Isaac Kalimi, *The Book of Chronicles: A Classified Bibliography* (Jerusalem: Simor, 1990), 105–6 (##727–38). The most recent commentary, Sara Japhet, *I and II Chronicles*, OTL (Louisville: Westminster/John Knox, 1993), 23–8, suggests a late fourth-century date. To some extent, its exact date depends on whether the genealogies in 1 Chronicles 1–9 and some other blocks of material are seen as primary or secondary. The compositional relationship between Chronicles, Ezra–Nehemiah and Esdras also affects scholars" dating of the book. (For a summary which disentangles the issues involved, see Peter Ackroyd, "Chronicles–Ezra–Nehemiah: The Concept of Unity," *ZAW* 100 Sup [1988], 189–201 [reprinted in his *The Chronicler in His Age*, JSOTSup 101 (Sheffield: Sheffield University Press, 1991), 344–59]. For the history of scholarship, see Kalimi, *The Book of Chronicles . . . Bibliography*, 72–4 (##363–89), to which Japhet, *I and II Chronicles*, 3–5 should now be added.)

8 These include Ezra–Nehemiah, Esther and the post-exilic prophets Haggai, Zechariah and Malachi.

9 I use the word "Chronicler" for the author of Chronicles only. I am convinced by the arguments that Chronicles was composed by a single person (though it may contain some later glosses) who is not responsible for writing Ezra–Nehemiah.

10 See now the summary in Japhet, *I and II Chronicles*, 14–19.

11 Howard Macy, "The Sources of the Books of Chronicles: A Reassessment," unpublished Ph.D. dissertation, Harvard University, 1975. Many important observations concerning sources are contained in the older study of Adrien-M. Brunet, "Le Chronist et ses Sources," *RB* 60 (1953), 481–508 and 61 (1954), 349–86.

12 *Ezra Studies* (New York: Ktav, 1970), 227–31.

13 An extreme position may be found in Baruch Halpern, "Sacred History and Ideology: Chronicles" Thematic Structure – Indications of an Earlier Source," *The Creation of Sacred Literature: Composition and Redaction of the Biblical Text*, Near Eastern Studies, 22 (Berkeley: University of California Press, 1981), 35–54. For more moderate positions concerning non-synoptic sources, see the literature referred to in Williamson, *1 and 2 Chronicles*, 19–23. For additional material on the Chronicler's sources, see Sara Japhet, *The Ideology of the Book*

of Chronicles and Its Place in Biblical Thought, BzEATAJ 9, trans. Anna Barbar (Frankfurt: Peter Lang, 1989), 8, n. 25.

14 Williamson, *1 and 2 Chronicles*, 23. Chronicles, however, is not the "last" example of this type of retelling; see the many examples cited in Yosef Hayim Yerushalmi, *Zakhor: Jewish History and Jewish Memory* (Seattle: University of Washington Press, 1982).

15 The debate concerning sources has been complicated by what may be considered "higher critical" and "lower critical" issues. On the level of higher or source criticism, the assumption that the Chronicler had the same edition of Samuel–Kings as we do, has been called into question, especially by Steven L. McKenzie, *The Chronicler's Use of the Deuteronomistic History*, HSM 33 (Atlanta: Scholars Press, 1985). McKenzie has argued that (the original version of) Chronicles was based on the first, Josianic, edition of the Deuteronomistic History, called Dtr[1]. If he is correct, many of the divergences between the Chronicler and his sources actually reflect the fact that the Chronicler had a substantially shorter version of these texts than the one currently extant. (See, however, the critical review of McKenzie's thesis by H. G. M. Williamson in *VT* 37 [1987], 107–14.) On the level of lower criticism, Werner E. Lemke, "The Synoptic Problem in the Chronicler's History," *HTR* 58 (1965), 349–63 has called attention to several cases where Chronicles differs from Samuel, but agrees with 4QSam[a] or with several LXX Samuel manuscripts frequently associated with the Lucianic recension. This suggests that the *Vorlage* of Chronicles was not the recension reflected in the MT, which would be identified by followers of Cross as Babylonian, but rather reflects an old Palestinian text type. (On the three-recension theory, see the articles collected in *Qumran and the History of the Biblical Text*, ed. Frank Moore Cross and Shemaryahu Talmon [Cambridge, MA: Harvard University Press, 1975], esp. those by Albright, Freedman and Cross.) Specifically on the relationship between non-MT Samuel and Chronicles, see Frank Moore Cross, Jr, "The Contribution of the Qumrân Discoveries to the Study of the Biblical Text," *Qumran and the History of the Biblical Text*, ed. Frank Moore Cross and Shemaryahu Talmon, 280. [A list of similarities between the texts may be found in Eugene Charles Ulrich, Jr, *The Qumran Text of Samuel and Josephus*, HSM 19 (Missoula, MT: Scholars Press, 1978), 273.] A valuable critique of this theory is by Matitiahu Tsevat, "Common Sense and Hypothesis in Old Testament Study," *Studies in the Book of Job*, 189–203, Emanuel Tov, "A Modern Textual Outlook on the Qumran Scrolls," *HUCA* 53 [1982], 11–27 and *The Text-Critical Use of the Septuagint in Biblical Research*, Jerusalem Biblical Studies 3 [Jerusalem: Simor, 1981], 253–75.) Thus, many cases of supposed pragmatic changes by the Chronicler actually reflect non-MT readings which were already in the Chronicler's *Vorlage*. Lemke is undoubtedly correct in certain instances, but has probably exaggerated the extent to which the Chronicler follows the Lucianic version of the LXX. Additionally, it is possible that the Lucianic edition of Samuel may reflect a partial assimilation to the text of Chronicles, and thus is not an ancient, independent tradition concerning Samuel which might have been known to the Chronicler. (On such assimilations, see Leslie Allen, *The Greek Chronicles: The Relation of the Septuagint of I and II Chronicles to the Massoretic Text. Part I: The Translator's Crafts*, SVT 25 [1974], 175–218 [Ch. 9: "Assimilation to Parallel Texts."] The whole issue of the relationship between the MT, LXX and 4QSam[a] is probably more complicated than assumed by Lemke; see the recent proposal of Frank H. Polak, "Statistics and Textual Filiation: The Case of 4QSam[a]/LXX (with a Note on

the Text of the Pentateuch)," *Septuagint, Scrolls and Cognate Writings*, SBLSCSS 33, ed. George J. Brooke and Barnabas Lindars [Atlanta: Scholars Press, 1992], 215–55.)

16 For two much more comprehensive studies which emphasize the Chronicler's creativity, see Thomas Willi, *Chronik als Auslegung: Untersuchungen zur literarischen Gestaltung der historischen Überlieferungen Israels*, FRLANT 106 (Göttingen: Vandenhoeck & Ruprecht, 1972) and Peter Welten, *Geschichte und Geschichtsdarstellung in den Chronikbüchern*, WMANT 42 (Neukirchen-Vluyn: Neukirchener Verlag, 1973). An important critique of the latter's methodology is found in Nadav Na'aman, "Pastoral Nomads in the Southwestern Periphery of the Kingdom of Judah in the 9th–8th Centuries B.C.E.," *Zion* 52 (1987), 261–78 (Hebrew with English summary, XI).

17 Others would use the term "proto-canonical." On the newer notions of canon, see James Barr, *Holy Scripture: Canon, Authority, Criticism* (Philadelphia: Westminster Press, 1983), esp. 49–74 and the essays collected in James A. Sanders, *From Sacred Story to Sacred Text: Canon as Paradigm* (Philadelphia: Fortress, 1987). I avoid the terms canonical and proto-canonical at this period, following the strictures of John Barton, *Oracles of God: Perceptions of Ancient Prophecy in Israel After the Exile* (New York: Oxford University Press, 1986). See, however, the important review of this book by R. T. Beckwith, "A Modern Theory of The Old Testament Canon," *VT* 41 (1991), 385–95.

18 Sid Z. Leiman, *The Canonization of Hebrew Scripture: The Talmudic and Midrashic Evidence* (Hamden, CT: Archon Books, 1976), esp. 26–30.

19 On the rhetorical devices that he used to accomplish this goal, see Rodney K. Duke, *The Persuasive Appeal of the Chronicler: A Rhetorical Analysis*, JSOT-Sup 88 (Sheffield: Almond Press, 1990), esp. 111–38.

20 David J. A. Clines, "The Old Testament Histories: A Reader's Guide," *What Does Eve Help? and Other Readerly Questions to the Old Testament*, JSOT-Sup 94 (Sheffield: Sheffield Academic Press, 1990), 104.

21 For a discussion with examples, see Peter Ackroyd, "The Chronicler as Exegete," *JSOT* 2 (1977), 10 (reprinted in his *The Chronicler in His Age*, 311–343), Williamson, *1 and 2 Chronicles, passim* (e.g. 97, 312) and most comprehensively, Willi, *Chronik als Auslegung*, 56–9. For the contrary view, see Fishbane, *Biblical Interpretation*, 382.

22 On 1 Chronicles 10 and its relationship to Samuel, see Saul Zalewski, "The Purpose of the Story of the Death of Saul in 1 Chronicles X," *VT* 34 (1989), 449–67.

23 Stephen Geller, letter of August 1, 1991; this is a major theme of Willi, *Chronik als Auslegung*.

24 See n. 7, above.

25 This is perceived by Wellhausen, who notes in the *Prolegomena*, 224, "It must be allowed that Chronicles owes its origin, not to the arbitrary caprice of an individual, but to a general tendency of its period."

26 A list of these may be found in Leiman, *Canonization*, 18. For a discussion, see William Michael Schniedewind, "Prophets, Prophecy and Inspiration: A Study of Prophets in the Book of Chronicles" (Ph.D. dissertation, Brandeis University, 1992), 250–73.

27 The Chronicler's success in antiquity was not total. By the late Second Temple period, the account of the Deuteronomistic History was generally preferred to that of the Chronicler; see Ehud Ben Zvi, "The Authority of 1–2 Chronicles in the Late Second Temple Period," *JSP* 3 (1988), 59–88.

28 So, for example, William Johnstone, "Guilt and Atonement: The Theme of 1

and 2 Chronicles," *A Word in Season: Essays in Honour of William McKane*, JSOTSup 42, ed. James D. Martin and Philip R. Davies, (Sheffield: JSOT Press, 1986), 113–38; note esp. 116, "Chronicles is better understood as primarily a theological essay than as a work of historiography" and Peter Ackroyd, "The Chronicler as Exegete," 2, following Rudolf Mosis, *Untersuchungen zur Theologie des Chronistischen Geschichtswerkes* (Freiberg: Herder, 1973). Cf. Ackroyd, *The Chronicler in His Age*, 280–9. Tomotoshi Sugimoto, "The Chronicler's Technique in Quoting Samuel–Kings," *Annual of the Japanese Biblical Institute* 16 (1990), 70 straddles the historian–theologian position. He notes, "Chronicles may be best identified as historical literature" and "Yet the Chronicler is more interested in theological lessons reflected by historical events than historical facts themselves."

29 Mordechai Cogan, "The Chronicler's Use of Chronology as Illuminated by Neo-Assyrian Inscriptions," *Empirical Models for Biblical Criticism*, ed. Jeffrey H. Tigay (Philadelphia: University of Pennsylvania Press, 1985), 209.

30 In her discussion of "Literary Genre and Forms," in *I and II Chronicles*, 31–4, Japhet also suggests that it is best to categorize the Chronicler as a historian.

31 For one example see p. 32. For lists of these changes, see S. R. Driver, *An Introduction to the Literature of the Old Testament* (Gloucester, MA: Peter Smith, 1972), 535–40. For a longer discussion, which extends the observations of A. Kropat, *Die Syntax des Autors der Chronik*, BZAW 16 (Weimar: Hof-Buchdruckerei, 1909), see Robert Polzin, *Late Biblical Hebrew: Toward an Historical Typology of Biblical Hebrew Prose*, HSM 12 (Missoula, MT: Scholars Press, 1976), 27–84.

32 Moshe Greenberg, "The Stabilization of the Text of the Hebrew Bible, Reviewed in Light of the Biblical Materials from the Judean Desert," *The Canon and Masorah of the Hebrew Bible: An Introductory Reader*, ed. Sid Z. Leiman (New York: Ktav, 1974), 314, "Piety is not always accompanied by a critical sense. To the devout reader, a text giving the substance of the sacred message is not invalidated by slight verbal divergences from other texts."

33 This is especially recognized by I. L. Seeligmann, "The Beginnings of *Midrash* in the Books of Chronicles," *Tarbiz* 49 (1979–80), 14–32 (Hebrew), esp. 20–3, 30–1, English summary, II–III. Most of the examples from the next pages are taken from Seeligmann's article. For a more comprehensive treatment of the issue, see Judson R. Shaver, *Torah and the Chronicler's History Work: An Inquiry into the Chronicler's Reference to Laws, Festivals, and Cultic Institutions in Relationship to Pentateuchal Legislation*, BJS 196 (Atlanta: Scholars Press, 1989). I cannot, however, agree with his conclusion that the Chronicler wrote before the Torah was canonized.

34 *Prolegomena*, 106; cf. Fishbane, *Biblical Interpretation*, 131–3.

35 There is some confusion on this issue, with MT suggesting that there were two seven-day festivals; see *BHS* and commentaries *ad loc.*

36 All translations from Hebrew are my own.

37 Hebrew בתורתי. Scholars are split concerning the translation of תורה (torah) in post-exilic texts, as "teaching" or "Torah." Cf. the literature cited in n. 33, above, Michael Fishbane, "Torah," *EB*, ed. Benjamin Mazar *et al.* (Jerusalem: Mosad Bialik, 1982), VIII, 469–83 (Hebrew) and Sara Japhet, "Law and 'The Law' in Ezra–Nehemiah," *Proceedings of the Ninth World Congress of Jewish Studies: Panel Sessions: Bible Studies and Ancient Near East*, ed. Moshe Goshen-Gottstein (Jerusalem: Magnes, 1988), 99–115.

38 "The Beginnings of *Midrash*," 20.

39 The rabbinic dictum is אלו ואלו דברי אלהי חיים (*b. ʿErub.* 13b and parallels),

literally, "These and these are the words of the powerful God." This dictum is cited by Willi, *Chronik als Auslegung*, 242, n. 94, following a nineteenth-century article by K. Kohler and M. Rosenberg.

40 Seeligmann, "The Beginnings of *Midrash*," 31–2 and Fishbane, *Biblical Interpretation*, 135–8.

41 This is the only proper translation of בשל ; see the lexica s.v. בשל and all the other occurrences of the word in the Bible. The rendering adopted in some translations and commentaries of "cook" is incorrect, and reflects harmonistic readings of the type found in the Chronicler.

42 On כמשפט and similar terms, contrast Fishbane, *Biblical Interpretation*, 209–10 with H. G. M. Williamson, "History," *It is Written: Scripture Citing Scripture: Essays in Honour of Barnabas Lindars*, ed. D. A. Carson and H. G. M. Williamson (Cambridge: Cambridge University Press, 1988), 27–31.

43 According to some scholars, David and Solomon, but especially David, were regarded as messianic figures; see Roddy Braun, "Solominic Apologetic in Chronicles," *JBL* 92 (1973), 503–4 and S. De Vries, "Moses and David as Cult Founders," *JBL* 107 (1988), 636–9; contrast Japhet, *Ideology*, 493–9 and H. G. M. Williamson, "Eschatology in Chronicles," *Tyndale Bulletin* 28 (1977), 115–54.

44 For an overview of the Chronicler's theology, see Sandra Beth Berg, "After the Exile: God and History in the Books of Chronicles and Esther," *The Divine Helmsman: Studies on God's Control of Human Events, Presented to Lou H. Silberman*, ed. James L. Crenshaw and Samuel Sandmel (New York: Ktav, 1980), 109–14. A more complete description is found in Japhet, *Ideology*.

45 It is found only in 2 Kgs 19:15 (//Isa 37:16), Jer 31:17 and Gen 2:4 (P), all of which are late pre-elixic or later.

46 Ps 115:15; 121:2, 124:8, 134:3; 135:6. On the editing of Psalms, see Gerald Henry Wilson, *The Editing of the Hebrew Psalter*, SBLDS 76 (Chico, CA: Scholars Press, 1985), who notes that the division between books four and five is artificial, and that these represent the latest collections.

47 H. G. M. Williamson, "The Temple in the Book of Chronicles," *Templum Amicitiae: Essays in the Second Temple Presented to Ernst Bammel*, JSNTSup 48, ed. William Horbury (Sheffield: Sheffield Academic Press, 1991), 15–31, esp. 25–30.

48 Elias Bickerman, *From Ezra to the Last of the Maccabees: Foundations of Postbiblical Judaism* (New York: Schocken, 1962), 22. However, for text-critical reasons, his interpretation of the relationship of that specific text to its *Vorlage* is questionable; cf. Williamson, *1 and 2 Chronicles*, 228–9.

49 Cf. Jacques Barzun and Henry F. Graff, *The Modern Researcher*, fourth edition (San Diego: Harcourt Brace Jovanovich, 1985), 109–44 ("Verification").

50 For a quick visual sketch, see Bendavid, *Parallels in the Bible*, 40–1 or Jürgen Kegler and Matthias Augustin, *Synopse zum Chronistischen Geschichtswerk*, BzEATAJ 1 (Frankfurt: Peter Lang, 1984), 117–19.

51 *Contra BHS*, there is no need to insert a relative pronoun after אל ; cf. Bruce Waltke and M. O'Connor, *An Introduction to Biblical Hebrew Syntax* (Winona Lake, IN: Eisenbrauns, 1990) § 9.6d.

52 MT cannot be translated as it stands. The verb עלי in the Hiphil is found in v. 3 and is contextually appropriate here as well. This emendation presumes that the perfect rather than the converted imperfect was used, as sometimes happens in late biblical Hebrew, and that העליתם was lost due to homoioteleuton. For a different possibility, see *BHS, ad loc.*

53 Japhet, *Ideology*, 481–2, Braun, "Solomonic Apologetic," 507–16 and H. G.

M. Williamson, "The Accession of Solomon in the Books of Chronicles," *VT* 26 (1976), 356–9. Cf. Mark A. Throntveit, "Hezekiah in the Book of Chronicles," *SBL 1988 Seminar Papers*, ed. David J. Lull (Atlanta: Scholars Press, 1988), 310–11.

54 Japhet, *Ideology*, 485; cf. 485–7.

55 The word בתים is used throughout. See 1 Kgs 7:1–12.

56 Hebrew כון ; see Williamson, *Israel in the Books of Chronicles* (Cambridge: Cambridge University Press, 1977), 54, Seeligmann, "The Beginnings of *Midrash*," 16–18, esp. 16, n. 7.

57 For a discussion of this motif, see Japhet, *Ideology*, 226–9. On the traditions concerning the creation of the Temple liturgy under David, see Alan Cooper, "The Life and Times of King David According to the Books of Psalms," *The Poet and the Historian: Essays in Literary and Historical Biblical Criticism*, HSS 26, ed. Richard Elliott Friedman (Chico, CA: Scholars Press, 1983), 117–31. For the possible historical reasons why David did not build the Temple, see Carol Meyers, "David as Temple Builder," *Ancient Israelite Religion: Essays in Honor of Frank Moore Cross*, ed. Patrick D. Miller, Jr *et al.* (Philadelphia: Fortress, 1987), 357–76.

58 Note the unconverted perfect נטה .

59 An additional illustration of this principle may be found in 2 Chr 7:12–15. The *Vorlage* in 1 Kgs 9:3 states in brief that God has heeded Solomon's prayer, while the Chronicler offers a short synopsis of that prayer (2 Chr 7:12–15), already quoted in 2 Chronicles 6.

60 1 Chr 19:7 is similar: the Chronicler adds up the figures in his *Vorlage*, offering new material which is totally consistent with his source.

61 The issue is compounded by the difficult word השל in 2 Sam 6:7, though this word might be a late error; see P. Kyle McCarter, Jr, *II Samuel*, AB (Garden City, New York: Doubleday, 1984), 165. On the danger associated with the ark and Uzza's death, see McCarter, *II Samuel*, 170.

62 Japhet, *Ideology*, 238, n. 130 emphasizes that the text does not mean to suggest that David is inventing this law, but is following earlier authoritative traditions.

63 Perhaps an explicit mention of this in ch. 13 would have reflected poorly on David, who allowed this infraction to transpire.

64 This commentary is probably not by Rashi; see Samuel Poznański, *Kommentar zu Ezechiel und den XII kleinen Propheten von Eliezer aus Beaugency* (Warsaw: H. Eppelberg, 1913), XIV, n. 1 (Hebrew).

65 He glosses v. 2, "That is to say, he chose the Levites, and not a cart [to convey the ark]. Because they transported it in a cart, Uzza was punished, as it says below [v. 13], 'Because initially, you did not {bring it up} YHWH our God broke out against us.' "

66 Cited by Williamson, *1 and 2 Chronicles*, 122. Similar legislation is found in Num 1:50–1, but it contains far less overlapping terminology with Chronicles (though note the similar use of the root שרת). The Numbers passage is important, however, for understanding why according to the Chronicler Uzza died – Num 1:51 establishes that the non-Levite who approaches the ark shall be killed.

67 See Japhet, *Ideology*, 37, n. 87 and 96–8.

68 See similarly 1 Chr 23:13.

69 Note the common use of the Hebrew root קהל.

70 Sara Japhet, "Conquest and Settlement in Chronicles," *JBL* 98 (1979), 205–18, esp. 208–10.

71 On this complex passage, see Williamson, *1 and 2 Chronicles*, 119–22.

72 For scholars who see the genealogies at the beginning of Chronicles as second-ary, the reference in 1 Chronicles 15 to ראשי האבות ללוים would be unique.

73 Williamson, *1 and 2 Chronicles*, 124.

74 See above, n. 52.

75 Hebrew דרש. Williamson, *Israel in the Books of Chronicles*, 54.

76 Hebrew כמשפט. Max Wagner, דרש, *TDOT*, III, 300–3, esp. 300. See the dis-cussion of this term above, n. 42 and see Neh 8:18; 2 Chr 4:20; 35:13; cf. Lev 9:16. It is never used in Deuteronomy, and is found only once in the Deuteronomistic History, in 2 Kgs 11:14.

77 This notion, however, should not be seen as dry legalism; note esp. 2 Chr 30:18.

78 Japhet, *Ideology*, 91.

79 Hebrew נשא rather than העלה.

80 This image is borrowed from Willi, *Chronik als Auslegung*, 176–84, who uses the term "*Musivstil*" in reference to the Chronicler.

81 Schniedewind, "Prophets, Prophecy and Inspiration," 151–7.

82 Japhet, *Ideology*, 242–3.

83 In addition to here, מוטה is found in H, the prose of Jeremiah, Ezekiel and Trito-Isaiah. For a different approach on distinguishing between these two words, see Japhet, *Ideology*, 242–4 and *I and II Chronicles*, 302.

84 See, for example, the retention of בדים rather than the late biblical Hebrew מוטות in 2 Chr 5:9.

85 V. 12a, which noted that YHWH blessed Obed-Edom, is moved by the Chronicler to 1 Chr 13:14. By removing this half-verse from its original context, the Chronicler eliminates the possibility that David's motivation was opportunistic.

86 E.g. 1 Chr 11:5; 13:13; most significantly, later in our chapter in v. 29.

87 Japhet, *I and II Chronicles*, 417–18, however, sees the change in light of a more general "'democratizing' trend" in Chronicles. This is possible as well, though the verbal similarities between 1 Chronicles 15 and 1 Kings 8 strongly suggest that the Kings passage influenced Chronicles.

88 2 Chr 5:2//1 Kgs 8:1; in contrast to שרי האלפים, the term מטות is never used in the Chronicler's free composition.

89 See esp. his use of this term in 2 Chr 17:14–18 for a select group of tribal leaders, similar to the ראשי המטות נשיאי האבות.

90 Cf., for example, 2 Sam 5:6b, 8; 8:2; 2 Kgs 11:6b.

91 For another case where the Chronicler responds to a practical problem raised by his *Vorlage*, see Brevard Childs, *Isaiah and the Assyrian Crisis*, SBT²3 (London: SCM, 1967), 107–9. In a similar vein, note how various problems that must have arisen during the Temple service, such as the presence of flies around the sacrificial meat, are "solved" by the Mishnah (Avot 5:5), which claims that miraculously no flies surrounded the sacrificial meat as it was butchered.

92 The Hebrew root עזר is used in the passages referred to in this paragraph.

93 Hebrew לעזרנו. For a discussion of this term, see H. G. M. Williamson, "'We Are Yours, O David': The Setting and Purpose of 1 Chronicles xii 1–23," *OTS* 21 (1981), 166–7. For an additional similar use of עזר, see 2 Chr 14:10.

94 Note the change at 1 Chr 18:17 (//2 Sam 8:18). The tendency in this case is not entirely consistent; see Williamson, *1 and 2 Chronicles*, 140 and texts such as 1 Chr 16:2 and 21:26.

95 See Avi Hurvitz, "The Date of the Prose-Tale of Job Linguistically Recon-sidered," *HTR* 67 (1974), 17–34.

96 שבעה פרים ושבעה[אילם איל]; cf. Lemke, "The Synoptic Problem," 353–4.

97 See Japhet, *I and II Chronicles*, 387.

98 Williamson, *Israel in the Books of Chronicles*, 62–4 and "The Temple in the Book of Chronicles," 21–2; cf. Sara Japhet, "Conquest and Settlement in Chronicles," *JBL* 98 (1987), 217–18.

99 On other possible influences of Genesis 23 on 1 Chronicles 21, see Williamson, *1 and 2 Chronicles*, 149. Additional possible typological elements in this narrative are offered in Sugimoto, "The Chronicler's Technique in Quoting Samuel–Kings," 64–5; cf. his general discussion of typology in Chronicles on 63–6, 68.

100 For this terminology and its application, see Benjamin David Sommer, "Leshon Limmudim: The Poetics of Allusion in Isaiah 40–66," Ph.D. dissertation, University of Chicago, 1994, esp. 37–40.

101 On the change in the verse order, see p. 42.

102 *1 and 2 Chronicles*, 222–3 and Mosis, *Untersuchungen*, 147–9.

103 The Chronicler only uses cloud (ענן) when he is copying from his *Vorlage*, in 2 Chr 5:13–14 (=1 Kgs 8:10–11). Note the use of glory (כבוד) in the post-exilic Hag 2:7 and Zech 2:9.

104 The Chronicler uses this expression in the more general sense of "in YHWH's presence" (e.g. 1 Chr 11:3), which may sometimes refer to the Temple (e.g. 2 Chr 20:13, 18), but never specifically to the ark.

105 For one example, cf. the non-synoptic 2 Chr 20:6 and Japhet, *Ideology*, 81–5.

106 Hebrew רנן.

107 Note esp. 1 Chr 16:41 and elsewhere in that chapter; 23:30; 25:3; 2 Chr 5:13; 7:6; 20:21. Ezra 3:11 suggests that the expression had an important role in the Temple cult in the Persian period.

108 On other cases of patterning of the Temple after the Tabernacle, see Japhet, *Ideology*, 73, esp. n. 199 and Seeligmann, "The Beginnings of *Midrash*," 24.

109 See Roddy L. Braun, "The Message of Chronicles: Rally 'Round the Temple,' " *CTM* 42 (1971), 502–14, esp. 509, 511–13 and Williamson, "The Temple in the Book of Chronicles."

110 On downplaying the exile, see Japhet, *Ideology*, 364–73; on the notion of continuity between the Temples, see the essays in Peter R. Ackroyd, *Studies in the Religious Traditions of the Old Testament* (London: SCM, 1987), 3–75 ("Continuity"), esp. 46–60 ("The Temple Vessels: A Continuity Theme").

111 Williamson, "The Accession of Solomon in the Books of Chronicles," 351–61.

112 Hebrew חזק ואמץ.

113 Williamson, "The Accession of Solomon in the Books of Chronicles," 356.

114 Williamson, "The Accession of Solomon in the Books of Chronicles," 357; cf. 357–9.

115 On the polemical nature of this verse, see Japhet, *I and II Chronicles*, 514.

116 Williamson, *Israel in the Books of Chronicles*, 119–25. This position is extended and modified in Throntveit, "Hezekiah in the Book of Chronicles," 302–11.

117 Some of the other points of comparison made by Williamson are less compelling because they appear in some form in Kings as well. In general, arguments for parallelism should show: (1) that the later source is not expanding its own *Vorlage* and (2) that the borrowed expression is highly unusual or unique, and was not used in several other contexts in Chronicles. In *1 and 2 Chronicles*, 382, he adds to his earlier arguments by noting that the encouragement formula (חזק ואמץ) is used of both Solomon and Hezekiah. It was originally used of Joshua; by literary patterning it is then used of Solomon, and because of another case of literary patterning is used of Hezekiah!

118 Williamson, "The Accession of Solomon in the Books of Chronicles," 125.

119 Williamson only sees the first similarity as significant. He incorrectly claims that the Chronicler develops the parallel between Solomon's and Hezekiah's wealth, while actually Chronicles is dependent on Kings for this.

120 As Williamson shows throughout *Israel in the Books of Chronicles*, the conception of the unity of Israel is a central conception of the Chronicler. In addition, the Chronicler was very concerned with prayer, especially the efficacy of prayer; note Japhet, *Ideology*, 85 and esp. 2 Chr 33:12–13, the prayer of Manasseh.

121 *1 and 2 Chronicles*, 188. Most scholars, however, consider David more significant for the Chronicler; cf., for example, Ackroyd, *The Chronicler in His Age*, 268–9, 285–6.

122 Williamson disputes this to some extent, and tends to see Solomon, the last king of the united monarchy, in some ways as greater than David.

123 Most commentators claim that the end of the verse is clumsy and secondary; cf., for example, Mordechai Cogan and Hayim Tadmor, *II Kings*, AB (Garden City, New York: Doubleday, 1988), 217. However, it seems to be known in this form to the Chronicler.

124 This verse does not appear in Chronicles, but the Chronicler elsewhere uses material that he does not cite in its "proper," expected place; for one example see Williamson, *Israel in the Books of Chronicles*, 124, n. 4.

125 Yairah Amit, "Studies in the Poetics of Chronicles," *Sefer H. M. I. Gebaryahu: Studies in the Bible and in Jewish Thought, Presented to him at Seventy*, ed. B. Z. Luria (Jerusalem: Kiryat Sepher, 1989), 288 (Hebrew).

126 See Gerson Cohen, "The Story of the Four Captives," *PAAJR* 29 (1960–1), 55–131, esp. 71, that "the account [of Ibn Daud] is a fiction and was probably not intended by its author to be read as factual history and that, on the other hand, the text and data which have come down to us in *Sefer ha-Qabbalah* are essentially as Ibn Daud wrote them" and 123, where Cohen notes that Ibn Daud's history was "a means to a higher end – the education of the masses to good conduct." This essay has been reissued in his *Studies in the Variety of Rabbinic Cultures* (Philadelphia: Jewish Publications Society, 1991), 158–208.

127 A similar point has been made in relationship to the schematic nature of biblical chronology in Jeremy Hughes, *Secrets of the Times: Myth and History in Biblical Chronology*, JSOTSup 66 (Sheffield: Sheffield Academic Press, 1990).

128 On this topic in general, see now David A. Glatt, *Chronological Displacement in Biblical and Related Literatures*, SBLDS 139 (Atlanta: Scholars Press, 1993), which offers a broad ancient Near Eastern and rabbinic context in which the issues explored here should be seen. I would only point out here that the Chronicler is far from unique in rearranging texts. Note especially the divergent orders of MT and LXX to Jeremiah; see the discussion of Emanuel Tov, "The Literary History of the Book of Jeremiah in Light of Its Textual History," *Empirical Models for Biblical Criticism*, ed. Jeffrey H. Tigay (Philadelphia: University of Pennsylvania Press, 1985), 217 and *Textual Criticism of the Hebrew Bible* (Minneapolis: Fortress Press, 1992), 321.

129 On chronological versus narrative order in the Bible, see W. J. Martin, " 'Dischronologized' Narrative in the Old Testament," SVT 17 (Leiden: E. J. Brill, 1969), 179–86.

130 Hebrew אין מוקדם ומאוחר בתורה. See *Sifre* to Numbers §64, H. S. Horovitz edition (Jerusalem: Wahrmann, 1966), 61 and the discussions in Ezra Zion Melammed, *Bible Commentators*, vol. 1 (Jerusalem: Magnes, 1975), 18–21

(Hebrew) and Glatt, *Chronological Displacement in Biblical and Related Literatures*, 3.
131 "History," 34–5.
132 For a similar rearrangement of material to highlight Judah, see my "The Book of Judges: Literature as Politics," *JBL* 108 (1989), 395–418.
133 Hebrew ברכ.
134 Similarly, Japhet, *I and II Chronicles*, 609.
135 Japhet, *Ideology*, 150–76.
136 "The Chronicler's Use of Chronology," 197–209; the reference to "pseudo-dating" is from p. 199. The article originally appeared in Hebrew in *Zion* 45 (1980), 165–72, where its Hebrew title, "Tendentious Chronology in the Book of Chronicles," is more descriptive of its content.
137 Cogan, "The Chronicler's Use of Chronology," 203.
138 Cf. 2 Chronicles 34, Cogan, "The Chronicler's Use of Chronology," 203–4 and Williamson, *1 and 2 Chronicles*, 397–8.
139 Note, for example, the immediate fulfillment of punishment in 2 Chr 26:19; note also the reverse idea, that penance is quickly rewarded, in 2 Chr 33:13. Cf. the discussion of Japhet, *Ideology*, 163, on " 'the imperative of reward and punishment' " and 159, on the problem of other sources" claims that YHWH postpones retribution.
140 Chronicles patterns this individual, Huram, after Bezalel, as noted by Williamson, *1 and 2 Chronicles*, 200–1. For the differences between Bezalel and Huram, see Japhet, *I and II Chronicles*, 545–6.
141 On the differences between the two texts, see Wilhelm Rudolph, *Chronikbücher*, HAT (Tübingen: J. C. B. Mohr, 1955), 200.
142 Cf., for example, 1 Kgs 21:2.
143 See McCarter, *II Samuel*, 16–19. Indeed, some modern scholars have concluded like the Chronicler that, "The list can be no later than David's Hebron period, and it might be as early as the wilderness period" (McCarter, *II Samuel*, 501).
144 See now the discussion in Glatt, *Chronological Displacement in Biblical and Related Literatures*, 57–60.
145 On these chapters, in addition to the commentaries, see Peter Welten, "Lade – Tempel – Jerusalem: Zur Theologie der Chronikbücher,"; *Textgemäß: Aufsätze und Beiträge zur Hermeneutik des Alten Testaments: Festschrift für Ernst Würthwein zum 70. Geburtstag*, ed. A. H. J. Gunneweg and Otto Kaiser (Göttingen: Vandenhoeck & Ruprecht, 1979), 169–83.
146 The Hebrew root פרצ is used consistently for this purpose. On פרצ unifying these chapters, see Glatt, *Chronological Displacement in Biblical and Related Literatures*, 60.
147 See Leslie C. Allen, "Kerygmatic Units in 1 & 2 Chronicles," *JSOT* 41 (1988), 27–8, following Mosis, *Untersuchungen*, 60–1 and Williamson, *1 and 2 Chronicles*, 114.
148 Glatt, *Chronological Displacement in Biblical and Related Literatures*, 59 also sees this verse as key to understanding the order of Chronicles, but he uses it in a different way.
149 This notion of fear caused by YHWH is found in other similar contexts in Chronicles (2 Chr 14:13; 17:10), and probably indicates that Deut 11:25 was on the Chronicler's mind.
150 Similarly, Glatt, *Chronological Displacement in Biblical and Related Literatures*, 59–60.
151 See Mosis, *Untersuchungen*, 59–60.
152 The Chronicler revises 2 Samuel to state that Solomon would build the Temple

because he was a man of peace (1 Chr 22:8–9). It is possible that this notion was to some extent transferred to David, so that only after he completes his first set of battles does he begin the preparations for the Temple.

153 See n. 28 above.

154 On the Chronicler as an exegete, see both Willi, *Chronik als Auslegung*, esp. 53–69 and Ackroyd, "The Chronicler as Exegete."

155 Ranke's understanding of history is frequently misunderstood; see Stephen Bann, "The Historian as Taxidermist: Ranke, Barante, Waterton," *Comparative Criticism* 3 (1981), 22; cf. 21–49.

156 On the historical reliability of Chronicles, see Sarah Japhet, "The Historical Reliability of Chronicles: The History of the Problem and its Place in Biblical Research," *JSOT* 33 (1985), 83–107 and Matt Patrick Graham, *Utilization of 1 and 2 Chronicles in the Reconstruction of Israelite History in the Nineteenth Century*, SBLDS 116 (Atlanta: Scholars Press, 1990).

157 The best summary, with extensive bibliography, is in Na'aman, "Pastoral Nomads."

158 See the article by Joseph Blenkinsopp, "Memory, Tradition, and the Construction of the Past in Ancient Israel" and my "Response" in the forthcoming *History and Memory in Jewish and Christian Tradition* (Notre Dame: Notre Dame Press). The studies of Paul Connerton, *How Societies Remember* (Cambridge: Cambridge University Press, 1989), David Lowenthal, *The Past is a Foreign Country* (Cambridge: Cambridge University Press, 1985) and Marie-Noëlle Bourguet *et al.*, eds, *Between Memory and History* (New York: Harwood Academic Publishers, 1990) are especially useful. For examples taken from recent times, see Michael Schudson, *Watergate in American Memory: How we Remember, Forget, and Reconstruct the Past* (New York: Basic, 1992) and Patrick H. Hutton, *History as an Art of Memory* (Burlington: University of Vermont Press, 1993).

159 This balance is emphasized in Ackroyd, *The Chronicler in His Age*, 64–70.

160 Mosis, *Untersuchungen*, 192–4. The placement of the exile of Manasseh in Babylon rather than Assyria makes the typological nature of this passage quite obvious.

161 This is fundamental to most pre-modern history, and much modern history writing as well; see Lowenthal, *The Past is a Foreign Country*, esp. 369.

162 Na'aman, "Pastoral Nomads," 261.

163 Ivan G. Marcus, "History, Story and Collective Memory: Narrative in Early Ashkenazic Culture," *Prooftexts* 10 (1990), 381.

164 Cf. Hag 2:3, 9 and Ezra 3:12. Note that according to Zechariah 7–8, the fasts commemorating the destruction of the First Temple continued to be observed in the early Second Temple period.

165 W. Den Boer, "Graeco-Roman Historiography in its Relation to Biblical and Modern Thinking," *H and T* 7 (1968), 71. For a similar view, see Niels Peter Lemche, "Review of Baruch Halpern's *The First Historians*," *JNES* 50 (1991), 217, "It is important to understand that the biblical historians tried to write history."

166 Dennis Nineham, *The Use and Abuse of the Bible: A Study of the Bible in an Age of Rapid Cultural Change* (London: SPCK, 1978), 122.

167 Cf. Cohen, "The Story of the Four Captives," 114.

168 See, for example, Walter Burkert, *Structure and History in Greek Mythology and Ritual* (Berkeley, CA: University of California Press, 1979), 28, "[M]yth can be defined as a metaphor at the tale level." On the connections between myth and history, see p. 153, n. 44.

169 K. Lawson Younger, Jr, *Ancient Conquest Accounts: A Study in Ancient Near Eastern and Biblical History Writing*, JSOTSup 98 (Sheffield: Sheffield Academic Press, 1990), 45–6; here Younger is heavily dependent on Hayden White. Additional perspectives for understanding this type of historical truth may be gleaned from Paul Veyne, *Did the Greeks Believe in their Myths?*, trans. Paula Wissing (Chicago: University of Chicago Press, 1988).

170 Contrast the use of animal names and scatology in the Ehud story (See Chapter Five) or the use of the symbolic names Machlon ("sickness"), Chilion ("death") and Orpha ("[she who turned her] back") in Ruth. On Ruth as a "historical novel," see Amos Funkenstein, *Perceptions of Jewish History* (Berkeley: University of California Press, 1993), 57–8.

3 THE TYPOLOGIES OF GENESIS

1 For the history of these positions, see G. W. Trompf, *The Idea of Historical Recurrence in Western Thought: From Antiquity to the Reformation* (Berkeley: University of California Press, 1979), esp. 117, n. 2, David Bebbington, *Patterns in History: A Christian Perspective on Historical Thought* (Leicester: Apollos, 1990), 21–48, Gerald A. Press, "History and the Development of the Idea of History in Antiquity," *H and T* 16 (1977), 280–1 and Herbert Butterfield, *The Origins of History* (New York: Basic, 1981), 88. On cyclical time in the Bible, see Northrop Frye, *The Double Vision: Language and Meaning in Religion* (Toronto: University of Toronto Press, 1991), 50–1.

2 James Barr, *Biblical Words for Time*, revised edition, SBT 33 (Naperville, IL: Allenson, 1969), 143–9 and Arnaldo Momigliano, "Time in Ancient Historiography," *Essays in Ancient and Modern Historiography* (Oxford: Basil Blackwell, 1977), 179–204; cf. Chester G. Starr, "Historical and Philosophical Time," *H and T* Beiheft 6 (1966), 24–35, John van Seters, *In Search of History: Historiography in the Ancient World and the Origins of Bibical History* (New Haven: Yale University Press, 1983), 8 and Hunter R. Rawlings III, *The Structure of Thucydides" History* (Princeton: Princeton University Press, 1981), 255.

3 Trompf, *The Idea of Historical Recurrence*, 118, 134–9, 156–60 and "Notions of Historical Recurrence in Classical Hebrew Historiography," SVT 30 (Leiden: E. J. Brill, 1979), 213–29. For the claim that Israelite historiography is predominantly cyclical, see John Briggs Curtis, "A Suggested Interpretation of the Biblical Philosophy of History," *HUCA* 34 (1963), 115–23.

4 This mixing is true of Western historiography in general; see John T. Marcus, "Time and the Sense of History: West and East," *Comparative Studies in Society and History* 3 (1960–1), 123–39. On the Bible, see Norman H. Snaith, "Time in the Old Testament," *Promise and Fulfilment: Essays Presented to Professor S. H. Hooke in Celebration of his Ninetieth Birthday*, ed. F. F. Bruce (Edinburgh: T. & T. Clark, 1963), 175–86.

I am here speaking of "depictions of historical events" rather than "time," following Peter Muntz, *The Shape of Time: A New Look at the Philosophy of History* (Middletown, CT: Wesleyan University Press, 1977), 223, "There is first of all the great debate whether the past is a series of cycles or one straight line. This is not really a debate about the past but about the manner in which we write historical narratives."

5 For this understanding of "cyclical," see Trompf, *The Idea of Historical Recurrence*, 2–3.

6 Frederick E. Greenspahn, "The Theology of the Framework of Judges," *VT* 36 (1986), 385–96.

7 Greenspahn, "The Theology of the Framework of Judges," 394–6. On this use of the past see J. H. Plumb, *The Death of the Past* (Harmondsworth: Penguin, 1973), 40, who notes that historians "romanticise the past in order to compensate themselves for what they no longer enjoy."

8 The literature on typology is immense. Some of the more important studies which bear on the issues discussed in this chapter are: Rudolph Bultmann, "Ursprung und Sinn der Typologie als hermeneutische Methode," *TLZ* 50 (1950), 205–12, G. W. H. Lampe and K. J. Woollcombe, *Essays on Typology*, SBT 22 (Naperville, IL: Allenson, 1957), Leonhard Goppelt, *Typos: The Typological Interpretation of the Old Testament in the New*, trans. Donald H. Madvig (Grand Rapids: Eerdmans, 1982), *idem*, *TDNT*, vol. 8, 246–59, s.v. "τύπος," J. Daniélou, "The New Testament and the Theology of History," *Studia Evangelica 1 (1959)*, 25–35, *idem*, *From Shadows to Reality: Studies in the Biblical Typology of the Fathers*, trans. Dom Wulstan Hibberd (London: Burns & Oates, 1960), Gerhard von Rad, "Typological Interpretation of the Old Testament," trans. John Bright, *Essays on Old Testament Hermeneutics*, ed. Claus Westermann (London: SCM, 1963), 17–39, Walter Eichrodt, "Is Typological Exegesis an Appropriate Method?" trans. James Barr, *Essays on Old Testament Hermeneutics*, ed. Claus Westermann, 224–45, M. D. Goulder, *Type and History in Acts* (London: SPCK, 1964), esp. 1–33, James Barr, *Old and New in Interpretation: A Study of the Two Testaments* (London: SCM, 1966), 103–48 ("Typology and Allegory"), Northrop Frye, *The Great Code: The Bible and Literature* (New York: Harcourt Brace Jovanovich, 1982), 78–138, A. C. Charity, *Events and Their Afterlife: The Dialectics of Christian Typology in the Bible and Dante* (Cambridge: Cambridge University Press, 1987) and Marc Saperstein, "Jewish Typological Exegesis after Nahmanides," *JSQ* 1 (1993/4), 158–70.

9 Goppelt, "τύπος," 252.

10 For a discussion of this passage, in addition to the commentaries, see Trompf, *The Idea of Historical Recurrence*, 141–2.

11 Trompf, *The Idea of Historical Recurrence*, 3.

12 See William H. Brownlee, *The Midrash Pesher Habakkuk*, SBLMS 24 (Missoula, MT: Scholars Press, 1979), 27. Some scholars would exclude interpretation of prophetic passages from "typology;" so Saperstein, "Jewish Typological Exegesis after Nahmanides," 158–9.

13 On *pesher* literature, see Michael Fishbane, "The Qumran Pesher and Traits of Ancient Exegesis," *Proceedings of the Sixth World Congress of Jewish Studies*, ed. Avigdor Shinan (Jerusalem: World Union of Jewish Studies, 1977), vol. 1, 97–114.

14 See O. S. Wintermute, "Introduction to Jubilees," *OTP* 2, 38.

15 See Isaac Heinemann's classic, *The Methods of Aggadah*, third edition, (Jerusalem: Magnes, 1970), 32–4 (Hebrew).

16 Jacob Neusner, "The Theory of History of Genesis Rabbah," *The Christian and Judaic Invention of History*, American Academy of Religion Studies in Religion 55, ed. Jacob Neusner (Atlanta, GA: Scholars Press, 1990), 209–30; the quotation is from 209.

17 See Neusner, "The Theory of History of Genesis Rabbah," 223–30 and the classic article by Gerson Cohen, "Esau as Symbol in Early Medieval Thought," *Jewish Medieval and Renaissance Studies*, ed. Alexander Altmann (Cambridge, MA: Harvard University Press, 1967), 19–48, reprinted in his *Studies in the*

Variety of Rabbinic Cultures (Philadelphia: Jewish Publications Society, 1991), 243–69.

18 Neusner, "The Theory of History of Genesis Rabbah," 227, translating Genesis Rabbah 62:6, J. Theodor and Ch. Albeck, *Bereschit Rabba* (Jerusalem: Wahrman, 1965), 682–3.

19 See esp. Michael Fishbane, *Biblical Interpretation in Ancient Israel* (Oxford: Oxford University Press, 1985), 350–79.

20 For this purpose, it is irrelevant whether there was an actual exodus or how that event might be related to the narrative in Exodus. Traditions rather than events typically form the basis of typologies. The most extensive discussion of typological use of the exodus is Yair Zakovitch, *"And You Shall Tell Your Son . . .": The Concept of the Exodus in the Bible* (Jerusalem: Magnes, 1991).

21 Fishbane, *Biblical Interpretation*, 358–9 and Zakovitch, *"And You Shall Tell Your Son . . ."*, 61–2.

22 Zakovitch, *"And You Shall Tell Your Son . . . "*, 57, 103, and Fishbane, *Biblical Interpretation*, 358–68, with bibliography there.

23 Hebrew בחפזון.

24 Cf., for example, Eichrodt, "Is Typological Exegesis an Appropriate Method?" 225.

25 See p. 173, n. 160.

26 Typologies which serve purely literary-aesthetic purposes are called "decorative typologies" by Robert Hollander, "Typology and Secular Literature: Some Medieval Problems and Examples," *Literary Uses of Typology from the Late Middle Ages to the Present*, ed. Earl Miner (Princeton: Princeton University Press, 1977), 7–10.

27 This is the term used in Susan Niditch, *Underdogs and Tricksters: A Prelude to Biblical Folklore* (San Francisco: Harper & Row, 1987), 23. The stories are sometimes called "ancestress of Israel in danger," but David J. A. Clines, *What Does Eve Help? and Other Readerly Questions to the Old Testament*, JSOTSup 94 (Sheffield: Sheffield Academic Press, 1990), 67 points out that it is the ancestor, not his wife, who is in danger.

28 For a detailed chart comparing these stories, see Niditch, *Underdogs*, 42–4.

29 In classical literature, see T. P. Wiseman, *Clio's Cosmetics: Three Studies in Greco-Roman Literature* (Leicester: Leicester University Press, 1979), 57–76; for rabbinic literature, see esp. Albert I. Baumgarten, "The Politics of Reconciliation: The Education of R. Judah the Prince," *Jewish and Christian Self-Definition, Vol 2: Aspects of Judaism in the Graeco-Roman Period*, ed. E. P. Sanders, A. I. Baumgarten and Alan Mendelson (Philadelphia, PA: Fortress, 1981), 213–20. For a discussion of parallels from the perspective of the study of narrative, see Barbara Herrnstein Smith, "Narrative Version, Narrative Theories," *On Narrative*, ed. W. J. T. Mitchell (Chicago: University of Chicago Press, 1980), 211–19.

30 For a survey, see Niditch, *Underdogs*, 23–7 and T. D. Alexander, "Are the Wife/Sister Incidents of Genesis Literary Compositional Variants?" *VT* 42 (1992), 145–53.

31 E. A. Speiser, "The Wife-Sister Motif in the Pentateuchal Narratives," *Biblical and Other Studies*, ed. Alexander Altmann (Cambridge, MA: Harvard University Press, 1963), 15–28 and *Genesis*, AB (Garden City, New York: Doubleday, 1983), 91–4.

32 Samuel Greengus, "Sisterhood Adoption at Nuzi and the 'Wife–Sister' in Genesis," *HUCA* 46 (1975), 5–31, Barry Eichler, "Another Look at the Nuzi Sisterhood Contracts," *Essays on the Ancient Near East in Memory of Jacob*

Joel Finkelstein (Hamden, CT: Archon, 1977), 45–59 and *idem*, " 'Say that you are my Sister': Nuzi and Biblical Studies," *Shnaton* 3 (1978–9), 108–23 (Hebrew; English summary, XIV).

33 John van Seters, *Abraham in History and Tradition* (New Haven, CT: Yale University Press, 1975).

34 Thomas L. Thompson, *The Historicity of the Patriarchal Narratives*, BZAW 133 (Berlin: Walter de Gruyter, 1974).

35 Klaus Koch, *The Growth of the Biblical Tradition: The Form-Critical Method*, trans. S. M. Cupitt (London: Adam & Charles Black, 1969), 111–32.

36 Susan Niditch, *Underdogs*, 23. For an additional critique of Koch's approach, see David Peterson, "A Thrice-Told Tale," *Biblical Research* 18 (1973), 3–43.

37 Hebrew נגעים גדלים.

38 Though I am indebted to several other scholars for my typological understanding of this unit (see n. 40), they have not adequately pointed out the problematics of the narrative flow of our unit. It is these narrative difficulties *in addition* to the strong similarities to the exodus which make the typological interpretation in this case so compelling.

39 This is the most likely sense of the unique Hebrew phrase כסות עינים.

40 Peter D. Miscall, *The Workings of Old Testament Narrative*, SBL Semeia Studies (Philadelphia: Fortress, 1983), 42. He then goes on to claim that Genesis 12 and the exodus story in Exodus are inversions of each other (43–5). I disagree with this section of his analysis, which is based on an overly close reading of the texts. It is usual for typological texts not to agree with each other in all aspects. The Genesis 12 story is discussed in terms of "foreshadow[-ing]" by Sharon Pace Jeansonne, *The Women of Genesis: From Sarah to Potiphar's Wife* (Minneapolis: Fortress, 1990), 13, 16. More complete discussions of the parallels between these stories may be found in Umberto Cassuto, *A Commentary on the Book of Genesis, Part II: From Noah to Abraham*, trans. Israel Abraham (Jerusalem: Magnes, 1964), 335–6, which is followed by Fishbane, *Biblical Interpretation*, 375–6 and Zakovitch, *"And You Shall Tell Your Son . . ."*, 18–20, 46–7. The latter considers the episode in a chapter "The Many Covert Faces of the Exodus Pattern" (46–98), and suggests (46) that Gen 12:10–20 is "cloaked in the Exodus pattern."

41 Theodor and Albeck, *Bereschit Rabba*, 385–6.

42 It may not be accidental that this is quoted by R. Phinehas, who elsewhere involves himself in anti-Christian polemic, since this passage may be seen as saying that the Hebrew Bible is typological, but its typologies do not refer to Jesus. See Benjamin Cohen, "Phinehas ben Ḥama Ha-Kohen," *EJ* 13, 468.

43 See Amos Funkenstein, "Nachmanides' Typological Reading of History," *Zion* 45 (1980), 35–59. A slightly abridged English version is "Nahmanides' Symbolical Reading of History," *Studies in Jewish Mysticism*, ed. Joseph Dan and Frank Talmage (Cambridge, MA: Association for Jewish Studies, 1982), 129–50. This study is also incorporated into his *Perceptions of Jewish History* (Berkeley: University of California Press, 1993), 98–121. For a list of Nachmanides' typologies, see Ezra Zion Melammed, *Bible Commentators*, 2 vols (Jerusalem: Magnes, 1975), 950–2 (Hebrew).

44 Funkenstein, "Nachmanides' Typological Reading," 53 and "Nahmanides' Symbolical Reading," 134; on the relationship of typology to history rather than words, see von Rad, "Typological Interpretation," 21.

45 D. E. Nineham, *The Use and Abuse of the Bible: A Study of the Bible in an Age of Rapid Cultural Change* (London: SPCK, 1978), 127; cf. 123–4. The concept of "paradigmatic event" is discussed in greater detail in Van Austin

Harvey, *The Historian and the Believer: The Morality of Historical Knowledge and Christian Belief* (London: SCM, 1967), 353–8. On the importance of the exodus throughout the Bible, see Samuel E. Loewenstamm, *The Evolution of the Exodus Tradition*, trans. Baruch J. Schwartz (Jerusalem: Magnes, 1992), 53–68.

46 Baruch M. Bokser, *The Origins of the Seder: The Passover Rite and Early Rabbinic Judaism* (Berkeley: University of California Press, 1984), 76–100.

47 Hebrew שלח in the *piel*.

48 For a more complete list of possible parallels, see the works of Cassuto, Fishbane and Zakovitch, cited above in n. 40. My list is narrower than theirs; I believe that they include several overgeneral similarities or cases of borderline similarities.

49 Nachmanides understands the patriarchal stories as analogous to the symbolic actions performed by the prophets; see Funkenstein, "Nahmanides' Symbolical Reading," 136–9 and "Nachmanides' Typological Reading," 50–3.

50 Fishbane, *Biblical Interpretation*, 379.

51 According to the first possibility, the motifs common to Genesis 12, 20 and 26 predate Gen 12:10–20, and took a new shape in this chapter under the influence of the exodus motifs; according to the second option, Genesis 20 and 26 are dependent on ch. 12, and their authors revised the stories in ways which eliminated the exodus typology. Though both models are possible, the first seems more likely, especially since the three stories are not all from the same Pentateuchal source.

52 On the importance of not merely noting typologies, but also seeking motives for them, see Goulder, *Type and History*, 10.

53 Cassuto, *Genesis*, 337.

54 On the biblical injunction to remember events, see Momigliano, "Time in Ancient Historiography," 195 and Ysef Hayim Yerushalmi, *Zakhor: Jewish History and Jewish Memory* (Seattle: University of Washington Press, 1982), 3–16.

55 He notes the "psychological effects" of this type of pre-enacted narrative, which suggests that "the future is foreseeable according to past events" (*"And You Shall Tell Your Son . . ."*, 20). Niditch, *Underdogs*, 48 does not emphasize the exodus connection, but notes that Gen 12:10–20 is an "underdog tale," that "addresses one's feeling of insecurity and smallness" by offering "wish fulfillment." The reassuring nature of typologies is noted by George P. Landow, *Victorian Types, Victorian Shadows: Biblical Typology in Victorian Literature, Art and Thought* (Boston: Routledge & Kegan Paul, 1980), 10. A similar point is made concerning cyclical time by Hans Meyerhoff, *Time in Literature* (Berkeley: University of California Press, 1960), 105: "It may provide a sense of continuity and unity between past, present and future."

56 Goulder, *Type and History*, 179–205 ("Symbol and History"); the quotation is from 204.

57 The relevant section of Genesis Rabbah noted above opens: "God said to Abraham our father, 'Go and prepare a path for your children.' "

58 See the discussion of intentionality, p. 12, in reference to Baruch Halpern's definition of history.

59 Goulder, *Type and History*, 8.

60 Note the title of a section in Hermann Gunkel, *The Legends of Genesis*, trans. W. H. Carruth (New York: Schocken, 1975), 19–23, "Patriarchs Represent Tribes."

61 Hugo Gressmann, *Ursprung und Entwicklung der Joseph Saga*, FRLANT 36,

NF 19 (Göttingen: Vandenhoeck & Ruprecht, 1923) 10–11. John Skinner, *Genesis*, ICC (Edinburgh: T. & T. Clark, 1910), 441 considers these elements "slight and secondary." See S. R. Driver, *The Book of Genesis* (London: Methuen, 1926), lvi for a list of scholars who understand some of the stories concerning the patriarchs as representative of peoples or tribes. On Reuben and Judah, see pp. lix–lx. A reading similar to Gressmann's is offered by Samuel E. Loewenstamm, "Reuben and Judah in the Joseph-Cycle," *Fourth World Congress of Jewish Studies, Papers*, vol. 1 (Jerusalem: World Union of Jewish Studies, 1967), 69–70 (Hebrew), translated in his *From Babylon to Canaan: Studies in the Bible and its Oriental Background* (Jerusalem: Magnes, 1992), 35–41. A more recent typological analysis of different aspects of patriarchal stories is Stanley Gevirtz, "Of Patriarchs and Puns: Joseph at the Fountain, Jacob at the Ford," *HUCA* 46 (1975), 33–54.

62 Donald B. Redford, *Egypt, Canaan, and Israel in Ancient Times* (Princeton: Princeton University Press, 1992), 429.

63 George W. Coats, *From Canaan to Egypt: Structural and Theological Context for the Joseph Story*, CBQMS 4 (Washington, DC: Catholic Biblical Association, 1976), 92, Donald B. Redford, *A Study of the Biblical Story of Joseph (Genesis 37–50)*, SVT 20 (Leiden: E. J. Brill, 1970), ix, "the discredited and (one had hoped) defunct practice of interpreting it [the Joseph story] as tribal history" (though his comment on 178 allows the reader to understand the final version of the story as "politico-historical propaganda") and W. Lee Humphreys, *Joseph and His Family: A Literary Study* (Columbia, SC: University of South Carolina Press, 1988), 199, "it is simply not colored by a strong political polemic of any sort."

64 For a reconstruction, see Roland de Vaux, *The Early History of Israel: To the Exodus and Covenant of Sinai*, trans. David Smith (London: Darton, Longman & Todd, 1978), 577–81 and Frank Moore Cross, "Reuben, First-Born of Jacob," *ZAW* 100 Sup (1984), 46–65. My understanding largely follows de Vaux.

65 For a discussion of the socio-historical functions of genealogy, see Robert R. Wilson, *Genealogy and History in the Biblical World*, YNER 7 (New Haven, CT: Yale University Press, 1977), and the more recent summary of Walter E. Aufrecht, "Genealogy and History in Ancient Israel," *Ascribe to the Lord: Biblical and Other Studies in Memory of Peter C. Craigie*, JSOTSup 67, ed. Lyle Eslinger and Glen Taylor (Sheffield: Sheffield Academic Press, 1988), 205–35.

66 Cf. Gen 46:9 and Num 26:5–6, of Carmi, and Num 26:6 and 26:21, of Hezron.

67 See the commentaries, e.g. Speiser, *Genesis*, 274.

68 For a discussion of literary interpretations of this doublet, see I. Willi-Plein, "Historische Aspekte der Josephgeschichte," *Henoch* 1 (1979), 312–13.

69 For a similar use of *lamed* in Chronicles, see 1 Chr 29:6. On נגיד as "king", see my *God is King: Understanding an Israelite Metaphor*, JSOTSup 76 (Sheffield: Sheffield Academic Press, 1989), 33–5.

70 Redford, *A Study of the Biblical Story of Joseph*, 191–2, 242.

71 De Vaux, *Early History*, 292–5, Redford, *A Study of the Biblical Story of Joseph*, 138–86, Humphreys, *Joseph*, 198–200 and van Seters, *Prologue to History*, 311–27. These scholars should be distinguished from Robert E. Longacre, *Joseph: A Story of Divine Providence: A Text Theoretical and Textlinguistic Analysis of Genesis 37 and 39–40* (Winona Lake, IN: Eisenbrauns, 1989), 3–12, who is generally unsympathetic to source-criticism on theoretical grounds.

72 *A Study of the Biblical Story of Joseph*, esp. 178–86; van Seters, *Prologue to History*, 315 concurs.

73 Redford, *A Study of the Biblical Story of Joseph*, 250 suggests a date between 650 and 425, and more recently, in *Egypt, Canaan, and Israel in Ancient Times*, 422–9, suggests a date in the seventh to sixth centuries. Redford, however, does not use the stringent criteria which Avi Hurvitz has developed for the exilic and post-exilic dating of biblical texts. In addition, among the biblical books which serve as his sample for late Hebrew (*A Study of the Biblical Story of Joseph*, 54) are works which many scholars would consider pre-exilic, such as Deuteronomy, Psalms and Proverbs.

74 Goulder, *Type and History*, 4–6.

75 Gressman, *Ursprung und Entwicklung*, 9–10.

76 E.g. Isa 7:2; Jer 31:9; Zech 9:10; see *HALAT*, I, 78 s.v. אפרים 3.

77 E.g. Amos 6:6; Ezek 37:16; see *HALAT*, II, 385, s.v. יוסף 2.

78 This is reflected in several biblical texts; cf. 1 Kgs 12:21–4; 14:30; 15:16, 32; 2 Kgs 14:14; 15:37; 16:5.

79 In a similar vein, I would suggest that Gen 32:23–33 sanctions the strife between God and Israel by placing it at the beginning of Israel's existence under that name.

80 This expression is borrowed from an article with that title by Keith Whitelam, *JSOT* 29 (1984), 61–87.

81 The clearest case is the Book of Judges; see my "The Book of Judges: Literature as Politics," *JBL* 108 (1989), 395–418.

82 This is overstated by Redford, *A Study of the Biblical Story of Joseph*, 27, "it is a *Märchen* of marvellous unity and drama and the literary interest which surrounds it is sufficient *raison d'être*," cf. 66–105 ("The Joseph Story as Literature").

83 "Typological Interpretation of the Old Testament," 17.

84 Typologies are also found in Mesopotamian texts, and should probably be seen as a basic feature of ancient Near Eastern historical writing. A likely case is the Sargon Birth Legend, concerning Sargon of Akkad, but probably written under Sargon II; see Brian Lewis, *The Sargon Legend: A Study of the Akkadian Text and the Tale of the Hero who was Exposed at Death* (Cambridge, MA: ASOR, 1980), esp. 99–107. Anachronisms suggest that the Weidner Chronicle is clearly typological; in the words of its most recent editor (A. K. Grayson, *Assyrian and Babylonian Chronicles*, TCS 5 [Locust Valley, New York: J. J. Augustin, 1975], 43), "The text, therefore, is a blatant piece of propaganda written as an admonition to future monarchs to pay heed to Babylon and its cult." Some scholars have even made the strong claim that typologies play a predominant role in most pre-eighteenth-century history writing; see e.g. Norman F. Cantor and Richard I. Schneider, *How to Study History* (New York: Cromwell, 1967), 58–63.

85 On the connection between typologies and cyclical thinking in non-biblical literature, see Hollander, "Typology and Secular Literature," 6 and Charity, *Events and Their Afterlife*, 3–4.

86 We need not believe in the historicity of the exodus to accept this model; all we need acknowledge is that ancient Israelites believed in an exodus, and that it had a central role in ancient Israelite life.

87 For details, see Chapter Six.

88 An additional example of a political typology is in Genesis 34, the conquest of Shechem, which, as we know from other texts, was a city of central

importance; see Stephen A. Geller, "The Sack of Shechem: The Use of Typology in Biblical Covenant Religion," *Prooftexts* 10 (1990), 1–15.

89 See Landow, *Victorian Types*, 3.

90 For example, the frequent claim that E and D are northern is possible, but not compellingly documented by evidence.

91 Contrast Philip R. Davies, *In Search of "Ancient Israel"*, JSOTSup 148 (Sheffield: Sheffield Academic Press, 1992), 18, who sees the central question concerning biblical historical texts as "For what purposes and under what conditions did this society create this Israel, obviously as a projection of itself?"

92 David J. A. Clines, *The Theme of the Pentateuch*, JSOTSup 10 (Sheffield: JSOT Press, 1978), 98. Contrast Peter F. Ellis, *The Yahwist: The Bible's First Theologian* (London: Geoffrey Chapman, 1969), 136–8 ("The Obstacle Story"), who treats the same structure from a literary-aesthetic perspective.

93 On the date of J, which is probably the earliest of the sources, see Kåre Berge, *Die Zeit des Jahwisten: Ein Beitrag zur Datierung jahwistischer Vätertexte*, BZAW 186 (Berlin: Walter de Gruyter, 1990) and the review of John van Seters in *JBL* 110 (1991), 501–3. The reasons typically given for a tenth-century date of J are not convincing; on the other hand, for linguistic reasons, the contention that this source should be viewed as exilic cannot be sustained. For an even more extreme position, see Niels Peter Lemche, "The Old Testament – A Hellenistic Book?" *SJOT* 7 (1993), 163–93.

94 Keith W. Whitelam, "Israel's Tradition of Origin," 22.

4 DEUTERONOMY AS INTERPRETATION

1 Baruch Halpern, *The First Historians: The Hebrew Bible and History* (San Francisco: Harper and Row, 1988).

2 Halpern, *The First Historians*, esp. 76–103 and his article "Doctrine by Misadventure," *The Poet and the Historian*, HSS 26, ed. R. E. Friedman (Chico, CA: Scholars Press, 1983), 41–73.

3 I continue to accept the standard position that JE precedes D, though this has been questioned in several recent works by John van Seters and others. (For a bibliography on the recent study of the Pentateuchal sources, which includes the current debate on dating J, see Alan Cooper and Bernard R. Goldstein, "Biblical Literature in the Iron(ic) Age: Reflections on Literary-Historical Method," *Hebrew Studies* 32 [1991], 52, n. 25.) For a critique of van Seters' revisionist chronology of the sources, see Bernard Levinson, "The Hermeneutics of Innovation: The Impact of Centralization upon the Structure, Sequence, and Reformulation of Legal Material in Deuteronomy," Ph.D. dissertation, Brandeis University, 1991, 106–13.

4 See Chapter Two.

5 The best source for the exegetical principles embedded in midrashic literature is Isaac Heinemann, *The Methods of Aggadah* (Jerusalem: Magnes, 1970; Hebrew), which unfortunately has not been translated. Provisionally, see the essays in Geoffrey H. Hartman and Sanford Budick, *Midrash and Literature* (New Haven: Yale University Press, 1986), which includes an English translation of Heinemann's introduction (41–55).

6 Morton Smith, "Pseudepigraphy in the Israelite Literary Tradition," *Pseudepigrapha I*, ed. Kurt von Fritz (Geneva: Fondation Hardt, 1972), 191–215.

7 For a translation with introduction and notes by R. P. Spittler, see *OTP*, I, 829–68.

8 H. C. Kee, "Satan, Magic, and Salvation in the Testament of Job," *SBL Seminar Papers* 1 (1974), 53–76.

9 Nahum Glatzer, *The Judaic Tradition* (Boston: Beacon Press, 1969), 101.

10 See Spittler, *OTP*, I, 829; for a brief synopsis, see John J. Collins, "Structure and Meaning in the Testament of Job," *SBL Seminar Papers* 1 (1974), 35–52.

11 For specific affinities between the Testament and midrashic literature, see K. Kohler, "The Testament of Job: An Essene Midrash on the Book of Job," *Semitic Studies in Memory of Rev. Dr. Alexander Kohut*, ed. George Alexander Kohut (Berlin: S. Cavalry & Co., 1897), 267–92 and Russell Paul Spittler, Jr, "The Testament of Job: Introduction, Translation, Notes," Ph.D. dissertation, Harvard University, 1971.

12 See Marvin H. Pope, *Job*, AB (Garden City, New York: Doubleday, 1973), xxiii–xxx and H. L. Ginsberg, "Job the Patient and Job the Impatient," SVT 17 (Leiden: E. J. Brill 1969), 88–111.

13 Following the LXX κοπρίας; MT reads "ashes."

14 On the name Jobab=Job, see Spittler *OTP*, I, 839, note b and ibn Ezra to Job 1:1.

15 Nahum M. Sarna, "Epic Substratum in the Prose of Job," *JBL* 76 (1957), 13–25.

16 Other examples of this may be seen throughout the Testament; see esp. ch. 2 in relationship to biblical and midrashic Abraham.

17 On this genre, see Spittler, *OTP*, 831–2 and Spittler, "The Testament of Job: Introduction, Translation, Notes," 35–43.

18 Contrast the assumptions of Gerhard von Rad, *Deuteronomy: A Commentary*, OTL, trans. Dorothea Barton (Philadelphia: Westminster, 1966), 38–9. Note esp. 38: "Could he [the author of the introduction of Deuteronomy] have cut up the [source] stories, which are far apart from each other in the earlier sources, and then combined them again? This hypothesis is quite impossible, as we have said." For the opposite view, see A. D. H. Mayes, *Deuteronomy*, NCBC (London: Marshall Morgan & Scott, 1979), 118–19.

19 Michael Fishbane, *Biblical Interpretation in Ancient Israel* (Oxford: Oxford University Press, 1985). Fishbane, however, deals predominantly with Chronicles and post-exilic psalms in his chapter on historical texts (380–407).

20 See Chapter Two, *passim*.

21 See p. 137.

22 Ben Halpern, "History as a Jewish Problem," *From Ancient Israel to Modern Judaism, Intellect in Quest of Understanding: Essays in Honor of Marvin Fox*, BJS 159, vol. 1, ed. Jacob Neusner *et al.* (Atlanta: Scholars Press, 1989), 3.

23 I use this term in the plural to reflect the widely accepted theory that the authors of Deuteronomy 1–3 and of the legal material in 12–26 are not identical, yet they are part of the same school and may be expected to interpret earlier material in a fundamentally similar (if not identical) fashion.

24 S. R. Driver, *Deuteronomy*, ICC (Edinburgh: T. & T. Clark, 1973 [f.p. 1895]), xvii.

25 E.g. A. D. H. Mayes, *The Story of Israel between Settlement and Exile: A Redactional Study of the Deuteronomistic History* (London: SCM, 1983), 26–7:

> Characteristic of the author of Deut. 1.1–3.29 is his use of sources and indeed perhaps even a certain expectation that his readers knew these sources.... [T]he deuteronomistic historian felt able to allude to and make free use of the sources available to him in order to promote his particular theological point of view.

Cf. Norbert Lohfink, "Darstellungskuns und Theologie in Dtn 1,6–3,29," *Bib* 41 (1960), 105–34, esp. 107–10.

26 My concern throughout is on the texts" depiction of the judicial system rather than the actual judicial system in ancient Israel, though it is likely that the reality helped to shape the literary depiction. For two reconstructions of the judicial structure in ancient Israel, see Georg Christian Macholz, "Zur Geschichte der Justizorganisation in Juda," *ZAW* 84 (1972), 314–40 and Robert R. Wilson, "Israel's Judicial System in the Preexilic Period," *JQR* 74 (1983), 229–48.

27 On this pericope, in addition to the commentaries, see Rolf Knierim, "Exodus 18 und die Neuordnung der Mosaischen Gerichtsbarkeit," *ZAW* 73 (1961), 146–71.

28 On this passage, in addition to the commentaries, see Henri Cazelles, "Institutions et Terminologie en Deut. I 6–17," *SVT* 15 (1966), 97–112.

29 Jeffrey H. Tigay, "Conflation as a Redactional Technique," *Empirical Models for Biblical Criticism*, ed. Jeffrey H. Tigay (Philadelphia: University of Pennsylvania Press, 1985), 63–8.

30 Judith E. Sanderson, *An Exodus Scroll from Qumran: 4QpaleoExod^M and the Samaritan Tradition*, HSS 30 (Atlanta: Scholars Press, 1986), 207–8. The text has just been published in Patrick W. Skehan, Eugene Ulrich and Judith E. Sanderson, *Qumran Cave 4 IV*, DJD 9 (Oxford: Clarendon Press, 1992), 53–130. For a discussion of this and similar manuscripts, see Esther Eshel, "4QDeut^n – A Text That Has Undergone Harmonistic Editing," *HUCA* 62 (1991), 117–54.

31 For a contrary view, see John van Seters, "Etiology in the Moses Tradition: The Case of Exodus 18," *HAR* 9 (1985), 355–61. The following paragraph is fundamental to van Seters" argument (357):

> Here we have a serious methodological contradiction. We are asked to believe that the Yahwist or Elohist, faced with different oral traditions, had no choice but to produce a combination of these traditions whose awkwardness is clearly apparent to any reader. Yet, the Deuteronomist, when faced with the written traditions of J and E, exercised complete freedom to combine the accounts, eliminate most of the details that did not suit him, and produce a homogeneous narrative with scarcely any trace of such editorial activity. That is too hard for me to swallow!

The point that van Seters fails to appreciate is that different biblical historians, authors or redactors could and did have different attitudes toward their sources; even a single author may not be fully consistent in his attitude toward sources, as we saw in the previous chapter concerning the Chronicler. Additionally, contrary to van Seters' claim, a careful reading of the text of Deuteronomy shows traces of editorial activity, so Deuteronomy cannot be seen as the earlier text. Martin Rose, *Deuteronomist und Jahwist: Untersuchungen zu den Berührungspunkten beider Literaturwerke*, ATANT 67 (Zürich: Theologischer Verlag, 1981), 224–63 also questions the literary chronology of these three passages, and suggests that Numbers 11 follows Deut 1:9–18.

32 Moshe Weinfeld, *Deuteronomy 1–11*, AB (New York: Doubleday, 1991), 139; cf. Siegfried Mittmann, *Deuteronomium 1₁–6₃: Literarkritisch und traditionsgeschichlich untersucht*, BZAW 139 (Berlin: Walter de Gruyter, 1975), 26, n. 14 for the tradition of this opinion in German scholarship.

33 Hebrew שָׂרֵי חֲמִשִּׁים.

34 A common source can always be posited, but this is unlikely; see the comments

of Levinson, "Hermeneutics," 101–6. Even if a common source did exist, at some point either JE or D would be making the type of interpretive moves suggested in this chapter.

35 For a summary of the differences, see Weinfeld, *Deuteronomy 1–11*, 139–40.

36 See Robert R. Wilson, *Prophecy and Society in Ancient Israel* (Philadelphia: Fortress, 1980), 157–66, George W. Coats, *Moses: Heroic Man, Man of God*, JSOTSup 57 (Sheffield: Sheffield Academic Press, 1988), 21–5 and *idem, The Moses Tradition*, JSOTSup 161 (Sheffield: Sheffield University Press, 1993), 40, 44, 67, 71–5.

37 I avoid calling him Jethro; he has that name in the unit preceding Exod 18:13–26, but it is not used in our unit.

38 Moshe Weinfeld, *Deuteronomy and the Deuteronomic School* (Oxford: Oxford University Press, 1972), 244–5. For more recent summaries of the wisdom milieu of Deuteronomy, see Tikva Frymer-Kensky, "The Sage in the Pentateuch: Soundings," *The Sage in Israel and the Ancient Near East*, ed. John G. Gammie and Leo G. Perdue (Winona Lake, IN; Eisenbrauns, 1990), 280–5 and Roland E. Murphy, *The Tree of Life: An Exploration of Biblical Wisdom Literature*, AB (New York: Doubleday, 1990), 104–6.

39 For additional examples, see the works referred to in the previous note.

40 I intentionally avoid the word exegesis, a word which is used predominantly in biblical scholarship and not in general literary studies, since the term suggests that biblical texts are somehow different from other works. Instead, I am attempting to emphasize the similarity between biblical and other historians. (See my "The Ancient Exegesis of Historical Texts," *The Hebrew Bible as Sacred Text and as Literature*, ed. Jacob Lassner and Peter Machinist, forthcoming.)

41 Hebrew בעת ההיא.

42 Samuel E. Loewenstamm, "The Formula בעת ההיא in Deuteronomy," *Tarbiz* 38 (1968–9), 99–103 (Hebrew with English summary), translated in his *From Babylon to Canaan: Studies in the Bible and its Oriental Background* (Jerusalem: Magnes, 1992), 42–50.

43 This view usually assumes that these chapters are the introduction to the Deuteronomistic History (and not only to Deuteronomy), and that the Deuteronomistic History is an exilic composition; see Martin Noth, *The Deuteronomistic History*, JSOTSup 15, trans. Jane Doull *et al.* (Sheffield: JSOT Press, 1981), 13–15, E. W. Nicholson, *Deuteronomy and Tradition* (Philadelphia: Fortress, 1967), 20 and Timo Veijola, "Principal Observations on the Basis Story in Deuteronomy 1–3," *"Wünschet Jerusalem Frieden,"* BzEATAJ 13, ed. Matthias Augustin (Frankfurt: Peter Lang, 1988), 252–3. It is noteworthy that even Weinfeld, *Deuteronomy 1–11*, 14, who prefers to date texts early whenever possible, suggests that this passage is exilic. A comprehensive summary concerning the date and redaction of Deuteronomy 1–3 is in Horst Dietrich Preuss, *Deuteronomium*, ErFor 164 (Darmstadt: Wissenschaftliche Buchgesellschaft, 1982), 75–84.

44 So Mark O'Brien, *The Deuteronomistic History Hypothesis: A Reassessment*, OBO 92 (Göttingen: Vandenhoeck & Ruprecht, 1989), 51.

45 For example, Driver, *Deuteronomy*, 10, does not list Deut 16:18–20 in his chart of texts which have influenced this pericope. Several German scholars have realized the connection, but have not noted how extensive it is; cf. Mittmann, *Deuteronomium* 1_1–6_3, 32. The scholar who has most clearly observed the importance of Deuteronomy 16 is van Seters, "Etiology in the Moses Tra-

dition." My comments build upon his, though we differ fundamentally in our understanding of the chronological relationship between the texts.

46 Hebrew שטרים.

47 Note, for example, ibn Ezra, who glosses v. 19, "He [Moses] is speaking to all of the judges."

48 Hebrew משפט־צדק.

49 Hebrew ושפטתם צדק.

50 It is typical for ancient copyists or authors to paraphrase rather than to copy exactly; in that sense, they are, as Sh. Talmon has said, "a minor partner in the creation of the literary process." Talmon has studied this process especially in relationship to synonymous readings; see his "Synonymous Readings in the Textual Traditions of the Old Testament," *ScrHier* 8 (1961), 335–83. For a synthesis which builds upon Talmon's views, see Eugene Ulrich, "The Canonical Process, Textual Criticism, and Later Stages in the Composition of the Bible," *"Sha'arei Talmon": Studies in the Bible, Qumran and the Ancient Near East Presented to Shemaryahu Talmon*, ed. Michael Fishbane and Emanuel Tov (Winona Lake, IN: Eisenbrauns, 1992), 267–91; the quote from Talmon is cited on p. 267.

51 2 Chr 19:7 suggests that this is the likely meaning of Deut 1:17aβ. Contrast Mayes, *Deuteronomy*, 125, who understands the phrase differently.

52 So Weinfeld, *Deuteronomy 1–11*, 138.

53 See Loewenstamm, "The Formula," 99–100.

54 See pp. 41–5.

55 Hebrew בעת ההיא.

56 Hebrew כל־הדברים.

57 Hebrew הדברים ואצוה. is a frequent designation for the law in Deuteronomy; cf., for example, 1:1; 6:6; 12:28. The *hiphil* of ידע is used in Deuteronomy only in 4:9 and 8:3; contrast the frequent use of the *piel* of צוי in Deuteronomy (cf. Weinfeld, *Deuteronomy and the Deuteronomic School*, 356–7, ## 7 and 8). It is also possible that הדברים refers to the decalogue (cf., for example, Deut 4:13; 10:2, 4), in which case Deuteronomy 1 is sensitive to the fact that Exodus 18 immediately precedes 19–24, the giving of the decalogue and the book of the covenant. On these possibilities, see Cazelles, "Institutions," 111.

58 Hebrew נשא לבד.

59 Hebrew וריבכם.

60 On the range of meanings of ריב, cf. BDB *s.v.* ריב (936–7). For a discussion of the ריב, with extensive bibliography, see Michael de Roche, "Yahweh's *rîb* Against Israel: A Reassessment of the So-Called "Prophetic Lawsuit" in the Pre-Exilic Prophets," *JBL* 102 (1983), 563–74.

61 The Hebrew term שטרים is used, the same term as is used in our unit.

62 See vv. 11, 12 (twice),14, 17 (twice). Driver, *Deuteronomy*, 15 says that the term in Deuteronomy 1 "is borrowed from" Numbers 11. This is not quite precise; the dynamic is of rewriting and combination, not borrowing.

63 Hebrew טרחכם and משאכם. It is noteworthy that *Sifre Deuteronomy*, ed. Louis Finkelstein (New York: Jewish Theological Seminary, 1969), §12 was implicitly aware of this problem, and solved it by giving a judicial sense to the terms טרחכם ומשאכם.

64 Indeed, according to the liturgical reading tradition, this verse is read using the melody of Lamentations.

65 See Driver, *Deuteronomy*, 16. The function of v. 11 in relationship to its source is not sufficiently appreciated by Mittmann, *Deuteronomium 1₁–6₃*, 24, who sees it as secondary.

66 The Deuteronomic phraseology is noted in the commentaries.

67 See the standard histories, e.g. Siegfried Horn, "The Divided Monarchy: The Kingdoms of Judah and Israel," *Ancient Israel: A Short History from Abraham to the Roman Destruction of the Temple*, ed. Hershel Shanks (Washington, DC: Biblical Archaeology Society, 1988), 147–9 and my "2 Kings 24:13–14 as History," *CBQ* 53 (1991), 541–52.

68 Additional radical examples of reinterpretation may be seen in Deuteronomy's handling of the spies" narrative. Most significant is his reversal in the order of Num 13:28 (=Deut 1:28) and Num 14:7 (=Deut 1:25), which helps to add to the culpability of the population as a whole.

69 Hebrew גר. For Deuteronomy's attitude to the גר, see Christiana van Houten, *The Alien in Israelite Law*, JSOTSup 107 (Sheffield: JSOT Press, 1991), 68–108.

70 Hebrew הקריב rather than הביא.

71 See n. 50.

72 So in the Mekhilta *ad loc.*; see Jacob Z. Lauterbach, *Mekhilta De-Rabbi Ishmael* (Philadelphia: Jewish Publication Society, 1961), vol. 2, 184.

73 Cf. Lauterbach, *Mekhilta*, vol. 2, 184. The same midrashic process is reflected in Weinfeld, *Deuteronomy 1–11*, 138, who translates the Exodus verse, "the difficult matter they will bring to Moses."

74 The Hebrew is ושמעתיו. On the root שמע in the technical, juridical sense, see BDB s.v. שמע 1h (1033).

This type of addition, making explicit what is implicit, may be seen for example in Deuteronomy's revision of the law of the Decalogue concerning proper treatment of parents: Exod 20:12 merely states, "so that you may live long on the land," while in Deut 5:16, that is expanded with the addition of, "so that it will go well with you." (I owe this observation to Michael Fishbane, in a class on inner-biblical interpretation, at Brandeis University in 1978. A similar case in the first three chapters of Deuteronomy may be seen in 1:25, which is based on Num 13:20. The relevant section of Deut 1:25 reads: "and they took in their hand from the fruit of the land" [ויקחו בידם מפרי הארץ]; it fills in the word בידם, "in their hand," which was lacking, but is certainly implicit, in the source of Num 13:20, "you should take from the fruit of the land" [ולקחתם מפרי הארץ]. Also note how this phrase, which is a command in Numbers, is found later in the narrative in Deuteronomy, and appears as a fulfilled action.)

75 On the continuity between vv. 8 and 19, cf., for example, Weinfeld, *Deuteronomy 1–11*, 139.

76 Note, for example, the Code of Hammurabi, which also opens with laws concerning the administration of justice. On this introduction to the laws, see Herbert Petschow, "Zur Systematik und Gesetztechnik im Codex Hammurabi," *ZA* 57 (1965), 148–9.

77 On the lack of consistency of the final, redacted work, see John A. Miles, Jr, "Radical Editing: *Redaktionsgeschichte* and the Aesthetic of Willed Confusion," *Traditions in Transformation: Turning Points in Biblical Faith*, ed. Baruch Halpern and Jon D. Levenson (Winona Lake, IN: Eisenbrauns, 1981), 9–31.

78 For a general discussion of Deuteronomy's traditions concerning the conquest of the Transjordan, see Weinfeld, *Deuteronomy 1–11*, 173–8. On parts of these chapters as interpretation, see Urs Koppel, *Das deuteronomische Geschichtswerk und seine Quellen: Die Absicht der deuteronomischen Geschichtsdarstellung aufgrund des Vergleiches zwischen Num 21,21–35 und Dtn 2,26–3,3*, Europäische Hochschulschriften, Reihe XXIII, Bd. 122 (Frankfurt am Main: Peter Lang, 1979), esp. 83–105. Though we share some conclusions, our

methods differ in that unlike Koppel, I emphasize the relationship between Deuteronomy and both general history writing and rabbinic interpretive methods.

79 So, tentatively, von Rad, *Deuteronomy*, 38–9.

80 So e.g. Weinfeld, *Deuteronomy 1–11*, 166.

81 So e.g. Menahem Haran, *Ages and Institutions in the Bible* (Tel-Aviv: Am Oved, 1972; Hebrew), 37–76, esp. 37–8, who emphasizes the direct dependence of D on the extant E source. John L. McKenzie, "The Historical Prologue of Deuteronomy," *Fourth World Congress of Jewish Studies Papers*, I (Jerusalem: World Union of Jewish Studies, 1967), 98 notes, "the passage [concerning the Edomites in Deuteronomy] is another example of theological rewriting." McKenzie's entire article (95–101) has been overlooked by many scholars of Deuteronomy, but contains significant insights, and is one of the strongest defenses for Deuteronomy 1–3 as an interpretation of the JE traditions. The position taken by J. Maxwell Miller, "The Israelite Journey Through (Around) Moab and Moabite Toponymy," *JBL* 108 (1989), 583 is especially perplexing; Miller recognizes that Deuteronomy "combines competing traditions," but does not consider JE to be one of these traditions.

82 Note the sympathetic attitude toward the Edomites in Deut 23:8; if our Deuteronomic author shared this attitude, it might have helped him reshape his sources.

83 See the sources cited in Louis Ginzberg, *Legends of the Jews*, vol. 6 (Philadelphia: Jewish Publication Society, 1968), 264, n. 92.

84 Hebrew ויכהו, "he smote him," is ambiguous; it may refer to Sihon alone, or may have a collective, his entire army, as its object.

85 This principle was known as סמוכין in rabbinic literature. The classic formulation of this principle is found in *Sifre Numbers* edition = *Siphre D'be Rab*, ed. H. S. Horovitz (Jerusalem: Wahrmann Books, 1966) § 131: למידה הימנה ר עקיבא אומר כל פרשה שהיא סמוכה לחברתה, "Rabbi Akiba says: every unit bears upon its adjacent unit." This device has been studied by Fishbane, *Biblical Interpretation*, 399–407 (cf. Wilhelm Bacher, *Die Exegetische Terminologie der jüdischen Traditionsliteratur* [Leipzig: Hinrics, 1905] vol. 1, s.v. סמך) in relation to midrashic techniques found already in the Hebrew Bible.

86 On the ḥerem in Deuteronomy, see now Philip D. Stern, *The Biblical ḥerem: A Window on Israel's Religious Experience*, BJS 211 (Atlanta: Scholars Press, 1991), esp. 89–121.

87 In addition, compare Deut 20:13 and 2:33, and 20:14 and 2:34 (והנשים והטף).

88 So Veijola, "Principal Observations," 255. A less likely option, that they both emanate from the same circle, is suggested by Stern, *The Biblical ḥerem*, 120–1.

89 See n. 43.

90 This problem was already noticed by the rabbis, who of course did not solve it by viewing it as coming from another source; see Weinfeld, *Deuteronomy 1–11*, 171.

91 Fishbane, *Biblical Interpretation*, 199–209 and Alexander Rofé, "The Laws of Warfare in the Book of Deuteronomy: Their Origins, Intent and Positivity," *JSOT* 32 (1985), 23–44, esp. 28–30.

92 Contrast BDB, 675, s.v. נשמה, 3, "every breathing thing." None of their examples clearly refers to non-humans, and one of their examples, from Josh 11:14, which is closely related to our text, clearly distinguishes between בהמה, "animal," and נשמה.

93 Moshe Greenberg, "Some Postulates of Biblical Criminal Law," reprinted in *The Jewish Expression*, ed. Judah Goldin (New Haven, CT: Yale University

Press, 1976 [1960]), 24, 31, *idem*, "More Reflections of Biblical Criminal Law," *ScrHier* 31 (1986), 14 and J. J. Finkelstein, *The Ox that Gored*, TAPS 71/2 (Philadelphia: American Philosophical Society, 1981), 48–85, esp. 48–58.

94 The serpent of Genesis 3 is an exception.

95 The LXX to Num 21:21 implies, "Moses sent"; see Alfred Rahlfs, *Septuaginta* (Stuttgart: Deutsche Bibelstiftung, 1935), 252. This is probably a secondary reading which attempts to harmonize Numbers to Deuteronomy.

96 The author of these chapters might have had access to a separate body of geographical traditions; cf. Lothar Perlitt, "Deuteronomium 1–3 im Streit der exegetischen Methoden," *Das Deuteronomium*, ed. Norbert Lohfink (Leuven: Leuven University Press, 1985), 149–63.

97 J. Maxwell Miller, "The Israelite Journey Through (Around) Moab and Moabite Toponymy," *JBL* 108 (1989), 583 suggests that perhaps we should emend to Kedesh: "possibly some confusion has occurred here between Kedemoth and Kedesh (cf. Deut 1:46)."

98 For a summary concerning Heshbon, see Lawrence T. Gerarty, "Heshbon: The First Casualty in the Israelite Quest for the Kingdom of God," *The Quest for the Kingdom of God: Studies in Honor of George E. Mendenhall*, ed. H. B. Huffmon *et al.* (Winona Lake, IN: Eisenbrauns, 1983), 239–48.

99 It is especially interesting that this verse mentioning דברי שלום ("terms of peace") is cited, since most commentators would see the injunction in it to open up with "terms of peace" as relevant only to the far-off cities, the subject of verses 11–14. The author of Deut 2:26ff., however, understood "terms of peace" as a general heading, appropriate to both far-off cities and the Canaanites, and used it in reference to the nearby Sihon of Heshbon. In Deut 20:10 "terms of peace" reflects a sincere offer of peace; in Deut 2:26ff. it becomes a ruse.

100 E.g. Num 21:22 and Deut 2:27, "let me pass through your land"; Num 21:22 and Deut 2:29, "until I/we pass."

101 The Samaritan Pentateuch has further harmonized Num 21:22 to Deuteronomy.

102 Exod 4:21; 10:20, 27, which are considered E by most scholars, while others have argued that E does not exist in the plague narrative. The passage closest in terms of terminology is Exod 7:3, but this is P. For the terminology surrounding the hardening of Pharaoh's heart, see Robert R. Wilson, "The Hardening of Pharaoh's Heart," *CBQ* 41 (1979), 18–36.

103 Hebrew ראה; see 1:8, 21; 2:24; 4:5; 11:26; 30:15.

104 Charles William Fornara, *The Nature of History in Ancient Greece and Rome* (Berkeley: University of California Press, 1983), 143–6.

105 God's presence on Israel's side is a major theme of the "holy war" according to Deuteronomy; see Gerhard von Rad, *Holy War in Ancient Israel*, trans. Marva J. Dawn (Grand Rapids, MI: Eerdmans, 1991), 115–27.

106 The exception is that the words "and his children" (ואת-בניו) of Num 21:35 are lacking in Deuteronomy. These words are not found in the Samaritan of Numbers, and it is possible that a similar text served as the *Vorlage* of Deuteronomy. Alternatively, Jacob Milgrom, *Numbers*, The JPS Torah Commentary (Philadelphia: Jewish Publication Society, 1990), 184 suggests, "It [ואת-בניו] may have been omitted in the Deuteronomic account of Og because it would have clashed with the claim that Og was the last of the giants (Deut. 3:11)." If Milgrom is correct, then the change in Deuteronomy reflects intepretation.

107 E.g. August Dillmann, *Die Bücher Numeri, Deuteronomium und Josua*, KHAT

(Leipzig: S. Hirzel, 1886), 133, George Buchanan Gray, *Numbers*, ICC (Edinburgh: T. & T. Clark, 1903), 306 and more recently, Jacob Licht, *A Commentary on the Book of Numbers*, II (Jerusalem: Magnes Press, 1991; Hebrew), 212. For a more general attempt to claim that the entire passage on Sihon in Numbers depends on Deuteronomy, see John van Seters, "The Conquest of Sihon's Kingdom: A Literary Examination," *JBL* 91 (1972), 182–97. His arguments are accepted in Miller, "The Israelite Journey," 587, but are successfully rebutted by John R. Bartlett, "The Conquest of Sihon's Kingdom: A Literary Re-examination," *JBL* 97 (1978), 347–51.

108 Compare the transformation in Deut 2:26, and the article cited above by Perlitt on that verse (n. 96, above). We may not, however, automatically assume that the information given in these verses is accurate; contrast von Rad, *Deuteronomy*, 41, "Nevertheless, here, too, there has no doubt been preserved a reliable early memory of a comparatively large region ruled by a king named Og."

109 The varying of terminology to avoid monotony is even the case with P, whose style is usually seen as highly monotonous; see Meir Paran, *Forms of the Priestly Style in the Pentateuch: Patterns, Linguistic Usages, Syntactic Structures* (Jerusalem: Magnes, 1989; Hebrew), index s.v. חזרה.

110 This is the title of Chapter 12 of Noth, *The Deuteronomistic History*, 84–8.

111 A series of papers assessing Noth's contributions to biblical studies were delivered at the 1993 meeting of the Society of Biblical Literature and are due to be published in the near future.

112 Esp. xvii, 29–32.

113 Noth, *The Deuteronomistic History*, 84.

114 Noth, *The Deuteronomistic History*, 86.

115 Noth, *The Deuteronomistic History*, 87.

116 For additional examples from Deuteronomy 1–3, see the article by W. L. Moran with the telling title "The End of the Unholy War and the Anti-Exodus," *Bib* 44 (1963), 333–42.

117 This is even the case with rabbinic interpretation, which is often characterized as harmonizing. Rabbinic harmonizing typically combines two texts, but one is foregrounded, while the other recedes into the background. See, for example, the laws concerning Hebrew slaves in *Mekhilta*, where Exodus 21, Leviticus 25 and Deuteronomy 16 are harmonized, but the notion that the servant may work "forever" (עד עולם), found in Exodus and Deuteronomy, recedes into the background as Leviticus" idea that he works until the jubilee year is accepted. (See Lauterbach, *Mekhilta*, vol. 3, 17.)

118 This question, of course, is connected to whether Deuteronomy should be seen as a (pious) forgery; see the discussion, with anecdotes, in Smith, "Pseudepigraphy," esp. 193.

119 See pp. 46–7.

120 Indeed, it is quite striking that Noth, like most other scholars, draws a clear contrast between the Deuteronomist and the Chronicler. In Noth's case, this is based on a mischaracterization of both corpora. For an exploration of the similarities between the Deuteronomistic History and Chronicles, see my "From the Deuteronomist(s) to the Chronicler: Continuities and Innovations," *Proceedings of the Eleventh World Congress for Jewish Studies. Division A: The Bible and its World* (Jerusalem: World Union of Jewish Studies, 1994), 83–90.

121 On this formula, see Michael Fishbane, "Varia Deuteronomica," *ZAW* 84 (1972), 349–50. The irony is studied at length throughout Levinson, "Hermeneutics."

122 H. St. J. Thackery, *Jewish Antiquities, Books I–IV*, The Loeb Classical Library (Cambridge: Harvard University Press, 1930), p. 9 (§ 1.17). On the meaning and origin of this claim, see most recently Gregory E. Sterling, *Historiography and Self-Definition: Josephos, Luke–Acts and Apologetic Historiography* (Leiden: E. J. Brill, 1992), 252–5.

123 This is the theme of many of Louis Feldman's studies concerning Josephus" biblical portrayals; see the bibliography in Louis H. Feldman and Gohei Hata, *Josephus, the Bible, and History* (Detroit: Wayne State University Press, 1989), 355–66, and most recently, Louis H. Feldman, "Josephus" Portrait of Gideon," *Revue des études juives* 152 (1993), 5–28, with a biliography of his other works on Josephus" depiction of biblical characters on p. 8, n. 6.

5 THE EHUD STORY AS SATIRE

1 Scholars disagree on the boundaries of the Ehud pericope; scholars' positions depend on whether the focus is the story in its current form or in one of its pre-redacted versions. I agree with Wolfgang Richter, *Die Bearbeitungen des "Retterbuches in der deuteronomischen Epoche*, BBB 21 (Bonn: Peter Hanstein, 1964), 3–6, J. Alberto Soggin, "᾿Ehud und ᶜEglon: Bemerkungen zu Richter III 11b-31," *VT* 29 (1989), 96, 98 and Uwe Becker, *Richterzeit und Königtum: Redaktionsgeschichtliche Studien zum Richterbuch*, BZAW 192 (Berlin: Walter de Gruyter, 1990), 120–2, that in its final form, this story is a Deuteronomistic reworking of an older story. Most of my observations, however, concern the pre-Deuteronomistic story. An earlier version of this study appeared as "Never the Twain Shall Meet? The Ehud Story as History and Literature," *HUCA* 62 (1991), 285–304. Another article that independently arrives at a similar conclusion is Lowell K. Handy, "Uneasy Laughter: Ehud and Eglon and Ethnic Humor," *SJOT* 6 (1992), 233–46; though our general conclusions are similar, our methods of arriving at them and our methodological concerns are quite different.

2 I do not attempt to comment in the notes on every difficulty that the text presents to translators. I concentrate on problems relevant to my interpretation and on issues that have not been adequately noted by previous scholars. For additional philological comments, see the commentaries, and most recently, Becker, *Richterzeit und Königtum*, 109–20.

3 Alternatively, "were more evil than before."

4 The decision not to translate הרע בעיני יהוה idiomatically as "what YHWH considered to be evil" is deliberate, and is meant to reflect the importance of body parts in the pericope.

5 The variation between singular וילד ויד and plural ויירשו is leveled in the LXX, whose reading is preferred by *BHS* and many commentators. My translation follows MT, which uses the singulars to give primary responsibility to Eglon, while the plurals reflect v. 13a, which states that Eglon and the Moabites did not act alone.

6 The novel suggestion of Gösta W. Ahlström, *The History of Ancient Palestine from the Paleolithic Period to Alexander's Conquest*, JSOTSup 146 (Sheffield: JSOT Press, 1993), 38, n. 2, that Ehud was not from Benjamin but from the land of Yemini (cf. 1 Sam 9:4), and thus an Asherite, is not compelling.

7 The expression אטר יד־ימינו, literally "bound with respect to his right hand," is probably idiomatic for "left-handed." Ehud's left-handedness is explicitly noted because it explains how he smuggled his sword in; the palace officials assumed he was right-handed, and checked his left side for weapons (cf.

George F. Moore, *Judges*, ICC [Edinburgh: T. & T. Clark, 1976 (f.p. 1895)], 93).

8 Literally, "a *gomed* long"; we do not know exactly how long a *gomed* is, though the versions, comparative lexicography and the context suggest that it is a short measure.

9 The awkwardness of the English attempts to depict the nuances of the Hebrew; see p. 81.

10 הפסילים may be a place name or a common noun; see *HALAT*, 894. If it refers to a place where there are idols, this detail may be narrated to explain where Ehud received the divine oracle noted in v. 20. The reference to the place again in v. 26, however, suggests that it was simply a well-known landmark.

11 The term עלית המקרה is difficult. It seems to be identical with or similar to חדר המקרה, which is mentioned in v. 24, though perhaps one is a subroom of the other. The context, namely Ehud delivering tribute, suggests that these refer to the throne room, as suggested by Baruch Halpern, *The First Historians: The Hebrew Bible and History* (San Francisco: Harper & Row, 1988), 45–58, though I do not find the additional specifics of his architectural reconstruction fully convincing. I will therefore translate עלית המקרה, חדר המקרה and המקרה as "throne room," though there probably was some difference between them. What is crucial for our understanding of the narrative (and was crucial in antiquity as well) is supplied by the narrator in v. 20 – אשר-לו לבדו, namely that this was a room in which the king could expect privacy.

12 Each of the three main clauses ends with an -ô; it is impossible to reflect this in the translation.

13 See most recently M. L. Barré, "The Meaning of *pršdn* in Judges iii 22," *VT* 41 (1991), 1–11.

14 Taking המסדרונה with many scholars from the root סדר. Halpern's understanding of this in *The First Historians*, 58 as a hidden area under the floor is based on questionable linguistic parallels.

15 See G. Bergsträsser, *Hebräische Grammatik* (Hildesheim: Georg Olms, 1962), vol. II, note to §9b–k.

16 An idiom for urinating; note the repeated use of a body part.

17 Instead of רדפו, רדו is expected. MT suggests that Ehud is being chased, rather than leading the chase. Either MT is wrong or reflects an anomalous usage of רדפו.

18 Hebrew יד.

19 Luis Alonso Schökel, "Erzählkunst im Buche der Richter," *Bib* 42 (1961), 149–57.

20 Robert Alter, *The Art of Biblical Narrative* (New York: Basic, 1981), 38–41.

21 *The Art of Biblical Narrative*, 40.

22 *The Art of Biblical Narrative*, 41.

23 Alonso-Schökel, "Erzählkunst im Buche der Richter," 151.

24 For a contrasting approach, see Wilfred G. E. Watson, *Classical Hebrew Poetry: A Guide to its Techniques*, JSOTSup 26 (Sheffield: JSOT Press, 1986), 229–33. Furthermore, the "rhyming" words share only the very common third masculine singular suffix, and at least according to most later, medieval Jewish rhyming schemes, this would not be considered a rhyme. (For a brief survey of rhyme in Hebrew poetry, see Benjamin Hrushovski, "Note on the Systems of Hebrew Versification," *The Penguin Book of Hebrew Verse*, ed. T. Carmi [Harmondsworth: Penguin, 1981], 68–70.)

25 Alonso-Schökel, "Erzählkunst im Buche der Richter," 149–50, Alter, *The Art of Biblical Narrative*, 39 and Yairah Amit, *The Book of Judges: The Art of*

Editing, Biblical Encyclopedia Library, vol. 5 (Jerusalem: Mosad Bialik, 1992), 171–2 (Hebrew). For more on the name Eglon, see n. 29.

26 Martin Noth, *Die israelitischen Personennamen im Rahmen der gemeinsemitischen Namengebung*, BWANT III/10 (Stuttgart: Kohlhammer, 1928), 230.

27 Hebrew ויקרב את-המנחה. Note that the typical verbs expected with מנחה in a non-sacrificial sense are הביא, הגיש, השיב, העלה, הוריד and נשא (e.g. Gen 4:3; 43:11; 1 Kgs 5:1; 2 Kgs 17:3, 4; Ps 96:8); see now Amit, *The Book of Judges*, 171, n. 19. For the verb הקריב in relation to sacrifice, see BDB *s.v.* קרב 2b (p. 898).

28 I am less hesitant on this matter than Gary A. Anderson, *Sacrifices and Offerings in Ancient Israel: Studies in Their Social and Political Importance*, HSM 41 (Atlanta: Scholars Press, 1987), 70, though he notes Ps 72:10 as a (single) additional case which does use the verb הקריב in a tribute context. Cf. Yairah Amit, "The Story of Ehud (Judges 3:12–30): The Form and the Message," *Signs and Wonders*, Semeia Studies, ed. J. Cheryl Exum (Society of Biblical Literature, 1989), 110, who makes a point similar to mine. Amit, however, is more interested in the religious overtones than in the specifically sacrificial ones.

29 Cf. Soggin, "'Ehud und 'Eglon," 96.

30 *The Art of Biblical Narrative*, 39. It is not surprising that the Bible should dwell on these matters, for it is much less prudish than typically thought; see Edward Ullendorff, "The Bawdy Bible," *BSAOS* 42 (1979), 425–56, though not all of the examples offered by Ullendorff are equally convincing. I would like to thank Gary Rendsburg for this reference.

31 Hebrew פתח and סגר; cf., for example, Michael V. Fox, *The Song of Songs and the Ancient Egyptian Love Songs* (Madison: University of Wisconsin Press, 1985), 144, 137.

32 Yigael Yadin, *The Art of Warfare in the Biblical Lands According to Archaeological Finds* (New York: McGraw Hill, 1963), 254–5.

33 For toilets in ancient Israel, see Halpern, *The First Historians*, 58, Ulrich Hübner, "Mord auf dem Abort? Überlegungen zu Humor, Gewaltdarstellung und Realienkunde im Ri 3, 12–30," *BN* 40 (1987), 131–40 and Jane Cahill *et al.*, "It Had to Happen – Scientists Examine Remains of Ancient Bathroom," *BARev 17/3* (May/June 1991), 64–9.

34 Hebrew בא אל. The significance of this term is noted by Alter, but he does not substantiate his point by contrasting this phrase to others that the author might have chosen, such as נגש אל, which is used in Gen 27:22. This point, however, should not be overemphasized, given that בא אל is a very common expression and is often used in a non-sexual sense.

35 Hebrew יד; contrast e.g. Judg 8:28.

36 On the phallic use of יד, cf. BDB 490, s.v. יד 4g and *HALAT*, vol. 2, 370, 1e. V. 30, which shares vocabulary with other passages from the framework of Judges, is probably later than the main part of the story (Richter, *Die Bearbeitungen*, 135), and might reflect the Deuteronomistic Historian's understanding of the sexual innuendo within the story.

37 אחלי! תבוא לי ויבוא הנצב אחר הלהב.; see the edition of David Yellin, *Gan Hammeshalim We-Hahidoth: Diwan of Don Tadros Son of Abu-'el-'äfiah* (Jerusalem: Weiss, 1934), vol. 2, part 1, 130–1, poem 724 (165). Some sense of Abulafiah's concern with love and his explicit use of sexual imagery is seen in the selection of his poems in T. Carmi, ed., *The Penguin Book of Hebrew Verse*, 410–16. I would like to thank Dr Noah Feldman for calling this poem to my attention.

38 See most recently Ahlström, *The History of Ancient Palestine*, 39.

39 On the editing of Judges, see Becker, *Richterzeit und Königtum*, esp. 1–17, 300–6, with literature there. On the possible origin of the original pre-Deuteronomistic narratives as tribal stories, see W. Beyerlin, "Gattung und Herkunft des Rahmens im Retterbuch," *Tradition und Situation, Studien zur alttestamentlichen Prophetie, Artur Weiser zur 70. Geburtstag* (Göttingen: Vandenhoeck & Ruprecht, 1963), 1–2, and on this story, see Moore, *Judges*, 90.

40 See Andrew Dearman, *Studies in the Mesha Inscription and Moab* (Atlanta: Scholars Press, 1989). For a survey, see J. R. Bartlett, "The Moabites and Edomites," *Peoples of Old Testament Times*, ed. D. J. Wiseman (Oxford: Oxford University Press, 1973), 229–58. For a sketch of the archeological evidence, see James A. Sauer, "Ammon, Moab and Edom," *Biblical Archaeology Today* (Jerusalem: Israel Exploration Society, 1985), 206–14.

41 ימנ.רבנ; see *KAI*, vol. 1, 33 #181.

42 The unusual positive attitude to Moab in 1 Sam 22:3–4 is noted by P. Kyle McCarter, Jr, *I Samuel*, AB (Garden City, New York: Doubleday, 1980), 357, "The tradition that David sequestered his parents in Moab during his outlaw days is an odd one."

43 I avoid discussing the attitude reflected in Ruth, which seems not to point in a clear direction; see most recently Yair Zakovitch, *Ruth*, Mikra Leyisra'el – A Bible Commentary for Israel (Tel-Aviv and Jerusalem: Am Oved and Magnes, 1990) [Hebrew] and in English, Jack M. Sasson, *Ruth: A New Translation with a Philological Commentary and a Formalist-Folklorist Interpretation* (Sheffield: JSOT Press, 1989).

44 J. Cheryl Exum and J. William Whedbee, "Isaac, Samson, and Saul: Reflections on the Comic and the Tragic Visions," *Sem* 32 (1984), 6. On humor in the Bible, see now Yehuda T. Radday and Athalya Brenner, *On Humour and the Comic in the Hebrew Bible*, JSOTSup 92 (Sheffield: Sheffield Academic Press, 1990). Bruce William Jones, "Two Misconceptions about the Book of Esther," *CBQ* 39 (1977), 171–81 raises issues concerning humor in Esther that are directly applicable to our passage in Judges. On the function of humor within religion, see Mahadev L. Apte, *Humor and Laughter: An Anthropological Approach* (Ithaca: Cornell University Press, 1985), 151–76. Specifically on satire and religion, see Robert A. Kantra, *All Things Vain: Religious Satirists and Their Art* (University Park, PA: The Pennsylvania State University Press, 1984).

45 Franz Rosenthal, *Humor in Early Islam*, (Philadelphia: University of Pennsylvania Press, 1956). For a discussion of Mesopotamian humor which is similarly indebted to Rosenthal, see Benjamin R. Foster, "Humor and Cuneiform Literature," *JANESCU* 6 (1974), 69–85.

46 *Humor in Early Islam*, 1.

47 Others have noted its humor, but have not attempted to discuss it in relationship to the general problem of deciding what the Israelites found funny; see Ulrich Hübner, "Mord auf dem Abort?" 130–40, Lillian R. Klein, *The Triumph of Irony in the Book of Judges*, JSOTSup 68 (Sheffield: Almond Press, 1988), 37–9 and Soggin, "'Ehud," 95.

48 Willliam H. Martineau, "A Model of the Social Function of Humor," *The Psychology of Humor: Theoretical Perspectives and Empirical Issues* (New York: Academic Press, 1972), 118–19.

49 It is further developed by Barry Webb, *The Book of Judges: An Integrated Reading*, JSOTSup 46 (Sheffield: JSOT Press, 1987), 129–30, but he, like Alter, does not adequately explore the social dynamics of this satire.

50 "U and ∩ in the Bible," *Sem* 32 (1985), 107–14, esp. 108–10.

51 See his posthumous work (completed by Joachim Begrich), *Einleitung in die Psalmen: Die Gattungen der religiösen Lyrik Israels* (Göttingen: Vandenhoeck & Ruprecht, 1966). A translation of his earlier *RGG* article has been published as *The Psalms: A Form-Critical Introduction*, trans. Thomas M. Horner (Philadelphia, PA: Fortress, 1967).

52 Tremper Longman III, *Fictional Akkadian Autobiography: A Generic and Comparative Study* (Winona Lake, IN: Eisenbrauns, 1991), esp. 3–21; cf. his *Literary Approaches to Biblical Interpretation* (Grand Rapids, MI: Zondervan, 1987).

53 Longman, *Fictional Akkadian Autobiography*, 7, 15–17.

54 Tsvetan Todorov, "The Origin of Genres," *NLH* 8 (1976), 163.

55 Ralph Cohen, "History and Genre," *NLH* 17 (1986), 206.

56 My use of the phrase "ancient function" makes it clear that the importance of isolating precise genres is connected to one's commitment to historical critical readings. For an example of misinterpretation based on "misgenrification," or on what one scholar calls "generic misfiring" (Dorrit Cohn, "Fictional *Versus* Historical Lives: Borderlines and Borderline Cases," *Journal of Narrative Techniques* 19 [1989], 15), note the confusion caused when the satiric work of the anti-Hasidic author Joseph Perl, *Megalleh Temirin* was initially received as a regular Hasidic work, offering true information about the wonders of a Hasidic Rebbe. The confusion concerning this work still continues; many libraries continue to catalogue it with Hasidic hagiographic tales, rather than with satire, where it properly belongs.

57 Longman, *Fictional Akkadian Autobiography*, 14.

58 Longman, *Fictional Akkadian Autobiography*, 13.

59 Longman, *Fictional Akkadian Autobiography*, 18–19.

60 James L. Kugel, *The Idea of Biblical Poetry: Parallelism and Its History* (New Haven: Yale University Press, 1981).

61 The biblical word שיר is more specific than "a poem"; it refers to a particular type of work sung or recited to musical accompaniment.

62 Kugel, *The Idea of Biblical Poetry*, 69; cf. 85 and 94.

63 Cf. Stephen Geller, "Theory and Method in the Study of Biblical Poetry," *JQR* 73 (1982), 75–7 and Francis Landy, "Poetics and Parallelism: Some Comments on James Kugel's *The Idea of Biblical Poetry*," *JSOT* 28 (1984), 68–70.

64 In contrast to calling a biblical text "poetry," the label "literature" does not foster a useful interpretive frame. "Literature," I have argued in Chapter One, encourages a particular type of evaluation not interpretation.

65 This point is made in the essays of both Todorov and Cohen, cited in nn. 54–5 above.

66 See n. 51, above.

67 They are used, for example, in the studies of Claus Westermann, *Praise and Lament in the Psalms*, trans. Keith Crim and Richard Soulen (Atlanta: John Knox, 1981).

68 E.g. שיר and תודה; see H. J. Kraus, *Psalms 1–59* (Minneapolis: Augsburg, 1988), 38–62; cf. Bernd Feininger, "A Decade of German Psalm-Criticism," *JSOT* 20 (1981), 91–103, esp. 97–8.

69 The situation is somewhat different for ancient Mesopotamia, where native form-critical terms are attested to; see William Hallo, "Individual Prayers in Sumerian: The Continuity of a Tradition," *JAOS* 88 (1968) [Essays in Memory of E. A. Speiser], 71–89. However, as noted by Longman, *Fictional Akkadian*

Autobiography, 14–15, many of these Sumerian or Akkadian designations are not actually *genre* labels.

70 The issue of *Sitz im Leben* has been appropriately de-emphasized since the time of Gunkel, as scholars have recognized that works of a similar genre may have different social settings; see Longman, *Fictional Akkadian Autobiography* 17–18. To the extent that genre can be closely related to *Sitz im Leben*, it is noteworthy that some scholars connect satire to ritual (e.g. Paul Frye, "Satire," *The Princeton Handbook of Poetic Terms*, ed. Alex Preminger [Princeton: Princeton University Press, 1986], 248–9), in which case Judg 3:12–30 might be explored as a text for the ritual humiliation of one's enemies.

71 For an extensive examination of satire in prophecy, see now Thomas Jemielty, *Satire and the Hebrew Prophet* (Louisville: Westminster/John Knox, 1992).

72 Northrop Frye, *Anatomy of Criticism* (Princeton: Princeton University Press, 1957), 224. For a discussion of the problems of defining the genre, see Patricia Meyer Spacks, "Some Reflections on Satire," *Satire: Modern Essays in Criticism*, ed. Ronald Paulson (Englewood Cliffs, NJ: Prentice-Hall, 1971), 360–78 and Don L. F. Nilsen, "Satire – The Necessary and Sufficient Conditions – Some Preliminary Observations," *Studies in Contemporary Satire* 15 (1988), 1–10. For a discussion which focusses on the word's etymology and its early use, see Carl Joachim Classen, "Satire – the Elusive Genre," *Symbolae Osloenses* 63 (1988), 95–121.

73 John R. Clark, "Bowl Games: Satire in the Toilet," *Modern Language Studies* 4 (1974), 43–58.

74 Irving Buchen, "Decadent Sexuality and Satire," *Paunch* 40–1 (1975), 64–77.

75 Edward A. Bloom and Lillian D. Bloom, *Satire's Persuasive Voice* (Ithaca: Cornell University Press, 1979), 218–21.

76 Gary Rendsburg (oral communication) has suggested to me that Ehud's father is named Gera, "cud". The etymology of Ehud is uncertain, but it cannot be related to any known animal name.

77 Edward R. Rosenheim, "The Satiric Spectrum," *Satire: Modern Essays in Criticism*, 317–18.

78 Paul Frye, "Satire," *The Princeton Handbook of Poetic Terms*, ed. Alex Preminger (Princeton: Princeton University Press, 1986), 248.

79 Leonard Feinberg, "Satire and Humor: In the Orient and in the West," *Costerus* 2 (1972), 33–61.

80 Feinberg, "Satire and Humor," 49.

81 Feinberg, "Satire and Humor," 53.

82 Feinberg, "Satire and Humor," 58.

83 Feinberg, "Satire and Humor," 60.

84 See Burke O. Long, "Historical Narrative and Fictionalizing Imagination," *VT* 35 (1985), 405–16, esp. 416 on the importance of recognizing the proper genre of historical texts.

85 Rosenheim, "The Satiric Spectrum," 312.

86 On this concept, see Eric Hobsbawm and Terence Ranger, eds, *The Invention of Tradition* (Cambridge: Cambridge University Press, 1983), which adduces modern cases of such inventions. These cases serve as important illustrations of how quickly falsehoods are believed and of the social mechanisms involved in the creation of new traditions.

87 An additional example of this tendency of biblical scholars has been recently pointed out by David J. A. Clines, "In Quest of the Historical Mordecai," *VT* 41 (1991), 129–36, who chastises scholars who improperly connect the Morde-

cai of the Book of Esther to a Marduka known from an Akkadian tablet from the Persian period and use this to develop the story's historical kernel.

88 Martin Noth, *The History of Israel*, third English edition (New York: Harper & Row, 1960), 156.

89 John Bright, *A History of Israel*, third edition (Philadelphia: Westminster, 1981), 179.

90 A. D. H. Mayes, "The Period of the Judges and the Rise of the Monarchy," *Israelite and Judaean History*, ed. John H. Hayes and J. Maxwell Miller (Philadelphia: Westminster, 1977), 312.

91 J. Maxwell Miller and John H. Hayes, *A History of Ancient Judah and Israel* (Philadelphia: Westminster, 1986).

92 Miller and Hayes, *A History of Ancient Judah and Israel*, 87.

93 Miller and Hayes, *A History of Ancient Judah and Israel*, 96.

94 J. Alberto Soggin, *A History of Ancient Israel from the Beginnings to the Bar Kochba Revolt, A.D. 135* (Philadelphia: Westminster, 1984), 175.

95 Ahlström, *The History of Ancient Palestine*, 38–40, 377–8.

96 My position that this text reflects its author's period rather than the period it purports to describe shares much with Julius Wellhausen, *Prolegomena to the History of Ancient Israel* (Gloucester, MA: Peter Smith, 1973), esp. what he says concerning the patriarchs on 318–19:

> It is true, we attain to no historical knowledge of the patriarchs, but only of the time when the stories about them arose in the Israelite people; this later age is here unconsciously projected, in its inner and its outward features, into hoar antiquity, and is reflected there like a glorified mirage.

Cf. Thomas L. Thompson, "Text, Context and Referent in Israelite Historiography," *The Fabric of History*, ed. Diana Vikander Edelman, 65–7. I do not mean to suggest that biblical historical texts may never be used to reconstruct the past. However, scholars have often been too careless in using them for this purpose. For a discussion of the biblical text and the modern historian, see the Conclusion to this book. On the problem of using the term "period of judges," see Philip R. Davies, *In Search of "Ancient Israel,"* JSOTSup 148 (Sheffield: Sheffield University Press, 1992), 27, who notes that the " 'period of judges' " cannot "be transformed into an epoch in the history of Palestine" and Thomas L. Thompson, *Early History of the Israelite People From the Written and Archaeological Sources*, Studies in the History of the Ancient Near East, 4 (Leiden: E. J. Brill, 1992), 95–105 ("The Historicity of the Period of the Judges").

97 It is tempting to read the story as a general declaration of Israel's superiority over all of its neighbors, but there are no indications that the Moabites are used symbolically in this manner.

98 For a discussion of this motif, see Peter Machinist, "The Question of Distinctiveness in Ancient Israel: An Essay," *ScrHier* 33 (1991) [=*Ah, Assyria. . . . Studies in Assyrian History and Ancient Historiography Presented to Hayim Tadmor*, ed. Mordechai Cogan and Israel Ephal], 196–212, reprinted in *Essential Papers on Israel and the Ancient Near East*, ed. Frederick E. Greenspahn (New York: New York University Press, 1991), 420–42.

99 The lack of repentance throughout most of Judges is noted in Frederick E. Greenspahn, "The Theology of the Framework of Judges," *VT* 36 (1986), 385–96. This point is worth emphasizing because many scholars insert repentance into the cycles of Israel's behavior in Judges; see for example Brevard Childs, *Introduction to the Old Testament as Scripture* (Philadelphia, PA:

Fortress, 1979), 260, who refers to a "schema [of] . . . the repetition of Israel's disobedience, God's anger, Israel's repentance, and God's salvation."
100 David Gunn, *The Fate of King Saul: An Interpretation of a Biblical Story* JSOTSup 14 (Sheffield: JSOT Press, 1980), 12.
101 Peter R. Ackroyd, *The First Book of Samuel*, CBC (Cambridge: Cambridge University Press, 1971), 6–7.
102 The one possible exception is Song of Songs, whose purpose remains elusive, despite a multiplicity of theories explaining its origin and putative function.
103 On irony in the unit in general, see Klein, *The Triumph of Irony in the Book of Judges*, 37–9.
104 Alter, *The Art of Biblical Narrative*, 41, following an observation by Alonso-Schökel.
105 See above, n. 24.
106 James L. Kugel, *The Idea of Biblical Poetry: Parallelism and its History* (New Haven: Yale University Press, 1981), 140–2.
107 See John Barton, *Reading the Old Testament: Method in Biblical Study* (Philadelphia: Westminster, 1984), esp. 11–16.
108 Diana Vikander Edelman, *King Saul in the Historiography of Judah*, JSOTSup 121 (Sheffield: Sheffield Academic Press, 1991), 13 and *passim*.

6 IDEOLOGY IN THE BOOK OF SAMUEL

1 A version of this chapter was given at a conference on "Literature and Politics in the Ancient Near East" at Cornell University, and benefited from the comments of the participants and audience.
2 Stefan Heym, *The King David Report*, (New York: G. P. Putnam's Sons, 1973). For an argument that non-biblical material is especially useful for understanding the biblical portrayal of David, see David L. Petersen, "Portraits of David Canonical and Otherwise," *Int* 40 (1986), 130–42. The usefulness of Heym for understanding the Bible is acknowledged by Walter Brueggemann, *David's Truth in Israel's Imagination and Memory* (Philadelphia: Fortress, 1985) 69–71.
3 For a synthetic summary of Israelite kingship, with bibliography, see Keith Whitelam, "Israelite Kingship. The Royal Ideology and Its Opponents," *The World of Ancient Israel: Sociological, Anthropological and Political Approaches*, ed. R. E. Clements (Cambridge: Cambridge University Press, 1989), 119–39.
4 Heym, *The King David Report*, 9.
5 Heym, *The King David Report*, 9.
6 Heym, *The King David Report*, 32.
7 Heym, *The King David Report*, 44.
8 Heym, *The King David Report*, 82.
9 Peter Hutchinson, "Problems of Socialist Historiography: The Example of Stefan Heym's *The King David Report*," *Modern Language Review* 81 (1986), 131–8.
10 Hutchinson, "Problems of Socialist Historiography: The Example of Stefan Heym's *The King David Report*," 134.
11 Hutchinson, "Problems of Socialist Historiography: The Example of Stefan Heym's *The King David Report*," 131.
12 See p. 13.
13 Leonhard Rost, *The Succession to the Throne of David*, trans. Michael D. Rutter and David M. Gunn (Sheffield: Almond Press, 1982).
14 Gerhard von Rad, "The Beginnings of Historical Writings in Ancient Israel,"

The Problem of the Hexateuch and Other Essays, trans. E. W. Trueman Dicken (London: SCM, 1984), 166–204, esp. 176–204. On the influence of von Rad, see Edward Ball, "Introduction" to Leonhard Rost, *The Succession to the Throne of David*, xxxii.

15 Various scholars who accepted the ideological stance of the story before the 1980s are mentioned in P. Kyle McCarter, Jr, " 'Plots, True or False': The Succession Narrative as Court Apologetic," *Int* 35 (1981), 359, nn. 9–10. In addition, see the iconoclastic Morton Smith, " 'The So-Called 'Biography of David' in the Books of Samuel and Kings," *HTR* 44 (1951), 167–9.

16 See the summary in James W. Flanagan, *David's Social Drama*, JSOTSup 73 (Sheffield, Almond Press, 1988), 17–22.

17 In early Hebrew manuscripts, Samuel is a single book. In the Greek tradition, it was split into two books; this is connected to ancient scribal practices and the technical problems presented by very long works. (See P. Kyle McCarter, Jr, *I Samuel*, AB [Garden City, New York: Doubleday, 1980], 3 and Christian D. Ginsburg, *Introduction to the Massoretico-Critical Edition of the Hebrew Bible* [New York: Ktav, 1966], 930–1.) Thus, the particular section of Samuel discussed above, often called the Succession Narrative, does not begin in 2 Sam 1:1. Its exact border is debated, and need not concern us here.

18 So McCarter, "Plots, True or False."

19 Keith Whitelam, "The Defence of David," *JSOT* 29 (1984), 61–87.

20 Whitelam, "The Defence of David," 79.

21 For that reason, this chapter is highly dependent on the observations of others, as indicated by the notes. The most recent scholar to join the anti-von Rad bandwagon is Donald B. Redford, *Egypt, Canaan, and Israel in Ancient Times* (Princeton: Princeton University Press, 1992), 301–6. The comparative perspective which Redford adduces makes his critique particularly trenchant.

22 This position continues to have its backers; see, for example, Hayim Tadmor, "Autobiographical Apology in the Royal Assyrian Literature," *History, Historiography and Interpretation: Studies in Biblical and Cuneiform Literatures*, ed. Hayim Tadmor and M. Weinfeld (Jerusalem: Magnes, 1983), 56.

23 For a late date, see John van Seters, *In Search of History: Historiography in the Ancient World and the Origins of Biblical History* (New Haven: Yale University Press, 1983), 290–1, who sees it as post-exilic. For a late date specifically for 1 Samuel 11, see Alexander Fischer, "David und Batseba: Ein literarkritischer und motivgeschichtlicher Beitrag zu II Sam 11," *ZAW* 101 (1989), 50–9. For a defense of a more conservative date of this work, and biblical historical texts in general, see Tomoo Ishida, "Adonijah the Son of Haggith and his Supporters: An Inquiry into Problems About History and Historiography," *The Future of Biblical Studies: The Hebrew Scriptures*, ed. Richard Elliott Friedman and H. G. M. Williamson (Atlanta, GA: Scholars Press, 1987), 165–87, esp. 183. For a survey of opinions on the date of the Successon Narrative, see Ball, "Introduction," xxxv–xxxviii and Douglas A. Knight, "Moral Values and Literary Traditions: The Case of the Succession Narrative (2 Samuel 9–20; 1 Kings 1–2)," *Sem* 34 (1985), 20–1. For a strong presentation of the problematics of taking this material as history, see Joel Rosenberg, *King and Kin: Political Allegory in the Hebrew Bible* (Bloomington, IN: Indiana University Press, 1986), 100–3.

24 For a summary of the royal cabinet in general, see R. N. Whybray, "The Sage in the Israelite Royal Court," *The Sage in Ancient Israel and the Ancient Near East*, ed. John G. Gammie and Leo G. Perdue (Winona Lake, IN: Eisenbrauns, 1990), 135–7, and literature cited there. For the possibility of an official court

annalist, see Tryggve N. D. Mettinger, *Solomonic State Officials: A Study of the Civil Government Officials of the Israelite Monarchy*, CBOT 5 (Lund: CWK Greerups, 1971), 40–2; his arguments, however, are not compelling.

25 For various examples, see R. Frankena, "The Vassal-Treaties of Esarhaddon and the Dating of Deuteronomy," *OTS* 14 (1965), 122–54, van Seters, *In Search of History*, 357, Peter Machinist, "Assyria and Its Image in the First Isaiah," *JAOS* 103 (1983), 719–37, Hayim Tadmor, "Sennacherib's Campaign to Judah: Historical and Historiographic Considerations," *Zion* 50 (1985), 78–9 (Hebrew) and John van Seters, "Joshua's Campaign of Canaan and Near Eastern Historiography," *SJOT* 1990, 6–8.

26 The most articulate example of this is Howard Eilberg-Schwartz, *The Savage in Judaism: An Anthropology of Israelite Religion and Ancient Judaism* (Bloomington, IN: Indiana University Press, 1990). See also the use of the story concerning "The Rise of Ibn Saud" in Flanagan, *David's Social Drama*, 325–41.

27 On annals, see A. Kirk Grayson, "Assyria and Babylonia," *Or* 49 (1989), 150–2 and Hayim Tadmor, "Observations on Assyrian Historiography," *Essays on the Ancient Near East in Memory of J. J. Finkelstein*, ed. Maria de Jong Ellis (Hamden, CT: Connecticut Academy of Arts and Sciences, 1977), 209–13. There is no recent synthesis of Assyrian historiography, though the study of Albert Ten Eyck Olmstead, *Assyrian Historiography* (Columbia, MO: University of Missouri, 1916), remains useful.

28 Mario Liverani, "The Ideology of the Assyrian Empire, *Power and Propaganda: A Symposium on Ancient Empires*, Mesopotamia 7, ed. Mogens Trolle Larsen (Copenhagen: Akademisk Forlag, 1979), 297–317. K. Lawson Younger, *Ancient Conquest Accounts: A Study in Ancient Near Eastern and Biblical History Writing*, JSOTSup 98 (Sheffield: Sheffield Academic Press, 1990), 61–124, offers an important survey of the ideology of the annals.

29 Mordechai Cogan, "A Plaidoyer on Behalf of the Royal Scribes," *ScrHier* 33 (1991), 126–7.

30 Frederick Mario Fales, "Narrative and Ideological Variations in the Account of Sargon's Eighth Campaign," *ScrHier* 33 (1991), 128–47; cf. the earlier study by A. Leo Oppenheim, "The City of Assur in 714 B.C.," *JNES* 19 (1960), 133–47, which is also acutely aware of the ideological force of this letter.

31 Fales, "Narrative and Ideological Variations in the Account of Sargon's Eighth Campaign," 130.

32 This is a theme of the papers in *Assyrian Royal Inscriptions: New Horizons in Literary, Ideological and Historical Analysis*, ed. Frederick Mario Fales (Rome: Instituto per L'Oriente, 1981). On the proper method for studying various recensions of a single king's annals, see Louis D. Levine, "Preliminary Remarks on the Historical Inscriptions of Sennacherib," *History, Historiography and Interpretation: Studies in Biblical and Cuneiform Literatures*, 69–74.

33 See the literature cited in Baruch Halpern, *The First Historians: The Hebrew Bible and History* (San Francisco: Harper & Row, 1988), 203, n. 40. For an older treatment, see Olmstead, *Assyrian Historiography*, esp. 53–9.

34 J. A. Brinkman, "Through a Glass Darkly: Esarhaddon's Retrospects on the Downfall of Babylon," *JAOS* 103 (1983), 35–42.

35 Brinkman, "Through a Glass Darkly: Esarhaddon's Retrospects on the Downfall of Babylon," 35.

36 Brinkman, "Through a Glass Darkly: Esarhaddon's Retrospects on the Downfall of Babylon," 41–2.

37 A convenient representative selection of these may be found in Julian Reade,

Assyrian Sculpture (Cambridge, MA: Harvard University Press, 1983). For a collection of reliefs from single kings, see Samuel M. Paley, *King of the World: Ashur-nasir-pal II of Assyria 883–859 B.C.* (Brooklyn: Brooklyn Museum, 1976) and John Malcolm Russell, *Sennacherib's Palace Without Rival at Nineveh* (Chicago: University of Chicago Press, 1991), esp. 191–267.

38 Irene J. Winter, "Royal Rhetoric and the Development of Historical Narrative in Neo-Assyrian Reliefs," *Studies in Visual Communication* 7 (1981), 2–38; the quotation is from p. 3. An additional source for the ideological nature of Assyrian art is Julian Reade, "Ideology and Propaganda in Assyrian Art," *Power and Propaganda*, 329–43.

39 On the complementary nature of the visual, written and oral types of propaganda, see Liverani, "The Ideology of the Assyrian Empire," 302.

40 See esp. Hayim Tadmor, "History and Ideology in the Assyrian Royal Inscriptions," *Assyrian Royal Inscriptions: New Horizons*, 32–3.

41 Bernard Lewis, *History Remembered, Recovered, Invented* (New York: Simon & Shuster, 1975), 61. See his entire discussion of this issue with a wide range of examples on pp. 61–9; he discusses the "Donation of Constantine" on p. 63.

42 R. C. C. Law, "The Heritage of Oduduwa: Traditional History and Political Propaganda Among the Yoruba," *Journal of African History* 14 (1973), 202–22. This study does suggest, however, that they could not always be radically revised with ease.

43 Henry A. Myers and Herwig Wolfram, *Medieval Kingship* (Chicago: Nelson-Hall, 1982), 129–30; the quote is from p. 129.

44 See Robin W. Winks, *The Historian as Detective: Essays on Evidence* (New York: Harper & Row, 1969), 192–212 (excerpted from Allan Nevins, *The Gateway to History* [Boston: D. C. Heath, 1938]).

45 See Janet L. Nelson, *Politics and Ritual in Early Medieval Europe* (London: Hambledon Press, 1986), 195–237. Other chapters of this book contain useful information concerning medieval historical writing, especially as it relates to the king.

46 Nelson, *Politics and Ritual in Early Medieval Europe*, 205.

47 Nelson, *Politics and Ritual in Early Medieval Europe*, 211.

48 This is the position, for example, of Whitelam, "The Defence of David."

49 Carole Fontaine, "The Bearing of Wisdom on the Shape of 2 Samuel 11–12 and 1 Kings 3," *JSOT* 34 (1986), 64 and Gale A. Yee, " 'Fraught with Background': Literary Ambiguity in II Samuel, 11" *Int* 42 (1988), 242–3. For the claim that this story is pro-Davidic, see Whitelam, "The Defence of David," 77.

50 R. A. Carlson, *David, the Chosen King: A Traditio-Historical Approach to the Second Book of Samuel* (Stockholm: Almqvist & Wiksell, 1964), 25, 131–259.

51 Karl Budde, *Die Bücher Samuel*, KHAT (Tübingen: J. C. B. Mohr, 1902), xvi, 244–5 and W. Nowack, *Richter, Ruth u. Bücher Samuelis* HKAT (Göttingen: Vandenhoeck und Ruprecht, 1902), xxi–xxiii, 185.

52 For a recent summary of the positions concerning the extent of the Succession Narrative, see Randall C. Bailey, *David in Love and War: The Pursuit of Power in 2 Samuel 10–12*, JSOTSup 75 (Sheffield: Sheffield Academic Press, 1990), 7–31.

53 One clear tool for determining borders is the discovery of unambiguous opening and closing formulae, such as those noted in Isaac B. Gottlieb, "*Sof Davar*: Biblical Endings," *Prooftexts* 11 (1991), 213–24. Other methods for determining units and subunits are discussed in H. van Dyke Parunak, "Transitional Techniques in the Bible," *JBL* 102 (1983), 525–48. Unfortunately, the

devices mentioned in both of these articles are lacking here. David Damrosch, *The Narrative Covenant: Transformations of Genre in the Growth of Biblical Literature* (Ithaca, New York: Cornell University Press, 1987), 197–8 suggests that 1 Samuel 17–2 Samuel 5 comprise a unit framed by mention of Philistines. But this is too vague a reference to delimit the unit.

54 See Peter R. Ackroyd, "The Succession Narrative (So-Called)," *Int* 35 (1981), 383–96 and Willem S. Vorster, "Readings, Readers and the Succession Narrative: An Essay on Reception," *ZAW* 98 (1986), 351–62.

55 See my "The Structure of 1 Kings 1–11," *JSOT* 49 (1991), 87–97, with additional examples there.

56 James W. Flanagan, "Court History or Succession Document? A Study of 2 Samuel 9–20 and 1 Kings 1–2," *JBL* 91 (1972), 177; cf. Ackroyd, "The Succession Narrative (So-Called)," 384 and James C. Vanderkam, "Davidic Complicity in the Death of Abner and Eshbaal: A Historical and Redactional Study," *JBL* 99 (1980), 523. There are several differences between the two lists. Such differences are not unusual in material used in this manner to structure units. For a discussion of these differences, see P. Kyle McCarter, Jr, *II Samuel*, AB (Garden City, New York: Doubleday, 1984), 257 and G. W. Ahlström, *Royal Administration and National Religion in Ancient Palestine* (Leiden: E. J. Brill, 1982), 29–31.

57 Tomoo Ishida, "Solomon's Succession to the Throne of David – A Political Analysis," *Studies in the Period of David and Solomon and Other Opportunities*, ed. Tomoo Ishida (Winona Lake, IN: Eisenbrauns, 1982), 178.

58 I use the word "editorial" to suggest that this division is likely secondary, and that the material incorporated within it is of diverse origin.

59 The verses that precede also fit in well with a climactic, concluding narrative; see the evidence adduced in Carlson, *David, the Chosen King*, 210–11.

60 Note the syntax of noun first followed by unconverted verb; cf. Mark F. Rooker, *Biblical Hebrew in Transition: The Language of the Book of Ezekiel*, JSOTSup 90 (Sheffield: Sheffield Academic Press, 1990), 108–10. It is, however, dangerous to date a verse on the basis of a single linguistic feature.

61 Chapter 9 introduces Mephiboshet and Ziba, who figure prominently in the rebellions against David narrated in chapters 16 and 19, while chapter 10, the humiliation of David's servant by the Ammonites, sets the scene for the following chapter, David's battle against the Ammonites.

62 For a general treatment of this theme see Patrick D. Miller, Jr, *Sin and Judgement in the Prophets*, SBLMS 27 (Chico, CA: Scholars Press, 1982). He does not, however, include this section of Samuel among his examples.

63 A subtheme of this unit is the transference of sin; see 2 Sam 12:13 (העביר) and Yohanan Muffs, *Love and Joy: Law, Language and Religion in Ancient Israel* (New York and Cambridge, MA: JTS and Harvard University Press, 1992), 16–24.

64 The general relevance of these chapters to all Israel within a Deuteronomic framework is emphasized by Carlson, *David, the Chosen King*.

65 Nelson, *Politics and Ritual in Early Medieval Europe*, esp. 233.

66 For a discussion of the extent of this pericope, see P. Kyle McCarter, "The Apology of David," *JBL* 99 (1980), 502, n. 25.

67 For a valuable summary of the secondary literature on this section through the early 1970s, see Joachim Conrad, "Zum geschichtlichen Hintergrund der Darstellung von Davids Aufstieg," *TLZ* 97 (1970), 321–2. The origin of the term "Aufstieg Davids," for this unit is Leonhard Rost, *Die Überlieferung von der Thronnachfolge Davids*, BWANT III, 6 (Stuttgart: W. Kohlhammer, 1926),

133–5. It was then used in the seminal work of Martin Noth, *Überlieferungsge-schichtliche Studien* (Tübingen: Max Niemeyer Verlag, 1967 [f.p. 1943], 62, and was borrowed from this in the first German large-scale study of the unit, by Hans-Ulrich Nübel, *Davids Aufstieg in der frühen israelitischer Geschichtssch-reibung* (Bonn: Rheinische Friedrich-Wilhelms-Universität, 1959). This term is a poor choice because it suggests that the narrator had historical/biographical interests in the material. Better suggestions are Artur Weiser, "Die Legitimation des Königs David: Zur Eigenart und Entstehung der sogen. Geschichte von Davids Aufstieg," *VT* 16 (1966), 325–54 and McCarter, "The Apology of David," 489–504. These articles, along with McCarter's Samuel commentaries, are especially well-argued, and I have based much of my analysis on their insights.

68 A similar position is advocated by David Jobling, "Saul's Fall and Jonathan's Rise: Tradition and Redaction in 1 Samuel 14:1–46," *JBL* 95 (1976), 371, n. 15, though my arguments are more extensive than his.

69 Cf. 1 Sam 13:8–14, though as noted by David M. Gunn, *The Fate of King Saul: An Interpretation of a Biblical Story*, JSOTSup 14 (Sheffield: JSOT Press, 1980), 33–40, Saul's sin is not expressed clearly in the text.

70 Peter A. Ackroyd, *The First Book of Samuel*, CBC (Cambridge: Cambridge University Press, 1971), 119 terms all of 14:47–52 "Saul's Reign – A Summary."

71 The Hebrew phrase is difficult, but it is not clear that McCarter's emendation (*ad loc.*) presents an easier text.

72 I am emending MT יְרִשׁוּי, following LXX and the scholarly consensus; cf., for example, Julius Wellhausen, *Der Text der Bücher Samuelis* (Göttingen: Vandenhoeck und Ruprecht, 1871), 95, S. R. Driver, *Notes on the Hebrew Text and the Topography of the Books of Samuel* (Oxford: Clarendon Press, 1960), 120, McCarter, *I Samuel*, 254.

73 On 14:52 as a dividing point between stories, see further Anthony F. Campbell, *Of Prophets and Kings (1 Samuel 1–2 Kings 10)*, CBQMS 17 (Washington, DC: Catholic Biblical Association of America, 1986), 129 and Tryggve N. D. Mettinger, *King and Messiah: The Civil and Sacral Legitimation of the Israelite Kings*, CBOT 8 (Lund: CWK Gleerup, 1976), 34.

74 For a discussion of the relationship between the two forms of the names Abner and Abiner, see Martin Noth, *Die israelitischen Personennamen im Rahmen der gemeinsemitischen Namengebung*, BWANT III/10 (Stuttgart: Kohlhammer, 1928), 34. On the likely meaning of the -î suffix, see Scott C. Layton, *Archaic Features of Canaanite Personal Names in the Hebrew Bible*, HSM 47 (Atlanta: Scholars Press, 1990), 145–50.

75 Some scholars read Edom, following the LXX and Peshitta.

76 *I Samuel*, 252.

77 For a discussion of this chapter and its development, see Fabrizio Foresti, *The Rejection of Saul in the Perspective of the Deuteronomistic School: A Study of 1 Sm 15 and Related Texts* (Rome: Edizioni del Teresianum, 1984). He surveys the opinions concerning the relationship of chapter 15 to the preceding and following chapters (16–24), and concludes that the Deuteronomistic History placed it at the dividing point between pro- and anti-Saul traditions (167–8), while later editors revised it so it was more firmly anti-Saul (177). This evidence suggests that the chapter belongs to *Aufstieg Davids*. For further links between chapters 15 and 16, which also foster my suggestion that chapter 15 belongs to the following material, see Moshe Garsiel, *The First Book of Samuel: A Literary Study of Comparative Structures, Analogies and Parallels* (Ramat Gan: Revivim, 1985), 112.

78 It is possible that in its final form, 1 Samuel 14 anticipates Saul's downfall, as suggested by David Jobling, "Saul's Fall and Jonathan's Rise: Tradition and Redaction in 1 Sam 14:1–46," *JBL* 95 (1976), 367–76. Yet, as Jobling comments, Saul's depiction there is not identical to that of the later chapters: in 1 Samuel 14 Saul (p. 368), "is not so much wicked as frustrated and foolish."

79 For the range of views of other scholars concerning the boundaries of the unit, see Tomoo Ishida, *The Royal Dynasties in Ancient Israel: A Study on the Formation and Development of Royal–Dynastic Ideology*, BZAW 142 (Berlin: Walter de Gruyter, 1977), 55–6. A position close to my own, namely that 1 Samuel 15–2 Samuel 8 forms a unit, is found in Julius Wellhausen, *Die Composition des Hexateuchs und der Historischen Bücher des Alten Testaments*, third edition (Berlin: Georg Reimer, 1899), 246–55, who calls the unit "Erste Geschichte Davids," and in Herbert Martin Wolf, "The Apology of Hattušiliš Compared with Other Political Self-Justifications of the Ancient Near East," Ph.D. dissertation, Brandeis University, 1967, 118–61, esp. 125.

80 Ben C. Ollenburger, *Zion the City of the Great King: A Theological Symbol of the Jerusalem Cult*, JSOTSup 41 (Sheffield: Sheffield Academic Press, 1987), 59–66; the quote is from 65–6. On the Davidic ideology, see in addition, Antti Laato, *Who is Immanuel? The Rise and the Foundering of Isaiah's Messianic Expectations* (Åbo: Åbo Academy Press, 1988), 69–79 and his "Psalm 132 and the Development of the Jerusalemite/Israelite Royal Ideology," *CBQ* 54 (1992), 49–66. Some of these concerns typify ancient Near Eastern kingship in general: see Ishida, "Solomon's Succession to the Throne of David – A Political Analysis," 179, "Royal lineage and divine election served as the fundamental principles for the legitimation of kingship in the ancient Near East, including Israel." For an extended defense of this position, see his *Royal Dynasties*, 6–25.

81 In enumerating the royal psalms, I follow the older position of Gunkel concerning them, rather than that of Eaton; see my *God is King: Understanding an Israelite Metaphor*, JSOTSup 76 (Sheffield: Sheffield Academic Press, 1989), 25.

82 Brettler, *God is King*, 136; see esp. Psalm 2:7 and probably 110–3.

83 The literature on this is immense; see most recently the bibliography offered by Baruch Halpern and David S. Vanderhooft, "The Editions of Kings in the 7th–6th Centuries B.C.E.," *HUCA* 62 (1991), 242–3.

84 Cf., for example, Psalms 2:8–9; 18:4, 18–20, 33–49; 20:10; 21:8–10; 45:4–6; 72:8–11; 110; 132:18; 144:10.

85 Views range from pre-exilic to post-exilic; see n. 80; on the date of the History of David's Rise, see McCarter, "The Apology of David," 495.

86 For the claim that this material has undergone two extensive Deuteronomistic editions, see Brian Peckham, "The Deuteronomistic History of Saul and David," *ZAW* 97 (1985), 190–209.

87 This is downplayed in some of the more recent literary studies of Samuel: see esp. Robert Polzin, *Samuel and the Deuteronomist: A Literary Study of the Deuteronomic History: 1 Samuel* (San Francisco: Harper & Row, 1989) and V. Philips Long, *The Reign and Rejection of King Saul: A Case for Literary and Theological Coherence*, SBLDS 118 (Atlanta: Scholars Press, 1989).

88 For a similar example, see p. 191, n. 36.

89 Roger Lemuel Ward, "The Story of David's Rise: A Traditio-Historical Study of I Samuel XVI–II Samuel V," Ph.D. dissertation, Vanderbilt University, 1967, 341.

90 "Davidic Complicity," 523.

91 See McCarter, *I Samuel*, 422–3. For other cases where material does not follow chronology, see Niels Peter Lemche, "David's Rise," *JSOT* 10 (1978), 10,

Vanderkam, "Davidic Complicity," 525 and Jakob H. Grønbœk, *Die Geschichte vom Aufstieg Davids (1. Sam. 15–2. Sam. 5): Tradition und Komposition* (Copenhagen: Prostant apud Munksgaard, 1971), 181–2.

92 See n. 23.

93 See 1 Samuel 9–10 and 11:14–15, which incorporate divergent traditions. For a brief survey of these texts, see my *God is King*, 126–7.

94 T. C. G. Thornton, "Studies in Samuel," *Church Quarterly Review* 168 (1967), 415.

95 It is irrelevant that this might not be a historical event (Diana Edelman, "Saul's Rescue of Jabesh-Gilead [1 Sam 11 1–11]: Sorting Story from History," *ZAW* 96 [1984], 195–209); all that is important is that some group in ancient Israel *believed* that it transpired.

96 Hebrew הקטן. This is noted by Garsiel, *The First Book of Samuel*, 115, who appropriately calls chapter 17 "David versus Saul."

97 For a different view which downplays Saul's sin, see Gunn, *The Fate of King Saul*, 41–56.

98 Hebrew מאס; with YHWH as its subject, see S. Wagner, "מאס," *TWAT* IV, 627–32.

99 The use of this image in 1 Samuel 15 and 24 is an important argument for seeing these chapters as a unity; cf. Mettinger, *King and Messiah*, 34.

100 We normally cannot assume that historical books presume Torah legislation, unless, like here, it is explicit in the text.

101 Elsewhere in the Bible, a person of a higher status generally has pity on (חמל) a person of a lower status.

102 On the depictions of Saul in this chapter, see W. Lee Humphreys, "The Rise and Fall of King Saul: A Study of an Ancient Narrative Stratum," *JSOT* 18 (1980), 80–2.

103 This is especially emphasized by Garsiel, *The First Book of Samuel*, 115–37, who suggests extensive antitheses between Saul and David, not all of which are fully compelling.

104 I have treated this on pp. 107–8, in relationship to the theme of hegemony, which is central to the Davidic ideology.

105 This is a remarkable contrast to the following unit; note, for example, the death of Uriah (2 Samuel 11) and David's testament to Solomon in 1 Kings 2.

106 For various treatments of these doublets see Klaus Koch, *The Growth of the Biblical Tradition: The Form-Critical Method*, trans. S. M. Cupitt (London: A. S. C. Black, 1969), 132–48, Robert C. Culley, *Studies in the Structure of Hebrew Narrative* (Philadelphia: Fortress, 1976), 49–54, Halpern, *The First Historians*, 61–5, Rosenberg, *King and Kin*, 133–9 and Robert P. Gordon, "David's Rise and Saul's Demise: Narrative Analogy in 1 Samuel 24–6," *Tyndale Bulletin* 31 (1980), 37–64. On the importance of doublets and repetition in the story, see Ward, "The Story of David's Rise," 199–200.

107 See Robert P. Gordon, "Word-Play and Verse-Order in 1 Samuel XXIV 5–8," *VT* 40 (1990), 139–44.

108 Weiser, "Die Legitimation," 337–8 and Polzin, *Samuel and the Deuteronomist*, 210–11.

109 See Lemche, "David's Rise," 14, Charles Mabee, "David's Judicial Exoneration," *ZAW* 92 (1980), 89–107, Walter Brueggemann, "2 Samuel 21–24: An Appendix of Deconstruction?" *CBQ* 50 (1988), 384 and *idem*, "Narrative Intentionality in 1 Samuel 29," *JSOT* 43 (1989), 21–35. David Gunn, "David and the Gift of the Kingdom (2 Sam 2–4, 9–10, 1 Kgs 1–2)," *Sem* 3 (1975), 18 notes that David's restraint as depicted here is "remarkable," and contrasts

sharply with the other characters, who are not depicted in such black-and-white terms.

110 On this theme, see John T. Willis, "The Function of Comprehensive Anticipatory Redactional Joints in 1 Samuel 16–18," *ZAW* 85 (1973), 294–314, esp. 300–1, 314, McCarter, "The Apology of David," 494, Mettinger, *King and Messiah*, 38 and Grønbœk, *Die Geschichte vom Aufstieg Davids*, 271–3.

111 Contrast McCarter, *I Samuel*, 356–7.

112 Hebrew משיח יהוה.

113 See my *God is King*, 125–58.

114 It does not matter that most scholars see this as historically inaccurate, and based on the prophetic anointing of Saul. (So, e.g. McCarter, *I Samuel*, 277–8.) As in other places in this narrative, we are examining the ideology behind the story, not the likely historical reality.

115 Thornton, "Studies in Samuel," 416. Weiser, "Die Legitimation," 349 considers it "the highpoint and endpoint" of the narrative; I agree with his first judgement, but not with the second. In contrast to many modern works, biblical episodes end anticlimactically, as in 2 Samuel 8; compare the anticlimactic end of the Ehud story in its final form in Judg 3:30.

116 Sigmund Mowinckel, "Israelite Historiography," *ASTI* 2 (1963), 14; cf. Mettinger, *King and Messiah*, 39.

117 Most scholars are not convinced by the arguments of Julian Morgenstern, "David and Jonathan," *JBL* 78 (1959), 322–5, where he contends that kingship in the earliest monarchy may have passed via the daughter's line, though a similar proposal was recently made by Flanagan, *David's Social Drama*, 243–4. In contrast, it was possible to rise to kingship by marrying a king's wife (see Matitiahu Tsevat, "Marriage and Monarchical Legitimacy in Ugarit and Israel," *JSS* 3 [1958], 237–43). This, however, is not attributed to David because that would have made him look like a usurper. Most scholars assume that kingship passed through primogeniture in ancient Israel, though this has been challenged recently by Frederick E. Greenspahn, *When Brothers Dwell Together: The Preeminence of Younger Siblings in the Hebrew Bible* (New York: Oxford University Press, 1994), esp. 69–83. This issue need not concern us, since it is certain that in this case, Jonathan, who seems to be the oldest living son of Saul, is viewed as his father's successor.

118 On the centrality of Jonathan for the transfer of the kingship, see David Jobling, *The Sense of Biblical Narrative: Three Structural Analyses of the Old Testament (1 Samuel 13–31; Numbers 11–12; 1 Kings 17–18)*, JSOTSup 7 (Sheffield: JSOT Press, 1978), 4–25, who has constructively used tools from folklore and narrative analysis. See also Diana Vikander Edelman, *King Saul in the Historiography of Judah*, JSOTSup 121 (Sheffield: Sheffield Academy Press, 1991) 317–18.

119 Both the opening of the verse, ועתה הנה, and the infinitive absolute מלך תמלוך are emphatic.

120 Hebrew אהב. See J. A. Thompson, "The Significance of the Verb *Love* in the David–Jonathan Narratives in 1 Samuel," *VT* 24 (1974), 334–8; cf. Peter R. Ackroyd, "The Verb Love – ʾāhēb in the David–Jonathan Narratives – A Footnote," *VT* 25 (1975), 213–14.

121 The Hebrew terms are אבי and בני.

122 So e.g. NJPS, which translates אבי as "sir."

123 See Damrosch, *Narrative Covenant*, 211–12, Ishida, *Royal Dynasties*, 61–2, and for a Freudian interpretation, Gunn, *The Fate of King Saul*, 94–5.

124 On the significance of these clothing exchanges, see Thompson, "The Signifi-

cance of the Verb *Love*," 335, Mettinger, *King and Messiah*, 39, Gunn, *The Fate of King Saul*, 80 and Damrosch, *Narrative Covenant*, 203–4.

125 Hebrew ועד.

126 James W. Flanagan, "Social Transformation and Ritual in 2 Samuel 6," *The Word of the Lord Shall Go Forth: Essays in Honor of David Noel Freedman in Celebration of His Sixtieth Birthday*, ed. Carol L. Meyers and M. O'Connor (Winona Lake, IN: Eisenbrauns/ASOR, 1983), 366.

127 See Lemche, "David's Rise," 2–25 and McCarter, "The Apology of David," 489–504.

128 Flanagan, "Social Transformation and Ritual in 2 Samuel 6," 361–2.

129 See Thornton's reminder, "Studies in Samuel," 413, "Behind the writing and compilation of a literary work lie not one, but several motives."

130 Ishida, *Royal Dynasties*, 59. For a different opinion, see Ward, "The Story of David's Rise," 191, who claims that the story is "substantially reliable," though he admits that its purpose is (p. 196) "to exculpate David." For other readings which downplay the author's political motives, see Polzin, *Samuel and the Deuteronomist* and Peter D. Miscall, *1 Samuel: A Literary Reading* (Bloomington, IN: Indiana University Press, 1986).

131 See above the insightful statement of Eric Voegelin, *Order and History*, vol.1: *Israel and Revelation* (Baton Rouge, LA: Louisiana University Press, 1956), 123, "Precisely when its [the Bible's] dubiousness as a pragmatic record is recognized, the narrative reveals its function in creating a people in politics and history." This idea could be very constructively applied in relationship to the exodus and settlement traditions within the framework of the recent archeological reconstructions.

132 See esp. Garsiel, *The First Book of Samuel*.

133 J. W. Wesselius, "Joab's Death and the Central Theme of the Succession Narrative (2 Samuel IX-1 Kings II)," *VT* 40 (1990), 340 uses the term "over-stress" to refer to the text's excessive emphasis on David's lack of culpability and on Saul's sorry state. He feels that this "over-stress" calls attention to these themes and forces the reader to reflect properly upon them.

134 See above, nn. 22–3, on the Succession Narrative.

135 This position would be necessary for those who question the existence of Saul, David and the united monarchy, such as Philip R. Davies, *In Search of "Ancient Israel,"* JSOTSup 148 (Sheffield: JSOT Press, 1992), 69 and Thompson, *Early History of the Israelite People*, 111, 114, with bibliography there.

136 See above, n. 72; the suggestion that in ירשיע we merely have a graphic error between a ר and a ו does not take into account why such errors occur. In addition, in that verse, it is possible that the verb לכד used in conjunction with המלוכה is pejorative and implies usurpation of power.

137 See 1 Sam 1:27–8, esp. 28aβ, הוא שאול ליהוה, which means "he is consecrated to YHWH," but could be translated "he is YHWH's Saul." This was defended clearly by Ivar Hylander, *Der literarische Samuel-Saul-Komplex (I. Sam 1–15)*, Uppsala: Almqvist & Wiksell, 1932) 11–39; for a summary of the issue and an unsuccessful attempt to connect the name Samuel to the etymology in 1 Samuel 1, see McCarter, *I Samuel*, 62, 65.

138 It is also possible that 1 Sam 13:8–14 is a secondary, anti-Saul reworking of material, created to anticipate 1 Samuel 15.

139 Pp. 109–11 reflect my "The Book of Judges: Literature as Politics," *JBL* 108 (1989), 414–16. For scholars who doubt that a historical Saul existed, this pro-Saul literature would reflect anti-Davidic propaganda.

140 Several major LXX manuscripts read מלכו(י)אל; this is probably a harmonization of a *hapax* Hebrew name מלך to names which are otherwise attested.
141 For additional material on this individual, see my article "Melech," *ABD* 4, 689.
142 James W. Flanagan, "Genealogy and Dynasty in the Early Monarchy of Israel and Judah," *Proceedings of the Eighth World Congress of Jewish Studies: Division A: The Period of the Bible* (Jerusalem: World Union of Jewish Studies, 1982), 25. For charts of the genealogies, see Flanagan, *David's Social Drama*, 343–6.
143 On other connections between Esther and Samuel, see W. McKane, "A Note on Esther IX and I Samuel XV," *JTS* NS 12 (1961), 260–1.
144 *HALAT* I, 132 בן 2, "Enkel."
145 For this reading, see most recently, Michael V. Fox, *Character and Ideology in the Book of Esther* (Columbia, SC: University of South Carolina Press, 1991), 26.
146 On the historicity of Esther, see Sandra Beth Berg, *The Book of Esther: Motifs, Themes and Structure*, SBLDS 44 (Missoula, MT: Scholars Press, 1979), 1–11 and Michael V. Fox, *Character and Ideology in the Book of Esther*, 131–40.
147 See Otto Eissfeldt, "The Promise of Grace to David in Isaiah 55:1–5," *Israel's Prophetic Heritage*, ed. B. W. Anderson and W. Harrelson (New York: Harper & Row, 1962), 196–207. The recent challenge to this interpretation by Walter C. Kaiser, Jr, "The Unfailing Kindness Promised to David: Isaiah 55.3," *JSOT* 45 (1989), 91–8 is not convincing.
148 On notions of messianism in the rabbinic period, see Jacob Neusner *et al.*, eds, *Judaisms and their Messiahs at the Turn of the Christian Era* (Cambridge: Cambridge University Press, 1987). For a survey of literature on biblical messianism, see R. E. Clements, "The Messianic Hope in the Old Testament," *JSOT* 43 (1989), 3–19.
149 H. L. Strack and G. Stemberger, *Introduction to the Talmud and Midrash*, trans. Markus Bockmuehl (Edinburgh: T. & T. Clark, 1991), 390–1.
150 *Midrash Shmuel*, ed. Solomon Buber (Cracow: Joseph Fischer, 1893), 24:6 (p. 120; Hebrew).
151 *b. Sanh.* 95a and *Midrash Shmuel* 25:2 (p. 122).
152 The preservation of extrabiblical traditions in rabbinic texts is often acknowledged, but has never been studied extensively. See provisionally Shalom Spiegel, "Introduction," Louis Ginzberg, *Legends of the Bible* (Philadelphia: Jewish Publication Society, 1968), xxxii–xxxiv, U. Cassuto, "The Israelite Epic," *Biblical and Oriental Studies* (Jerusalem: Magnes, 1975), vol. 2, 69–109 and many of the studies by Samuel E. Loewenstamm, including *The Evolution of the Exodus Tradition*, trans. Baruch J. Schwartz (Jerusalem: Magnes, 1992), and by Judah Goldin, *Studies in Midrash and Related Literature*, ed. Barry L. Eichler and Jeffrey H. Tigay (Philadelphia: Jewish Publication Society, 1988).
153 Louis Feldman, "Josephus' Portrait of Saul," *HUCA* 53 (1982), 45–99.
154 Whitelam, "The Defence of David," 76.
155 See especially Lam 4:20, and my *God is King*, esp. 46; note the similar observation concerning the class to whom this material was addressed in Edelman, *King Saul*, 23.
156 Rosamond McKitterick, *The Carolingians and the Written Word* (Cambridge: Cambridge University Press, 1989), 236–41.

7 TEXT IN A *TEL*: 2 KINGS 17 AS HISTORY

1 New examination of the evidence suggests that 586 is more likely than 587; see Gershon Galil, "The Babylonian Calendar and the Chronology of the Last Kings of Judah," *Bib* 72 (1991), 367–78, *idem*, "A New Look at the Chronology of the Last Kings of Judah," *Zion* 56 (1991), 5–19 (Hebrew: English summary V-VI) and Ormond Edwards, "The Year of Jerusalem's Destruction. 2 Addaru 597 B.C. Reinterpreted," *ZAW* 104 (1992), 101–6. Despite the emerging new consensus that 586 is correct, we must remember the problems of absolute chronology in the pre-modern world; see Julian Reade, "Mesopotamian Guidelines for Biblical Chronology," *Syro-Mesopotamian Studies* 4/1 (May 1981), 1–7, esp. 6–7.

2 Christopher R. Seitz, "The Crisis of Interpretation over the Meaning and Purpose of the Exile: A Redactional Study of Jeremiah xxi-xliii," *VT* 35 (1985), 78–97 and *idem, Theology in Conflict: Reactions to the Exile in the Book of Jeremiah*, BZAW 176 (Berlin: Walter de Gruyter, 1989).

3 It is very difficult to reconstruct the details of this event, specifically the roles of Shalmaneser and Sargon. For the standard view, see Mordechai Cogan and Hayim Tadmor, *II Kings*, AB (Doubleday, 1988), 198–201, and in more detail, (over-)using the prophetic book of Hosea as a source for history, John H. Hayes and Jeffrey K. Kuan, "The Final Years of Samaria (730–720)," *Bib* 72 (1991), 153–81; for a revisionist position, which claims that Shalmaneser had no role in the conquest, which is to be attributed to Sargon in 720, see Nadav Na'aman, "The Historical Background to the Conquest of Samaria (720 BC)," *Bib* 71 (1990), 206–25.

4 See Bustenay Oded, *Mass Deportations and Deportees in the Neo-Assyrian Empire* (Wiesbaden: Dr Ludwig Reichert Verlag, 1979).

5 I disagree with the contention of Shemaryahu Talmon, "Polemics and Apology in Biblical Historiography – 2 Kings xvii 24–41," *The Creation of Sacred Literature: Composition and Redaction of the Biblical Text*, Near Eastern Studies, 22, ed. Richard Elliott Friedman (Berkeley, CA: University of California Press, 1981), 60–6, who claims that part of 2 Kings 17 is of northern origin. (This essay is now reprinted in his *Literary Studies in the Hebrew Bible: Form and Content* [Jerusalem: Magnes, 1993], 134–59.) On evidence for northern sources in Kings, see Ziony Zevit, "Deuteronomistic Historiography in 1 Kings 12–2 Kings 17 and the Reinvestiture of the Israelian Cult," *JSOT* 32 (1985), 57–73.

6 Short works would not survive alone; note how, for example, the twelve prophets were copied together as a single work, probably because each book was too small to circulate individually. On copying books together, see Menahem Haran, "Book-Size and the Device of Catch-Lines in the Biblical Canon," *JJS* 36 (1985), 1–3.

7 See esp. prophetic books such as Isaiah or Jeremiah.

8 Although scholars differ in their exact delineation of sources, almost everyone agrees that the chapter is composite. An exception is Charles C. Torrey, *Ezra Studies* (New York: Ktav, 1970), 327–8.

9 On 1 Kings 8, see my "Interpretation and Prayer: Notes on the Composition of 1 Kings 8.15–53," *Minḥa Le-Naḥum: Biblical and Other Studies Presented to Nahum M. Sarna in Honour of his 70th Birthday*, JSOTSup 154, ed. Marc Brettler and Michael Fishbane (Sheffield: Sheffield Academic Press, 1993), 17–35; on the events surrounding 701, see esp. Brevard S. Childs, *Isaiah and the Assyrian Crisis*, SBT² 23 (London: SCM, 1967), Cogan and Tadmor, *II Kings*, 246–51 and Francolino J. Gonçalves, *L'expédition de Sennachérib en*

Palestine dans la littérature hébraïque ancienne, Ebib n. s. 7 (Paris: Libraire Lecoffre J. Gabalda, 1986). The redactional similarity between 2 Kings 17 and 1 Kings 8 has previously been noted by Steven L. McKenzie, *The Trouble with Kings: The Composition of the Book of Kings in the Deuteronomistic History*, SVT 42 (Leiden: E. J. Brill, 1991), 133. 2 Samuel 7 is likely another magnet text.

10 Moshe Greenberg, "Exodus, Book of," *EJ*, VI, 1056. This debate continues into the rabbinic period; see Abraham Joshua Heschel, *Theology of Ancient Judaism*, vol. 2 (London: Soncino Press, 1965; Hebrew).

11 The structure I am suggesting for this chapter is not entirely original, and is based on the insights of previous scholars. The observations of Bernhard Stade, "Miscellen: 16. Anmerkungen zu 2 Kö. 15–21," *ZAW* 6 (1886), 163–70 are an essential beginning point for any analysis of this chapter.

12 Some of what follows is based on my article "Ideology, History and Theology in 2 Kings XVII 7–23," *VT* 39 (1989), 268–82. In contrast to that article, this chapter deals with the entire chapter of 2 Kings 17, incorporates recent literature and attempts more consciously to understand the place of that chapter within biblical history writing. I could not, however, incorporate the two studies in Dutch by Bob Becking, "De Ondergang van Samaria, historische, exegetische en theologische opmerkingen bij II Koningen 17," dissertation RU Utrecht, 1985 and "Theologie na de Onergang: Enkele Opmerkingen bij 2 Koningen 17," *Bijdragen* 49 (1988), 150–72; English summary, 173–74, though I have used his recent *The Fall of Samaria: An Historical and Archaeological Study* (Leiden: E. J. Brill, 1992).

13 For a list of these, see McKenzie, *The Trouble with Kings*, 124 or Antony F. Campbell, S. J., *Of Prophets and Kings: A Late Ninth-Century Document (1 Samuel–2 Kings 10)*, CBQMS 17 (Washington, DC: The Catholic Biblical Association of America, 1986), 144, 209.

14 There are later traditions which offer various suggestions; it is unclear whether these reflect ancient traditions or are later attempts to explicate the odd phrase. See Cogan and Tadmor, *II Kings*, 196 and Zevit, "Deuteronomistic Historiography," 63. For a different attempt to explain this statement, see Campbell, *Of Prophets and Kings*, 153.

15 Too much, however, should not be made out of this theological problem. In contrast to the Chronicler, the Deuteronomistic Historian did not assume immediate retribution upon the nation for a king's actions, as may be seen by contrasting the treatment of Manasseh and Zedekiah in Kings and Chronicles.

16 Becking, *The Fall of Samaria*, 49.

17 Hebrew עליו עלה.

18 Hebrew בימיו עלה.

19 Mordechai Cogan and Hayim Tadmor, "Ahaz and Tiglath-Pileser in the Book of Kings: Historiographic Considerations," *Bib* 60 (1979), 493–9, which builds on James A. Montgomery, "Archival Data in the Book of Kings," *JBL* 53 (1934), 48 and James A. Montgomery and Henry Snyder Gehman, *The Books of Kings*, ICC (Edinburgh: T. & T. Clark, 1951), 30–7. For a different opinion concerning some of these "archival" sources, see Ehud Ben Zvi, "Tracing Prophetic Literature in the Book of Kings: The Case of II Kings 15, 37," *ZAW* 102 (1990), 100–5.

20 Some of these points were first raised by Hugo Winckler, *Alttestamentliche Untersuchungen* (Leipzig: Eduard Pfeiffer, 1892), 16–25, esp. 23–4. See A. Sanda, *Die Bücher der Könige*, vol. 2 (Münster i. West.: Aschendorffsche Verlagsbuchhandlung, 1912), 217 and more recently Martin Rehm, *Das zweite*

NOTES

Buch der Könige: Ein Kommentar (Würzburg: Echter Verlag, 1982), 167 and Ernst Würthwein, *Die Bücher der Könige, 1 Kön. 17–2 Kön. 25*, ATD (Göttingen: Vandenhoeck & Ruprecht, 1984), 393–4. This position is not accepted by Hayes and Kuan, "The Final Years of Samaria," *passim*, esp. 165, n. 26; this allows them a historical reconstruction which differs from the one suggested here. Vv. 3–6 are now examined in detail in Becking, *The Fall of Samaria*, 47–60.

21 For the history of research, see Shemaryahu Talmon, "The Presentation of Synchroneity and Simultaneity in Biblical Narrative," *ScrHier* 27 (1978), 12–14; this essay is now reprinted in his *Literary Studies in the Hebrew Bible: Form and Content* (Jerusalem: Magnes, 1993), 112–33.

22 For a bibliography, see my "Jud 1,1–2,10," *ZAW* 101 (1989), 433, n. 9.

23 Hebrew מועדים.

24 See my "Jud, 1,1–2,10," 434. For a more detailed discussion, see Israel Knohl, "The Priestly Torah Versus the Holiness School: Sabbath and the Festivals," *HUCA* 58 (1987), 72–3.

25 There is an additional insertion, with another *Wiederaufnahme* at the end of the unit, but this need not concern us here.

26 See above, n. 3, and Becking, *The Fall of Samaria*, who argues for a double conquest of Samaria (by Shalmaneser V and Sargon II); contrast, however, Hayes and Kuan, "The Final Years of Samaria," 158–9.

27 The reference to "So, king of Egypt" has not been entirely resolved. For a synthesis of the issues, see Duane Christensen, "The Identity of 'King So' in Egypt (2 Kings XVII 4)," *VT* 39 (1989), 140–53. A bibliography of central articles is in Becking, *The Fall of Samaria*, 47, n. 2, to which Donald Redford, *Egypt, Canaan, and Israel in Ancient Times* (Princeton: Princeton University Press, 1992), 346 should now be added.

28 The idea that vv. 5–6 are a separate source rather than the composition of a redactor is bolstered by the fact that they lack a synchronic reference to Judah, as noted by Shemaryahu Talmon, "Biblical Tradition on the Early History of the Samaritans," *Eretz Shomron: The Thirtieth Archaeological Convention September 1972*, ed. J. Amiram (Jerusalem: Israel Exploration Society, 1973), 24 (Hebrew).

29 So Na'aman, "The Historical Background," but see the trenchant critique of Becking, *The Fall of Samaria*, esp. 233–4, 252.

30 Sources closer to events are not always more accurate than those chronologically more removed from them, but this is typically the case.

31 Albert Kirk Grayson, *Assyrian Royal Inscriptions*, part 2 (Wiesbaden: Otto Harrassowitz, 1976), 140–1. Many Assyrian inscriptions mention the destruction of a foreign city. For additional references, see *CAD* N1, 273–4, *s.v. napālu*, for the idiom *appul aqqur*. This element, however, is absent in the Bible and in the Assyrian material relating to the conquest of the northern kingdom; see Stephanie Dalley, "Foreign Chariotry and Cavalry in the Armies of Tiglath-Pileser III and Sargon II," *Iraq* 47 (1985), 34–6.

32 Dalley, "Foreign Chariotry," 34; cf. Becking, *The Fall of Samaria*, 26.

33 For further examples in the Neo-Assyrian royal inscriptions, see *CAD* K, 276b, *s.v. kašādu*.

34 See the complete list in Oded, *Mass Deportations*, 116–35.

35 See for example, A. G. Lie, *The Inscriptions of Sargon II King of Assyria, Part I: The Annals* (Paris: Librairie Orientaliste Paul Greuthner, 1929), lines 23, 67, 74, 76, 90.

36 Oded, *Mass Deportations*, 30.

37 בשנת + definite article + numeral in construct + ל; see Gesenius §134p, who fails to notice the late distribution of this form. A complete list is Num 33:38; 2 Kgs 17:6; 25:1; Jer 28:1; 32:1; 46:2; 51:59; 1 Chr 26:31; 2 Chr 13:1; Ezra 7:8.

38 We have לכד instead of the expected וילכד.

39 So Na'aman, "The Historical Background," 221 and Antti Laato, "New Viewpoints on the Chronology of the Kings of Judah and Israel," ZAW 98 (1986), 217; however, much of Laato's analysis is misguided because he does not recognize that 2 Kgs 17:3–4 and 5–6 are from separate sources.

40 Becking, The Fall of Samaria, 49 offers little supporting evidence that the basis for these verses in the "archives or annals of the Northern Kingdom."

41 See CAD K 360b, s.v. bīt kīli.

42 See my "2 Kings 24:13–14 as History," CBQ 53 (1991), 547–8. On this source, see E. Theodore Mullen, Jr, "Crime and Punishment: The Sins of the Kings and the Despoliation of the Treasuries," CBQ 54 (1992), 231–48, Baruch Halpern, The First Historians: The Hebrew Bible and History (San Francisco: Harper & Row, 1988), 209–11 and the similar suggestion by Hugo Gressmann, "The Oldest History Writing in Israel," trans. David Orton, ed. David M. Gunn, Narrative and Novella in Samuel: Studies by Hugo Gressmann and Other Scholars 1906–1923 (Sheffield: Almond, 1991), 11, concerning what he calls "temple chronicles."

43 See p. 198, n. 25.

44 This is suggested by the use of Akkadian loanwords in Hebrew; see Édouard Lipinski, "Emprunts seméro-akkadiens en hébreu biblique," Zeitschrift für Althebraistik 1 (1988), 61–73, Eduard Yechezkel Kutscher, A History of the Hebrew Language (Jerusalem: Magnes, 1982), 48–9 (with bibliography). For the late second millennium, see Aaron Demsky, "The Education of Canaanite Scribes in the Mesopotamian Cuneiform Tradition," Bar-Ilan Studies in Assyriology dedicated to Pinhas Artzi, ed. Jacob Klein and Aaron Skaist (Ramat Gan: Bar Ilan University Press, 1990), 157–70.

45 See 2 Kgs 18:26. The historicity of the whole episode is irrelevant to this issue; the verse reflects the assumption of its author that Aramaic would have been well known to Assyrian and Judean officials, though not to the general populace. On Aramaic as the lingua franca, see Hayim Tadmor, "The Aramaization of Assyria: Aspects of Assyrian Impact," Mesopotamien und seine Nachbarn, Berliner Beiträge zum Vorderen Orient 1/2, ed. H. J. Nissen and J. Renger (Berlin: Dietrich Reimer, 1983), 449–70, esp. 451–5 and Raymond A. Bowman, "Arameans, Aramaic, and the Bible," JNES 7 (1948), 65–90.

46 See Na'aman, "The Historical Background."

47 Note that the fettering and the exile of Manasseh to Babylon (!) in 2 Chr 33:11 are probably based on the account of Zedekiah.

48 See, for example, John Macdonald, "The Structure of II Kings xvii," Transactions of Glasgow University Oriental Society 23 (1969), 29–41, Talmon, "Polemics and Apology," 57–62, Cogan and Tadmor, II Kings, 204–7, Pauline A. Viviano, "2 Kings 17: A Rhetorical and Form-Critical Analysis," CBQ 49 (1987), 548–59 and Mark A. O'Brien, The Deuteronomistic History Hypothesis: A Reassessment, OBO 92 (Freiburg: Universitätsverlag, 1989), 208.

49 II Kings, 203, 208.

50 Cogan and Tadmor, II Kings, 207, n. 1. For a survey of opinions concerning the sources incorporated into this section, see McKenzie, The Trouble with Kings, 140–2.

51 Hebrew בני ישראל.

52 Hebrew ישראל.

53 Hebrew כל זרע ישראל.

54 The overlapping phrases in a *Wiederaufnahme* need not be identical; see the examples cited on p. 116.

55 To the best of my knowledge, this exact analysis has not been proposed, though I certainly have built it on the insights of others.

56 For a broader discussion of this issue, see Moshe Weinfeld, "The Period of the Conquest and of the Judges as Seen by the Earlier and the Later Sources," *VT* 17 (1967), 93–113.

57 See Deut 12:29–31, which presents the same paradox.

58 Hebrew ויצבו.

59 Hebrew ויעשו.

60 The exact nature of the *asherah*, i.e. whether it is a pole or a tree, is irrelevant to this context; for a discussion, see John Day, "Asherah in the Hebrew Bible and in Northwest Semitic Literature," *JBL* 105 (1986), 385–408, Saul M. Olyan, *Asherah and the Cult of Yahweh in Israel*, SBLMS 34 (Atlanta: Scholars Press, 1988) and Baruch Margalit, "The Meaning and Significance of Asherah," *VT* 40 (1990), 264–97.

61 The standard rendering of "high places" is problematic; see Patrick H. Vaughan, *The Meaning of "bāmâ" in the Old Testament* (Cambridge: Cambridge University Press, 1974). On "high places" in Kings, see Ian Provan, *Hezekiah and the Books of Kings: A Contribution to the Debate about the Composition of the Deuteronomistic History*, BZAW 172 (Berlin: Walter de Gruyter, 1988), 57–91.

62 On the proper translation of קטר, see Diana Edelman, "The Meaning of Qiṭṭēr," *VT* 35 (1985), 395–404.

63 The likelihood that 2 Kings 17 is quoting from 1 Kings 14 is furthered by noting the chiastic ordering of the verses between the two texts (1 Kgs 14:23// 2 Kgs 17:10 and 1 Kgs 14:24//2 Kgs 17:8a); on these chiastic quotations, sometimes called Seidel's law, see Moshe Seidel, "Parallels between Isaiah and Psalms," *Sinai* 38 (1955–6), 149–72, 229–40, 272–80, 335–55 (Hebrew), and Pancratius Beentjes, "Inverted Quotations in the Bible: A Neglected Stylistic Pattern," *Bib* 63 (1982), 506–23.

64 Morton Cogan, *Imperialism and Religion: Assyria, Judah and Israel in the Eighth and Seventh Centuries B.C.E.*, SBLMS 19 (Missoula, MT: Scholars Press, 1974), 103, Viviano, "2 Kings 17," 552, O'Brien, *The Deuteronomistic History Hypothesis*, 210 and Provan, *Hezekiah and the Book of Kings*, 72 have all noted that several of the sins attributed to the north in this chapter are used elsewhere to typify Judah, but have not adduced from their observation the conclusions reached here.

65 See, provisionally, James Flanagan, "Judah in All Israel," *No Famine in the Land: Studies in Honor of John L. McKenzie*, ed. James Flanagan and Anita Weisbrod Robinson (Missoula, MT: Scholars Press, 1975), 101–16.

66 This is one of the arguments adduced by Frank Moore Cross, *Canaanite Myth and Hebrew Epic* (Cambridge, MA: Harvard University Press, 1972), 288 for the double redaction of Kings; cf. McKenzie, *The Trouble with Kings*, 127.

67 "Ahaz and Tiglath-Pileser," 508.

68 Brettler, "2 Kings 24:13–14 as History," 549–51.

69 Hebrew גם, which can mean "also" but, in this context, is more likely emphatic ("indeed").

70 Provan, *Hezekiah and the Book of Kings*, 74–7 advocates the translation of "also" for גם in this context.

71 See pp. 71–2.

72 I follow most scholars in considering יהודה (Judah) a gloss; see pp. 71–2.
73 A structure similar to section E3 is evident in 1 Kgs 11:9ff., which like our unit uses ויתאנף יהוה ("YHWH was very angry") following the actions being condemned and preceding their punishment.
74 Though the *qeri* and the *kethib* are both difficult, the reading כל נביא וכל חזה (assuming that the *wāw* was erroneously placed after the *'aleph* [see Friedrich Delitzsch, *Die Lese- und Schreibfehler im Alten Testament* (Berlin: Walter de Gruyter, 1920), 2, C. F. Burney, *Notes on the Hebrew Text of the Books of Kings* (Oxford: Clarendon Press, 1903), 332, and others]) or כל נביאי כל חזה (assuming synonymous constructs [see Yitzhak Avishur, *Stylistic Studies of Word-Pairs in Biblical and Ancient Semitic Literatures*, AOAT 210 (Neukirchen-Vluyn: Neukirchener Verlag, 1984), 153–211]) are both acceptable.
75 An additional example of this "theology of guilt" is found in Deut 8:14–16a.
76 This does not mean, however, that the king is always viewed as responsible for the nation's welfare, as is often stated; see my *God is King: Understanding Israelite Metaphor*, JSOTSup 76 (Sheffield: Sheffield Academic Press, 1989), 181, n. 45.
77 The fourth case is in the great rebuke in Deut 28:68.
78 The exact nuance of the different terms used for divination is not known.
79 *Prophetie und Geschichte: Eine redaktionsgeschichtliche Untersuchung zum deuteronomistischen Geschichtswerk*, FRLANT 108 (Göttingen: Vandenhoeck & Ruprecht, 1972), 45. See more recently Ehud Ben Zvi, "The Account of the Reign of Manasseh in II Reg 21,1–18 and the Redactional History of the Book of Kings," *ZAW* 103 (1991), 363.
80 On this worship, see Susan Ackerman, "And the Women Knead Dough: The Worship of Sixth-Century Judah," *Gender and Difference in Ancient Israel*, ed. Peggy L. Day (Minneapolis: Fortress, 1989), 109–24.
81 On the debate concerning the meaning of this phrase, see George C. Heider, *The Cult of Molek: A Reassessment*, JSOTSup 43 (Sheffield: JSOT Press, 1985) and John Day, *Molech: A God of Human Sacrifice in the Old Testament* (Cambridge: Cambridge University Press, 1989).
82 Richard D. Nelson, *The Double Redaction of the Deuteronomistic History*, JSOTSup 18 (Sheffield: JSOT Press, 1981), 56 and Provan, *Hezekiah and the Book of Kings*, 70, n. 35 bring compelling evidence that the phrase "the descendants of Israel" includes Judah.
83 I. Benzinger, *Die Bücher der Könige*, KHAT (Freiburg: J. C. B. Mohr, 1899), 174, following Stade, "Miscellen," 167.
84 See Provan, *Hezekiah and the Book of Kings*, 71, n. 40, to which Burney, *Notes on the Hebrew Text*, 330 should be added.
85 On the translation of כי קרע, see pp. 124–5.
86 Both the *qeri* and the *kethib* וידח/א seem to have the same meaning; see Robert Gordis, *The Biblical Text in the Making: A Study of Kethib–Qere* (New York: Ktav, 1971), 151 and 200, n. 538.
87 They are innovations from the biblical perspective only. In reality, depending on one's understanding of the dating and redaction of Exodus 32, they may have been examples of religious conservatism. For several possibilities, see Moses Aberbach and Leivy Smolar, "Aaron, Jeroboam, and the Golden Calves," *JBL* 86 (1967), 129–40 and Jörg Debus, *Die Sünde Jeroboams: Studien zur Darstellung Jeroboams und der Geschichte des Nordreichs in der deuteronomistischen Geschichtsschreibung*, FRLANT 93 (Göttingen: Vandenhoeck & Ruprecht, 1967).

88 It also appears in Gen 20:9, in reference to adultery; this suggests that its use with idolatry may fit the pattern of a covenant infraction being viewed as adultery; see Nahum M. Sarna, *Genesis*, JPS Torah Commentary (Philadelphia: Jewish Publication Society, 1989), 143 and Elaine June Adler, "The Background for the Metaphor of Covenant as Marriage in the Hebrew Bible," Ph.D. dissertation, University of California at Berkeley, 1989, 127–9a.

89 Cf., for example, Exod 22:21–3 and 1 Sam 15:23, 26. See the "talion style" noted in Sean McEvenue, *The Narrative Style of the Priestly Writer* (Rome: Pontifical Biblical Institute, 1971), 70–1 and Patrick D. Miller, *Sin and Judgment in the Prophets* (Chico, CA: Scholars Press, 1982). The smooth seam between vv. 22 and 23, however, does not compensate for the substantial differences between them. See the discussion of "The Disappearing Redactor" in John Barton, *Reading the Old Testament: Method in Biblical Study* (Philadelphia: Westminster, 1984), 56–8. This point is especially important given the current tendency of some scholars to over-emphasize the unity of the Deuteronomistic History or Kings; cf., for example, J. G. McConville, "Narrative and Meaning in the Books of Kings," *Bib* 70 (1989), 31–49.

90 RSV, following the KJV. NEB, JB, REB, NRSV are similar.

91 Hebrew קרע.

92 Hebrew את.

93 Either הממלכה or in one case ממלכות ישראל.

94 This has not been noted by McKenzie, *The Trouble with Kings*, 45–6, who puts 2 Kgs 17:21 in the same category as the other texts. In contrast, O'Brien, *The Deuteronomistic History Hypothesis*, 175–6 is partially aware of the uniqueness of 2 Kgs 17:21.

95 *Tanakh: The New Translation of the Holy Scriptures According to the Traditional Hebrew Text* (Philadelphia: Jewish Publication Society, 1985), 595; cf. Würthwein, *Die Bücher der Könige, 1 Kön. 17–2 Kön. 25*, 391, "Als Israel 'sich losgerissen hatte' vom Hause Davids."

96 Alexander Sperber, *The Bible in Aramaic*, II (Leiden: E. J. Brill, 1959), 309 (ארי אתפליגו בית ישראל על דבית דויד).

97 *The Old Testament in Syriac According to the Peshitta Edition*, ed. Peshitta Institute, II, 4 (Leiden: E. J. Brill, 1976), 132 (דפרקו דבית איסריל מן בתר דויד מטל). Contrast, however, the reading attested in two manuscripts as cited in the apparatus: מטל דאפרק לאיסראיל מן בית דויד, which presumes that Israel (note the accusative *lamed*) is the direct object of "to tear" (note פרק in the *Aphel*).

98 Although the middle voice is often expressed in the *niphal* (Bruce K. Waltke and M. O'Connor, *An Introduction to Biblical Hebrew Syntax* [Winona Lake, IN: Eisenbrauns, 1990] § 22.2.2), the phrase גזר ממכלה צאן, "the sheep are destroyed from the enclosure" (Hab 3:17) suggests that verbs in the semantic field of "separating" with a medial sense may appear in the *qal* (Contrast *BHS* to Hab 3:17, which emends גזר to נגזר.) The Targum and the Peshitta thus reflect a correct understanding of this verse. (The suggestion that these versions" *Vorlage* reads נקרע [Benzinger, *Die Bücher der Könige*, 174 and John Gray, *I and II Kings*, second, fully revised edition OTL (Philadelphia: Westminster, 1970), 650, n. a] is not compelling.)

99 The translation with Israel as the verb's subject initially seems problematic because it presumes a fluctuation of the verb's number; in v. 21aα the verb whose subject is Israel is in the singular (קרע), while later in the verse Israel is referred to in the plural (וימליכו). However, the verb appears in the singular in 21aα because it precedes the noun, which is a logical, not a grammatical

plural, while in v. 21aβ, after the subject, it is appropriately in the plural. V. 19 presents a similar syntagma.

100 The likelihood of an allusion is enhanced by noting that קרע, "to tear," is typically used of clothing, so its use in 2 Kings 17 is unusual.

101 Hebrew פשע.

102 See esp. 2 Kgs 3:4–5, Moshe Weinfeld, *Deuteronomy and the Deuteronomic School* (Oxford: Oxford University Press, 1972), 138 and Rolf Knierim, *Die Hauptbegriffe für Sünde im Alten Testament* (Gütersloh: Gütersloher Verlagshaus Gerd Mohn, 1965), 150. However, this verse in 1 Kings 12 is probably secondary, as indicated by the atypical attitude that it has toward the northern kingdom and by its use of the formula "until this very day," which very frequently indicates notices which are secondary. (See Brevard S. Childs, "A Study of the Formula, 'Until this Day,' " *JBL* 82 [1963], 279–92.)

103 H. G. M. Williamson, *Israel in the Books of Chronicles* (Cambridge: Cambridge University Press, 1977), esp. 110–18 and Sara Japhet, *The Ideology of the Book of Chronicles and Its Place in Biblical Thought*, BzEATAJ 9, trans. Anna Barbar (Frankfurt: Peter Lang, 1989), 308–24.

104 Chronicles recognizes this prophecy once, in 2 Chr 10:15; for an attempt to reconcile this with the Chronicler's more typical views toward kingship, see the previous note.

105 The contentions of Richard D. Nelson, *The Double Redaction of the Deuteronomistic History*, JSOTSup 18 (Sheffield: JSOT Press, 1981), 56, that vv. 19–20 may be from the same hand as the surrounding verses, and are "pointing forward to what is coming," are difficult to maintain. The exilic origin of these verses has been advocated from at least the time of Abraham Kuenen, *Historisch-kritische Einleitung in die Bücher des alten Testaments* I, 2 (Leipzig: O. R. Reisland, 1897), 91.

106 The relationship between these texts has been noted to some extent by Nelson, *The Double Redaction*, 63. However, he incorrectly suggests that vv. 21–3a are later than all of vv. 7–20, 23b.

107 Note אשר עשו, which the Jeremiah text shares with 2 Kgs 17:19.

108 See O'Brien, *The Deuteronomistic History Hypothesis*, 282.

109 Compare v. 19b.

110 The secondary nature of this half-verse concerning Sheshakh is also indicated by its absence in the LXX; see e.g. William McKane, *Jeremiah*, vol. 1, ICC (Edinburgh: T. & T. Clark, 1986), 640.

111 The use of a cipher for its name suggests that this half-verse was added between 586, the exile, and 539, the conquest of Babylon by Cyrus the Great.

112 For various formulations of this position, see Šanda, *Die Bücher der Könige*, 233, Würthwein, *Die Bücher der Könige, 1 Kön. 17–2 Kön. 25*, 397–403, John Gray, *I & II Kings*, second edition, OTL (Philadelphia: Westminster Press, 1970), 654–5 and McKenzie, *The Trouble with Kings*, 142. The position that these verses reflect an expectation that the Samaritans should fully observe the Torah was stated as recently as Hans-Detlef Hoffmann, *Reform und Reformen: Untersuchungen zu einem Grundthema der deuteronomistischen Geschichtschreibung*, ATANT 66 (Zürich: Theologischer Verlag, 1980), 138.

113 Mordechai Cogan, "Israel in Exile – The View of a Josianic Historian," *JBL* 97 (1978), 4–44.

114 In general, the fact that Kings ends with the release of Jehoiachin from prison rather than the Cyrus proclamation, like Chronicles, argues against extensive post-exilic editing of Kings. This point speaks against those who see extensive sections of 2 Kings 17 as post-exilic, such as Shemaryahu Talmon,

"Polemics and Apology in Biblical Historiography: 2 Kings 17:24–41," *The Creation of Sacred Literature: Composition and Redaction of the Biblical Text*, 57–68, ed. Richard E. Friedman (Berkeley: University of California Press, 1981), [reprinted in Talmon's *Literary Studies in the Hebrew Bible: Form and Content* (Jerusalem: Magnes, 1993), 134–59]. The presence of several late biblical Hebrew features does not necessarily require a post-exilic date; see the study of the exilic language of Ezekiel by Mark F. Rooker, *Biblical Hebrew in Transition: The Language of the Book of Ezekiel*, JSOTSup 90 (Sheffield: Sheffield Academic Press, 1990).

115 Since I am interested here in the ideological issues raised by these sections, I will not deal with the historical issues that they raise, including the extent of the exile of the north. For this, see Bustanay Oded, "II Kings 17: Between History and Polemic," *Jewish History* 2 (1987), 37–50.

116 This has been misunderstood by McKenzie, *The Trouble with Kings*, 142, who claims that "The tension between v 33a and 34b concerning whether or not the Samaritans fear Yahweh is obvious." This causes him to understand the history of this unit differently from what I propose here. O'Brien, *The Deuteronomistic History Hypothesis*, 212 also misunderstands vv. 29–34a, suggesting that it "looks like a thinly veiled attack on the northern priesthood."

117 It is possible that the story concerning the lions is somehow related to the tradition recorded in Esarhaddon's vassal treaties which connects the deity Anat-bethel with "the claws of the devouring lion"; see Cogan and Tadmor, *II Kings*, 210. There are other possible Assyrian influences on this unit as well; see Hayim Tadmor, "On the History of Samaria in the Biblical Period," *Eretz Shomron*, ed. J. Amiram, 70 (Hebrew), on the possibility that the sending of a priest to Bethel is related to the traditions found in the Assyrian annals.

118 The evaluation of these people is not, however, entirely positive. V. 33 suggests that these foreigners were like the Israelites who had just been exiled. This opens up the possibility that even though they partially revere YHWH, they too would be exiled, to make room for a group (like Judah) which should properly reside there and knows (in theory) how properly to revere YHWH.

119 Hebrew כמשפטים הראשנים (v. 34) and כמשפט הראשון (v. 40); see Cogan, "Israel in Exile," 42, n. 13.

120 This is noted to some extent in A. D. H. Mayes, *The Story of Israel Between the Settlement and Exile: A Redactional Study of the Deuteronomistic History* (London: SCM, 1983), 127. His analysis (pp. 125–7) differs from mine in that he finds fewer sources in 2 Kgs 17.

121 Shemaryahu Talmon, "The Presentation of Synchroneity and Simultaneity in Biblical Narrative," *ScrHier* 27 (1978), 9–26.

122 See similarly R. J. Coggins, "The Old Testament and Samaritan Origins," *ASTI* 6 (1968), 39–41.

123 Hebrew משפט.

124 See the multiple references to these verses in the index of Weinfeld, *Deuteronomy and the Deuteronomic School*, 437.

125 Some Deuteronomistic features of this section are noted by Mordechai Cogan, "For We, Like You, Worship Your God: Three Biblical Portrayals of Samaritan Origins," *VT* 38 (1988), 289–90, but they are not as predominant as he implies and they are certainly not as extensive as those found in the following verses.

126 Talmon, "Polemics and Apology," 64–5 and Cogan and Tadmor, *II Kings*, 211.

127 On these cities, see Becking, *The Fall of Samaria*, 95–104.

128 Cogan and Tadmor, *II Kings*, 211–12.

129 The presence of a list of exiled nations and the use of Assyrian administrative

diction in v. 27 support the idea that our author used a source. On the last
point, see Shalom Paul, "Sargon's Administrative Diction in II Kings 17:27,"
JBL 88 (1969), 73–4.

130 See Nadav Na'aman and Ran Zadok, "Sargon II's Deportation to Israel and
Philistia," *JCS* 40 (1988), 36–46, esp. 37–8, for a (broken) text listing people
deported to Samaria.

131 The syntagma היי + participle, found for example in v. 25 (ויהיו הרגים בהם), is
especially frequent in late Hebrew and is probably an Aramaism; see MacDonald, "The Structure of II Kings xvii," 33–5 and Paul Joüon, *Grammaire de
L'Hebreu Biblique* (Rome: Pontifical Biblical Institute, 1923) § 121g. The
additional examples for late biblical Hebrew adduced by MacDonald, 33–8,
are not fully compelling. A similar syntagma is used, however, in some clearly
early pre-exilic contexts, including in the Yabneh Yam inscription, line 3 (*KAI*,
vol. I, p. 36, # 200).

132 The presence of a single Aramaism, however, is not sufficient to prove that a
verse is exilic; see A. Hurvitz, "The Chronological Significance of 'Aramaisms'
in Biblical Hebrew," *IEJ* 18 (1968), 234–40.

133 See Ezek 37:15–28.

134 Mordechai Cogan, "The Men of Nebo – Repatriated Reubenites," *IEJ* 29
(1979), 37–9. On similar passages concerning the restoration of the north, see
David C. Greenwood, "On the Jewish Hope for a Restored Northern Kingdom," *ZAW* 88 (1976), 376–85.

135 This is significant because Manasseh is after Josiah, under whom the first
edition of Kings was composed according to many scholars.

136 Cogan and Tadmor, *II Kings*, 211.

137 Baruch Halpern and David S. Vanderhooft, "The Editions of Kings in the 7th–
6th Centuries B.C.E.," *HUCA* 62 (1991), 179–244.

138 On ideology as incorporating both religious and political factors, see p. 13.

139 J. G. McConville, "Narrative and Meaning in the Books of Kings," 48. The
parenetic nature of the chapter has been properly appreciated by Viviano, "2
Kings 17."

140 Burke O. Long, *2 Kings*, FOTL (Grand Rapids, MI: Eerdmans, 1991), 189.

141 Long, *2 Kings*, 181.

142 This is significant, because vv. 3–6 are usually taken at face value. True, in
contrast to the rest of the chapter they look rather straightforward, but careful
internal analysis suggests otherwise.

143 This is increasingly acknowledged by scholars who study the origin of the
Samaritans; see, for example, R. J. Coggins, *Samaritans and Jews: The Origins
of Samaritanism Reconsidered* (Atlanta: John Knox, 1975), 13–15. A more
recent study of the early history of the Samaritans by Menachem Mor, "Samaritan History: The Persian, Hellenistic and Hasmonean Period," *The Samaritans*,
ed. Alan D. Crown (Tübingen: J. C. B. Mohr, 1989), 1–39, esp. 1–2, almost
entirely sidesteps 2 Kings 17.

144 This is similar to what we have seen in other chapters of this book as well;
material which previous modern historians have used (improperly) to reconstruct political history should actually be used to reconstruct the history of
ideologies.

CONCLUSION: THE CREATION OF BIBLICAL HISTORY

1 Edward Hallett Carr, *What is History?* (London: Macmillan, 1961), 17.

2 A less successful analogy is proposed by Gösta W. Ahlström, *The History of Ancient Palestine from the Paleolithic Period to Alexander's Conquest*, JSOT-Sup 146 (Sheffield: JSOT Press, 1993), 53, "The available facts are the potsherd, but their history comes about in the reconstruction." When we excavate, we know that a potsherd is a potsherd, and can reconstruct a jar even if many pieces are missing, but it is much more difficult to determine whether a particular item buried in the biblical historical corpus is indeed a fact.

3 I do not mean to suggest, however, that there is a correlation between lack of historicity and distance from the event being described.

4 David Damrosch, *The Narrative Covenant: Transformations of Genre in the Growth of Biblical Literature* (Ithaca, New York: Cornell University, 1987), 233.

5 Others have used "invention" (so e.g. Philip R. Davies, *In Search of "Ancient Israel,"* JSOTSup 148 [Sheffield: Sheffield University Press, 1992], and in reference to non-biblical history, Eric Hobsbawm and Terence Ranger, eds, *The Invention of Tradition* [Cambridge: Cambridge University Press, 1983]). I believe that "creation" is a better term; "invention" to me suggests massive or total fabrication, in other words little or no relation between the text and the reality it purports to depict, while "creation" fits a range of situations, from *creatio ex nihilo* to the reworking of an event into a relatively faithful narrative by the historian who is interested in depicting the past as he or she perceives it.

6 For a summary, see Yosef Hayim Yerushalmi, *Zakhor: Jewish History and Jewish Memory* (Seattle: University of Washington Press, 1982), 5–16.

7 The clearest example of this in popular circles is Werner Keller, *The Bible as History*, trans. William Neil, second revised edition (New York: William Morrow, 1981). In his introduction (p. 23), he notes, "Nevertheless, the events themselves are historical facts and have been recorded with an accuracy that is nothing less than startling." The popularity of this book, which had by 1981 sold over 10,000,000 copies in 24 languages, attests to the prevalence of this (misguided) position.

8 For a discussion with extensive bibliography, see John H. Hayes and Frederick Prussner, *Old Testament Theology: Its History and Development* (Atlanta: John Knox, 1985), 241–4, 260–4.

9 Yerushalmi, *Zakhor*, 5–12; for a discussion and additional literature, see H. Eising, "זכר," *TDOT* IV, 64–82.

10 Yerushalmi, *Zakhor*, 10.

11 This term is used by Nahum M. Sarna, "Israel in Egypt: The Egyptian Sojourn and the Exodus," *Ancient Israel: A Short History from Abraham to the Roman Destruction of the Temple*, ed. Hershel Shanks (Washington, DC: Biblical Archaeology Society, 1988), 51.

12 There are some cases where past events are commemorated religiously in other ancient Near Eastern cultures (see, for example, the conclusion of the *Enuma Elish*), but the notion that the past must be recalled does not predominate in any ancient Near Eastern culture to the extent that it predominates in the Hebrew Bible.

13 Bertil Albrektson, *History and the Gods: An Essay on the Idea of Historical Events as Divine Manifestations in the Ancient Near East and in Israel*, CBOT 1 (Lund: CWK Gleerup, 1967). On this work, see W. G. Lambert, "History and the Gods: A Review Article," *Or* 39 (1970), 170–7.

14 Albrektson, *History and the Gods*, 115.

15 J. H. Plumb, *The Death of the Past* (Harmondsworth: Penguin, 1973). See also David Lowenthal, *The Past is a Foreign Country* (Cambridge: Cambridge University Press, 1985). The problems presented to the practicing historian by this tendency are discussed under the rubric of "the pragmatic fallacy" by David Hackett Fischer, *Historians" Fallacies: Toward a Logic of Historical Thought* (New York: Harper & Row, 1970), 82–7. They are applied to biblical texts in great detail in Thomas L. Thompson, "Text, Context and Referent in Israelite Historiography," *The Fabric of History: Text, Artifact and Israel's Past*, JSOTSup 127, ed. Diana Vikander Edelman (Sheffield: Sheffield Academic Press, 1991), 65–92.

16 Ben Halpern, "History as a Jewish Problem," *From Ancient Israel to Modern Judaism: Intellect in Quest of Understanding, Essays in Honor of Marvin Fox*, vol. 1, ed. Jacob Neusner *et al.* (Atlanta: Scholars Press, 1989), 3–21; the quotation is from p. 3.

17 See p. 179, n. 65.

18 This position is especially associated with H. H. Rowley; for a summary see George W. Ramsey, "Zadok," *ABD* VI, 1034–6.

19 Note, however, the contrast between ancient and modern historians pointed out in Donald B. Redford, *Egypt, Canaan, and Israel in Ancient Times* (Princeton: Princeton University Press, 1992), 334.

20 For a discussion on the use of models to explicate biblical problems, see Jeffrey H. Tigay, "Introduction," *Empirical Models for Biblical Criticism*, ed. Jeffrey H. Tigay (Philadelphia: University of Pennsylvania Press, 1985), 1–20.

21 See Davies, *In Search of "Ancient Israel,"*, 31, "It is impossible to discern any grounds for deciding that on the one hand the Joseph story is not historical, while on the other hand the accounts of the life and times of David or Ezra are." Most scholars assume, without a decisive methodological basis, that material from early sections of the canon may not be used to reconstruct the events that they convey, but at some point, typically in Exodus, Joshua or Samuel, the Bible becomes a useful historical source. (This point is sometimes called the "datum point"; for a discussion see J. Alberto Soggin, "The History of Ancient Israel – A Study in Some Questions of Method," *EI* 14 [1978] [H. L. Ginsberg Volume], 44*–51*. Soggin's suggestion is not compelling.)

22 See Robin W. Winks, ed., *The Historian as Detective: Essays on Evidence* (New York: Harper & Row, 1969), 181–91, esp. 186–7 concerning the famous Göttingen experiment in which professionals were asked to describe a staged incident that they had just witnessed, and many of the reports showed gross inaccuracies. For contemporary examples, see Michael Schudson, *Watergate in American Memory: How we Remember, Forget, and Reconstruct the Past* (New York: Basic, 1992).

23 Hermann Gunkel, *Legends of Genesis*, trans. W. H. Carruth (New York: Schocken, 1975), 41; this is quoted in Eduard Nielson, *Oral Tradition*, SBT 11 (London: SCM, 1958), 11.

24 See John van Seters, "Oral Patterns or Literary Conventions in Biblical Narrative," *Sem* 5 (1976), 139–54 and the response by David M. Gunn, "On Oral Tradition: A Response to John van Seters," *Sem* 5 (1976), 155–63.

25 Ruth Finnegan, *Oral Poetry: Its Nature, Significance and Social Context* (Cambridge: Cambridge University Press, 1977).

26 See Ernst Axel Knauf, "From History to Interpretation," *The Fabric of History: Text, Artifact and Israel's Past*, JSOTSup 127, ed. Diana Vikander Edelman

(Sheffield: Sheffield Academic Press, 1991), 46, n. 2 and Davies, *In Search of "Ancient Israel."*

27 Robert B. Coote and Keith Whitelam, *The Emergence of Early Israel in Historical Perspective*, SWBA 5 (Sheffield: Almond Press, 1987).

28 Niels Peter Lemche, *Ancient Israel: A New History of Israelite Society*, (Sheffield: Sheffield Academic Press, 1988).

29 Fredric Brandfon, "The Limits of Evidence: Archaeology and Objectivity," *Maarav* 4 (1987), 5–43. For a critique of those who claim to ignore the Bible, see J. Maxwell Miller, "Is It Possible to Write a History of Israel Without Relying on the Hebrew Bible?" *The Fabric of History*, ed. Diana Vikander Edelman, 93–102. On fitting archeology and the text together, given the limitations of both, see Gösta W. Ahlström, "The Role of Archaeological and Literary Remains in Reconstructing Israel's History," *The Fabric of History*, ed. Diana Vikander Edelman, 116–41.

30 So according to the ongoing study of the Belgian archeologists, the Donceels, but see Hershel Shanks, "The Qumran Settlement: Monastery, Villa or Fortress?" *BARev* 19/3 (May/June 1993), 62–5. Another well-known case is the continuing debate over the (Solomonic) stables at Megiddo; see the summary in Israel Finkelstein and David Ussishkin, "Back to Megiddo," *BARev* 20/1 (Jan./Feb. 1994), 39–40.

31 Davies, *In Search of "Ancient Israel,"* 51.

32 Martin Noth, John Bright and J. Alberto Soggin are obvious examples.

33 One of the few exceptions is the section on "The Period of the First Temple, the Babylonian Exile and the Restoration" by H. Tadmor in *A History of the Jewish People*, ed. H. H. Ben-Sasson (Cambridge, MA: Harvard University Press, 1976), 91–182.

34 On the accepted canons of historical method, see Jacques Barzun and Henry F. Graff, *The Modern Researcher*, fourth edition (New York: Harcourt Brace Jovanovich, 1985); for a more polemical approach, see Fischer, *Historians" Fallacies*. For these criteria in relationship to biblical history, see the sketch of Diana Vikander Edelman, "Doing History in Biblical Studies," *The Fabric of History*, ed. Diana Vikander Edelman, 13–25. Note also the following statement by Thomas L. Thompson, *Early History of the Israelite People From the Written and Archaeological Sources*, Studies in the History of the Ancient Near East, 4 (Leiden: E. J. Brill, 1992), 388, concerning the use of evidence for reconstructing biblical history:

> Without concrete external evidence, such selective preference [of one biblical tradition rather than another] is not critical. As long as we continue to work with historical contexts that are not based on independent evidence, plausibility and verisimilitude cannot be recognized as valid criteria for historicity. Plausibility and verisimilitude are characteristics that are to be attributed far more to good fiction. Reasonableness is a characteristic of the fictional not the historical genres of literature. History happens, and our knowledge of it is based on evidence not reason.

35 J. A. Brinkman, *A Political History of Post-Kassite Babylonia 1158–722 B.C.*, AnOr 43 (Rome: Pontifical Biblical Institute, 1968).

36 Brinkman, *A Political History of Post-Kassite Babylonia 1158–722 B.C.*, 3–36.

37 For example, from the perspective of a biblical scholar, the evidence sifted through, evaluated and synthesized in the recent book by David Hackett Fischer, *Albion's Seed: Four British Folkways in America* (New York: Oxford University Press, 1989) is absolutely staggering.

38 For a discussion of the sources for the monarchy, where we have the most evidence, see Nahum M. Sarna, "The Biblical Sources for the History of the Monarchy" and N. Avigad, "Hebrew Epigraphic Sources," *The World History of the Jewish People: The Age of the Monarchies: Political History*, ed. Abraham Malamat (Jerusalem: Massada Press, 1979), 3–19, 20–43.

39 For a more optimistic view, see William W. Hallo, "Biblical History in Its Near Eastern Setting: The Contextual Approach," *Scripture in Context: Esays on the Comparative Method*, ed. Carl D. Evans *et al.* (Pittsburgh: Pickwick Press, 1980), 1–26, esp. 5. Contrast the view of Alan Cooper and Bernard R. Goldstein, "Exodus and Maṣṣôt in History and Tradition," *Maarav* 8 (1992), 15–37, which to my mind is more realistic and theoretically sound.

40 See esp. 185–7. In addition, see now Knauf, "From History to Interpretation," *The Fabric of History*, ed. Diana Vikander Edelman, 53–63.

41 Compare the following observation of Thompson, *Early History of the Israelite People*, 365:

> [Q]uestions of historicity have a strong negative *Tendenz*; that is, answers to such questions of historicity are often most clearly and satisfactorily answered when that answer is negative. Moreover, even such negative answers are rarely decisive, but relate to the lack of or inadequate evidence for affirming historicity.

42 See the study of Francolino J. Gonçalves, *L'expédition de Sennachérib en Palestine dans la littérature hébraïque ancienne*, Ebib n. s. 7 (Paris: Librairie Lecoffre J. Gabalda, 1986), who advocates the one-campaign theory. For a summary which advocates the one-campaign account, see Mordechai Cogan and Hayim Tadmor, *II Kings*, AB (Garden City, New York: Doubleday, 1988), 246–51; for the contrary opinion see William H. Shea, "Sennacherib's Second Palestinian Campaign," *JBL* 104 (1985), 401–18.

43 R. G. Collingwood, *The Idea of History*, (Oxford: Clarendon Press, 1946), 266–8 ("Who Killed John Doe?"). This section is reprinted in the useful collection *The Historian as Detective: Essays on Evidence*, ed. Robin W. Winks (New York: Harper & Row, 1969), 41–4. On the historian as detective, see also Joseph M. Levine, "The Autonomy of History: R. G. Collingwood and Agatha Christie," *Clio* 7 (1978), 253–64. The image of historian as juror has also recently been applied by Davies, *In Search of "Ancient Israel,"* 40–1.

44 For the standard definitions of these terms, see Henry Campbell Black, *Black's Law Dictionary*, fifth edition (St Paul: West Publishing Co., 1979), 147, 1064.

45 For the Mesopotamian evidence, see A. K. Grayson, *Assyrian and Babylonian Chronicles*, TCS 5 (Locust Valley, New York: J. J. Augustin, 1975), 102 and *ANET*, 308.

46 See my "The Book of Judges: Literature as Politics," *JBL* 108 (1989), 395–418.

47 For such skepticism about David's existence, see Knauf, "From History to Interpretation," 39, Davies, *In Search of "Ancient Israel,"* esp. 69, Thompson, *Early History of the Israelite People*, 111. Some scholars have noted that the discovery of the name David (actually ביתדוד) on a stele from Tel Dan (Avraham Biran and Joseph Naveh, "An Aramaic Stele Fragment from Tel Dan," *IEJ* 43 [1993], 81–98) merely proves the existence in the ninth century of a dynasty that saw David as its ancestor, but does not prove the historicity of David; others suggest that it is a place name. As an indication of how recent this deep skepticism is, contrast Ronald E. Clements, "History and Theology in Biblical Narrative," *Horizons in Biblical Theology* 4 (1982), 52–3,

Whereas virtually all scholars have been willing to concede that there exists considerable difficulty in bringing the stories of the Hebrew patriarchs out of the shadows into a clear historical light, no such uncertainty surrounds the figures of Israel's first kings: Saul, David, and Solomon.

48 An example of one such attempt is P. Kyle McCarter, Jr, "The Historical David," *Int* 40 (1986), 117–29.

49 See esp. *Clio* and *H and T*. An important older essay which primarily deals with Ranke in Charles A. Beard, "That Noble Dream," *American Historical Review* 41 (1935–6), 74–87. For recent examples, see many of the essays in W. J. Van Der Dussen and Lionel Rubinoff, eds, *Objectivity, Method and Point of View: Essays in the Philosophy of History* (Leiden: E. J. Brill, 1991) and Joseph M. Levine, "Objectivity in History: Peter Novick and R. G. Collingwood," *Clio* 21 (1992), 109–27.

50 Lionel Gossman, "The Rationality of History," *Between History and Literature* (Cambridge, MA: Harvard University Press, 1990), 285–324.

51 Gossman, *Between History and Literature*, 317–18.

52 See Peter Kosso, "Observation of the Past," *H and T* 31 (1992), 21–36 for an application of the problems of objectivity in science to the study of history.

53 This is a departure from the radical skepticism of some scholars (e.g. Thomas L. Thompson), who have recently suggested that biblical texts can only be trusted when they are confirmed by reliable, outside sources. I am suggesting instead that we must use the evidence at hand to inquire after the historical reliability of each text, and that there will be cases where we will affirm biblical traditions which do not have outside confirmation because the assumption that these traditions reflect some historical reality is the most suitable explanation of their existence in a particular form. Particular reconstructions may be, in the words of Gossman (*Between History and Literature*, cited above, n. 51), "rationally justifiable," though lacking outside verification.

54 On the first issue, see Cooper and Goldstein, "Exodus and Maṣṣôt in History and Tradition"; on the second, see Israel Finkelstein, *The Archaeology of the Israelite Settlement* (Jerusalem: Israel Exploration Society, 1988), esp. 295–314, William G. Dever, *Recent Archaeological Discoveries and Biblical Research* (Seattle: University of Washington Press, 1990), 37–84, Amihai Mazar, "The Iron Age I," *Archaeology of Ancient Israel*, trans. R. Greenberg (New Haven, CT: Yale University Press, 1992), 281–8 and Diana Edelman, ed., "Toward a Consensus on the Emergence of Israel in Canaan," *SJOT* 2 (1991), 1–116.

SELECT BIBLIOGRAPHY

The following is a selection of English sources on biblical historical texts and on connected topics, such as the nature of history and literature. I have concentrated on works which have contributed significantly to my understanding of biblical historical texts, though I have included several important works with which I fundamentally disagree. For reasons of space, I have not cited any biblical commentaries or the standard histories of Israel, although these contain much useful material. More comprehensive bibliographies may be found in K. Lawson Younger, Jr, *Ancient Conquest Accounts: A Study in Ancient Near Eastern and Biblical History Writing* and Thomas L. Thompson, *Early History of the Israelite People From the Written and Archaeological Sources*, which are cited below.

Ackroyd, Peter, *The Chronicler in His Age*, JSOTSup 101, Sheffield: Sheffield Academic Press, 1991.

Ahlström, Gösta W., *The History of Ancient Palestine from the Paleolithic Period to Alexander's Conquest*, JSOTSup 146, Sheffield: JSOT Press, 1993.

Albrektson, Bertil, *History and the Gods: An Essay on the Idea of Historical Events as Divine Manifestations in the Ancient Near East and in Israel*, CBOT 1, Lund: CWK Gleerup, 1967.

Alter, Robert, *The Pleasures of Reading in an Ideological Age*, New York: Simon & Schuster, 1989.

Althusser, Louis, *For Marx*, trans. Ben Brewster, New York: Pantheon, 1969.

Anchor, Robert, "Narrativity and the Transformation of Historical Consciousness," *Clio* 16 (1987): 121–37.

Barr, James, "Story and History in Biblical Theology," *JR* 56 (1976): 1–17.

Barton, John, *Reading the Old Testament: Method in Biblical Study*, Philadelphia: Westminster, 1984.

Becking, Bob, *The Fall of Samaria: An Historical and Archaeological Study*, Studies in the History of the Ancient Near East, 2, Leiden: E. J. Brill, 1992.

Ben Zvi, Ehud, "The Account of the Reign of Manasseh in II Reg 21,1–18 and the Redactional History of the Book of Kings," *ZAW* 103 (1991): 355–74.

Bloom, Edward A. and Lillian D. Bloom, *Satire's Persuasive Voice*, Ithaca, NY: Cornell University Press, 1979.

Brandfon, Fredric, "The Limits of Evidence: Archaeology and Objectivity," *Maarav* 4 (1987): 5–43.

Brettler, Marc, "The Book of Judges: Literature as Politics," *JBL* 108 (1989): 395–418.

—— "The Structure of 1 Kings 1–11," *JSOT* 49 (1991): 87–97.

Brinkman, J. A., "Through a Glass Darkly: Esarhaddon's Retrospects on the Downfall of Babylon," *JAOS* 103 (1983): 35–42.

Brueggemann, Walter, *David's Truth in Israel's Imagination and Memory*, Philadelphia, PA: Fortress, 1985.

Burke, Peter, ed., *New Perspectives on Historical Writing*, University Park, PA: Pennsylvania State University Press, 1992.

Burkert, Walter, *Structure and History in Greek Mythology and Ritual*, Berkeley, CA: University of California Press, 1979.

Carlton, Eric, *Ideology and Social Order*, London: Routledge & Kegan Paul, 1977.

Childs, Brevard S., "A Study of the Formula, 'Until this Day,' " *JBL* 82 (1963): 279–92.

―― *Isaiah and the Assyrian Crisis*, SBT²3, London: SCM, 1967.

Clines, David J. A., "The Old Testament Histories: A Reader's Guide," in *What Does Eve Help? and Other Readerly Questions to the Old Testament*, JSOTSup 94, ed. David J. A. Clines, Sheffield: Sheffield Academic Press, 1990, 85–105.

Cogan, Morton, *Imperialism and Religion: Assyria, Judah and Israel in the Eighth and Seventh Centuries B.C.E.*, SBLMS 19, Missoula, MT: Scholars Press, 1974.

―― "Israel in Exile – The View of a Josianic Historian," *JBL* 97 (1978): 40–4.

Coggins, R. J., "History and Story in Old Testament Study," *JSOT* 11 (1979): 36–46.

Cohen, Gerson, "The Story of the Four Captives," *PAAJR* 29 (1960–1): 55–131. Reprinted in his *Studies in the Variety of Rabbinic Cultures*, Philadelphia, PA: Jewish Publications Society, 1991, 155–208.

Cohen, Ralph, "History and Genre," *NLH* 17 (1986): 203–18.

Collins, John, "The 'Historical Character' of the Old Testament in Recent Biblical Theology," *CBQ* 41 (1979): 185–204.

Connerton, David A., *How Societies Remember*, Cambridge: Cambridge University Press, 1989.

Cooper, Alan and Bernard R. Goldstein, "Exodus and Maṣṣôt in History and Tradition," *Maarav* 8 (1992): 15–37.

Damrosch, David, *The Narrative Covenant: Transformations of Genre in the Growth of Biblical Literature*, Ithaca, NY: Cornell University, 1987.

Davies, Philip R., *In Search of "Ancient Israel*," JSOTSup 148, Sheffield: Sheffield Academic Press, 1992.

Edelman, Diana Vikander, *King Saul in the Historiography of Judah*, JSOTSup 121, Sheffield: Sheffield Academic Press, 1991.

―― ed., *The Fabric of History: Text, Artifact and Israel's Past*, JSOTSup 127, Sheffield: Sheffield Academic Press, 1991.

―― ed., "Toward a Consensus on the Emergence of Israel in Canaan," *SJOT* 2 (1991): 1–116.

Ellis, John M., *The Theory of Literary Criticism: A Logical Analysis*, Berkeley, CA: University of California Press, 1974.

Evans, J. A. S., "Father of History of Father of Lies; The Reputation of Herodotus," *The Classical Journal* 64 (1968): 11–17.

Fales, F. M., ed., *Assyrian Royal Inscriptions; New Horizons in Literary, Ideological, and Historical Analysis*, Rome: Istituto Per L'Oriente, 1981.

Feinberg, Leonard, "Satire and Humor: In the Orient and in the West," *Costerus* 2 (1972): 33–61.

Finley, M. I., *Ancient History: Evidence and Models*, New York: Viking, 1986.

Fishbane, Michael, *Biblical Interpretation in Ancient Israel*, Oxford: Oxford University Press, 1985.

Flanagan, James W., "Court History or Succession Document? A Study of 2 Samuel 9–20 and 1 Kings 1–2," *JBL* 91 (1972): 172–81.

Fornara, Charles, *The Nature of History in Ancient Greece and Rome*, Berkeley, CA: University of California Press, 1983.

Funkenstein, Amos, *Perceptions of Jewish History*, Berkeley, CA: University of California Press, 1993.

Gabba, Emilio, "True History and False History in Classical Antiquity," *Journal of Roman Studies* 71 (1981): 50–62.

Geller, Stephen A., "The Sack of Shechem: The Use of Typology in Biblical Covenant Religion," *Prooftexts* 10 (1990): 1–15.

Glatt, David A., *Chronological Displacement in Biblical and Related Literatures*, SBLDS 139, Atlanta, GA: Scholars Press, 1993.

Goldenberg, Robert, "History and Ideology in Talmudic Narrative," *Approaches to Ancient Judaism, Vol IV: Studies in Liturgy, Exegesis, and Talmudic Narrative*, ed. William Scott Green, Chico, CA: Scholars Press, 1983, 159–71.

Gordon, Robert P., "David's Rise and Saul's Demise: Narrative Analogy in 1 Samuel 24–6," *Tyndale Bulletin* 31 (1980): 37–64.

Gossman, Lionel, *Between History and Literature*, Cambridge, MA: Harvard University Press, 1990.

Graf, Gerald, *Professing Literature: An Institutional History*, Chicago: University of Chicago Press, 1987.

Gunkel, Hermann, *The Legends of Genesis*, trans. W. H. Carruth, New York: Schocken, 1975.

Gunn, David, *The Story of King David: Genre and Interpretation*, JSOTSup 6, Sheffield: JSOT Press, 1978.

—— *The Fate of King Saul: An Interpretation of a Biblical Story*, JSOTSup 14, Sheffield: JSOT Press, 1980.

Hallo, William, W., "Biblical History in its Near Eastern Setting: The Contextual Approach," in *Scripture in Context: Essays on the Comparative Method*, ed. Carl D. Evans *et al.*, Pittsburgh, PA: Pickwick Press, 1980, 1–26.

Halpern, Baruch, "Doctrine by Misadventure," in *The Poet and the Historian*, HSS 26, ed. R. E. Friedman, Chico, CA: Scholars Press, 1983, 41–73.

—— *The First Historians: The Hebrew Bible and History*, San Francisco: Harper & Row, 1988.

—— and David S. Vanderhooft, "The Editions of Kings in the 7th–6th Centuries B.C.E.," *HUCA* 62 (1991): 179–244.

Halpern, Ben, "History as a Jewish Problem," in *From Ancient Israel to Modern Judaism: Intellect in Quest of Understanding. Essays in Honor of Marvin Fox*, vol. 1, ed. Jacob Neusner *et al.*, Atlanta, GA: Scholars Press, 1989, 3–21.

Hernadi, Paul, ed., *What is Literature?* Bloomington, IN: Indiana University Press, 1978.

Heym, Stefan, *The King David Report*, New York: G. P. Putnam's Sons, 1973.

Hobsbawm, Eric and Terence Ranger, eds, *The Invention of Tradition*, Cambridge: Cambridge University Press, 1983.

Huizinga, Johan, "A Definition of the Concept of History," in *Philosophy and History: Essays Presented to Ernst Cassirer*, ed. Raymond Klibansky and H. J. Paton, Gloucester, MA: Peter Smith, 1975 [1936], 1–10.

Iggers, Georg G., *New Directions in European Historiography*, revised edn, Middletown, CT: Wesleyan University Press, 1984.

Ishida, Tomoo, *The Royal Dynasties in Ancient Israel: A Study on the Formation and Development of Royal–Dynastic Ideology*, BZAW 142, Berlin: Walter de Gruyter, 1977.

Japhet, Sara, *The Ideology of the Book of Chronicles and Its Place in Biblical Thought*, BzEATAJ 9, trans. Anna Barbar, Frankfurt: Peter Lang, 1989.

Kugel, James, "On the Bible and Literary Criticism," *Prooftexts* 1 (1981): 217–36.

—— "Controversy: James Kugel Responds," *Prooftexts* 2 (1982): 328–32.

Larsen, Mogens Trolle, ed., *Power and Propaganda: A Symposium on Ancient Empires*, Mesopotamia 7, Copenhagen: Akademisk Forlag, 1979.

Lassner, Jacob, " 'Doing' Early Islamic History: Brooklyn Baseball, Arabic Historiography and Historical Memory," *JAOS* 114 (1994): 1–10.

Lasswell, Harold D., Daniel Lerner and Hans Speier, eds, *Propaganda and Communication in World History*, Honolulu: University Press of Hawaii, 1979–80.

Le Goff, Jacques and Pierre Nora, eds, *Constructing the Past: Essays in Historical Methodology*, trans. David Denby *et al.*, Cambridge: Cambridge University Press, 1974.

Lemche, Niels Peter, "David's Rise," *JSOT* 10 (1978): 2–25.

—— *Early Israel: Anthropological and Historical Studies on the Israelite Society Before the Monarchy*, SVT 37, Leiden: E. J. Brill, 1985.

Levinson, Bernard, "The Hermeneutics of Innovation: The Impact of Centralization upon the Structure, Sequence, and Reformulation of Legal Material in Deuteronomy," Ph.D. dissertation, Brandeis University, 1991.

Lewis, Bernard, *History Remembered, Recovered, Invented*, New York: Simon & Schuster, 1975.

Ligota, C. R., " 'This Story is not True.' Fact and Fiction in Antiquity," *Journal of the Warburg and Courtlauld Institutes* 45 (1982): 1–13.

Loewenstamm, S. E., *From Babylon to Canaan: Studies in the Bible and its Oriental Background*, Jerusalem: Magnes, 1992.

Long, Burke O., "Historical Narrative and Fictionalizing Imagination." *VT* 35 (1985): 405–16.

Longman, Tremper, III, *Fictional Akkadian Autobiography: A Generic and Comparative Study*, Winona Lake, IN: Eisenbrauns, 1991.

Lowenthal, David, *The Past is a Foreign Country*, Cambridge: Cambridge University Press, 1985.

McCarter, P. Kyle, " 'Plots, True or False': The Succession Narrative as Court Apologetic," *Int* 35 (1981): 355–67.

—— "The Historical David," *Int* 40 (1986): 117–29.

Machinist, Peter, "The Question of Distinctiveness in Ancient Israel: An Essay," *ScrHier* 33 (1991) [=*Ah, Assyria ...: Studies in Assyrian History and Ancient Historiography Presented to Hayim Tadmor*, eds Mordechai Cogan and Israel Ephal]: 196–212. Reprinted in Frederick E. Greenspahn, ed., *Essential Papers on Israel and the Ancient Near East*, New York: New York University Press, 1991, 420–42.

McKenzie, John L., "The Historical Prologue of Deuteronomy," in *Fourth World Congress of Jewish Studies Papers*, vol. I, Jersualem: World Union of Jewish Studies, 1967, 95–101.

Marcus, Ivan G., "History, Story and Collective Memory: Narrativity in Early Ashkenazic Culture," *Prooftexts* 10 (1990): 365–88.

Millard, A. R., James Hoffmeier and David Baker, eds, *Faith, Tradition and History: Old Testament Historiography in Its Near Eastern Context*, Winona Lake, IN: Eisenbrauns, 1994.

Momigliano, Arnaldo, *Essays in Ancient and Modern Historiography*, Oxford: Basil Blackwell, 1977.

—— *On Pagans, Jews and Christians*, Middletown, CT: Wesleyan University Press, 1987.

—— *The Classical Foundations of Modern Historiography*, Berkeley, CA: University of California Press, 1990.

Moye, Richard H., "Thucidides' 'Great War': The Fiction in Scientific History," *Clio* 19 (1990): 161–80.

Muntz, Peter, *The Shape of Time: A New Look at the Philosophy of History*, Middletown, CT: Wesleyan University Press, 1977.

Na'aman, Nadav, "The Historical Background to the Conquest of Samaria (720 BC)," *Bib* 71 (1990): 206–25.

Nelson, Richard D., *The Double Redaction of the Deuteronomistic History*, JSOTSup 18, Sheffield: JSOT Press, 1981.

Neusner, Jacob, ed., *The Christian and Judaic Invention of History*, American Academy of Religion Studies in Religion, 55, Atlanta, GA: Scholars Press, 1990.

Nineham, Dennis, *The Use and Abuse of the Bible: A Study of the Bible in an Age of Rapid Cultural Change*, London: SPCK, 1978.

Noth, Martin, *The Deuteronomistic History*, JSOTSup 15, Sheffield: JSOT Press, 1981.

O'Brien, Mark A., *The Deuteronomistic History Hypothesis: A Reassessment*, OBO 92, Göttingen: Vandenhoeck & Ruprecht, 1989.

Oded, Bustanay, "II Kings 17: Between History and Polemic," *Jewish History* 2 (1987): 37–50.

Paulson, Ronald, ed., *Satire: Modern Essays in Criticism*, Englewood Cliffs, NJ: Prentice-Hall, 1971.

Plumb, J. H., *The Death of the Past*, Harmondsworth: Penguin, 1973.

Polzin, Robert, *Samuel and the Deuteronomist: A Literary Study of the Deuteronomic History: 1 Samuel*, San Francisco: Harper & Row, 1989.

—— *David and the Deuteronomist: 2 Samuel*, Bloomington, IN: Indiana University Press, 1993.

Press, Gerald A., *The Development of the Idea of History in Antiquity*, Kingston: McGill-Queen's University Press, 1982.

Provan, Ian, *Hezekiah and the Books of Kings: A Contribution to the Debate about the Composition of the Deuteronomistic History*, BZAW 172, Berlin: Walter de Gruyter, 1988.

Reade, Julian, "Mesopotamian Guidelines for Biblical Chronology," *Syro-Mesopotamian Studies* 4/1 (May 1981): 1–7.

Redford, Donald B., *A Study of the Biblical Story of Joseph (Genesis 37–50)*, SVT 20, Leiden: E. J. Brill, 1970.

—— *Egypt, Canaan, and Israel in Ancient Times*, Princeton, NJ: Princeton University Press, 1992.

Seitz, Christopher R., *Theology in Conflict: Reactions to the Exile in the Book of Jeremiah*, BZAW 176, Berlin: Walter de Gruyter, 1989.

Smith, Morton, "Pseudepigraphy in the Israelite Literary Tradition," in *Pseudepigrapha I*, ed. Kurt von Fritz, Geneva: Foundation Hardt, 1972, 191–215.

Stern, Fritz, ed., *The Varieties of History from Voltaire to the Present*, New York: Vantage, 1973.

Sternberg, Meir, *The Poetics of Biblical Narrative: Ideological Literature and the Drama of Reading*, Bloomington, IN: Indiana University Press, 1985.

Tadmor, Hayim and Mordechai Cogan, "Ahaz and Tiglath-Pileser in the Book of Kings: Historiographic Considerations," *Bib* 60 (1979): 493–9.

Tadmor, Hayim and Moshe Weinfeld, eds, *History, Historiography and Interpretation: Studies in Biblical and Cuneiform Literatures*, Jerusalem: Magnes, 1983.

Talmon, Shemaryahu, "Polemics and Apology in Biblical Historiography – 2 Kings xvii 24–41," *The Creation of Sacred Literature: Composition and Redaction of the Biblical Text*, Near Eastern Studies, 22, ed. Richard Elliott Friedman, Berkeley, CA: University of California Press, 1981, 57–68. Reprinted in his *Literary Studies in the Hebrew Bible: Form and Content*, Jerusalem: Magnes, 1993, 134–59.

Thompson, Thomas L., *The Historicity of the Patriarchal Narratives*, BZAW 133, Berlin: Walter de Gruyter, 1974.

—— *Early History of the Israelite People From the Written and Archaeological Sources*, Studies in the History of the Ancient Near East, 4, Leiden: E. J. Brill, 1992.

Tigay, Jeffrey H., ed., *Empirical Models for Biblical Criticism*, Philadelphia, PA: University of Pennsylvania Press, 1985.

Todorov, Tsvetan, "The Origin of Genres," *NLH* 8 (1976): 159–70.

Trompf, G. W., *The Idea of Historical Recurrence in Western Thought: From Antiquity to the Reformation*, Berkeley, CA: University of California Press, 1979.

Tsevat, Matitiahu, "Israelite History and the Historical Books of the Old Testament," *The Meaning of the Book of Job and Other Biblical Studies: Essays on the Literature and Religion of the Hebrew Bible*, New York: Ktav, 1980, 177–83.

Van Beek, Gus W., ed., *The Scholarship of William Foxwell Albright: An Appraisal*, HSS 33, Atlanta, GA: Scholars Press, 1989.

Van Der Dussen, W. J. and Lionel Rubinoff, eds, *Objectivity, Method and Point of View: Essays in the Philosophy of History*, Leiden: E. J. Brill, 1991.

van Seters, John, *Abraham in History and Tradition*, New Haven, CT: Yale University Press, 1975.

—— *In Search of History: Historiography in the Ancient World and the Origins of Biblical History*, New Haven, CT: Yale University Press, 1983.

Veyne, Paul, *Did the Greeks Believe in their Myths?*, trans. Paula Wissing, Chicago: University of Chicago Press, 1988.

Weinfeld, Moshe, "The Period of the Conquest and of the Judges as Seen by the Earlier and the Later Sources," *VT* 17 (1967): 93–113.

Wellhausen, Julius, *Prolegomena to the History of Ancient Israel*, Gloucester, MA: Peter Smith, 1973 [1878].

Westermann, Claus, ed., *Essays on Old Testament Hermeneutics*, London: SCM, 1963.

White, Hayden, *Tropics of Discourse: Essays in Cultural Criticism*, Baltimore, MD: Johns Hopkins University Press, 1978.

—— *The Content of Form: Narrative Discourse and Historical Representation*, Baltimore, MD: Johns Hopkins University Press, 1987.

Whitelam, Keith, "The Defence of David," *JSOT* 29 (1984): 61–87.

—— "The Symbols of Power: Aspects of Royal Propaganda in the United Monarchy," *BA* 49 (1986): 166–73.

—— "Between History and Literature: The Social Production of Israel's Traditions of Origin," *SJOT* (1991/2): 60–74.

Williamson, H. G. M., *Israel in the Books of Chronicles*, Cambridge: Cambridge University Press, 1977.

—— "History," *It is Written: Scripture Citing Scripture: Essays in Honour of Barnabas Lindars*, ed. D. A. Carson and H. G. M. Williamson, Cambridge: Cambridge University Press, 1988, 25–38.

Wilson, Robert R., *Genealogy and History in the Biblical World*, YNER 7, New Haven, CT: Yale University Press, 1977.

Winks, Robin W., ed., *The Historian as Detective: Essays on Evidence*, New York: Harper & Row, 1969.

Winter, Irene J., "Royal Rhetoric and the Development of Historical Narrative in Neo-Assyrian Reliefs," *Studies in Visual Communication* 7 (1981): 2–38.

Wiseman, T. P., *Clio's Cosmetics: Three Studies in Greco-Roman Literature*, Leicester: Leicester University Press, 1979.

Yerushalmi, Yosef Hayim, *Zakhor: Jewish History and Jewish Memory*, Seattle: University of Washington Press, 1982.

Younger, K. Lawson, Jr, *Ancient Conquest Accounts: A Study in Ancient Near Eastern and Biblical History Writing*, JSOTSup 98, Sheffield: Sheffield Academic Press, 1990.

Zakovitch, Yair, "Story versus History," *Proceedings of the Eighth World Congress of Jewish Studies: Panel Sessions: Bible Studies and Hebrew Language*, Jerusalem: World Union of Jewish Studies, 1983, 47–60.

—— "And You Shall Tell Your Son . . .": *The Concept of the Exodus in the Bible*, Jerusalem: Magnes, 1991.

INDEX OF SUBJECTS

References are (almost exclusively) to the body of the text, and not to the endnotes; references to the notes may be found in the other two indices, or by looking up the notes to the body of the text in this index.

INDEX OF MODERN AUTHORS

INDEX OF CITATIONS FROM
THE HEBREW BIBLE